THUNDER AT SUNRISE

THUNDER AT SUNRISE

*A History of the Vanderbilt Cup, the Grand Prize
and the Indianapolis 500, 1904–1916*

John M. Burns

McFarland & Company, Inc., Publishers
Jefferson, North Carolina, and London

Library of Congress Cataloguing-in-Publication Data

Burns, John M., 1951–
Thunder at sunrise : a history of the Vanderbilt Cup,
the Grand Prize and the Indianapolis 500, 1904–1916 /
by John M. Burns.
p.   cm.
Includes bibliographical references and index.

ISBN-13: 978-0-7864-2474-0
ISBN-10: 0-7864-2474-5
(illustrated case binding : 50# alkaline paper) ∞

1. Vanderbilt Cup Race — History.   2. Indianapolis Speedway Race — History.
3. Automobile racing — History.   4. Grand Prix racing — History.   I. Title.
GV1029.15.B87   2006   796.72 — dc22   2006022426

British Library cataloguing data are available

Front cover: Howard "Howdy" Wilcox's number 29 Premier,
Indianapolis 500, 1916; Back cover: Indianapolis, 1915 — the drivers and
their teams arrayed across the front straight prior to the start of the race (IMS Photo)

Manufactured in the United States of America

McFarland & Company, Inc., Publishers
Box 611, Jefferson, North Carolina 28640
www.mcfarlandpub.com

Table of Contents

Preface

This book arose from two articles I wrote which were intended for magazines. The first, a history of the Mercer Raceabout and Mercer's racing program, entitled "Mercer Raceabout — The First Sports Car," was published in issue 1998/4 of *Vintage Motorsport*. The second, a history of the Fairmount Park races in Philadelphia held between 1908 and 1911, which was provisionally titled "Saturday in the Park with George — And Len and Erwin," never saw the light of day.

Prior to that time, I was vaguely aware of the Vanderbilt Cup races, but I had no real understanding of their importance to motor racing, both in America and worldwide, nor of their place in the pantheon of spectator sports that were proliferating in America during the first and second decades of the twentieth century. As for the International Grand Prize, I am not sure that I was aware of its existence at all. If I was, I certainly was not aware that it was an American version of the French *Grand Prix*, run under the same rules, or formula, and attracting the same international competition as its slightly older French counterpart. I, like more than a few of my contemporaries with an interest in the field of motorsports history, had chosen to ignore the races of the era prior to America's entry into World War I and to focus instead on the era beginning with the 1920s — with the Duesenbergs and Millers battling on America's ovals, and the Bugattis and Alfa Romeos vying for supremacy over Europe's road circuits. Equipped with those blinders, Jimmy Murphy's victory for Duesenberg in the French *Grand Prix* in 1921 became the first American victory in international motorsports competition, while the prior victories of Locomobile, Alco, Lozier and Mercer in the Vanderbilt Cup and International Grand Prize were either ignored or unknown.

Upon my discovery of the international significance of the Vanderbilt Cup and the Grand Prize, and their important place in maintaining motorsports competition on an international scale in the wake of the Paris-Madrid disaster of 1903 and during the French boycott of racing between 1908 and 1912, I resolved that their story had to be made known. Few books of any era had taken up the subject, and even the best of them had dealt with the races in a vacuum, either covering only selected races within each series, or dealing with the Vanderbilt Cup and Grand Prize in isolation, as though the races existed separate and apart from each other and from the larger picture of motorsports in general.

Originally, I intended to cover only the Vanderbilt Cup and International Grand Prize in detail, with passing references to other races to give the context that I felt was missing from prior efforts, but as my research progressed, it became apparent that a detailed history of the Indianapolis 500 would also have to be included. The 1904 Vanderbilt Cup attained its singular significance as a motor race not merely because it was the brainchild of William K. Vanderbilt, Jr., but because it was the first international motorsports competition held in America. It was a position of prominence the Vanderbilt Cup would hold through the 1906 season. The International Grand Prize, with its inaugural running in 1908, would, in its turn, assume the distinction of being the motor race that brought the factory teams over from Europe. It would hold that position until 1913 when the European teams discovered Indianapolis, lured by prize money all out of proportion to that offered by the Vanderbilt Cup or the Grand Prize. So it was the preeminence of the Indianapolis 500 and its introduction of oval track racing to the American public, as much as the dangers and difficulties associated with racing over public roads, that would ultimately be responsible for the demise of America's first two races of international stature.

In researching these races, I have tried to rely on contemporary accounts from newspapers or automotive journals of the era whenever possible. Obviously, the closer the reporter was to the subject matter, the more reliable the resulting account. On occasion, I have relied on secondary sources, but only where those sources were not inconsistent with accounts made contemporaneously with the races. Thus, you will see no reference to an AAA championship for any year prior to 1916. While some modern writers take it as a given that a racing champion was crowned every year from 1904 onward, in point of fact those "championships" prior to 1916 are works of fiction concocted by latter day journalists.

In discussing the subject matter of this book with friends and colleagues during the research stage, I was repeatedly confronted by a few misconceptions about the cars and drivers of this so-called "brass era" of automobile development. The first was that the cars were ridiculously slow. The second was that the technology was primitive. The third was that the drivers, while admittedly brave, were not really possessed of the skills of their more modern brethren. While these misconceptions can be attributed in large part to a simple lack of knowledge, I believe some of the reason for them can be found in the fact that we tend to view the world from the perspective of our own time, in this instance from the long lens that is the length of the twentieth century. So the Wright Flyer that was cutting edge technology in 1903 tends to look like such an antique as to be comical when viewed from a world where commercial jets traveling at 500 mph, five miles above the earth, are part of our everyday lives. Similarly, we tend to view the cars of the pre–World War I era without any realization that the engineering that went into them was as cutting edge as that involved in the Wright Flyer.

In point of fact the cars of that era were fast — by 1906 their top speeds exceeded 100 mph. They embodied a surprising amount of "modern" technology. The first supercharged engine appeared in 1906. The basic configuration for the "modern" racing engine, the configuration you will find in every Indianapolis and *grand prix* racer today, dates back to 1912. The cars of the "brass era," while not the ground-hugging, wing-laden machines of today, were nevertheless the product of brilliant engineers: men like J. Walter Christie, who designed the gun turrets for the battleship USS *Maine* and would go on to design much of the Russian T-34 tank, considered by many the finest tank ever produced. And the drivers of this era were not only brave, but highly skilled — by 1910 touching top speeds in races that were nearly as fast as man had ever traveled, taking corners in spectacular slides or four-wheel drifts, dancing on the edge of control despite the skinny tires of their cars and the variety of road surfaces and conditions with which they were faced.

In an effort to disabuse the reader of these misconceptions, and once again to provide a context for these races, I have tried to provide the reader with a snapshot of the salient political, cultural, scientific and technological events of each year covered by this book. My hope is to allow the reader to set down his long lens and to stand in the shoes of a person in the crowd at these most prestigious of sporting events — to provide some insight into that spectator's frame of reference as he watches the technological marvels of his time hurtle by at unimaginable speeds.

I hope my effort has been successful. More significantly, I hope you enjoy it.

Introduction

Ask almost any history or motorsports buff about the beginnings of motor racing in America and he will likely tell you about the first Indianapolis 500 in 1911—about Ray Harroun, and his single-seat Marmon Wasp, and his invention of the rear-view mirror. There are only two problems with that version of the story—nobody is sure if Harroun really won, and Indy wasn't really the beginning.

Before Indianapolis there were two motor races even bigger—the Vanderbilt Cup and the International Grand Prize. Both drew crowds larger than Indy. In fact, the Vanderbilt Cup was the largest single-day sporting event of its time, drawing in a crowd of over a quarter-million people—and this in 1906.

The Vanderbilt Cup was the product of William K. Vanderbilt, Jr., the poster boy for America's Gilded Age. It was the first motor race in America to draw international competition. It was the *raison d'être* for the first modern highway, Long Island's Motor Parkway. And it gave America its first great motorsports heroes, not Harroun and the Marmon Wasp, but George Robertson and the Locomobile known forever after as "Old 16."

Savannah's International Grand Prize was the first *grand prix* outside France. Beginning in 1908, it gave the world America's first driver of international stature, Ralph DePalma. It was the site where the *grand prix* tradition of pouring champagne over the head of the winner began. And it was host to two successive races that would each, in turn, be christened with the title "the world's greatest."

So why are these races all but unknown today? It's hard to say. Perhaps it's because they were races conducted over closed sections of public roads which never enjoyed a permanent home, despite the best efforts of Willie K. Vanderbilt and the ACA in Savannah. Perhaps it's because they were last raced so long ago. Perhaps it's because, unlike Indianapolis, no modern racing series traces its traditions back to them.

Regardless of the reason, these are races that deserve to have their stories told. They did much to shepherd the young sport of automobile racing through the disaster of Paris-Madrid in 1903 and the French boycott of motor racing between 1908 and 1912. But more than that, the Vanderbilt Cup and International Grand Prize provided an America that was just entering the modern age of spectator sports with spectacles that rivaled any other. And in doing so, they gave the motorsports fan of the time heroes to match any to be found in the more traditional sports of baseball or football or boxing. Any sports fan who knows the names of Cy Young, Ty Cobb, Jim Thorpe, Knute Rockne, or Jack Johnson should also know the stories of George Robertson, Ralph Mulford, Ralph DePalma, David Bruce-Brown, and Caleb Bragg.

So climb aboard. The year is 1904. I'd tell you to put on your helmet and strap yourself in, but crash helmets and seat belts haven't been invented yet. Just turn your cap around backwards so it doesn't blow off in the wind, pull down your goggles to keep the dust out of your eyes, and hang on. Let's go for a ride.

1

A Cloud of Dust

It was good to be an American in the autumn of 1904. The world seemed full of promise, full of new possibilities. Politically, the United States was in a position to flex its muscles. In the wake of the Spanish-American War, it had become an international power of the first order. In 1903, President Roosevelt had used that status and a bit of gunboat diplomacy to engineer Panama's secession from Colombia and to establish the U.S. controlled Canal Zone for the building of a canal linking the Atlantic and Pacific oceans. On the technological front, Ransom E. Olds was in the third year of production of his Curved Dash Oldsmobile, the first commercially successful car in America. Less than a year before, the Wright brothers had made the first successful powered flight. Perhaps more relevant to the average person in 1904, the St. Louis World's Fair introduced the American public to hamburgers, iced tea and ice cream cones.

True, the world has its problems. The Russo-Japanese War rages across Manchuria, introducing the large-scale use of automatic weapons to warfare and demonstrating the basic incompetence and vulnerability of the czarist regime. Perhaps more significantly, it will set Japan on a course of expansionism that will culminate in the firestorms of Hiroshima and Nagasaki. Britain and France have signed the Entente Cordiale, agreeing to respect each other's imperialist designs in Egypt and Morocco. The agreement will isolate Germany, setting in motion a series of events that will ultimately lead to World War I. But in the autumn of 1904, political problems involving Manchuria and North Africa seem very far away, and their far-reaching ramifications lie a decade or more in the mist.

Even in this year of American power and prosperity, Harold Rigby can well think of himself as a particularly lucky man. At age twenty-five, he has secured a position as chauffeur for Herbert Lytle, one of the increasing number of wealthy men who have embraced the new technology of the automobile. Such a position will give Rigby credentials that he hopes will put him in increasing demand as automobile usage, and the need for skilled professionals to drive them, become more widespread. And Rigby's position is not merely that of an ordinary chauffeur. Herbert Lytle is more than just another rich man who can afford a car and a driver — he is a sportsman whose passion is the growing sport of automobile racing. As Lytle's chauffeur, Harold is part of the racing team, driving his boss to the races, working on the car. In effect, Harold gets a free pass to the best seat in the house at every race Lytle enters. And not merely as a spectator — he is part of the show, changing tires, adding oil and water, helping with repairs. The whole thing is incredibly exciting, and the experience cannot help but enhance Harold's stature in his chosen profession. Maybe he will even get an opportunity to drive a race car. As with events involving Manchuria and North Africa, who could say what the future would bring?

If things weren't good enough for Harold already, the autumn of 1904 brought increased excitement. William K. Vanderbilt, Jr., great-grandson of the famous Commodore, announced that he, in conjunction with the American Automobile Association, would hold an automobile race unlike any ever held in America before. It would be an international competition, patterned after the Gordon Bennett Cup races in Europe, with cars and drivers from all over Europe as well as the United States. The Vanderbilt Cup, as the race would be called, would clearly be the most important sporting event of the year, with the rich and famous of society coming out to Long Island to watch. And Harold would be right there in the front row. Herbert Lytle was entered in a Pope-Toledo, one of the fastest of the American entries.

Herbert Lytle had an uncanny knack for being involved in crashes that would impact the entire race in which they took place. First, his crash in practice for the inaugural Vanderbilt Cup, which fatally injured his mechanic, Harold Rigby, nearly derailed that race before a lap was even run. Seven years later at Indianapolis, his parked Apperson would be a central player in the multi-car wreck that would cause chaos in the timing and scoring booth (IMS Photo).

So it was that on the evening of October 3, 1904, the Monday before the race, Harold found himself riding on the left step of the Pope-Toledo racer as Lytle piloted the machine around the thirty-mile circuit of roads that would be closed to the public on Saturday and become the course for the inaugural Vanderbilt Cup. Riding on the right step was H. C. Anderson, another member of Lytle's team. The two men watched the action of the racer's suspension as Lytle made three laps of the course, hitting speeds in excess of 50 mph on the Jericho Turnpike while Rigby and Anderson hung on. The racer's engine was running well and its suspension handling the sandy, rutted roads as well as could be expected. It was time to get the car back to the garage. Lytle slowed to about 25 mph after making the turn from the Jericho Turnpike onto Massapequa Road, heading back to the Garden City Hotel. Then, just as the big racer reached the outskirts of Hicksville, its left front tire blew. The car swerved sharply and crashed into a picket fence. Lytle and Anderson were flung headlong into the road. Neither of them was seriously hurt. But Harold's luck had just run out: he was caught between the big car and the fence, and three of his ribs were crushed. One of the shards of bone punctured his left lung. He was rushed to Nassau Hospital, but by 3 a.m.

he was dead. The Vanderbilt Cup, America's first international automobile race, had claimed its first victim before a single lap had been run.

❖ ❖ ❖

Rigby's death and the negative publicity it generated were not the only problems facing the young William Kissam Vanderbilt, Jr., or Willie K. as the press liked to call him, in the days leading up to the race. Despite the fact that teams had assembled from as far away as Europe, the Nassau County Board of Supervisors had yet to give the race their final approval, an absolute necessity since the race was to be run on public roads. Under normal circumstances, obtaining such approval would have been no problem for a man with Vanderbilt's money and influence, but the circumstances surrounding the race, and surrounding Vanderbilt himself, were anything but normal. By sanctioning the race through the AAA, Vanderbilt had alienated himself from its arch-rival, the Automobile Club of America, a club whose members included many of the rich and powerful of New York and of which Vanderbilt himself had once been vice-president. Many ACA members looked on Vanderbilt's defection to the more representative and less elite AAA as nothing less than treason, and while few of them spoke publicly about their feelings they were not above exerting pressure on the press or local officials to sabotage Vanderbilt's race. The *New York World*, no friend of the automobile, a newspaper that had coined the term "Autofat" in 1903[1] (claiming that wealthy men and women were becoming obese from giving up bicycling, golf, tennis and polo in favor of a pastime that required no physical effort), blasted the race: "In order that the speed-madness monomaniacs may drive their man-maiming engines at an excessive and illegal pace, the residents and taxpayers of the island are bidden to keep off the road." The *World* went on to level particular criticism at Willie K. and his wealthy friends who supported the project, moaning paternalistically that "It is an extraordinary condition of affairs when a coterie of idlers, rich men's sons and gilded youth can take possession of the public highways."[2]

Local reaction to the race was not what Vanderbilt had expected either. He had hoped that the prospect of wealthy sportsmen and large crowds of spectators gravitating to rural Long Island would provide sufficient economic incentive to overcome any negative reaction the race might generate among the local populace. In some circles, no doubt, it did. But by many of the residents, the race was seen as a major inconvenience, at best. At worst, it could prove downright dangerous to life and property. At the October 4 hearing before the board of supervisors, local resident John A. Taylor voiced an opinion shared by many. The gray-bearded farmer complained of the dangers of the automobile, citing a recent incident in which a boy from the area had been killed. He went on to tell the supervisors it was high time they stopped granting special privileges to wealthy men, and he suggested that if men like Vanderbilt wanted to hold races, they should purchase private land and build a suitable track there. John Myers, a resident of Hempstead, said that since practice for the race had started he was in constant fear for his family. They became virtual prisoners in their home whenever the cars came speeding past their house at 60 mph or more. When asked why he didn't take down the numbers of the cars speeding past and report them, Myers responded, "all I can ever see is a cloud of dust."[3]

In the end, the board of supervisors agreed to allow the race after being assured that the AAA would be responsible for any damage that might occur. But that was not the end of the matter. In the wake of the board's vote, E. M. Bennett, acting for a group calling itself the People's Protective Association, filed a motion seeking an injunction barring the race. Not until Friday afternoon did Vanderbilt and the AAA know whether they had a race to run, or not. At the injunction hearing, Judge Wilmot Smith denied the motion. Vanderbilt's race was on. For the next dozen years, until America's entry into World War I, the Vanderbilt Cup would be one of the world's pre-eminent motor races. But in 1904, it may just have saved racing.

❖ ❖ ❖

If the automobile was born in Germany in the workshops of Gottlieb Daimler and Karl Benz, the sport of automobile racing was born in France, with inter-city races run over its vast system of roads — a legacy from the Napoleonic and Roman empires. France held the first sanctioned automotive competition, the Paris-Rouen Trial, in 1894. Pierre Giffard, the owner of the Paris news magazine *Le Petit Journal*, offered a prize of 5,000 francs to demonstrate the safety and reliability of *voitures sans chevaux*, "horseless carriages." The trial was not a race *per se*, but a judged competition over the seventy-eight-mile distance between Paris and Rouen to determine the best performance by a practical road vehicle. The organizers received 102 entries. From that number, they selected 21 to take part in the trial, with 8 of the starters being powered by steam and 13 by gasoline. Of the 13 gasoline-powered starters, 12 were Daimler-engined Peugeots or Panhard-Levassors, both marques powering their cars with Daimler engines built under license. The fastest car over the distance was a De Dion steam tractor, but the judges, in what some might call typically French fashion, disqualified it, deciding that — despite its pre-race selection as a starter from among the 102 entries — it was not, in fact, a "practical road vehicle." In a further demonstration of Gallic political correctness, the judges refused to declare a winner at all. Instead, the prize was awarded jointly to the leading Peugeot, driven by Doriot, and the Panhard that finished close behind. Doriot's average speed was 11.5 mph.

A year later, on June 11, 1895, France was the site of the first sanctioned automobile race, run between Paris and Bordeaux. Significantly, two Americans were among those contributing the prize money: James Gordon Bennett, the Paris-based owner and publisher of the *New York Herald*, and the teenaged William K. Vanderbilt, Jr. The race spanned the 732-mile distance from Paris to Bordeaux and back. Its organizers expected it to take four days, but no one had told that to Emile Levassor. At the wheel of a two-cylinder, four-horsepower Panhard-Levassor known as "No. 5," which boasted a top speed of 18.5 mph, Levassor drove through the night using candle-powered headlights. He reached Bordeaux the morning following the start. Pausing only briefly, he set off again, driving through a second night before arriving back in Paris at lunchtime on June 13. His arrival was met by wild enthusiasm from a huge crowd. His time: 48 hours, 48 minutes — over two full days of nearly continuous driving at an average speed of 15 mph.

But, as in 1894, being first to the finish line did not assure victory. In another display of Gallic rule enforcement, race officials disqualified Levassor because his Panhard had only two seats. The rules required four. (One might think that this fact would have been pointed out to Levassor and Panhard *before* the race, but as anyone with any knowledge of French racing history can tell you, that is not their way.) First prize was awarded to M. Koechlin, whose Peugeot finished eleven hours behind. Nevertheless, the people of France had anointed their hero — and it was Levassor, not Koechlin. While the race records still officially list Koechlin as the winner, it was Levassor's statue that was later erected overlooking the finish line at the Port Maillot.

Paris-Bordeaux was followed in 1896 by Paris-Marseilles, another round trip city-to-city race, this time organized by the newly formed Automobile Club de France, or ACF. Again Levassor was entered, but south of Avignon he swerved to avoid a dog. His Panhard crashed. With Levassor out, the 1,063-mile race was won by his teammate, Mayade. Levassor was hospitalized. The official diagnosis was concussion, but the full extent of his injuries was far more serious. He never completely recovered, dying on April 14, 1897.

In the wake of the Paris-Marseilles race, Paris became a hub for a whole series of open-road races. Eighteen ninety-eight saw Fernand Charron win the 889-mile Paris-Amsterdam race, again in a Panhard, with a time of 33 hours, 4 minutes, 34 seconds, an average speed of 26.9 mph. Charron followed up his Paris-Amsterdam victory with another win for Panhard in the 1899 Paris-Bordeaux race. And another Panhard, this time driven by Réne de Knyff, won the inaugural Tour de France.

As the century turned, France became the site of the first international automobile competition, but the man behind it was an American. James Gordon Bennett, one of the contributors to the inaugural Paris-Bordeaux race, had voiced concern that the American automobile industry was lagging behind that of France and other European nations. Inspired by American car builder Alexander Winton's challenge to France's most famous driver, Fernand Charron, Bennett commissioned the creation of a permanent trophy, *La Coupe Internationale*, to be awarded to the winner of an annual race contested by three-car national teams. The idea was to spur the fledgling American auto industry to produce faster, better cars and to provide it with a venue to demonstrate the quality of its technology in competition against the recognized world leader. *La Coupe Internationale*, which quickly became known worldwide as the Gordon Bennett Cup, not only established the concept of international competition with cars painted in national colors (originally blue for France, red for the U.S., yellow for Belgium, and white for Germany), it also introduced the concept of a racing formula, or set of rules, to even the competition. That formula consisted of a weight limitation, with the cars required to weigh between 400 kg (880 lbs.) and 1,000 kg (2,204 lbs.).

The first of the Gordon Bennett Cup races was held on June 14, 1900, between Paris and Lyons. The 353-mile race was contested by entries from France, the United States, Belgium, and Germany, but only the French could muster a three-car team, with Panhards for Fernand Charron, Réne de Knyff and Léonce Girardot. The U.S. was represented by two Wintons driven by Alexander Winton and Andrew Riker. Belgium was represented by a single Snoek-Bolide driven by its automotive speed record holder, Camille Jenatzy, who, in 1899, had become the first man to break the mile-a-minute barrier in his speed machine, *Jamais Contente*. Germany fielded a single Benz driven by Eugen Benz, the son of the company's founder.

If the Gordon Bennett Cup was designed to demonstrate the competitiveness of the American auto industry, its first running did nothing of the sort. Riker withdrew his Winton before the start. Winton, himself, failed to finish. The German and Belgian entries fared no better, with Benz being forced to withdraw and Jenatzy retiring. In the end, Charron won at an average speed of 38.6 mph. Among the French entries, only de Knyff failed to finish.

France's victory in the inaugural Gordon Bennett Cup did nothing to warm it and its auto industry to the American-sponsored competition, however. The complaint was with the three-car-per-nation team limitation, which was seen as a clever way to minimize French competition. Unlike other nations, which could not field a single three-car team, France could have fielded several, had the rules permitted. In fact, the limitation had created quite a controversy among the French manufacturers, many of whom sought to represent their nation in the race. In the end, a vote had been taken to settle the dispute, but when the ballot produced three drivers from Panhard and none from arch-rival Mors, there were whispers of scandal.

Even as the Gordon Bennett Cup began drawing international attention to motor racing, France continued its city-to-city races centered around Paris, and French marques continued to dominate. In 1900, the Paris-Toulouse race was won by Levegh in a Mors. This was followed by Henri Fournier's win in a Mors in the Paris-Berlin race of 1901. France's domination continued in the 1901 Gordon Bennett Cup, this time held between Paris and Bordeaux, with Léonce Girardot winning in a Panhard after Charron, in a second Panhard, succumbed to tire problems and the sole Mors entry crashed. The only significant challenge to the French was the lone British entry, a Napier driven by Selwyn Edge, but, like Charron, he was forced to retire due to tire problems.

Still dissatisfied with the rules of the Gordon Bennett Cup despite their two convincing victories, the ACF arranged to have the 1902 Gordon Bennett Cup race held in conjunction with its own Paris-Vienna race. The Gordon Bennett Cup, however, would cover only the 350-mile distance between Paris and Innsbruck. The idea was to minimize the importance of the Gordon Bennett Cup by holding a longer, and therefore more significant, race in conjunction with it. The strategy would backfire as completely as France's ill-fated "Plan 17" a decade later.

Teams from France and Britain were entered in the Gordon Bennett Cup race. In the end, it came down to a fight between Réne de Knyff's Panhard and Selwyn Edge's Napier. Then, just thirty miles short of Innsbruck, the Panhard broke, handing the victory to Edge, Napier, and — most significantly — Britain. France was aghast. Edge's victory was a double-edged sword to the heart of French pride. Not only had Britain wrested the Gordon Bennett Cup from its rightful home, Marcel Renault's victory in the longer Paris-Vienna race was almost completely overshadowed, despite the fact that it was the first major victory for one of the new lighter cars represented by Renault and Darracq over the heavier, larger engined machines epitomized by Panhard and Mors. Like it or not, the French were forced to accept the fact that the Gordon Bennett Cup was the race that drew international attention — and that after seven years of complete and utter dominance in the sport, they had finally been beaten.

While the French defeat in the 1902 Gordon Bennett Cup may have been viewed as a disaster in France, it only served to re-kindle interest in the series, and in motor racing in general, throughout the rest of Europe and the United States. That same year, the Belgian Motor Club organized its first race — a six-lap event over a 53.5-mile circuit of closed roads known as the *Circuit des Ardennes*. By using a closed circuit of roads, rather than the city-to-city format, the Belgian Motor Club sought to increase race safety by relieving the racers of the burden of dealing with other traffic, always a potential danger in the city-to-city races. The organizers also hoped to attract more spectator interest, since they could now see the cars go by repeatedly and could watch both start and finish. In this they were wildly successful. The race attracted seventy-five entrants and a huge crowd. Unfortunately, the circuit format, while doing away with the danger of collisions between racers and other traffic, only exacerbated the most significant hazard faced by drivers of the day — dust.

Blinding clouds of dust plagued the racers from the outset. First Camille Jenatzy crashed. Then race organizer Pierre de Crawhez crashed into Evance Coppice's car, unable to see it through the fog. Léon Théry hit a cow. Pierre de Caters, blinded by the dust cloud thrown up by Charles Jarrott's Panhard, drove into a wall. The huge clouds of dust did not merely blind the drivers, it got behind goggles and masks, into eyes, into noses, into mouths, nearly choking them. Drivers tried to revive themselves with large swallows of champagne straight from the bottle. But despite the difficult conditions, the crowd was enthralled by the race, which came down to a battle between Jarrott's Panhard and a Mors driven by Fernand Gabriel. In the end, Jarrott won, but not before nearly crashing into the Mors when Gabriel stopped to replace a broken chain.

If the 1902 Gordon Bennett Cup had demonstrated that the French could be beaten, the *Circuit des Ardennes* had demonstrated that they were still the dominant power in racing. Of course, the *Circuit des Ardennes* had also demonstrated the dangers inherent in conducting races over unprepared dirt roads, whether or not they were open to the public, but nobody was paying attention. Not yet.

The French government had initially been reluctant to sanction the Paris-Madrid race of 1903. With top speeds now nearing 90 mph, there was a feeling that the cars had become too fast and the sport too dangerous to be permitted on open roads. But in the end, pressure from the French automobile industry, coupled with public sentiment strongly in favor of the race, proved too much for the politicians. The race was scheduled to take place over three days, with the first day's run covering the distance between Paris and Bordeaux, the second day's from Bordeaux to the Spanish border, and the third day's from the border to Madrid. In all, 314 cars were entered, although many of them, like the cars of Americans Foxhall Keene, Tod Sloan, and W. J. Dannat, failed to make the start. Still, the vast number of racers only added to the danger of the race, not only by creating congestion on the course, but also by forcing the race organizers to start the cars at shorter intervals than they otherwise would, just one minute apart. Ultimately, the number of competitors and their relatively close proximity could lead to only one thing — dust, thick blinding clouds of it.

A crowd estimated at one hundred thousand flooded the little town of Versailles on the outskirts of Paris in the early hours of May 24, 1903, to watch the start of the race. Soldiers armed with fixed bayonets lined the course for more than a mile on either side, keeping the road clear of spectators as the De Dietrich of Charles Jarrott was flagged away at 3:45 a.m. In all, between two and three million people lined the course between Paris and Bordeaux. Among the racers they had come to see were the cream of the French racing fraternity, Fernand Charron, Réne de Knyff, Fernand Gabriel, Léon Théry, and brothers Louis and Marcel Renault.

While Jarrott alone among the racers had a clear view of the course, that did not stop Louis Renault from making up his three-minute starting-time deficit. By the time the cars reached the old cathedral town of Chartres, Renault had powered his lightweight machine past both de Knyff and Jarrott to take the overall lead. Throughout the morning, reports sent back from along the course documented his progress. Clarence Moore, reporting from outside Chartres, clocked Renault at nearly 75 mph going up a steep incline. An observer on the Bourdinierre straight between Chartres and Bonneval timed him at over 88 mph. Reports from Vendôme, Tours and Poitiers had him on a record pace, well under Henri Fournier's record of 8 hours, 44 minutes. When he pulled into Bordeaux at 12:15 p.m., he had beaten the old record by 17 minutes.

Behind Renault, Jarrott had lost ground when a huge mastiff wandered into his path outside Chartres. Unable to avoid the dog for fear of losing control of his machine and crashing into one of the trees that lined the road, Jarrott plowed squarely into it, carrying its body for over half a mile before it dropped between the wheels. The force of the impact had been so great that when the carcass was later examined, virtually every bone in its body was found to be broken. Despite the incident, Jarrott finished only fourteen minutes behind Renault, tying Fournier's prior record.

While Louis Renault's record pace was the story at the outset, it was the performance of Fernand Gabriel that would truly astonish the huge crowd. Starting eighty-second in the field, he piloted his 70-horsepower Mors at incredible speed through the blinding conditions. By the time he reached Bordeaux at 1:14 p.m., he had passed 79 of the 81 cars that had started in front of him, finishing behind only Renault and Jarrott. His time, a record-shattering 8 hours and 7 minutes; his average speed, 65.3 mph.

While the morning's dispatches from various points on the course had been filled with descriptions of speed and racing drama, the afternoon's race reports took on a new and more ominous tone. First, Lorraine Barrow was reported to have crashed near Libourne, only seventeen miles from Bordeaux. Like Jarrott, he had been confronted with a dog in the road. Unlike Jarrott, he had tried to avoid it. He lost control and hit a tree, smashing his racer to pieces. Pierre Roderiz, his riding mechanic, had been killed. Barrow was reported in critical condition.

The next report into Bordeaux was even more chilling to the small group of racers gathered there. Marcel Renault, Louis' brother, had crashed just south of Poitiers, 125 miles from Bordeaux. He had been closely following Léon Théry as the racers approached the village of Couhe-Verac, trying to find a way past. Suddenly, Théry swerved sharply left, following the road. Renault, unable to see in the blinding dust, plowed straight on. His car nosed into a ditch and rolled. Renault was seriously injured. He was not expected to survive. Upon hearing of Marcel's crash, Louis gave orders that all Renault cars be withdrawn from the race. Then he jumped back into his racer and headed for Poitiers, hoping to reach his brother in time.

Throughout the remainder of the afternoon reports of accidents, injuries, and deaths swirled in from all parts of the course. A racer had overturned and caught fire at a railroad crossing near Libourne, pinning the riding mechanic beneath it and burning him to death. Two soldiers and a child had been killed at Angoulême. A peasant woman had wandered into the road at Ablis and been run down. Racers had crashed into each other while speeding along wheel to wheel, leaving drivers and mechanics badly injured. A bicyclist had been kicked by a startled horse and dumped into the road, where she was run over, her legs amputated. With all the reports, sometimes conflicting, sometimes incredible, that poured in over the course of the afternoon, it was difficult to tell what was really happening. One thing was certain, however — the news was all very, very bad. As proof of that fact, at day's end, only 111 of the 300-odd starters had made it to Bordeaux.

Without waiting for a final list of the killed, injured and maimed, the French government halted the race. When some of the racers argued against the stoppage, suggesting that they might drive to the Spanish border and pick up the race there, the Spanish government did likewise. In the end, the tally was eight dead, including both Renault and Barrow, and ten seriously injured. Paris-Madrid had become the deadliest race in the sport's brief history. The days of city-to-city racing were over.

With city-to-city races now banned, the sport of motor racing had lost virtually all of its traditional venues. Its sole remaining major series, the Gordon Bennett Cup, now assumed even more importance, but for a time it appeared that it would not be run. Reaction to the carnage of Paris-Madrid had prompted governments to talk of banning motor racing outright. While no such actions were ultimately taken, the 1903 Gordon Bennett Cup still faced a somewhat sticky problem. Under the terms of the series established by James Gordon Bennett, the nation winning the race hosted the following year's competition. That had never been a problem as long as French cars kept winning. Britain, however, had always forbidden racing on public roads. In fact, until 1896 British law had required a man with a red flag to precede any moving car. The problem was solved by holding the race at a circuit near Athy in Ireland, where such races were permitted. Teams from Britain, France, the U.S. and Germany were entered.

After one look at the circuit, the French team was aghast — it was designed for lightweight machines with a maximum of 30 or 40 horsepower, totally ill-suited to the 13.7-liter (836-cubic-inch), 80-horsepower Panhards and the 11.6-liter (707-cubic-inch), 70-horsepower Mors that made up their team. The German team had problems of its own. Its three 90-horsepower Mercedes racers had been destroyed in a fire at the Canstatt works where the cars had been stored in the wake of Paris-Madrid. They were forced to substitute three 60-horsepower machines for their front-line cars. However, one of their drivers, Camille Jenatzy, was able to locate an 85-horsepower engine and shoehorn it into the 60 chassis.

In the race, despite the problems faced by the continental teams, neither the English nor the Americans could capitalize. The English team of three Napiers were never a factor. Selwyn Edge, the 1902 winner, was plagued by tire problems. He would finish no better than fifth and later be disqualified for receiving outside assistance — his racer was push started. His teammates Jarrott and Stocks fared even worse. Stocks failed to complete one lap and Jarrott crashed at Stradbally on lap two. The American team, composed of two Wintons (one packing a massive 17-liter (1,037-cubic-inch), 8-cylinder 80-horsepower engine) and an 80-horsepower Peerless, failed to get even one car to the finish, the Peerless being disabled after only completing one lap, and the Wintons being withdrawn on the fourth and fifth laps, hours behind the leaders and hopelessly out of contention.

American amateur Foxhall Keene's Mercedes led the first lap by twenty seconds, but by lap two he began to fade. A bent rear axle would sideline him on lap four. Jenatzy in his cobbled together 85-horsepower Mercedes then took over, seizing a two-minute lead over Réne de Knyff's Panhard on lap two and extending it lap by lap to the finish. In the end, the French showed that they were the dominant team, with the Panhards of de Knyff and Henri Farman and Fernand Gabriel's Mors finishing second, third, and fourth, but none of them could catch the red-bearded Belgian in the flying Mercedes.

For the second time in as many years, the French public was appalled by the outcome. Again France had been beaten in the sport it invented, and this time not by the

British, whom the French merely disliked, but by the hated Germans. Little more than thirty years before, in the wake of their victory in the Franco-Prussian War, Germany had annexed the French provinces of Alsace and Lorraine. Its army had marched down the *Champs Élysées*. To be beaten again by the hated *Boche*, even in something as politically insignificant as a motor race, was almost more than the Gallic soul could bear.

As the 1904 racing season began, the sport was in disarray in its French birthplace. City-to-city racing was dead. The Gordon Bennett Cup was in the hands of the Germans. French manufacturers and sportsmen alike felt that they desperately needed a victory in the 1904 Gordon Bennett Cup race to return it, and motor racing in some form, to France. French manufacturers came out in force to contest the 1904 race — a field of twenty-nine entries in all. Perhaps the best gauge of the French seriousness about the competition is the fact that none of the normal intrigue marred the selection process. The three-car team, an 80-horsepower Richard-Brasier for Léon Théry, a 100-horsepower Turcat-Méry for Rougier, and a 100-horspower Mors for Salleron, was determined by an elimination race.

Facing the French was the strongest field in Gordon Bennett Cup history. Germany fielded a team of two 90-horsepower Mercedes for Jenatzy and De Caters and an Opel-Darracq for Fritz Opel. Austria fielded a team of three 90-horsepower Austrian-made Mercedes for Braun, Werner, and Warden. Belgium entered three 100-horsepower Pipes for Hautvast, De Crawhez, and Augieres. Italy fielded a team of three 75-horsepower Fiats for Lancia, Cagno and Storero. England entered a 96-horsepower Wolseley for Jarrott, a 72-horsepower Wolseley for Girling, and an 80-horsepower Napier for Edge. Even little Switzerland had an entry, an 80-horsepower Dufaux. There were nineteen starters in all, but not a single American entry.

The race, which was held at the Taunus circuit near Frankfurt, featured an exciting battle between Jenatzy's 12-liter (731-cubic-inch) Mercedes and the 9.9-liter (604-cubic-inch) Richard-Brasier of Léon Théry. After one 79.46-mile lap, the two were only one second apart, with Selwyn Edge's Napier hanging onto third some five minutes behind. But Jenatzy could easily have been leading, or dead. As he'd flogged his Mercedes downhill at full throttle on the fastest part of the course, he'd noticed spectators alongside the road shouting and waving their arms frantically. He slowed. Behind a blind curve at the bottom of the hill he found the reason for all the commotion — a locomotive blocking the road completely. Had he not slowed, he surely would have crashed. As it was, he lost only a minute to Théry.

By the end of lap two, half-distance, Théry's lead over Jenatzy was just ninety-eight seconds. But here, the German machine showed its Achilles heel. Mercedes used exhaust gases to pressurize the fuel tank, but during fuel stops the pressure would be lost when the tank was opened, requiring someone to pump up the pressure by hand once the tank was full. It was a process that took several minutes. While Jenatzy sat fuming at the wheel of his motionless Mercedes, the Frenchman inexorably pulled away, opening his lead on lap three to nearly ten minutes. It was a lead he would hold to the end. The Gordon Bennett Cup was headed back to France.

No sooner had France recovered the Cup than factions within the ACF began plotting its demise. The French continued to dislike the format of the series, believing that the three-car team limitation was unfair. There was talk of supplanting the Gordon Bennett Cup with a grand prize race, a *grand prix*, but in the end the various factions within the ACF could not come to an agreement on its format. The Gordon Bennett Cup would be run at least one more time, but everyone involved in racing knew that its days were numbered.

❖ ❖ ❖

This was the turbulent state of the sport when William K. Vanderbilt, Jr., announced the running of his Vanderbilt Cup in 1904. For much of the next ten years, the Vanderbilt Cup would provide stability to an infant sport rocked by turmoil — but not without creating turmoil of its own.

2

The Invasion of Nassau County

That William K. Vanderbilt, Jr., was fabulously wealthy goes without saying. His great-grandfather, Cornelius "Commodore" Vanderbilt, was a tycoon of the first magnitude, making his fortune in shipping and, later, at the helm of the New York Central Railroad. When Willie K. was just seven years old, his father, William K. Vanderbilt, Sr., inherited $65 million, an amount worth $1 billion or more in today's dollars. He also succeeded the Commodore as the chairman of the board and CEO of the New York Central. During his teens, Willie K. spent his summers at his parents' palatial "cottage," Marble House, in Newport, Rhode Island, built at a cost of $11 million — the marble used in its construction alone was valued at $7 million. It was America's Gilded Age and Willie K. was right in the thick of it, attending formal balls in the marble mansions along Fifth Avenue, traveling through Europe on the Grand Tour, spending part of each year at Idlehour, the family's 900-acre estate at Oakdale on Long Island's south shore.

After prep school, Willie K. attended Harvard, but unlike his brother Harold, who earned a degree in law, he had little interest in studies. He left Cambridge after only eighteen months. In 1899, he married Virginia Fair of San Francisco, whose father was a partner in the Comstock Silver Mine in Nevada and reputedly worth $200 million. The young couple were the center of attention wherever they went. The newspapers reported every detail of their wedding and brief honeymoon, including the fact that the 100-room mansion at Idlehour burned to the ground during the newlyweds' stay at the estate.

But Willie K. was more than just a wealthy patron for the young sport of motor racing, he was an active automobilist and racer himself. He had taken his first ride in a motorcar at age eleven, while in Monte Carlo. In 1899, he bought his first car, a Stanley Steamer, and was promptly cited by the police for operating it without an engineer's license. When he and Virginia visited Newport in the wake of the Idlehour conflagration, he brought his own automobile with him — and caused quite a stir in the community. Routinely driving through town "at a speed equal to a railroad train," Vanderbilt had the staid and sober community up in arms. Fifty residents petitioned the city

One by one the cars (photos of each scattered throughout chapter) in the inaugural Vanderbilt Cup come to the line and are flagged away. *Top:* Car No. 1 in the Vanderbilt Cup, S.B. Stevens' 60-horsepower Mercedes driven by A.L. Campbell (image courtesy Smithtown [N.Y.] Library, Long Island Room). *Bottom:* Fernand Gabriel's factory-backed, 80-horsepower De Dietrich started second in the 1904 Vanderbilt Cup (image courtesy Smithtown [N.Y.] Library, Long Island Room).

government to impose speed limits protecting them from the speed-demon automobilist. In 1900, their petition was answered, a speed limit was imposed — 6 mph in central areas and 10 mph elsewhere. Willie K. ignored it. He was cited and summoned to appear in court. "Arrest me every day if you want to," he said. "It's nothing to pay fines for such sport."[1] But by 1901, the constant complaints became tiresome. Willie K. and Virginia departed Newport for a place with good roads where the automobile was reputedly much better accepted — Long Island.

The Vanderbilts built a colonial home on a hilltop overlooking Lake Success. They named their country estate Deepdale. It was modest by Vanderbilt standards. Willie K. and Virginia had settled on the site only after their plan to buy all of the lakeshore, the lake itself, and all public access roads leading to the shoreline had been thwarted by the voters of the town of North Hempstead. Still, relations between the residents of Nassau County and their wealthy new neighbor were generally congenial. Little attention was paid to his Paris purchase of a 33-horsepower Daimler with a top speed of 65 mph that he affectionately named the "White Ghost." But that is not to say that all was smooth sailing; he continued to have his share of problems with the law regarding his driving. The village of Hempstead enacted its first speed limit — 6 mph — after one of Willie K.'s forays into town. In 1902, a reporter from *The New York American* published a story claiming that Nassau County residents were living in fear of being run down by Willie K. in his "Red Devil" Mercedes.

But Willie K.'s love of the automobile was not merely confined to fast drives through the countryside; he was a serious racer as well. In 1902, the twenty-four year-old piloted his 60-horsepower Mors to a third-place finish behind the Panhard of Charles Jarrott and Fernand Gabriel's Mors at the inaugural *Circuit des Ardennes*. Later that year, he drove the Mors to an automotive speed record of 76.08 mph, beating out the old record of 75 mph set by Frenchman Léon Serpollet at the wheel of *La Baleine* (the Whale) and becoming America's first holder of the title. (The New York Central's famous locomotive "999" was still the fastest thing on land, with a record speed of 112.5 mph, but that distinction would go to an automobile, Fred Marriott's Stanley Steamer, by 1906.) In 1903, Vanderbilt participated in the ill-fated Paris-Madrid race. Perhaps fortunately, he made it no farther than Chartres before mechanical problems put him in a ditch. In 1904, he purchased a 90-horsepower Mercedes which he used to set a new outright speed record of 92.30 mph at Ormond Beach, near Daytona. But at age twenty-six, he stepped out from behind the wheel to devote his energies to the race that would bear his name.

The Vanderbilt Cup, itself, was an impressive trophy, a massive, Tiffany-designed, sterling silver affair, weighing

William K. Vanderbilt, Jr., was not only the driving force behind America's first race of international stature, the Vanderbilt Cup, he was also a driver of great renown with two automotive speed records to his credit (image courtesy Smithtown [N.Y.] Library, Long Island Room).

Top: Car No. 3 in the 1904 Vanderbilt Cup, Joe Tracy's 35-horsepower Royal. Tracy, a former bicycle racer, would complete only one lap in the 1904 race, but in the 1906 Vanderbilt Cup he would achieve some measure of success, setting the lap record behind the wheel of a Locomobile, a first for an American entry (image courtesy Smithtown [N.Y.] Library, Long Island Room). *Bottom:* Car No. 4 in the 1904 Vanderbilt Cup, A.C. Webb's 60-horsepower Pope-Toledo. Tire troubles would sideline Webb on the third lap (image courtesy Smithtown [N.Y.] Library, Long Island Room).

forty pounds and standing nearly three feet high with its ebony base. On it was depicted the figure of Vanderbilt seated at the wheel of his record-setting Mercedes. The race was calculated to be no less impressive, ten laps of a triangular 30.2-mile course laid out along the Jericho, Bethpage and Hempstead turnpikes between Queens Village, Jericho and Bethpage, with cars from France, Germany, and Italy competing against

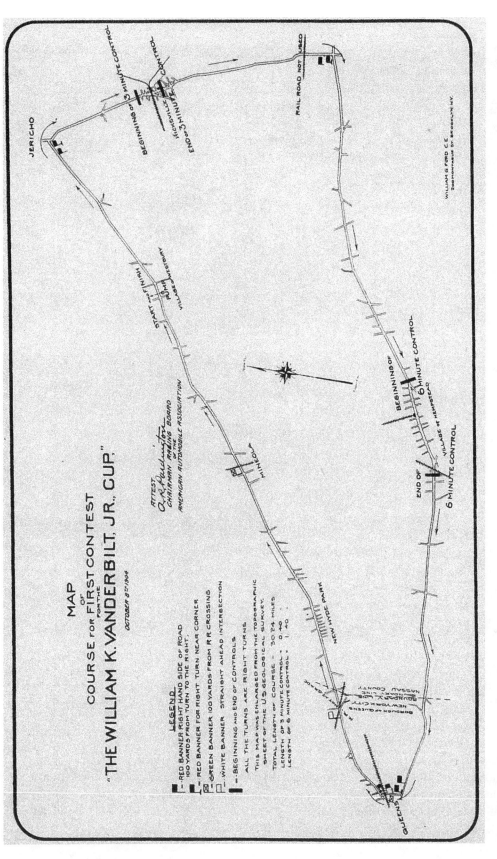

The course for the 1904 Vanderbilt Cup was a 30.2-mile triangle connecting Queens Village, Jericho and Bethpage (image courtesy Smithtown [N.Y.] Library, Long Island Room).

the cream of the American crop. Unlike a modern race course, however, it also contained two control sections, one just west of the village of Hempstead and one just south of Hicksville, where the cars were stopped and re-started on each lap. (The control sections comprised 1.8 miles of the course and held the cars up for nine minutes per lap. The time and distance of the control sections were not included in the race distance or lap times.) To keep the race rules simple, Vanderbilt and the AAA adopted the formula of the Gordon Bennett Cup, with two notable exceptions — the three-car team limitation was dispensed with and the requirement of national colors was abandoned. Even before the competitors logged their first mile, no less an authority than *The New York Times* proclaimed that "the first international race on American soil" ranked behind only the Gordon Bennett Cup in worldwide importance.[2]

Also lending the race an air of importance was the fact that the field was truly an international one, even if many of the European cars were American owned. Germany was represented by five privately owned Mercedes for drivers Al Campbell, George Arents, Jr., E. E. Hawley, Wilhelm Werner and W. C. Luttgen. Both Werner's and Hawley's cars were wasp-tailed racers that had taken part in the 1904 Gordon Bennett Cup. In fact, Werner's car, now owned by Clarence Grey Dinsmore, was the 12-liter (732 cubic inch), 90-horsepower model driven by Camille Jenatzy to second place in that event, while the other four were 9.2-liter (561 cubic

THE VANDERBILT CUP

Compliments of
A. R. PARDINGTON
Sept. 15, 1910

The Vanderbilt Cup, forty pounds of sterling silver standing nearly three feet high and depicting William K. Vanderbilt, Jr., at the wheel of his speed-record Mercedes, was calculated to be a trophy worthy of the international stature of the race it celebrated (image courtesy Smithtown [N.Y.] Library, Long Island Room).

inch), 60-horsepower models. Italy was represented by two privately owned 10.6-liter (647 cubic inch), 90-horsepower Fiats (more properly F.I.A.T.s, the initials standing for *Fabbrica Italiana Automobili Torino*). One was owned and driven by William Wallace, while the second was owned by Alfred Vanderbilt and driven by Paul Sartori. Matched against these teams, the American contingent consisted of a 6.4-liter (390 cubic inch), 35-horsepower Royal driven by former bicycle racer Joe Tracy, Herbert Lytle's ill-fated 5.7-liter (348 cubic inch), 24-horsepower Pope-Toledo, a second Pope-Toledo sporting a 13-liter (793 cubic inch), 60-horsepower engine for A. C. Webb, a 4.5 liter (275 cubic inch), 24-horsepower Packard for Charles Schmidt, and a 14.7-liter (897 cubic inch),

Top: Car No. 5 in the 1904 Vanderbilt Cup, George Arents' 60-horsepower Mercedes. On lap two, a blown tire caused Arents to lose control. The car stood on its nose and overturned, throwing Arents clear. His mechanic, Carl Mensel, was not so lucky. He was fatally injured when the racer rolled with him still in his seat (image courtesy Smithtown [N.Y.] Library, Long Island Room). *Bottom:* Car No. 6 in the 1904 Vanderbilt Cup, Herbert Lytle's 24-horsepower Pope-Toledo. Despite its lack of power, the little Pope-Toledo would put together the best showing of any American entry (image courtesy Smithtown [N.Y.] Library, Long Island Room).

75-horsepower Simplex driven by novice racer Frank Croker, the son of a notorious Tammany Hall boss.

While the two Gordon Bennett Cup Mercedes may have given the Vanderbilt Cup some credibility, the cars that anointed it with instant status were the six from France — Fernand Gabriel in a factory-backed 12.8-liter (781 cubic inch), 80-horsepower

Top: Car No. 7 in the 1904 Vanderbilt Cup, George Heath in the factory-backed 90-horsepower Panhard. Despite being an American, Heath was captain of the powerful Panhard team. He would go on to win the race by 1:28 over the Clément-Bayard of Albert Clément (image courtesy Smithtown [N.Y.] Library, Long Island Room). *Bottom:* Car No. 8 in the 1904 Vanderbilt Cup, E. R. Thomas' 60-horsepower Mercedes driven by E. E. Hawley. Hawley was only one minute behind Heath's Panhard on lap four when the Mercedes succumbed to suspension failure (image courtesy Smithtown [N.Y.] Library, Long Island Room).

De Dietrich; Maurice Bernin in a privately owned 12.1-liter (738 cubic inch), 90-horsepower Renault; the twenty-one-year-old Albert Clément, son of the car's designer, at the wheel of a radically streamlined 11.3-liter (689 cubic inch), 80-horsepower Clément-Bayard; and a three-car factory team of huge 15.4-liter (940 cubic inch), 90-horsepower Panhards, their flat-topped engine cowlings standing nearly as high as a man's chest. They

Top: Car No. 9 in the 1904 Vanderbilt Cup, C. G. Dinsmore's 90-horsepower Mercedes driven by Wilhelm Werner. This car, with Camille Jenatzy behind the wheel, had finished second in the 1904 Gordon Bennett Cup. In the Vanderbilt Cup it would be sidelined on lap two with a cracked cylinder (image courtesy Smithtown [N.Y.] Library, Long Island Room). *Bottom:* Car No. 10 in the 1904 Vanderbilt Cup, A. G. Vanderbilt's 75-horsepower Fiat driven by Paul Sartori. Clutch trouble on the way to the start delayed him for nearly two hours (image courtesy Smithtown [N.Y.] Library, Long Island Room).

would be driven by Frenchmen George Teste and Henri Tart, and American team captain George Heath.

With so many French drivers available it may seem odd that an American was captain of the powerful Panhard team, but George Heath was no ordinary driver. Although virtually unknown today, he was the first American to achieve international stature as

Top: Car No. 11 in the 1904 Vanderbilt Cup, W. G. Brokaw's 90-horsepower Renault driven by Maurice Bernin. It would be sidelined on lap two with a broken driveshaft (image courtesy Smithtown [N.Y.] Library, Long Island Room). *Bottom:* Car No. 12 in the 1904 Vanderbilt Cup, the 80-horsepower Clément-Bayard driven by Albert Clément. Clément would finish second, only 1:28 behind Heath's Panhard (image courtesy Smithtown [N.Y.] Library, Long Island Room).

a racer. A native New Yorker born in Astoria, Long Island, he had spent most of his adult life in Europe. He was a resident of Paris when it became the center of European city-to-city racing in the late 1890s and, almost immediately, was bitten by the racing bug. The first race he entered was the 1898 Paris-Amsterdam, a grueling six-day event covering 889 miles. A year later in the inaugural Tour de France, an even more demanding 1,350-mile circuit of the country, he finished sixth. He followed that up six days later with a fourth place finish in the Paris-St. Malo race. By 1904, the tall, handsome man with the handlebar mustache had become a member of the Panhard factory team.

Top: Car No. 14 in the 1904 Vanderbilt Cup, the 90-horsepower Panhard driven by Henri Tart. Tire trouble would cost him nearly an hour, but he was still running when the race was stopped (image courtesy Smithtown [N.Y.] Library, Long Island Room). *Bottom*: Car No. 15 in the 1904 Vanderbilt Cup, the 90-horsepower Panhard driven by George Teste. He would lead the first three laps of the race, but would retire on lap four due to damage sustained as a result of a shredded tire (image courtesy Smithtown [N.Y.] Library, Long Island Room).

Earlier in the year, he had survived a slow penultimate lap at the *Circuit des Ardennes* to beat out teammate George Teste. As in Belgium, Heath would be one of the pre-race favorites, along with Teste and the De Dietrich of Fernand Gabriel.

❖ ❖ ❖

The year 1904 marked the beginning of the modern age of spectator sports in America. The first World Series had been held only one year previously, with the Boston

Pilgrims (later to become the Red Sox), led by pitcher Cy Young, defeating the Pittsburgh Pirates and their standout shortstop Honus Wagner. The second would not be held until 1905 owing to John McGraw's refusal to allow his National League pennant-winning New York Giants to compete in 1904. Except for the occasional boxing match or the Triple Crown of horse racing, sporting events featuring large crowds were a new and poorly understood phenomenon. So it was that Vanderbilt and the AAA gave little thought to the crowd that would be coming to attend their event when they scheduled it to start at 6:00 a.m. In doing so they insured that the race would be finished by mid-afternoon, but their starting time compelled spectators from New York to either spend the night before the race in rural Long Island, or commute by train or automobile in the pre-dawn darkness. The Long Island Railroad had no better grasp of the situation. It scheduled special trains for the race, but made no further provisions for the unusual crowd. The ticket booth was closed until shortly before departure time, and only a single ticket taker was on duty. The result can be easily imagined — a howling mob of people clamoring for tickets, hammering on the booth. Once it opened, the lone ticket taker was swamped by the rush. Out in Nassau County, every hotel room was sold out, most at what were described as "Waldorf-Astoria prices." In the pre-dawn darkness, bridges and ferries from Manhattan to Long Island were clogged with motorists driving to the race, often in cars grossly overloaded with extra passengers and supplies. If the roads and rail lines to the course were a madhouse, the area surrounding the course itself was worse. Crowds at the Westbury station milled around, unsure of the way to the circuit. Roads to the circuit were choked with traffic, both motorized and horse-drawn. Motorists abandoned their cars in any convenient location. Knots of people wandered everywhere, most without any clear understanding of where they were going. Two roadhouses outside Westbury were packed to the walls with thirsty motorists on their way to the race. Local farmers hitched teams

The press and timing stand at the inaugural Vanderbilt Cup (image courtesy Smithtown [N.Y.] Library, Long Island Room).

Top: Car No. 16 in the 1904 Vanderbilt Cup, the little, streamlined 24-horsepower Packard "Gray Wolf" driven by Charles Schmidt. He would still be running when the race was called off, but would never be a factor (image courtesy Smithtown [N.Y.] Library, Long Island Room). *Bottom:* Car No. 17 in the 1904 Vanderbilt Cup, the 75-horsepower Simplex driven by Frank Croker. Note the holes drilled in the frame and seat surround; these were necessary to bring the racer within the maximum weight limitation (image courtesy Smithtown [N.Y.] Library, Long Island Room).

of horses to their hay wagons and served as makeshift taxis for the spectators, as often as not charging outrageous prices for the privilege. As the *New York Times* put it, "it was like Nassau County had been invaded."[3]

Somehow, amid the chaos the crowd found its way to vantage points surrounding the track. The task was somewhat easier for the society set, for whom grandstand seats had been arranged at the Westbury start-finish line. They treated the race like any other

Car No. 18 in the 1904 Vanderbilt Cup, Isidor Wormser's 60-horsepower Mercedes driven by William Luttgen. He would still be running when the race was stopped, but was never among the leaders (image courtesy Smithtown [N.Y.] Library, Long Island Room).

society outing, bringing along their servants and setting up camp kitchens behind the grandstand. Breakfast was served on china plates at 7:00 a.m., one hour into the race. A second informal repast was arranged for 9:00. Throughout the morning coffee, bottled beer, mineral water and Scotch whisky were delivered to the well-heeled spectators by their liveried staff. For the less-well-to-do, hastily constructed coffee and lunch stands dotted the area surrounding the course.

By the 6:00 a.m. start, the grandstands were packed, not only the official one at the start-finish line, but others which had been hastily erected by many of the landowners adjacent to the course. Those who couldn't find, or couldn't afford, a seat in one of the grandstands lined nearly every inch of the track, standing ten deep in places. As starter C. H. Gillette sent off the first car, Al Campbell's red Mercedes, a great shout filled the air. Two minutes later, Fernand Gabriel, the second starter, received Gillette's signal. But just as he was about to accelerate away, a steam-powered touring car motored into the roadway, its driver oblivious to the shouts of the crowd. Gabriel waited impatiently as race officials mobbed the car and manhandled it to the side of the road amid shouts of "Throw him out!" and "Put him off!" At this, the motorist, a balloonist, artist, and publicity hound by the name of Augustus Post, floored the throttle of his tourer, nearly crushing a couple of spectators against a barricade. Not until Willie K. spoke personally to Post did the headline hunter finally move his car out of the way. Once the furor subsided, Gabriel dropped the clutch and his white De Dietrich thundered off.

Off they went, one by one, Tracy's Royal, Webb's Pope-Toledo, Arents' Mercedes; but when it came time for car No. 10 to approach the starting line, none appeared. Paul Sartori in Alfred Vanderbilt's Fiat had suffered clutch trouble near Garden City on his way to the start. While Sartori and his mechanic feverishly tried to repair their broken machine, the rest of the starters were flagged away. All got off cleanly except W. C. Luttgen's Mercedes. The big German machine was firing on only three of its four

These four photographs show the condition of the course in the 1904 Vanderbilt Cup, with the crowd completely blocking the roadway during lulls in the action and only clearing the course as Lytle's Pope-Toledo comes by. It was the inability to control this behavior that would ultimately lead to the Vanderbilt Cup leaving Long Island (images courtesy Smithtown [N.Y.] Library, Long Island Room).

Hawley's Mercedes hugs the left side of the road as the crowd grudgingly gives it room in the 1904 Vanderbilt Cup. Its day would end after four laps (image courtesy Smithtown [N.Y.] Library, Long Island Room).

cylinders. Finally, William Wallace in the No. 19 Fiat sped off, leaving the crowd staring at each other and marveling at the silence that had supplanted the deafening roar of the engines. Within minutes they became restless. Spectators climbed down from the grandstand and strolled onto the track, peering into the far distance, trying to be first to get a view of the returning racers. Conversations were struck up. Wagers were made. Then, as the first car came into view, race announcer Peter Prunty shouted, "Back of the fence! Car coming!" and the crowd returned to their seats. So it would go for the rest of the race, each racer owning the road for a moment as he flashed by, only to have the crowd reclaim it once he had passed.

Naturally, the American crowd had high hopes for the home team, but the knowledgeable among them knew that victory for an American car was unlikely. While the German and Italian machines were private entries and possibly vulnerable, the French team, composed as it was primarily of factory-backed cars, looked far too strong. With that in mind, many of the spectators began cheering for the Panhard of George Heath: if an American car couldn't win, perhaps an American driver would.

At the end of lap one, Gabriel was first across the line. Despite the delay caused by Post and his touring car, Gabriel had powered his De Dietrich past Campbell's Mercedes by the time the cars reached Queens Village. The crowd now looked to their watches, or to the scoreboard, to see if his time would hold up. As the rest of the racers flashed by, Gabriel fell to second, behind George Teste. The Panhard pilot was simply flying, setting fastest lap of the race with a time of 24:04, an average speed of nearly 71 mph. His lead over Gabriel was nearly two minutes already. But the biggest surprise to the

Car No. 19 in the 1904 Vanderbilt Cup, the 75-horsepower Fiat owned and driven by William Wallace. Wallace had the misfortune of running over his own mechanic while trying to stop at the Hicksville control (image courtesy Smithtown [N.Y.] Library, Long Island Room).

American crowd was Frank Croker, lying third. No one had expected much from the first-time racer, and his Simplex, although powered by the largest and most powerful engine of any of the American entries, was an unknown quantity. Prior to the race, most would have told you that Croker was not even among the fastest of the Americans, but here he was, not only leading the American contingent, but also ahead of all but two of the powerful French team. Maybe the home team would have something to cheer after all.

Lap one also saw the attrition begin. Joe Tracy's Royal coasted to a stop at Queens Village with a broken driveshaft. William Wallace tried to stop at the Hicksville control and found his Fiat had no clutch. In trying to stop the machine, his mechanic, Antonio Donderi, jumped out, was caught by its rear wheel and run over. Fortunately, the wheel merely ran over his thigh and he was not seriously injured. Although limping, he began his attempts to repair the crippled racer.

George Teste extended his lead on lap two, while further back Heath and Hawley climbed past Albert Clément into fourth and fifth. Clément and Frank Croker came past the grandstand nearly wheel to wheel, only ⅔ of a second separating them. Many in the crowd gasped as the two racers sped past side by side on the narrow roadway, then, as one, they craned their necks and peered off down the straight toward Jericho to see if the American could hold off the French challenge. He couldn't. A groan erupted as the rakish blue Clément-Bayard slipped past. Croker still held an eight-minute lead on Clément by virtue of his later starting time, but his Simplex was beginning to fade. The car's heavy frame had been drilled like Swiss cheese to meet the weight limitation. It was beginning to sag from the strain. By the end of lap three, it would nearly collapse, the racer's underpan scraping the roadway. Still, Croker would soldier on gamely, if slowly, to the end.

But Croker's was not the only racer in trouble. Werner's Mercedes cracked a cylinder at Mineola. Maurice Bernin's slope-nosed Renault broke its driveshaft at Plain Edge. George Arents, Jr., was even less fortunate. The amateur driver who had disdained the need for practice in the days leading up to the race, claiming to know every foot of the course, was having a very bad day. He had bungled the start, nearly stalling his Mercedes. He had overrun a control zone. Twice, his racer had swapped ends, on one occasion throwing his mechanic, Carl Mensel, into the roadway and nearly running him down. On lap two, after piloting his Mercedes carefully through the turn at Elmont, he poured on the power down the two-mile-long straight that followed. As the racer reached its top speed of nearly 90 mph, a front tire blew. Arents stomped on the brakes, trying to bring the machine under control, but the left rear wheel locked, shredding its spokes. The Mercedes pirouetted on its nose and rolled viciously in the center of the road. Arents was thrown clear and landed head first on the roadway. He was unconscious and seriously injured, but would survive. Mensel would not. Still in his seat, he was hammered head first into the track as the racer slammed onto its back. His skull was fractured. Unconscious, he was taken to Nassau Hospital, but efforts to save him proved unsuccessful. The Vanderbilt Cup had claimed its second victim, this one leaving behind a wife and three small children, the youngest just two months old. It was not the last time the Cup would bring tragedy to those around it.

As word of the accident filtered through the crowd, Teste continued to stretch his lead. By lap three, he had opened up a six-minute cushion over Panhard teammate Heath, with Hawley's Mercedes another minute back. Gabriel's De Dietrich had fallen to fourth, a further eight minutes behind, but even this position was not unchallenged. Clément was only one minute down and his streamline-bodied, blue Clément-Bayard was rapidly closing.

On lap four, mechanical problems sidelined leader George Teste. His record pace proved too much for his Panhard's tires and one blew. Normally, a blown tire would not have been fatal to his chances, but this one shredded, tearing up the Panhard's suspension and drivetrain. He was through for the day. Heath took over the lead with Hawley, just one minute back, looking poised to make his move. It would never happen. The terrific pounding of three high-speed laps was too much for the German car's suspension. Two of its springs snapped. Hawley nursed the machine back to the start-finish line to complete lap four, then pulled to the side of the road, his race over.

With Teste and Hawley out, Heath had a seemingly insurmountable lead—fourteen minutes over Gabriel's De Dietrich, thirty-three minutes over Clément, who had been slowed by the need to repair a gas tank cracked by the incessant pounding. Lying fourth was the little 24-horsepower Pope-Toledo of Herbert Lytle. With less than one-third the power of the French machines, Lytle couldn't hope to threaten, but he could turn in lap after consistent lap at the fastest pace his machine could survive. This he did with consummate skill. It was not the last time that Lytle would do wonders with an under-powered racer. Still, with the Italian threat but a memory, three of the German entries out and the other two well over an hour behind, and the Americans behind Lytle bunched in sixth, seventh, and eighth positions all more than an hour behind Heath, the only question was which of the French cars would win — and the nationality of its driver.

As the leading trio made their way around the course on the fifth circuit, the crowd at the start-finish grandstand was treated to an unexpected show. From out of nowhere, Paul Sartori appeared in the Vanderbilt Fiat, blasting down the front straight at top speed. As he passed the grandstand, the judges tried to stop his machine so it could make an official start. Sartori wasn't having any. Not only was he late and determined to make up time, his Fiat had no clutch. He ignored the violent gestures from the sidelines and sped on. Somewhat miffed, race chairman Arthur R. Pardington and the judging committee initially decided to contact the Hicksville control and have Sartori stopped and instructed to return to Westbury, but Alfred Vanderbilt prevailed upon them to let the Fiat continue. The Italian Ambassador was in attendance. The absence of Sartori at the start and Wallace's retirement in less than one lap was already enough of an embarrassment. In the end, it wouldn't matter, the car never reappeared.

While Sartori's Fiat was providing the crowd with some light entertainment, it was Gabriel's turn to fall back. He was slowed with tire trouble on the sixth round. Then on the seventh, a cracked cylinder sidelined the De Dietrich at Hicksville. Gabriel began working feverishly to effect repairs, but upon finding the full extent of the damage he threw down his tools and sat disconsolately on the ground, momentarily bursting into tears. In broken English, he explained to the small crowd around the racer that he had overcome his tire troubles and was poised to take the lead when Heath had his, as inevitably he would. He was certain he could have won, if only the De Dietrich had held together.

Whether Gabriel really could have won will never be known, but his prediction of tire problems for the leader was deadly accurate. No sooner had Heath established a thirty-seven minute lead over Clément than a tire cost him sixteen of those minutes. Another blown tire on lap eight cost him the rest. With just two laps left, Clément took over the lead, his rakish blue racer holding a margin of 3:08 over the big Panhard. Things looked grim for the American driver and the home town crowd, but Heath wasn't finished.

The crowd presses out onto the roadway to get a better view of the oncoming racer (image courtesy Smithtown [N.Y.] Library, Long Island Room).

There was a reason he was captain of the powerful Panhard team, after all. On the ninth circuit, he put the boot to his tired racer, turning in a time of 28:52. It wasn't a record, such a thing was out of the question this late in the race with a tired machine and a torn up racetrack, but it was damned fast, enough to cut Clément's lead nearly in half. When the young Frenchman appeared just over eight minutes later, the scoreboard told the tale. His lead was down to 1:48. If Heath could just squeeze a little more out of the Panhard on the final round he could win. But he had to find still more speed, another lap like the ninth would leave him twenty-eight seconds back.

Every watch in the grandstands was out. Every eye looked back down the straight toward Mineola. Every ear listened for the telltale rumble of an approaching racer. Finally, the big Panhard appeared in the distance. When it flashed over the finish line, the scoreboard read 27:05. The crowd burst into wild cheers. Their man Heath had done it — or had he? Certainly, Heath had turned in a time fast enough to beat Clément, unless the young Frenchman turned in a hot lap of his own. Would he? Could he? Clément had ten minutes in hand by virtue of his later starting time. The crowd sat down to wait.

If every watch was out as Heath made his tenth circuit, every eye was glued to one as the crowd waited for Clément. The seconds ticked by, turning to minutes. No sign of the rakish blue Clément-Bayard. And as 9:59 became 10:00, there arose a strange roar as the huge crowd began to cheer at nothing. No car sped down the straight. No rumble could be heard in the distance. With no sign of Clément, they were cheering Heath's victory, but the moment had a strange, surreal quality. Yet on they cheered for their American hero, for a minute or more until the rumble of the Clément-Bayard could be heard. And as Clément piloted his racer across the finish line, the cheers swelled again for the valiant but vanquished competitor. When the final tally was made, Heath's margin of victory was a mere 1:28 — the closest race of its kind ever run.

Two laps back, Lytle's Pope-Toledo, Campbell's Mercedes and Schmidt's Packard tried to soldier on to the finish. It was a vain attempt. The crowd had had their race. They had their winner. And now, race or no race, they were reclaiming their roads and making for home. Within minutes of Clément's crossing of the finish line, huge throngs of people and hundreds of cars filled the roads. To avoid a disaster, the controls at Hempstead and Hicksville stopped the remaining racers. Whether the race officials and remaining competitors liked it or not, the first running of the Vanderbilt Cup was history. Not for the last time, the crowd had dictated events.

In the wake of his heartbreaking loss, Clément protested, claiming he had been unfairly detained at the Hicksville control. While there was some evidence to support his claim, the protest was quickly denied. This wasn't France, after all.

❖ ❖ ❖

Among the throng of people returning to New York on that October afternoon was an unknown twenty-one-year-old Italian immigrant. His family had come to New York from their home in Troia, Italy, when he was only ten and had settled in Brooklyn. During his teens, he had done some motorcycle racing, but this was the first automobile race he had seen. The speed of the spectacle had thrilled him. He knew then that he wanted to race like these men, like Heath and Teste and Clément. It was a day that would change forever the life of the young man. In less than ten years, his name, Ralph DePalma, would be as well known to American sports fans as those of Honus Wagner or Cy Young.

3

Devil-Wagon Holiday

Two events perhaps more than any others provide some insight into how different the world was in 1905, and where the events of the century would take it. On Sunday, January 9, 1905, 300,000 workers under the leadership of the radical priest Georgy Gapon marched on the Winter Palace in St. Petersburg to deliver a petition to Czar Nicholas II of Russia. In the petition, the workers demanded improved working conditions, the right to vote, and a representative body in the government. The Czar, not the last remaining absolute monarch in Europe and a man who only eight years before had described his occupation as "Owner of all Russia," thought these demands were unwarranted. He instructed his soldiers to disperse the marchers. When the marchers refused, the soldiers opened fire, killing over one hundred and wounding hundreds more.

The events of "Bloody Sunday," as it came to be called, galvanized the Russian people. Cities were crippled by strikes; universities were shut down by dissenting students; peasants rioted in the countryside, burning the estates of the wealthy. In June, sailors on the battleship *Potemkin* mutinied. In the end, Czar Nicholas, in his "October Manifesto," was forced to make concessions: agreeing to the establishment of an elected legislative body, the *Duma*, granting freedom of speech and assembly, and granting the right to vote to citizens of every class. Still, it would not be enough. The concessions would open the door for revolution only a dozen years later. By 1918, Nicholas would be dead. More significantly, every absolute monarch in Europe would be gone.

Meanwhile, in Bern, Switzerland, an unknown, German-born, twenty-six-year-old patent examiner published three papers in a German scientific journal. In the three, the young Albert Einstein confirmed the atomic structure of the universe, provided the basis for quantum theory, and established the theory of special relativity. The world would never be the same again.

❖ ❖ ❖

If the beginnings of change were evident on the political and scientific fronts in 1905, they were equally evident in the world of motor racing. The last running of the Gordon

Bennett Cup was held in July over the 85.35-mile Auvergne circuit in France. Eighteen entrants from six nations — France, Italy, Germany, Britain, Austria and the United States — made the start. Perhaps for the first time in history, the French team found themselves outgunned. Against their pair of 11.3-liter (687 cubic inch), 96-horsepower Richard-Brasiers, the Italians fielded a trio of 16.3-liter (994 cubic inch), 110-horsepower Fiats. Worse yet, the Germans and Austrians were equipped with a sextet of 14-liter (857 cubic inch), 120-horsepower Mercedes. Among the French, only the 17-liter (1,038 cubic inch), 130-horsepower De Dietrich, piloted by Arthur Duray, could boast more power than the Italian, German and Austrian entries.

Sadly, the American team still lagged, although not as badly as in years past. Two 8.6-liter (523 cubic inch), 60-horsepower Pope-Toledos were fielded for Herbert Lytle and Bert Dingley. While not as hopelessly under-powered as Lytle's Vanderbilt Cup car, they were still giving up 200 cubic inches and 30 horsepower to every other entry in the race. Not so the Locomobile fielded for Joe Tracy. It featured a massive 17.7-liter (1,077 cubic inch), 90-horsepower engine under its hood. Unfortunately, none of the Yanks would be a factor in the race. Dingley broke his gearbox after less than one lap. Tracy, likewise, was hopelessly slowed by gearbox trouble until a broken clutch ended his misery at half distance. Only Herbert Lytle would finish — twelfth and last, nearly two and one-half hours behind the leader.

From the outset, the Fiats showed their speed, with Vincenzo Lancia opening up an eight-minute lead after one lap and teammates Alessandro Cagno and Felice Nazzaro running third and fourth. Among the French, only the Richard-Brasier of Léon Théry could stay with the Italian machines, holding down second. But Théry had an advantage: starting first, he was free from the dust that blinded his pursuers.

By half distance, Lancia had stretched his lead over Théry to thirteen minutes and was seemingly running away with the race when a holed radiator overheated his engine. A piston seized, putting him out. Arthur Duray momentarily wedged his De Dietrich past Cagno and Nazzaro, only to quickly fade from the leaders. Over the last half of the race, Théry and the Fiats played fox and hounds, but as the conditions deteriorated the front-running Frenchman was too much for the powerful Italians. At the flag, Théry's margin of victory was sixteen minutes over Nazzaro, with Cagno another two minutes back.

In the wake of the race, the ACF informed the Gordon Bennett Cup committee that it declined the honor of organizing the event for 1906. The Cup committee then offered the race to the Italians. They also declined. After six years as the world's most important motor race, the Gordon Bennett Cup was dead. True, not all of this was a certainty when the second running of the Vanderbilt Cup was held in October of 1905, but every insider knew that the handwriting was on the wall. The French were anxious to organize their own *grand prix* race with rules more to their liking, and the Italians already had the *Coppa Florio*, so they had no reason to organize another race to compete with it for importance. So it was that a vacuum was about to exist at the highest level of motor racing. It would remain to be seen whether the Vanderbilt Cup would fill that pre-eminent position.

For 1905, the Vanderbilt Cup course was changed. The race length remained at 283 miles, within a mile of its length in 1904, but the control sections were gone, the circuit was shortened, and its route changed almost completely. Where the Jericho Turnpike had formed the northern leg of the triangular course in 1904, the section of it between Hyde

Park and Jericho now formed the southern leg. In addition, the course was no longer triangular. A kink had been inserted in the new northern leg, giving the circuit the shape of a badly tied bow tie. From the start on the Jericho Turnpike, the course went straight east for 6.3 miles to Jericho, where it turned north toward East Norwich, snaking along the Jericho and Oyster Bay Road for 3.5 miles. Turning west at East Norwich, the course then followed the North Hempstead Turnpike for 5.5 miles through Brookville to Bull's Head (also known as Greenvale), where it turned south toward Albertson, 3 miles distant. The road between Bull's Head and Albertson, officially named Willets Road but better known as "the Guinea Road," was dark and narrow, with overhanging trees on either side and an evil S-curve at the Albertson end. At Albertson, the circuit turned west on Glen Cove Road and proceeded up a grade toward Lakeville, about 5 miles away. At Lakeville, the circuit turned sharply south and made a downhill run toward Hyde Park, where the racers once again picked up the Jericho Turnpike 2.5 miles west of the start–finish line.

The new course was designed to be fast. While Vanderbilt and the AAA would not admit to laying out a course calculated to break the then-existing race record of 64.8 mph set in August by Reggio in the *Coppa Florio* at the Brescia circuit, it seems clear that such a record was on their minds. After all, a speed record could only serve to heighten the stature of the Vanderbilt Cup in the eyes of the public. Renault driver Ferenc Szisz pronounced the course "extremely fast," but went on to note that the section of the circuit between the S-curve and Albertson was filled with loose dirt that had not been oiled or rolled, making it impossible to maintain a high speed. He calculated that passing was impossible for five miles of the twenty-eight-mile lap, but went on to say that several sections of the course would safely support speeds of 100 mph for quite a distance.

The course was not without its other perils as well. During the week before the race, Robert Lee Morrell of the AAA Racing Board and Asa Goddard, a road expert, noted several dangerous spots on the course, one at the Mineola railroad crossing along the Jericho Turnpike, another on the North Hempstead Turnpike between East Norwich and the Bull's Head turn where the road crossed a culvert at the base of a depression, and a third below Bull's Head on the Guinea Road where a macadamized road intersected the course. At each of these places, racers traveling at speed would leave the ground and fly, perhaps as much as fifty feet, before touching down again. Goddard and Morrell arranged to have the loose portion of the course near Albertson oiled and rolled, and improved the grade crossing at Mineola, but there was little they could do for the spots along the North Hempstead Turnpike and Guinea Road. The racers would just have to accept the dangers.

Given the money injected into the local economy by the 1904 race, local sentiment was much improved. However, that is not to say that every Nassau County resident was in favor of it. Some were not, and they made their displeasure known. A few days before the race, bits of glass were found embedded in the racing surface at various points around the course. Worse yet, an old bicycle camouflaged under shopping baskets was found in the middle of the road waiting for an unsuspecting car to plow into it. To prevent further incidents, Vanderbilt ordered the circuit patrolled day and night. Nor was the vandalism confined to the course itself. There was also speculation that Herb Lytle's Pope-Toledo had been sabotaged after a cotton rag was found in its fuel line. But inasmuch as the car had been under lock and key since its arrival from the factory, it was wondered how anyone could have gotten in to do the deed. Despite the uncertainty, the teams took every precaution. They posted guards over their racers whenever they were not on the course.

If the new course layout was designed to call attention to the speed of the race, the list of entrants was one that could easily produce record-shattering laps. Five-car teams representing France, Italy, Germany and the United States were entered, and while the German team was again composed of privately owned cars, the French and Italian teams were clearly world class. The French team was composed entirely of factory-sponsored cars with a 17-liter (1,038 cubic inch), 130-horsepower De Dietrich for Arthur Duray, two 9.9-liter (604 cubic inch), 80-horsepower Darracqs for Louis Wagner and Victor Hemery, the winner of the 1905 *Circuit des Ardennes*, a 13-liter (792 cubic inch), 90-horsepower Renault for Ferenc Szisz, and a 15.4-liter (942 cubic inch), 120-horsepower Panhard for 1904 winner George Heath. Arrayed against this French factory might, the Italians fielded three 16.3-liter (994 cubic inch), 110-horsepower Fiats entered by Fiat's American distributor, Hollander & Tangeman. These would be driven by factory-team drivers Vincenzo Lancia, Felice Nazzaro, and Emanuele Cedrino. Rounding out the Italian team were two privately owned 10.6-liter (645 cubic inch), 90-horsepower Fiats, one owned by Major C. J. Miller and driven by Louis Chevrolet (who had crashed his 110-horsepower model in practice), and the second Alfred Vanderbilt's Fiat from the 1904 race, again driven by Paul Sartori.

If the German team could not match the factory involvement of the French or Italians, it nevertheless looked formidable on paper. New 14-liter (857 cubic inch), 120-horsepower Mercedes were entered for 1903 Gordon Bennett Cup winner Camille Jenatzy, veteran amateur Foxhall Keene, and John Warden. Al Campbell, a 1904 Vanderbilt Cup participant, returned in a 12-liter (731 cubic inch), 90-horsepower model. A fifth Mercedes owned by Clarence Grey Dinsmore was scheduled to round out the team, but it failed to make its transatlantic connections in time for the race.

HEMERY

Victor Hemery won the 1905 Vanderbilt Cup as a member of the Darracq team. Later, driving for Benz, he would come agonizingly close to winning the Grand Prize on two occasions, finishing second to Louis Wagner's Fiat in 1908 and a scant 1.42 seconds behind teammate David Bruce-Brown in 1910 (image courtesy Smithtown [N.Y.] Library, Long Island Room).

Against these teams of European machines, the American team looked less over-matched than in 1904, but, in truth, the team was in complete disarray. In the months leading up to the race, there had been twelve entrants for the five spots on the team. Pope-Toledo fielded its Gordon Bennett Cup car for Bert Dingley and a six-cylinder, 90-horsepower track racer for Herbert Lytle. Locomobile entered its Gordon Bennett Cup racer for Joe Tracy. Royal and Haynes each fielded single-car 40 horsepower production-based entries, while Matheson fielded a pair. Franklin and Premier, both builders of cars with air-cooled engines, each fielded a single entry, Franklin's a 60-horsepower straight-8. White entered a steam-powered car rated at 40-horsepower, while Thomas fielded a radical racer sporting a 12.3-liter (750 cubic inch), 60-horsepower, 6-cylinder engine, and featuring a hood 96 inches in length, its driver and mechanic seated aft of its rear wheels. But perhaps the most radical of the American entries was the Christie, a 60-horsepower, transverse-engined, front-wheel-drive machine, which had occasionally appeared in four-wheel-drive configuration with a second engine bolted into its tail.

The large number of entries mandated an elimination race, and here the problems began. The race was originally scheduled for ten laps over the Vanderbilt Cup course, but opponents of the race again reared their heads, complaining of the further usurpation of Nassau County's roads for the benefit of a few speed-demons. A deal was struck limiting the elimination race to four laps, at which point the sponsors of the production-based entries cried foul. At the shortened distance, their low-powered machines had little chance to outlast the temperamental racing specials.

Bert Dingley at the wheel of a 50-horsepower Pope-Toledo in practice for the 1905 Vanderbilt Cup. Unfortunately, Dingley would be the first to fall victim to Vincenzo Lancia's flying Fiat in the opening lap of the race. His race would end on lap three with his Pope-Toledo sustaining a cracked cylinder (image courtesy Smithtown [N.Y.] Library, Long Island Room).

Only ten starters appeared for the elimination race. Tom Cooper's Matheson had seized a shaft the day before, and the Premier never arrived, unable to meet the 2,204-lb. weight limit. In the race, the attrition continued. The second Matheson retired after five miles with the same malady as Cooper's. Lytle's Pope-Toledo, second after one lap, was withdrawn at thirty miles, its frame fractured. At fifty miles, the Franklin sheared its drive shaft. The White steamer did likewise. The Christie, piloted by George Robertson, threw tires like a ring-toss machine, broke a wheel, and was nearly two laps in arrears when the race was flagged.

Bert Dingley's Pope-Toledo won by fifty-nine seconds over Tracy's Locomobile. The two had swapped the lead throughout the race, with Dingley making three short stops for repairs. Tracy had made a conservative nonstop run, content to be assured a place on the team. They were followed by Jardine's Royal, which had survived a rollover at the Guinea Woods S-curve to finish third, eighteen minutes behind the leader, the Haynes (which had plugged along steadily, if slowly), and the Thomas driven by Montague Roberts. Despite the shortened distance, two of the stockers had made the team — or so it seemed.

At that point, the AAA Racing Board stepped in. Relying on the fact that it was vested with final authority to choose the team, it threw out the results of the elimination race and replaced the third, fourth and fifth place finishers with Lytle's Pope-Toledo, Robertson's Christie, and the White steamer. In the words of the board, they were "deemed as better fitted."[1] The reaction was immediate. The motoring press blasted the board's action. Factory representatives from Royal, Haynes and Thomas, along with sponsors and crew members, protested vehemently. The matter was taken up by the Vanderbilt Cup Commission, where Andrew Riker, designer of the Locomobile, and J. L. Breese, sponsor of the Christie, were both members. Riker and Breese abstained from the voting, but the commission upheld the board's selections. The whole situation was cause for embarrassment and hard feelings. After the eleventh-hour shortening of the elimination race, the selection process made it appear that the board and commission were conspiring to eliminate production-based machines at all cost in favor of more powerful racing specials.

And perhaps they were. With the least-powerful of the European factory teams packing 80 horsepower, it is understandable that both the AAA Racing Board and the Vanderbilt Cup Commission wanted the American team to be composed of the most powerful and race-worthy machines possible. They all remembered 1904, when Lytle drove a flawless race in his Pope-Toledo, but simply lacked the power to be any threat to the leaders. With 90 horses under his hood, Lytle might be a factor. The same could be said for the Christie. Although carrying only 60 horsepower, the car was the product of J. Walter Christie, a brilliant engineer and the designer of the revolving gun turrets for the famous battleship USS *Maine*. He would go on to pioneer front-wheel drive, V-engines, and a variety of other innovations, including the suspension system utilized on the Russian T-34 tank in World War II. If the car's penchant for flinging rubber and other reliability problems could be cured, it might well be a contender. The only selection that is difficult to fathom is the White steamer. It was not only unreliable, it was just plain slow. Just how slow was demonstrated on the Wednesday before the race. Members of the French and Italian teams confronted White and accused him of purposely slowing down on the course during practice to disrupt their lap times. They threatened to push his steamer into a ditch if he persisted. The matter became so heated that the parties ended up in front of Willie K., explaining their positions. There, White said that he wasn't trying to obstruct anyone, but merely trying to learn the course. He offered to try to stay to the side of the road so as not to impede his competitors. The Europeans cooled down and nothing further came of the incident, but it clearly demonstrated that White would not be among the front-runners.

Practice was held on the days leading up to the race between 5:30 and 7:30 a.m. During the early part of the week, most of the cars were lapping in the 27- to 28-minute range, but Ferenc Szisz turned in two laps at 26:30 in the slope-nosed red Renault that journalists would come to call the "Red Beetle." Vincenzo Lancia pushed his Fiat to a lap in the 25-minute range. As Lancia demonstrated, the factory Fiats, despite giving away between ten and twenty horsepower to the most powerful of the French and German machines, were clearly as fast as anything in the field — just as they had been in the Gordon Bennett Cup.

On Wednesday, Szisz reclaimed fastest lap from the Italian contingent with a time of 24:15, an average speed of 70 mph. The Hungarian-born Szisz, who had been Louis Renault's riding mechanic in the ill-fated Paris-Madrid race two years before, had taken over as Renault's top driver when Louis retired from racing in the wake of brother Marcel's death. Despite giving away even more power than the Fiats to the most powerful of the French and German machines, Szisz's Renault, like Lancia's Fiat, clearly had to be considered one of the pre-race favorites.

But favorites were not limited to Lancia and Szisz. A variety of stars caught the public's attention. Some liked Heath, based on his 1904 victory. Others favored Jenatzy, the "Red Devil," former speed record holder and winner of the 1903 Gordon Bennett Cup — at 120 horsepower, his Mercedes could run with anyone. Still others put their money on

Vincenzo Lancia in his 110-horsepower Fiat prior to the 1905 Vanderbilt Cup. Lancia would set the lap record, lap the entire field, and completely dominate the race until an accident with Walter Christie's machine that would sideline the Fiat for nearly an hour (image courtesy Smithtown [N.Y.] Library, Long Island Room).

the other Belgian, Duray, his De Dietrich the most powerful car in the race; or on the little Darracqs of Hemery and Wagner that seemed faster than anything else over the course's treacherous turns.

Heavy rain on Wednesday night precluded the possibility of a Fiat reply to Szisz's fast time. The rainwater combined with oil recently spread over the dirt sections of the course to turn them into a greasy paste. High speeds were impossible and few of the racers went out on either Thursday or Friday. Fortunately, by race day the course had dried sufficiently to be in near-perfect condition.

As in 1904, the Vanderbilt Cup was scheduled to start at 6:00 a.m., and as in 1904, the early morning start resulted in an overnight invasion of Nassau County. At 2:00 a.m., the Waldorf-Astoria began serving breakfast to race-goers. From 3:00 to 5:00, 34th Street in Manhattan was packed with cabs, cars and pedestrians, all making their way to the Long Island ferries. Cars streamed down Broadway bound for the race by way of the Brooklyn Bridge. The city was literally alive. As *The New York Times* reported, "From the Battery up to Harlem big cars boomed through the darkness."[2] Out on Long Island, things were much the same. Hundreds slept on cots in the halls of the Garden City Hotel. Others found accommodations for the night in haylofts, on billiard tables, sitting up in armchairs, or even on camp stools. Many more slept in their cars. Prices for lodging were so high that many a millionaire refused to pay them, preferring to spend the night roaming around under the open sky.

William K. Vanderbilt, Jr., race official Arthur Pardington, driver and car owner Foxhall Keene, and Fiat importer E.R. Hollander in conversation at the 1905 Vanderbilt Cup (image courtesy Smithtown [N.Y.] Library, Long Island Room).

By daybreak, the course was a mass of humanity. Additional grandstands had been constructed due to the number of requests for seats, but all of these had been sold out long before the race. The society set was out in force; it was rumored that even the Roosevelt children from Oyster Bay were among the throng at the East Norwich turn. An overflow crowd estimated at well over 100,000 stood ten deep along the Jericho Turnpike as Jenatzy's shuddering, silver Mercedes approached the starting line, smoke from the booming pulses of its open exhausts creating a fog around Vanderbilt and starter Fred Wagner. Willie K. shook the hand of the bearded Belgian with the flaming red hair, then, with a shout and a slap on the shoulder, Wagner flagged him away. At one-minute intervals, they followed — Duray's De Dietrich, its driver clad in a cloth helmet in the colors of the *tricouleur*, Dingley's Pope-Toledo, Lancia's Fiat. As Foxhall Keene approached the line in his Mercedes, a roar of applause led by the Vanderbilt box consumed the grandstand. Keene was a close friend of the Vanderbilts. Virginia Vanderbilt and her entourage, which included the Duchess of Marlborough, was not about to let him go without a cheer. They continued until Keene acknowledged them with a small wave. Seconds later he was off.

Keene was followed by the remainder of the field. Each of them got away cleanly except J. Walter Christie, who was now at the wheel of his racer, in place of Robertson. His engine wouldn't start. For twenty-eight minutes, as the remaining cars took to the course, Christie worked frantically on his machine. Finally, its recalcitrant engine fired and he was off, but it was just the beginning of a very long day for the engineer from River Edge, New Jersey.

As Paul Sartori, the last starter, spurred his Fiat away from the start-finish line and disappeared into the distance toward Jericho, the crowd, as it had in 1904, became restless. Spectators again wandered out onto the track, standing in the middle of the roadway, craning their necks to catch the first glimpse of an oncoming racer. But there were many more of them this year. To the racers, the effect of the crowd ebbing from the track as they passed, only to flow out behind them, was like racing into a "living wall." As one commentator reported, it was "as if each car were equipped with an invisible wedge a quarter of a mile long with which it smoothly plowed its way through the human clods."[3] George Heath was not so charitable. He would later complain, "It was like trying to race on a Broadway sidewalk."[4]

The fans did not have long to wait for the return of their heroes. Less than five minutes after Sartori's departure, Jenatzy flashed past the start-finish line in his silver Mercedes. His time, 24:52, was only thirty-seven seconds off Szisz's record-setting practice round, and Jenatzy had accomplished it from a standing start. A mammoth blackboard atop the press pavilion across from the main grandstand kept the spectators informed. But even before they had had a chance to consider Jenatzy's time, or its meaning, a second car flashed by, the Fiat of Vincenzo Lancia.

Lancia had started fourth, passing both Dingley and Duray on the opening lap. That he had gotten by the Pope-Toledo was not really a surprise, despite the American's minute in hand. Lancia had been one of the fastest in practice, after all, and the Pope-Toledo gave up 50 horsepower to the Fiat. But his pass of Duray, whose De Dietrich held a two-minute advantage and was the most powerful car in the race, was really something. Then again, maybe Duray had run into trouble. But when Lancia's lap time of 23:49 was posted, the spectators knew it was not trouble that had overtaken the big, blue machine. It was a burly Italian in a faded red sweater.

As the rest of the field streaked by, the blackboard began to tell the tale. White's steam car was sidelined at Bull's Head. Campbell's Mercedes was out with a cracked gas tank. But among most of the leaders, the race was a close one. Jenatzy's time had been good enough for second. Szisz in the underslung "Red Beetle" Renault was only three seconds behind, with Louis Wagner in the leading Darracq only one second further back. But ahead of them all, already by more than a minute, was Lancia's flying Fiat.

If George Teste had taken control of the opening laps of the 1904 race, Vincenzo Lancia positively dominated them in 1905. On lap two he lowered the lap record to 23:31, and cut Jenatzy's lead on the track to just 55 seconds. For his part, Jenatzy had fallen to third overall, overtaken by Szisz on lap two, but by less than a second. Further back, Victor Hemery in the second Darracq jumped from thirteenth on lap one to sixth on lap two. The Panhard of 1904 champion George Heath was eighth. And Arthur Duray in the De Dietrich had fallen to eleventh, a blown tire early in lap two dropping him from among the leaders.

The finish of lap two also treated the grandstand throng to a couple of incidents that demonstrated the skill of the drivers and the dangerous nature of their sport. Just as Louis Wagner came past the grandstand, his Darracq blew a rear tire. It went off like a gunshot. The black machine, still traveling at nearly top speed, swerved drunkenly. It rocked up on two wheels. Wagner and his mechanic crouched down in their seats, anticipating the rollover to come, but the car settled back down and Wagner was able to bring it to a stop a quarter mile down the straight.

No sooner had the crowd caught its breath than two cars appeared in the distance — the silver Mercedes of Foxhall Keene and Ferenc Szisz's red Renault. Szisz had caught the Mercedes and was trying to pass. Closer and closer the Renault crept as the cars approached the narrow section of roadway between the main grandstand and the press pavilion. As they passed the grandstand, they were side by side, only inches apart on the narrow road, only inches from the fans on either side. Szisz's Renault, less than six inches from the spectators in the front row, almost grazed the rope that held back the crowd. As they whizzed past, one spectator shouted, "You couldn't have put a sheet of paper between them."[5] While that may have been overstatement, the two actually were close enough that Keene's mechanic could have touched Szisz without extending his arm full length. As the two racers sped on past Wagner's inert Darracq, the red car crept ahead.

On lap three, Lancia continued his domination of the race, passing Jenatzy and posting another record — 23:25. As he rocketed by the grandstand, his Fiat spitting jets of blue flame from its open exhausts, the crowd let out a huge cheer. Virginia Vanderbilt rushed to the rail of her box and stood on it while a friend held her there, just to get a better look at the speeding racer. Lancia responded with a hand in the air. With a combined time of 70:45, his average speed for the first three laps stood at an incredible 72 mph. Szisz continued in second, while Hemery vaulted to third. But the Darracq was already ten minutes behind the flying Italian. Heath held fourth, another minute back. Arthur Duray, finally able to let his big, blue De Dietrich display its vaunted power, climbed from eleventh to fifth. Back in the pack, Emanuele Cedrino's Fiat broke a wrist pin at the Bull's Head turn and dropped out. The Pope-Toledo of Bert Dingley, Lancia's first victim, succumbed to a cracked cylinder.

Still, both of them were probably more fortunate than Herbert Lytle. The American who had had so much bad luck in 1904 began his third lap by running over a dog just as he passed the grandstand. Then, as he made the turn at Bull's Head and started down the narrow Guinea Road, his Pope-Toledo's chain snapped, sending the car skidding out of control. Tattersall, his mechanic, was thrown from the car before Lytle could get it stopped. Fortunately, Tattersall reported that he was "not damaged" and the Pope-Toledo's chain could be repaired, but the delay dropped Lytle hopelessly out of contention.

At the front, Lancia continued his assault on the record books, lowering the lap record to 23:18 on lap four. As one fan described it, he was "faster than any wind save a hurricane."[6] His rival, Szisz, was not so fortunate. Just short of the grandstand, the slope-nosed Renault coasted to a stop. A water pipe had broken on lap three and the engine was overheating. Eventually, the Hungarian was able to make temporary repairs and get back in the race, ultimately completing nine laps, but frequent stops for water would keep him out of contention. Jenatzy, whose Mercedes had been falling back over the preceding two laps, suffered a similar fate. The German car blew a cylinder at Bull's Head, forcing his retirement. Things were little better in the Darracq camp. After his tire problem, Wagner's mount succumbed to seized bearings. Hemery also had a tire give up. He was able to get back in the race, but the repairs ate up over ten minutes. His lap times, which had been in the 26 minute range, skyrocketed to 38:18 for lap four.

Further back in the pack, Joe Tracy had been nursing a nasty vibration. His Locomobile had blown its engine just ten hours before the start, requiring an all-night rebuild. On lap four, Tracy finally felt the engine smooth out. He poured on the power, trying to make up for lost time, but when he tried to take the S-curve on the Guinea Road at full throttle, he got in over his head. The tail of his big, maroon racer slewed around until he was facing the way he had come. Without stopping, Tracy stomped the throttle again, spun the machine back around like a figure skater and was back on his way. Despite his luck and quick reflexes, the spin would cost him nearly four minutes.

With all the attrition at the front, George Heath, who had been running at a conservative pace, turning lap times in the twenty-seven-minute range, found himself in second place as the cars approached half distance. Still, he was nearly fifteen minutes behind Lancia. Barring accident or mechanical problems, it seemed clear that no one would catch the burly Italian in the flying Fiat, but accidents and mechanical problems were all too common in motor racing in 1905 — and the race had a long way yet to run.

On lap five, a chink did appear in the Fiat's armor. Tire troubles slowed the leader, but a quick repair cost him less than five minutes. Still, it narrowed the gap between the No. 4 Fiat and Heath's Panhard to thirteen minutes. From Heath's perspective, it was at least a start. Behind Heath, Foxhall Keene had finally found his rhythm, or perhaps his Mercedes had found some extra horses. After falling back as far as ninth early in the race, he had climbed to third by lap five, up from sixth on the previous lap and only five minutes behind Heath. With half the race still to run, he was within shouting distance of the leader.

If Lancia had given his competition reason for hope on lap five, he whisked it off the table on lap six. Returning to his twenty-three-minute lap times, he stretched his lead over Heath to more than sixteen minutes. Still, Heath continued to drive his conservative race, turning in his mid-twenty-six-minute lap. Foxhall Keene, on the other hand, had taken the bit in his teeth. As he entered the Guinea Road S-turn, pressing hard in an effort to catch Heath and Lancia, the drive chain of his Mercedes snapped. The engine screamed wildly. With no power to balance the machine through the turn, Keene lost control. The silver Mercedes with the "5" on its cowling skidded off the side of the road and got airborne. It collected a telephone pole, splintering it and snapping it in two. Keene and his mechanic were thrown out. One of the Mercedes' wheels sheared off, hitting Keene's mechanic a glancing blow in the chest. Fortunately, it did nothing more than knock the wind out of him. Keene was completely unhurt, but his racer was smashed, as were his dreams of victory. As Keene would exclaim to Virginia Vanderbilt upon his return to her box, still grimy from the race, "Damn my luck!"[7] It was language a gentleman didn't use in front of a lady in 1905 — especially a lady named Vanderbilt.

Like George Heath, Victor Hemery knew that races are seldom won by the man who turns the fastest lap. As the old adage goes, "To finish first, you must first finish." After a slow first lap left his Darracq mired in thirteenth place, the dark-eyed Frenchman with the reputation for irascibility and the scraggly mustache had begun turning laps in the twenty-six-minute range, running comfortably in third, until his tire troubles on lap four. Thereafter, feeling the need to make up lost time, he had pushed his low, black racer harder, dropping his laps to twenty-five minutes. Between laps four and six, he had begun to claw his way back, reducing Heath's lead by nearly three minutes. And with Keene now out of the race, he had taken over third. Lancia might be uncatchable if his Fiat held up, but if it didn't, Hemery was poised to duel the American in the Panhard head to head. He would need a little luck — Heath still held a seven-minute advantage — but only a little.

By the time he finished his seventh lap, Lancia had lapped the field. Another flying lap of 24:02 put him twenty minutes ahead of Heath, his closest competitor, on overall time. On the road, by virtue of his earlier start, he was running a full lap ahead. That lead only increased as Lancia continued his blazing pace on lap eight, but as he neared the repair station just outside Albertson he felt one of his tires give way. Carefully, Lancia nursed his machine to the station. Quickly, the team changed tires. In less than six minutes, he was ready to go. Heath's Panhard still had not appeared. As he jumped in his Fiat and readied to pull out, the low, square silhouette of Christie's racer loomed on the straight behind him. Heath couldn't be far behind. Lancia couldn't wait. He knew that the road to Lakeville was narrow and winding, making it impossible to pass. Despite his lap in hand, he didn't want to be stuck behind Christie, to give Heath any chance of catching him. He floored the throttle of his big red machine and pulled out, but the gap was already closing — closing too fast!

After spending the early part of the race just trying to get his car to run, J. Walter Christie finally had a horse he could ride. Its engine had finally come on song and Christie was booming toward Albertson as fast as his big blue creation could take him. True, he was already four laps down, but even if he couldn't win, he wanted to show the crowd what his car could do. Suddenly, Lancia's Fiat pulled out in front of him, filling the road. He stomped on the brakes and fought for control, but it was useless. The Christie spun slowly, its wheels locked, as it bore down on the Italian machine. The Fiat fought for every ounce of speed. The cars' wheels interlocked; then, with a grinding and wrenching of metal, came impact. Christie was thrown to the roadway. His mechanic turned three somersaults before hitting the ground hard, breaking his left arm. Except for a few bruises, the other participants were unhurt. Lancia's Fiat was not so lucky. Its rear tire was sliced in half, its wheel bent grotesquely. The Italian contingent swarmed over the machine, but the repairs would take nearly an hour. In the space of an instant Vincenzo Lancia had lost his insurmountable lead, his record, and his race.

Next on the scene was Heath. He pulled his Panhard up short as he saw the two entangled cars filling the road. Nearly stopping to avoid another collision, he negotiated a path around the wreckage. Recognizing Lancia's machine, he knew what it meant — he was now in the lead. But it also meant Hemery was closing, somewhere behind him with three minutes in hand.

As Heath and Hemery raced back to the line, Louis Chevrolet neared the Guinea Road S-curve. His Fiat had been mired back in the pack for most of the day, but now it was running well. Chevrolet, always a charger, was determined to show what it could do. He entered the dangerous curve at 80 mph, confident he could handle the speed. Perhaps he could, but his Fiat couldn't. As he turned into the corner, its front axle snapped just inside the wheel. The car yawed sickeningly, following the route of Foxhall Keene's Mercedes, its rear wheel hub carving a furrow in the butt of the telegraph pole that Keene had splintered just a lap before. Somehow Chevrolet kept control. He ground his three-wheeled racer to a halt and stepped out. One look told him his race was through.

A pleasant surprise was waiting for Victor Hemery when he crossed the start-finish line at the end of lap seven. The scoreboard above the press pavilion told him that Heath's lead had been cut in half. He already knew about Lancia, but until now he didn't know that Heath had been slowed by the accident. Now he was in with a chance; with three long laps to go, he was just 3:21 behind.

Six miles ahead near the Jericho turn, Heath's thoughts were much the same. He couldn't be sure where Hemery was, but he knew that his slow lap seven, the seconds lost skirting Lancia's accident, had cost him. While his previous laps had been mid-twenty-sixes, lap seven took twenty-nine minutes. And Hemery had been cutting a minute a lap from his lead as it was. Quick calculations told him half of his lead had just vanished. With three laps to go, the Darracq was just three minutes behind — and closing at a minute a lap. It was anybody's race.

Heath faced a dilemma — should he increase his speed to keep Hemery behind him and risk a mistake or a broken machine, or stay at the pace that had given him the lead and let Hemery continue to close? In the end, a tire made the decision for him. It blew. Heath rushed to change it, but as he put the new wheel on and lowered the Panhard back down, the low black shape of the Darracq flashed by. Now there was nothing to resolve. His lead was gone.

At the end of lap eight, the first car past the grandstand was Hemery's. Ninety-two seconds later came Heath. But the real deficit was three times as large due to Hemery's later start. Knowing that he could not lose if he just kept Heath behind him, Hemery began to cruise. Heath closed, but his Panhard was starting to tire; the best he could do for the lap was 27:10, forty seconds off his mid-race times. Still, as Hemery crossed the line for lap nine, Heath was just eight seconds behind.

It was as close as he would get. Over the last lap, Hemery slowly pulled away, taking back twenty-four of the seconds he had given away on lap nine. And as the black machine trailing a haze of blue smoke made its way across the finish line for lap ten, followed thirty-two seconds later by the American in the Panhard, the crowd made their feelings known with a round of polite applause.

Victor Hemery's Darracq crosses the finish line to win the 1905 Vanderbilt Cup and is greeted by polite applause, but the crowd reserves its biggest ovation for Vincenzo Lancia, who had lapped the field in his Fiat and seemed a sure winner until a crash with Walter Christie's racer cost him the victory (image courtesy Smithtown [N.Y.] Library, Long Island Room).

If their cheers seemed restrained, it was because they were waiting. Waiting for their hero to arrive. The burly Italian in the faded red sweater had gotten his car back on the road. True, he was hopelessly out of contention, back in sixth place behind Nazzaro, Tracy and Szisz. But with two laps remaining he had put on a charge, another of his patented twenty-three-minute laps. One by one he'd picked off the Renault, the Locomobile, and his teammate. Crossing the line at the end of lap nine, he was third. And with that the balloon seemed to burst. Hemery and Heath were just too far ahead. He cruised through lap ten, going just fast enough to keep Tracy behind him.

Approaching the crowd at the start-finish line, Lancia shut off the engine of his big Fiat and coasted, stopping right under the wire. The crowd let loose with a roar for their man, but Lancia's dejection was obvious. He smiled weakly as shouts of "Bravo!" and "Bully for you, Lancia!"[8] rang through the crowd. Lancia may not have won, but his performance that day was one that no one who witnessed it would ever forget.

Still, the race wasn't over, despite the huge mob at the start-finish line. There were other cars out on the course, and one of them was racing for position. Joe Tracy could do the math. He knew that Lancia had started three minutes ahead of him. Now all he had to do was close the gap to put his Locomobile in third, ahead of the Fiat. His big, maroon Loco hadn't been running particularly well, turning laps in the thirty-minute range for much of the last half of the race, and Lancia had come past him like he was standing still, but still there was a chance and he was going to go for it. So it was that Tracy's Locomobile appeared in the distance going hell-for-leather toward a finish line mobbed with people. A flagman rushed up the road, waving a yellow flag. Tracy saw it in time, but just barely. He slowed, the crowd parting as he crossed. But he made it, snatching third from the Italian by less than two minutes.

After Tracy's near crash, the race was stopped. As in 1904, the mob on the course was too large to control. But this crowd was in no rush to leave. Apparently, the excitement of the day had been too much for many of the fans. Hundreds of tired spectators curled up under trees along the road between Albertson and Mineola to nap. One village constable said he would only let them sleep until sundown. "We're peaceable folk around here on the sabbath," he said, "and we don't want any leftovers from a devil-wagon holiday."[9]

4

A Miracle That Hundreds Weren't Killed

On April 18, 1906, at 5:16 a.m., the city of San Francisco was jolted awake by an earthquake measuring nine on the Richter scale. Forty-seven seconds later it was over — but in those forty-seven seconds nearly every non-wooden structure in the city had been damaged or destroyed. The recently completed city hall collapsed "like a giant house of cards." Buildings slid down hillsides, collecting others like tenpins. The cupola of the California Hotel slammed through the roof of a nearby fire station like an artillery round, burying San Francisco's sleeping fire chief in rubble. Still, most of the city's wooden buildings and virtually all of its houses still stood. But the quake had done damage that would prove to be even more disastrous — it had severed gas pipes, shredded electrical wiring and ruptured water mains. The inevitable result was fire, raging and out of control, with no way to fight it. San Francisco burned for three days. In the end, the flames consumed 3,400 acres and destroyed 28,000 buildings. Well over half of its population of 450,000 lost their homes. The death toll was set at 670. Another 350 were listed as missing. In some circles, it was being referred to as "the Disaster of the Century."

But the century was still young, after all.

On the other side of the continent, a calamity of another sort entirely gripped the populace of New York City. Mary Mallon, a robust woman who had worked in kitchens across the Northeast, knew nothing about germs and microbes. In truth, few people did. The work of Robert Koch into the spread of tuberculosis and other diseases, research that had earned him the Nobel Prize in medicine in 1905, was still little known outside the medical community. What Mary did know for sure was that some "hoodoo" followed in her footsteps. Wherever she went, illness followed. Dr. George Soper, a New York City health official investigating an outbreak of typhoid in the home of a wealthy family, was the first person, other than Mary, to make the connection. He looked into Mary's employment history and found that the dreaded disease had appeared in seven of the eight households in which she had worked. But when he went to question the itinerant cook, she had vanished. "Typhoid Mary," as the newspapers came to call her, was loose in the city. By the time of her capture in March 1907, she would be linked to twenty-five cases of the disease and one fatality.

❖ ❖ ❖

The Vanderbilt Cup would face a calamity of its own in October of the year, one that would threaten its very existence. But as 1906 began, all of the omens were favorable. The international racing season began in May with the inaugural Targa Florio, run over a ninety-mile circuit of roads beginning alongside the beach at Campofelice on the north coast of Sicily and winding through the nearby Madonie Mountains. Given the difficulty of the terrain, rising from sea level to over 3,600 feet, it was feared that the race would be a car killer. Many teams chose to stay home. Only ten cars made the start. And while some of the cars did crack under the strain, six of them, led by the Italas of Alessandro Cagno and Ettore Graziani, made it to the finish.

In late June, the ACF held its inaugural *Grand Prix* at the Sarthe circuit on the outskirts of Le Mans. In order to establish the preeminence of its new race, the ACF set its distance at a whopping 769 miles, twelve laps of the 64.12-mile circuit. It was run over two days, with the cars locked up overnight in a paddock and released the following morning to restart at the time intervals they had held at the finish of day one. The ACF had also done away with the hated concept of national teams, instead allowing three-car teams from each manufacturer. The result was a Gallic onslaught, at least in numerical terms. Of the twelve teams entered, nine were French — Clément-Bayard, Darracq, De Dietrich, Gobron-Brillié, Grégoire, Hotchkiss, Panhard, Renault, and Richard-Brasier. Italy was represented by Fiat and Itala, Germany by Mercedes. The Americans stayed home.

Ferenc Szisz took the early lead in his 90-horsepower Renault, but could not shake the pursuit of the faster 105-horsepower Richard-Brasiers. Fortunately, Szisz had an advantage. His Renault was equipped with the new detachable rims, allowing him to change tires in only two or three minutes. The new rims proved to be invaluable over the Sarthe circuit, composed as it was of long, fast straights paved with small, sharp, tire-shredding stones. The stones not only tore up tires, they became flying projectiles, forcing the drivers to wear leather facemasks in addition to their goggles. In the end, Szisz brought his Renault home first, thirty-one minutes ahead of Felice Nazzaro's Fiat, with Albert Clément in a Clément-Bayard finishing third. Jules Barillier in the leading Richard-Brasier came home fourth, followed by the Fiat of Vincenzo Lancia and the Panhard of George Heath.

Despite being outnumbered by French cars by nearly four to one in the race, the Italians continued to demonstrate the competitiveness they had begun to show in 1905, with Fiats finishing second and fifth. With a win at the *Circuit des Ardennes* in August they would have broken the Gallic stranglehold on the sport. Sadly, it was not to be. Arthur Duray's De Dietrich continued the French victory tradition.

So it was that as the racing fraternity came to Long Island in October, the French marques maintained their position of dominance, with the Italians seeming to be the only ones who could give them a run for their money. This state of affairs was looked on rather coldly by the American public. After all, hadn't the Vanderbilt Cup, like the Gordon Bennett Cup before it, been organized to foster better-built and faster American cars? Yet after six years of competition in one or both races, the best finish that an American manufacturer could boast was the rather distant third-place finish of Joe Tracy's Locomobile in the 1905 Vanderbilt Cup. Those looking to gild the lily could point to Herbert Lytle's effort in the 1904 Vanderbilt Cup, running third, two laps down, when the race was red-flagged; but, in truth, he had not been classified as a finisher. In the wake of the poor showing in 1905, the AAA Racing Board came under renewed criticism for its method of selection of the American team. Americans were sick of watching their cars run back in the pack. They were ready to blame anybody and everybody connected with the effort. In truth, the blame lay not with the drivers or organizers but with many of the manufacturers' commitment to winning. The simple fact was that most American manufacturers, although capable of building competitive machines, were preoccupied with building cars for the general public. They saw little point, and no profit, in building special high-powered racers. As a result, the American teams, with a few notable exceptions, had been composed of cars that were little more than stripped down production models. They couldn't hope to compete with the all-out racing machines from Panhard, Darracq, or Fiat. But in 1906, all that was about to change. The results would not be immediate, but the handwriting was there on the wall.

In the wake of the American showing in 1905, eight manufacturers began construction of all-out racing machines to compete in the Vanderbilt Cup. Many of them were of radical design. In an era when most engines were of four cylinders and many manufacturers had difficulty developing a reliable six, Maxwell built an 80-horsepower straight-8, and an 80-horsepower V-12. The V-12 was a particularly outlandish design, with twin radiators mounted on each bank of cylinders and neither a water pump nor a flywheel. Walter Christie was back with a revamped track car he called the "Big Bear." It sported a 13.6-liter (830 cubic inch) engine and its crankshaft also served as its front axle. Frayer-Miller fielded a trio of cars with air-cooled 16.2-liter (991 cubic inch) engines. Their seats were set flat on the frame with their pedal controls below the transmission.

In place of the conventional radiator and engine cowling, the cars had their engines completely exposed, with massive air scoops mounted above and alongside. More conservative designs came from B.L.M. and Apperson. The B.L.M. was a good-looking, if unproven, design — a lightweight chassis carrying an 85-horse-power engine. The Apperson packed 80 horsepower and had been demonstrably fast in the hands of George Robertson.

But the designs with the best chance for success came from the firms that had built Cup racers before — Pope-Toledo, Thomas and Locomobile. Tired

Lee Frayer, the man chiefly responsible for one of the most radical American race cars of 1906, the air-cooled Frayer-Miller (IMS Photo).

of giving away power to the Europeans, Col. Albert R. Pope fielded a car with a massive 18.4-liter (1,122 cubic inch), 120-horsepower engine calculated to do 100 mph at 1,200 rpm. Thomas, the Buffalo-based manufacturer headed by E. Russell Thomas, employed French talent and techniques in the creation of its trio of new machines. It established an office in Paris and engaged Amédée Longeron to do the design work. It hired technicians at Richard-Brasier away from the French firm to aid in the construction of the 115-horsepower racers. It also recruited two French drivers, Hubert Le Blon and Gustave Caillois, as teammates for Monty Roberts.

French reaction was immediate. Despite the fact that the ACF had taken no part in the selection of the French Vanderbilt Cup team and had nothing to do with the race, its chairman, former driver René de Knyff (who was also a representative of Panhard) cabled AAA officials to protest the Thomas on the grounds that its aluminum engine castings had been made in France, in contravention of the requirement that each car be completely manufactured in its country of origin. After a lengthy meeting between Thomas and Vanderbilt, the protest was denied. (It probably didn't hurt matters that Thomas was a member of the Vanderbilt Cup Commission).

Unlike Thomas, Locomobile looked to homegrown talent for the design of its racer, and the Bridgeport, Connecticut-based firm had just the man it needed. Andrew Riker was a veteran of the ill-fated Winton challenge in the first Gordon Bennett Cup. Previously, he had designed and built an electric-powered speed-record car. In 1905, he had been the man behind Joe Tracy's Vanderbilt Cup racer. But in 1906 Locomobile gave him carte blanche. Twenty thousand dollars later (more than five times the price of the average American's house), Locomobile had its racer, a machine that was fast and strong, if not revolutionary. Its frame and suspension were fairly standard fare for the era, a heavy-duty ladder frame with four cross-members riding on semi-elliptical springs, an I-beam front axle and double chain drive to the rear. Only in the engine department did the new Locomobile depart from the norm. To begin with, the four-cylinder engine, while not as large as the Pope's, was still massive. Displacing 16.2 liters (988 cubic inches), it was every bit the equal in size of the French and Italian machines. By comparison, the Renault in which Ferenc Szisz won the 1906 French *Grand Prix*, while admittedly a lightweight by European standards, displaced a mere 12.9 liters (787 cubic inches). It was also over-square, meaning that the diameter of its pistons was larger than their stroke. But perhaps most significantly, while most engines of the era, whether for racing or production cars, employed either an L-head or T-head valve arrangement, with both the intake and exhaust valves seated in the top of the block alongside each cylinder, Riker employed an F-head design, with the intake valves seated in the head directly above the cylinders. The result was better flow for the air-fuel mixture — and better flow meant more power. Officially, the new racer was rated at 90 horsepower, but many insiders claimed it was more — perhaps as much as 30 horsepower more. For once, an American driver would come to a race toting a gun that could shoot.

With all of the racing specials being built and production-based entries from Haynes, Matheson and Oldsmobile, the organizers were again compelled to hold an elimination race for the five spots on the team. This time they made it ten laps, the full Vanderbilt Cup distance. Unfortunately, the attrition began before the race had even started. Both Maxwells and the B.L.M. failed to make the weigh-in, victims of eleventh-hour mechanical bugs. Christie's "Big Bear" crashed into a telegraph pole in practice and was immediately replaced by the designer's little 50-horsepower car. Robertson's Apperson, one of the favorites, also wrapped itself around a pole after its steering linkage broke, sending young George and his mechanic, Arthur Warren, to the hospital. The impact was so severe that blowtorches were needed to cut the wreck from the pole.

In the race itself, things went almost according to the pre-race predictions, but not quite. Herbert Lytle in the powerful Pope-Toledo took the early lead, with Le Blon's Thomas and the little Christie holding down second and third. Inside of one lap, Mongini's Matheson and Lee Frayer's Frayer-Miller were out, the Frayer-Miller breaking a radius rod, the Matheson finding a ditch and yet another telegraph pole. Monty Roberts' Thomas was in little better shape; stripped gears in its transmission left it limping along at a snail's pace, taking nearly four hours to complete the first lap.

By lap two, the Oldsmobile was gone with a broken front axle, and the group at the top was beginning to take shape. Lytle still led, followed by Le Blon's Thomas and Tracy's Locomobile, but unexpectedly Hugh Harding in the production-based Haynes was fourth. The other Thomas and the remaining two Frayer-Millers, despite outgunning the Haynes and the fifth-place Christie by at least 50 horsepower, were already falling back.

As the laps unwound, the front five remained constant: Le Blon's Thomas, the Locomobile and the Pope-Toledo tightly bunched at the front, followed at some distance by the Haynes and the Christie. Try as they might, the others just couldn't crack the stranglehold at the top. Nearing half distance, the second Frayer-Miller broke a wheel, ending its day in a ditch. One lap later, Caillois' Thomas, after finally breaking into the top five, retired with a failed magneto. That left only six cars running with four laps to go.

At the front, the race was a crowd-pleaser, with the Locomobile and the Thomas trading places for the lead, never more than three minutes between them until Le Blon slowed on lap eight, giving the victory to Tracy and cementing second place for himself. Further back, Lytle had run into mechanical problems on lap six. The repairs took nearly an hour, but it was an hour that Lytle and the Pope-Toledo camp could easily afford. Although falling behind Harding's third-place Haynes, the big Pope finished fourth, one lap back. At the tail of the train, another lap back, Walter Christie held off Lawell's Frayer-Miller challenge by a scant four minutes after having had a twenty-four-minute cushion earlier in the race. Nevertheless, it was enough to garner the Christie a place on the team.

The fact that only one of the powerful Thomas racers had made the team was surprising. The fact that the trio of Frayer-Millers had been completely shut out was unthinkable, at least in the mind of W. J. Miller. He lost no time in filing a protest, claiming that the Frayer-Miller and the Christie should have been permitted to run the full distance, not just eight laps, before being flagged (once again, crowd control, or its absence, had made that impossible). He also claimed that Lytle's Pope-Toledo should be disqualified for receiving outside assistance, inasmuch as it had been towed to restart its engine after the repairs on lap six. While the issue of race length was not one that moved the AAA Racing Board, the issue of the Pope's receiving outside assistance was one that they could not ignore. Lytle was disqualified. Lawell's Frayer-Miller took its place on the team.

Sometime later, Col. Pope and Harry C. Leyman belatedly petitioned for their car's reinstatement, claiming that many of the competitors had received similar assistance. Whatever the merit of the claim, in prior years the racing board would probably have listened since the Pope-Toledo was clearly among the fastest of the American entries, but with the furor of 1905 still ringing in their ears, the matter was a *fait accompli*. The petition was denied as untimely.

❖ ❖ ❖

For the third time in three years, the course layout for the Vanderbilt Cup was new. While the Jericho Turnpike remained the southern leg of the course, and the eastern half of the course through Jericho, East Norwich, and Bull's Head remained the same as in 1905, the western half of the course was substantially changed. After making the turn at Bull's Head down Willets Road, the course bore off southeast to Old Westbury, thus eliminating the old Guinea Road section and the dreaded S-turn at Albertson. At Old Westbury, the course made a hairpin turn to the right, following the road northwest to Roslyn and the Manhasset Turnpike. The course then followed that turnpike west to Lakeville Road, where it turned south. In Lakeville, the course turned down the Glen Cove Road, running east as far as Plattsdale, where it again turned south for 2.5 miles, meeting the Jericho Turnpike at the Krug's Hotel corner in Mineola. The new course was longer, at 29.7 miles. It was hoped that the elimination of the Guinea Road section, the S-turn at Albertson, and the section of Lakeville Road between Lakeville and New Hyde Park would make for a less dangerous circuit with more opportunity for passing. Unfortunately, the most significant danger would prove to be one that no course change could remedy.

The teams for the 1906 race featured many former participants, along with some new cars and new faces. For the French, 1904 winner George Heath was back, as always driving a Panhard. This one carried an 18.3-liter (1,116 cubic inch), 130-horsepower engine. Louis Wagner was back as well, again driving a little Darracq much like his 1905 machine, but this one packed 12.7 liters (774 cubic inches) and 100 horsepower under its hood, up from 80 the year before. Back too were Arthur Duray in his *Circuit des Ardennes*-winning De Dietrich, an 18.1-liter (1,104 cubic inch), 130-horsepower monster, and Albert Clément in a 12.9-liter (787 cubic inch), 100-horsepower Clément-Bayard. New to the team was an American, Elliot Shepard, a cousin of William K. Vanderbilt, Jr. Shepard would be driving the 16.3-liter (994 cubic inch), 130-horsepower Hotchkiss he had driven in his first race, the French *Grand Prix*. Italy fielded two-car factory teams from Fiat and Vanderbilt-newcomer Itala. The 16.3-liter (994 cubic inch), 120-horsepower Fiats were piloted by veterans Vincenzo Lancia and Felice Nazzaro, the 16.7-liter (1,019 cubic inch), 120-horsepower Italas by newcomers Maurice Fabry and Alessandro Cagno, winner of the *Targa Florio*. In addition, Aldo Weilschott, a millionaire Italian doctor, had entered his privately owned Fiat, also a 16.3-liter model.

In the face of these powerful factory-backed teams, the German effort looked a bit second-rate, with only three privately owned cars entered. Camille Jenatzy, the "Red Devil," was again driving for Robert Graves, this year in a 14.4-liter (878 cubic inch), 120-horsepower Mercedes. Foxhall Keene was back too, at the wheel of the Mercedes he had crashed in 1905. In the wake of that race, he had sent the car back to the factory where it had been totally rebuilt and modified. Rounding out the team was 1904 veteran W. C. Luttgen at the wheel of George McKesson Brown's 14-liter (857 cubic inch), 120-horsepower Mercedes.

Despite the increased engine size and power of the European machines over their 1905 racers, the American team, or at least part of it, still looked competitive. Le Blon's Thomas and Lawell's Frayer-Miller both packed nearly the punch of the most powerful

European cars. And if Tracy's Locomobile was rated at just 90 horsepower, they were very strong horses indeed. True, some weak links remained. Both the 8.5-liter (519 cubic inch) Haynes, which would be driven by John Haynes in the Cup race, and J. Walter Christie's little 50, with its 7.7-liter (470 cubic inch) engine, looked much overmatched. Their engines were half the size and produced half the power of the big boys, but the board had had little choice in leaving them on the team, despite unspoken wishes among many of them that one or the other of the little cars could be replaced with the powerful Pope-Toledo. Right up until the start of the race, Col. Pope kept his racer and its crew in readiness at their camp in Bull's Head, waiting for the call that would put his machine in the race. It was a call that would never come.

If the German team looked a bit thin in the weeks leading up to the race, its chances dimmed even further as practice opened on Monday. On the previous afternoon, Foxhall Keene had been getting in some test laps at Belmont Park. When he arrived back at his garage in Cedarhurst on Sunday evening, his racer seemed fine. But the following morning, it was found that one of the Mercedes' cylinders was cracked. The damage proved to be irreparable and Keene had no spares. The only person who did, Robert Graves, refused to let Keene have them, believing that to do so would jeopardize his own car's chances. Before a single lap had been turned, the already-outnumbered German team had lost one-third of its entry.

When practice opened on Monday, Tracy wasted little time in displaying the speed of his Locomobile, turning one lap of twenty-eight minutes and a second of twenty-nine. Equally fast were the Fiats of Lancia and Weilschott, who reported that they were completely satisfied with their machines. But if things were going well for the Italians and Americans, the French team appeared to be in disarray. George Heath was unable to get under thirty-five minutes in his Panhard. Worse yet, Louis Wagner's Darracq, the one that had set fastest lap at the *Circuit des Ardennes*, had not yet arrived. It was mired in customs. The best times for the team were turned in by Arthur Duray and Elliot Shepard, but neither of them could break thirty minutes, no faster than Jenatzy's Mercedes.

Tuesday brought the first of a series of rumors that would keep the railbirds and the press buzzing all week. In its first incarnation, the rumor was of a match race between Willie K. in his 90-horsepower Mercedes and Harry Payne Whitney in his Richard-Brasier, the one in which Jules Barillier had placed fourth at the French *Grand Prix*. By Friday, the rumored race had expanded to include S. B. Stevens, who now owned Hemery's 1905 Vanderbilt Cup-winning Darracq. Although the race never came off, its possibility was the talk of New York, and the three millionaires all played to the crowd, taking laps of the course in their cars during practice.

If rumors of the match race had Tuesday's crowd buzzing, Louis Wagner did as well. Still faced with the fact that customs had not released his racer and anxious to turn some laps owing to the changes in the course, he borrowed S. B. Stevens' ex-Hemery Darracq. With it, he proceeded to turn a twenty-eight-minute lap, equaling the Locomobile and the Fiats. It remained to be seen what he could do with his own car and the 20 more horses it carried.

By Wednesday, the course was a mess. The turns at East Norwich and Lakeville were deeply rutted. The Manhasset Turnpike was equally bad. One racer described the Westbury hairpin as "little less than a plowed field."[1] It was doubtful that anyone could set a fast time given the conditions. Then again, Louis Wagner finally had his car. With a full

100 horsepower now under his right foot, the Alsatian blasted his pale blue, coffin-shaped Darracq through the ruts and danced it across the furrows, turning in a lap of twenty-six minutes. The French team was back—with a vengeance.

If the French prospects looked brighter on Wednesday, American hopes took a turn for the worse. Lawell spun his Frayer-Miller on Manhasset Hill and crashed into a telegraph pole. He and his mechanic were uninjured, but the crash badly damaged their racer, bending the frame at the front and snapping off one of the wheels. It was questionable whether the repairs could be finished in time for the race. Fortunately, Lee Frayer's own car was available as a backup, if necessary.

For the remainder of the week, there was little to report. With bad weather late Thursday and Friday, only Arthur Duray could better his time from earlier in the week, the blond Belgian turning in a twenty-eight-minute lap in his big De Dietrich. And so the race favorites looked set—Wagner, clearly the fastest, in his Darracq, followed by the Fiats, Tracy's Locomobile and Duray's De Dietrich, in no particular order. The 1906 Vanderbilt Cup looked as wide open as any race in history.

In its third year, the Vanderbilt Cup had become the nation's biggest single-day sporting event, outdrawing even the venerable Kentucky Derby and posting crowd numbers that nearly equaled those for the entire World Series. In the week leading up to the race, Nassau County sold out completely, with every hotel room filled and every available house anywhere near the course rented. The railroad siding at Westbury was home to two seven-car trains of Pullmans filled with wealthy Westerners who had come from St. Louis and Chicago to see the race. They made the trains their headquarters in order to avoid the depredations of the already infamous local population. Privately constructed grandstands blossomed like weeds, some of them so poorly constructed that race officials demanded they be strengthened or condemned by the county board of supervisors.

By the time of the Friday night exodus from Manhattan, Nassau County was already full to overflowing, with people bunking ten to a room in the hotels and overcrowded tents littering every available field. From Manhattan to Montauk, the whole area seemed to be one huge pre-race party. Posh hotels like the Waldorf served "Vanderbilt Breakfasts" to their race-bound patrons. The Long Island Railroad ran "Vanderbilt Specials" filled with all-night revelers. At the homes of the wealthy, fabulous "night-before" extravaganzas were thrown, while out in the fields, caravans of car-borne campers built fires, pulled out their banjos, guitars, harmonicas and accordions, and sang, danced and drank the night away.

As the sun rose on Saturday morning behind low gray clouds threatening rain, fully 300,000 people lined the course. As in years past, the main grandstand, now enlarged to seat 3,000, was the province of the society set, with such notables as Col. John Jacob Astor and AAA president Jefferson De Mont Thompson in evidence, in addition to the Whitneys and Vanderbilts. But elsewhere around the track things were not so orderly, with mobs jostling for space at vantage points like Krug's corner and the Westbury hairpin.

The enormous throng was more than even Willie K. and the AAA Racing Board had expected—and far more than they were prepared for, despite the crowd control and safety measures they had undertaken. They had ringed the course with wire fencing six feet high, topped by two strands of barbed wire, and hired scores of locals to act as "special constables" in charge of crowd control. They had even gone so far as to bring in detectives from the famous Pinkerton firm, who were scattered throughout the crowd with orders to run off gamblers, crooks and troublemakers. But despite all their precautions, before the day was out, the enormous throng would render the best efforts of all of them useless.

No less sophisticated were their measures to keep spectators informed of race events — telephone lines ringing the course fed news to race announcer Peter Prunty, the "megaphone man," who then transmitted the information to the crowd. Simultaneously, timers would provide him with lap times and speed data that would also be transmitted. For those out of earshot, a team of clerks would mark the place of each car on a giant map atop the grandstand. For the first time, a spectator in or near the grandstand would know what was happening at all points on the course almost as fast as the events themselves took place.

The race got started seventeen minutes late, after a dispute over the legality of Jenatzy's Mercedes. Le Blon in the Thomas was first away, the red car piloted by the red-bearded driver spouting blue and white flames from its exhausts as it thundered off into the distance. Next up was Heath in his Panhard. Starter Fred Wagner consulted his watch, shouted "Go!" and slapped Heath on the back. Amid a *basso profundo* roar, the blue car was gone. Then Jenatzy's Mercedes came to the line, painted a bright silver and sporting leather mudguards along its sides in deference to the soft track conditions. The Red Devil and his mechanic were no less impeccable, wearing matching white sweaters. With a shout and a slap they too were gone. And so it went — Lancia in the steel gray Fiat, Lawell in the Frayer-Miller "skeleton car," Shepard in the Hotchkiss — one by one they came to the line, their machines shuddering and shaking with the pulse of each bucket-sized piston, waiting for the signal, then gone with a boom of mechanical thunder and a lightning flash of flaming exhaust. Starting ninth, Joe Tracy in the gun-metal gray Locombile got a huge round of applause as he came to the line. Clearly, the crowd had a favorite. In contrast, the next starter, Louis Wagner, was met with relative silence, perhaps already cast as the villain. If so, Wagner looked sufficiently sinister to play the part — his long mustache protruding from a hooded and goggled face. The rest came and went: Cagno, Haynes, Clément, Weilschott, Christie, and Fabry. After twenty minutes of thunder, the main straightaway grew quiet. The mechanized symphony was over for the moment, its first movement complete.

The frontrunners had barely reached East Norwich when the day's first incident took shape. A constable patrolling the course near the Bull's Head Tavern was shocked to see a local farmer blithely pedaling his bicycle down the North Hempstead Turnpike. The farmer apparently had no idea that he was about to have company on the road in the form of seventeen racers moving at over 100 mph. The constable shouted to the farmer to get off the course. The farmer ignored him. He shouted again and again was ignored. At that point, the first of the racers appeared in the distance. With little choice now, the constable tackled the farmer, driving both men and the bicycle to the ground at the side of the road. But as the farmer went down on his hip, a sound of shattering glass and escaping liquid could be heard over the still-distant roar of the machines. He got to his feet and glared at the constable, the contents of his flask now running down his leg. For a moment the two men just stood there, each unsure what further unpleasantness the other had in store. But before an arrest could be made, or a brawl started, a few friends of the farmer's whisked him away to the happy confines of the Bull's Head Tavern, where he could "restore his spirits."

If the leading cars made it through Bull's Head without incident, at least one further back wasn't so lucky. Joe Tracy's Locomobile had been all over the road from the start. Its tires were completely ill suited to the soft, slippery road conditions. After turning on to Willets Road, he stopped to change to nonskid tires in hopes that their steel treads would give him some traction. His stop was announced to the crowd, which immediately erupted with a groan — less than one lap, and already their favorite was in trouble.

Further back in the pack, Dr. Weilschott was scorching the course. He and Clément had made quick work of Haynes, and as the Fiat pilot approached Old Westbury, he saw Cagno's Itala a short way ahead. As the two cars neared the hairpin, Weilschott closed the distance. Then, as Cagno braked for the turn, Weilschott dove to the inside, carrying speed. He slid around the hairpin in front. The next car ahead would be Clément or Wagner. Weilschott knew that if he could get them in sight he would be near the lead. As he pointed his Fiat out the Manhasset Turnpike, he stood on the throttle. He skated hard around the left at Manhasset, taking the corner as fast as he dared, and powered up Manhasset Hill toward Lakeville.

As the Lakeville Road approaches the town of Lakeville, it descends the back side of Manhasset Hill in a chute known as Spinney Hill. At the end of the chute is an S-curve. The journalists had dubbed it the "Dip of Death" (a favorite nickname for downhill curves among motoring journalists of the era) in the wake of Mongini's accident there in the elimination race. A grandstand had also been erected at the curve to give spectators a better view. Weilschott would give them a bit more than they wanted.

According to the good doctor's report in the wake of the crash, his steering gear jammed. Whether true or not, as he powered his Fiat down the treacherous chute, he lost all control. The racer, reportedly "running wild," first blasted past the flagman at the entrance to the S-curve, tearing the flag from his hand and nearly running him down. The Fiat then skidded across the front of the grandstand, scattering spectators. At the far end of the grandstand a couple of bicycles had been parked. The runaway machine hit them square. The bikes' owners and their friends tried to run, but the whirling projectiles knocked four of them flat. Still the Fiat wasn't done. It turned and smashed into a telegraph pole, demolishing itself and launching Weilschott and his mechanic into a flowerbed some thirty feet away. The now abandoned car then climbed an embankment and rolled, coming to rest upside down like some huge dead animal.

Fortunately, the boys were not seriously hurt, although two of them, Robert Ten Eyck and John Brooks, were taken home to have their cuts and bruises attended. Likewise, Weilschott and his mechanic were lucky, although they probably didn't think so at the time. The crowd nearby at first thought they were dead, but they were quickly up and out of the flowerbed and examining their wrecked machine. As Weilschott looked at the extent of the damage, tears welled up in his eyes. "I had set every store on this race," he said, "hoping to win even against the high-class competitors entered. And this is the result — out of it without even making one round."[2]

If Weilschott's racer posed a danger to the crowd at the Dip of Death, it was the crowd itself that posed the danger at Krug's Corner. Before the first racers had reached it on lap one, the crowd had trampled the fence in places and torn huge holes in it in others. They piled out onto the roadway. Jenatzy and Nazzaro were nearly forced to stop to get through the wall of humanity. Lancia and his mechanic stood up in their seats and shook their fists to warn the crowd away. Nothing did much good.

While Weilschott was out of the running and Tracy's stop had put him off the pace, the remaining favorites were keeping it close. Jenatzy barreled past the main grandstand first at the end of lap one, having passed Heath and Le Blon. Lancia was little more than a minute behind. But when the times were all in, it was Wagner in front, and already by nearly two minutes. To make matters worse for those in the crowd looking for an American upset, European cars occupied the rest of the top five positions, with Jenatzy running second, just seconds ahead of Duray, Lancia and Nazzaro. The best-placed American was Lawell's Frayer-Miller in eighth, already three minutes behind Nazzaro. The other serious U.S. contender, Le Blon's Thomas, had fallen to dead last with engine trouble.

Behind the leaders, Tracy braked to a stop and pulled off the road as his Locomobile reached the main grandstand. Again the crowd groaned, thinking Tracy's day was finished, but there was nothing wrong with his machine. He had merely stopped to warn Vanderbilt about the crowd in the road at Krug's and the hairpin. As Tracy sped away, Vanderbilt dispatched security personnel on motorcycles to help with crowd control. A short time later, they reported back — the job was impossible. As the race went on, things would only get worse.

As the leaders completed lap two, Jenatzy retained his lead on the track, followed closely by Lancia, but Wagner was catching them quickly. Wagner's lead overall was already three minutes over Duray, who now occupied second, with Lancia and Jenatzy less than a minute back, and only seconds apart themselves. It was almost a miracle that the leaders had all made it through. The crowd at the hairpin made it nearly impassable. People packed the roadway so densely that Wagner closed his eyes and piloted his Darracq by blind instinct, brushing at least a dozen coats and expecting at any minute to mow down a row of onlookers. If anything, Krug's Corner was worse. On his approach to the turn, Lancia began weaving his Fiat back and forth across the road to scare the crowd back. Duray intentionally took a wide line to back them away. Wagner actually took his hands off the wheel and punched at the spectators.

By the close of lap three, Lancia was only ten seconds behind Jenatzy, but Wagner and Duray were closing on both of them and, in the process, extending their leads on overall time. Still, the race within the race, the one that enthralled the crowd, was the one between the Fiat and the Mercedes: the steel gray machine, piloted by the burly Italian in the blousy shirt that bulged like a balloon in the wind, chasing down the impeccable white-clad, red-bearded driver in the brilliant silver racer. For nearly two hours they raced within striking distance of one another, each summoning every last ounce of speed. And all the while, Lancia inexorably closed the gap. On lap three, as the duo braked hard for the turn at Bull's Head, their engines' rapid-fire detonations sounding like a battery of artillery, Lancia inched alongside. The two machines slid through the corner together, the silver Mercedes on the inside showering the gray Fiat with dirt and stones. Then both of them roared off toward the hairpin, Jenatzy in front, a cacophony of thunder broken only by gear changes. Finally, on lap five Lancia powered by, driving his gray machine past the Mercedes like a stake through the heart of his rival. Still, Jenatzy gave ground grudgingly. Crouched low over the cowl of his racer he sped on, a demonic grin flashing from behind his red beard.

While Lancia and Jenatzy were captivating the crowd, the French contingent found trouble. Tire trouble slowed Duray on lap four, dropping the De Dietrich back to fourth. A similar fate found Wagner's Darracq on lap five, but his stop left him still in the lead.

Nevertheless, all but fifty seconds of the margin he had worked so hard to attain was now gone. As the leaders reached half distance, it was anyone's race, with less than eight minutes separating the first four positions.

On the crowd control front, things were only getting worse. Despite the number of spectators in the roadway, the first half of the race had been practically incident free. Fabry's Itala had grazed a little boy slightly on lap four, and in trying to avoid the youngster, Fabry had nearly lost control, his car fish-tailing drunkenly back and forth across the road. Still, the fact that no one had been killed or maimed was nothing short of amazing. But as the sun came out at half distance, the unruly mob at Krug's corner became even more brazen. Whole sections of the fencing were trampled. Holes as much as two feet wide were cut in it by spectators, who allegedly had brought wire cutters with them for just this purpose. The mob was far more than the constables could handle. As *The New York Times* later reported, many among them did nothing but "make a pretense of policing the course."[3] But even those who did try to do their job came in for criticism, the *Times* opining, rather unfairly, that "it took twice as many Long Island special constables as it would have taken of ordinary men to control the situation."[4] Shortly after half distance, the situation became so bad that Vanderbilt himself drove to Krug's. He yelled at the crowd in the roadway, urging them to back away, but his words had no effect. At that point, he put his shoulder into the men in the front row and moved them back physically, but the crowd merely spilled out around him, amoeba-like. From now on, the crowd was in charge.

Like Wagner, Jenatzy was slowed on lap five by the need to change tires. On lap six, it was Lancia's turn. At the same time, Wagner pulled out all the stops, trying to rebuild his lost lead. The result was his fastest lap of the race, 27:22. In the process, the Alsatian caught and passed Lancia's Fiat. As the pale blue Darracq flashed across the start-finish line thirty seconds ahead of the steel gray Fiat, the Fiat team sat up in shock and horror. Despite the announcements and course map, they hadn't seen it coming. But if the Fiat team hated it, the crowd loved it. Wagner might have six minutes in hand on overall time, but overall time be damned, here were the frontrunners going at it head to head. The grandstand went wild. Others, mired in the mob and unable to see the proceedings, amused themselves with reports of the ongoing fights between crowd and police.

By lap five, Joe Tracy was out of the fight, now over a lap in arrears. It wasn't that the Locomobile and "Daredevil Joe" weren't a fast combination, it was just that he, like all of the American entries, had no tires suited to the soft track conditions. The American nonskids, unlike the Michelins used by the Europeans, were virtually useless. The need for repeated tire changes and a series of niggling mechanical problems had slowed him on every lap. But Joe Tracy wasn't a quitter, and he knew how to put on a show. On lap five it all came together. With the track now drying, the Locomobile ran like a champion, and when Tracy crossed the start-finish line he had set the race's fastest lap at 26:21, more than a minute better than Wagner's best. Upon hearing the announcement, the crowd roared its approval — the race today might belong to the Europeans, but the Yanks had a car that was faster, at least for one lap.

Sometimes circumstances conspire to kill you. So it was with Kurt Gruner, a thirty-three-year-old father of two from Passaic, New Jersey. At first blush, there would seem to be no reason why this superintendent in the starch department of a mosquito netting factory would be at the race at all, let alone in the vicinity of Krug's Corner. But circumstances of friendship and marriage put him there with a predestination that only a Presbyterian could really understand. You see, Gruner was acquainted with one of the drivers, Elliott Shepard, and so wanted to cheer on his friend. And if that weren't enough, he had track-side accommodations. His wife was the former Helen Krug, part of the family that owned the hotel that gave Krug's Corner its name. And so it was inevitable that he would be at the race, and somewhere near the now-famous corner. By lap six, Gruner had made his way a short distance down the Jericho Turnpike from Krug's to the spot where the road crossed the Long Island Railroad tracks. There, he and some others watched breathlessly as the cars became airborne, leaning out into the roadway to get a better look at them as they landed and sped down the straight.

For his part, Elliott Shepard was having a respectable drive, particularly for a man with but a single race under his belt. Lying in sixth place since lap three, he only had Albert Clément and the lead gang of four in front of him. He felt good as he slowed the big Hotchkiss at Krug's and made the turn through the crowd. From his right-hand driving position, the big racer's hood obscured his view to the left, but he lost little time through the mass of humanity. He could tell because the two cars he had been chasing before Krug's, which were locked in a wheel-to-wheel struggle, were still only fifty yards ahead.

Kurt Gruner and the crowd at the railroad crossing saw the two cars coming toward them, nearly wheel to wheel at seventy miles per hour. They gave ground as the racers

Krug's Hotel, the establishment that gave Krug's Corner its name. This portion of the course was beset with crowd control problems during the 1906 Vanderbilt Cup, ultimately culminating with Elliot Shepard's Hotchkiss running down and fatally injuring spectator Kurt Gruner (image courtesy Smithtown [N.Y.] Library, Long Island Room).

approached and took flight over the treacherous rails, then jumped out into the road to see who would take the lead. Kurt never saw the speeding Hotchkiss only fifty yards back, not even when it smashed him with a sledgehammer blow that sent him glancing off a woman in the crowd and straight into a telegraph pole. His skull was shattered by the impact, his body broken like a rag doll. For her part, the woman sustained only cuts and bruises, although the impact had flung her ten yards through the air. She was, however, understandably hysterical, there amid the shrieks of other onlookers, and was led away from the scene by her friends.

If Kurt Gruner never knew what hit him, Elliott Shepard never did either. With his vision obstructed low and to the left, he never saw the figure in the roadway, and the jolt of the landing after the flight over the tracks masked any shock from the impact. Speeding along at 70 mph, his Hotchkiss easily outdistanced the screams of the horrified crowd. It was not until he stopped at East Norwich for tires and found that the car's crank had been bent that he asked his mechanic if they had hit something. "Yes," the mechanic responded, "a spectator. I think it was a man."[5] Still not wanting to believe the horrible truth, Shepard called Jefferson De Mont Thompson of the AAA Racing Board to find out if anyone had been injured. Upon hearing the news he withdrew from the race.

If lap six was a disaster for Elliott Shepard, it was nearly as bad for Joe Tracy. Fresh from his record-setting lap and wanting to lower the record even further, he was pushing his racer for all it was worth. But as he powered the Locomobile through the turn at East Norwich onto the North Hempstead Turnpike, the big gray car slid wildly in the loose dirt, hitting three men and a boy broadside. Not done with its carnage, the broad-sliding racer then grazed a car parked alongside the track, dumping the large party standing in the tonneau off into the dirt.

Neither the party in the tonneau, nor the men at the roadside, part of a crowd of 200 who were watching the race from the outside edge of the curve, were seriously injured. The boy, Ralph Baldwin of Norwalk, Connecticut, was not so lucky. Both his ankles and one leg were broken, and it was feared that he had suffered internal injuries. Unconscious, he was taken to the East Norwich Hotel. Fortunately, he regained consciousness there and was able to return home on the yacht that had brought him to the race, attended by an Oyster Bay doctor.

Through the crowd and the carnage, the leaders continued their duel. On lap seven, Wagner stretched his lead on the track to a full minute, continuing his succession of fast laps. The little Darracq was running like clockwork — in a very fast clock. With the exception of lap five, when he had stopped for tires, all of his laps had been in the twenty-seven- or low twenty-eight-minute range. If the pale blue machine could keep up this pace there was no way to catch it. Even Lancia's best was a mere 28:06. But those who remembered the races in 1904 and 1905 were not ready to crown Wagner with the victor's laurels just yet. After all, hadn't George Teste built up an eight-minute lead in just three laps in 1904 only to see his Panhard sidelined by a blowout? Hadn't Lancia carried a seemingly insurmountable lead into lap eight just last year, only to see his dreams shattered by a single error in judgment? There was no doubt about it, the Vanderbilt Cup had not been kind to frontrunners. So the crowd watched and waited, to see if the Frenchman could succeed where his predecessors had failed.

The first chink in the armor appeared on lap eight. When the cars reappeared, Lancia was in front. Those predicting a Darracq demise nodded sagely. The pale blue machine crossed a full minute back — two minutes lost to the Fiat in a single lap. Two more laps like that and Vincenzo Lancia might just get the victory many thought he deserved in 1905. What the crowd didn't know, couldn't know, was that one of the Darracq's tires had thrown a tread. The car was still healthy — and fast.

Still, five minutes was not a comfortable lead in a race run in 1906. A single tire failure or mechanical problem could gobble it up in an instant. So on lap nine, Wagner again put his boot to the floor in a final push to the finish. Again, he caught Lancia and passed him, opening up a sixteen-second lead as the two crossed the start-finish line. Through Jericho and East Norwich the blue machine continued to pull away from the steel gray Fiat, opening the lead. Then the unthinkable happened.

As Wagner swung the little Darracq into the stretch leading to the Bull's Head turn at eighty miles an hour, his rear tire struck a broken glass bottle that had been thrown into the road. The tire collapsed with a bang, and Wagner's hopes collapsed with it. His repair station was still some two miles further on. Without slackening speed, he powered the crippled racer to its destination, then jumped out as his crew went to work on the tire. As the seconds passed by like centuries, Wagner downed two raw eggs and a glass of champagne. Still, the frenzied mechanics wrestled with the tire as a speck appeared up the roadway. In seconds, the speck became a cloud, then a car, and the Fiat thundered by and was gone.

Back in the grandstand, the crowd heard the news. Everybody knew what it meant. Could Wagner get back on the track in time to hold off the charging Lancia? And could Lancia hold off the De Dietrich of Arthur Duray? The two had been separated by just ninety seconds at the end of lap nine, with Duray cutting the gap between them by nearly a minute. The crowd waited breathlessly, watches in hand, to see what the next few minutes would bring.

From Wagner's perspective, there was nothing left to do but to stand on it. Unlike the Fiat team, which had been surprised by Wagner's pass of Lancia on lap six, the Darracq team had developed a system of signals that had let Wagner know where his competitors were throughout the race. But no system of signals could help him now. There was no telling whether he had any lead left. As Wagner said later, "There was no more stopping or slackening at turns, no further fear or concern over the reckless crowd."[6] He pitched the pale blue machine headlong down the straights, drifted it in long power slides through the turns, trying to carve seconds or milliseconds from his lap, trying to make time stand still.

First to the line was the steel gray Fiat. As Lancia braked to a halt a quarter-mile beyond the start-finish line and looked back down the road toward Mineola, awaiting his pursuers, admiring mobs overwhelmed him. Others in the crowd that now filled the road turned their gaze westward, trying to be first to catch a glimpse of the speeding Darracq. Two minutes went by. Then a shape appeared in the distance. But who was it? The shape became larger, then turned pale blue. It was Wagner — the winner.

The band struck up the *Marseillaise* in honor of the third straight French victory as the crowd mobbed Wagner, just as they had Lancia. By this time, the start-finish line was a wall of humanity. Race officials frantically tried to clear a path through the throng as Jenatzy, then Duray, then Clément blasted full-throttle over the line, each racing for position. In the end, Duray would be credited with third, Clément fourth, and Jenatzy fifth. With each finisher, the crowd in the roadway swelled larger, just as it had in years past,

Louis Wagner's Darracq wins the 1906 Vanderbilt Cup as the band strikes up the *Marseillaise* and the crowd bursts out onto the roadway seeking to congratulate their new champion (image courtesy Smithtown [N.Y.] Library, Long Island Room).

until finally race officials were forced to flag it to a halt, leaving six racers out on the course. As the band repeated the *Marseillaise* over and over, journalists thronged Wagner, wanting a statement. The quiet, mild mannered Alsatian looked every inch the "speed fiend," his face covered in soot. He had little to say to the newsmen; he spoke little English. But one quote from him would resound through the Sunday morning tabloids and echo in the thoughts of the AAA and the Vanderbilt Cup Commission for weeks and months to come. "The miracle was not in my winning," he said, "but that hundreds were not killed in my doing so."[7]

5

An Appian Way for the Motorist

Wagner's words were startlingly honest. They highlighted the precarious position in which the race organizers and the AAA found themselves in the wake of the race. On the one hand, the race had been a smashing success. Not only had the crowd been huge, the race had been a great spectacle, *The New York Times* hailing it as "perhaps the most thrilling sporting event ever witnessed in America."[1] On the other hand, it had nearly been a complete disaster. The single spectator fatality could easily have been dozens and the Vanderbilt Cup, or even the whole sport of motor racing in America, banned thereafter, gone the way of Paris-Madrid. Only hours after the race, Willie K. issued a statement: "I am deeply distressed that the contest should have been marred by any fatalities, but I am sure it was unavoidable. Every possible precaution was taken. The unfortunate and deplorable accident in which Mr. Shepard figured is the cause of the keenest sorrow for me, and I sympathize, not only with the families of those who were victims of the accidents, but with Mr. Shepard and the other drivers, who could not prevent them."[2]

The AAA, anxious to police itself before a governmental entity felt the need to step in and do so, decided in short order that it would sanction no further races on the course due to the impossibility of keeping the crowds in check. In the wake of the race, Willie K. and his sportsman friends retired to the Garden City Hotel to discuss their options. None seemed particularly good. They discussed the possibility of moving the course to a less populous site further out on Long Island, but quickly realized that, in truth, such a move would solve nothing. The Vanderbilt Cup had become such a marquee event that huge crowds could be expected wherever it was held — and huge crowds meant crowd control problems. The race had become a victim of its own enormous success. The only other option appeared to be the establishment of a private course somewhere, preferably on Long Island, but that would entail a huge outlay of money for the acquisition and improvement of the site. With cars starting at one-minute intervals and lapping at over 60 mph, a course at least twenty miles in length would be necessary. Even Willie K. Vanderbilt wasn't ready to spend that kind of money without a better return on his investment than a race course could provide.

Then the group hit on an elegant solution. They would build not merely a race course, but an automobiles-only toll road running the length of Long Island, from Queens to Riverhead. It could provide income to its backers and serve as the site for their race as well. Before long, they had formed a corporation capitalized with $2.5 million in stock. Not unexpectedly, Willie K. was elected its president. The board of directors included such notables as John Jacob Astor and Harry Payne Whitney. But the man assigned the job of actually making the dream a reality was the corporation's vice president, Willie K.'s right-hand man in all things connected with the Vanderbilt Cup, Arthur R. Pardington.

Pardington, a pharmacist by profession, and a master salesman, began with a massive public relations campaign to gain support for the project, now christened the Long Island Motor Parkway. He went from town to town touting the Parkway's advantages. "The Long Island Motor Parkway is a necessity," he preached, quoting the corporation's prospectus. "The use of the much-frequented highways of the Island by motorists is becoming irksome."[3] He wrote an article for *Harper's* magazine, where he likened the Parkway to a "modern Appian Way for the motorist."[4] He even went so far as to meet with individual Long Island landowners in an attempt to convince them to donate strips of their land for the project, claiming that the Parkway would greatly increase their property values.

Reaction to the project among the local populace ran the gamut from whole-hearted support to staunch resistance. Several farmers agreed to donate portions of their land for the Parkway, some even convincing their neighbors to do likewise. Others were more skeptical. "Mr. Pardington thinks landowners ought to give their land to millionaires for their pleasure," said one, "I think millionaires should pay for what they want."[5] Not all criticism was leveled at the requests for donated land; some people just didn't like the idea of the Parkway, itself— one writer calling it "an experiment to cut an island practically in two separate parts."[6]

The land acquisition proved more time consuming than originally expected. The 1907 Vanderbilt Cup was canceled — construction of the Parkway had not even started. But by June of 1908, the corporation was ready to build. It had acquired 137 parcels of land, often purchasing entire farms when necessary. The Parkway's route would have a number of twists and turns, necessitated by the inability to get certain parcels, but it would be a beauty — a sixteen-foot-wide

Arthur R. Pardington, pictured here at Daytona Beach, was not only the AAA representative for many of the races of this era, he was also one of the prime movers on behalf of William K. Vanderbilt, Jr.'s, Long Island Motor Parkway (image courtesy Smithtown [N.Y.] Library, Long Island Room).

The Long Island Motor Parkway was the first highway to use overpasses. Here a country road meanders beneath the parkway (image courtesy Smithtown [N.Y.] Library, Long Island Room).

ribbon of concrete for automobiles only, with bridges and overpasses isolating it from other roads. It would be like nothing the nation had ever seen before. Concrete roads existed only in a few cities, and then only for stretches of five miles or less. Bridges and over-passes such as the Parkway's could only be found in the roads through New York's Central Park.

At the ground-breaking, Arthur Pardington imparted his vision of the future. "Think of the time it will save the busy man of affairs," he said. "Speed limits are left behind, the Great White Way is before him, and with the throttle open he can go, go, go and keep going, 50, 60, or 90 miles an hour until Riverhead or Southampton is reached, in time for a scotch at the Meadow Club, a round of golf and a refreshing dip in the surf, and all before dinner is served, or the electric lights begin to twinkle."[7]

Nearly a century later, it remains a fine vision indeed.

❖ ❖ ❖

While Willie K. and the Vanderbilt Cup Commission spent 1907 in the land-acquisition and road-building business, the world, both inside and outside of motor racing, spun relentlessly on. In Spain, a young artist chose as the subject for one of his paintings a group of prostitutes from a brothel on Barcelona's Carrer d'Avinyo. Seeking to express a "truth" in his work that was something more than met the naked eye, the artist set the world on a course toward an artistic revolution unlike anything since the Renaissance. In *Les Demoiselles d'Avignon*, Pablo Picasso created what is arguably the most important painting of the century, ushering in a style that would later become known as Cubism.

While Picasso was setting the art world on its ear, Britain's Cunard Steam Ship Company was launching the biggest, fastest and most lavishly appointed liners that the world had yet seen, the *Lusitania* and her sister ship *Mauretania*. The two would go on to set trans-Atlantic speed records as part of the international fleet carrying European immigrants to the United States in record numbers in the first decade of the twentieth century — 1.2 million in 1907 alone. And the torpedoing of the *Lusitania* on May 7, 1915, would bring the United States another step closer to participation in World War I.

In American sports, the fourth World Series saw the Chicago Cubs, led by the double-play combination of Joe Tinker, Johnny Evers and Frank Chance, defeat the Detroit Tigers and their superstar rookie, Ty Cobb, four games to one. The phrase "Tinker to Evers to Chance" had become part of the American sporting lexicon.

Meanwhile, in the sleepy southern California fishing village of San Pedro, just outside Los Angeles, a new product was being developed that, if more mundane than art works, ocean liners or sports heroes, probably did more to change the life of the average American over the next century than all of them combined — canned tuna.

❖ ❖ ❖

On the racing front, the season again opened with the *Targa Florio* in April. The race attracted a field of forty-nine cars and shaped up as a classic battle between the all-conquering French teams and the Italian manufacturers that had been knocking on the door for the past two seasons. Vincenzo Lancia's Fiat took the early lead with a host of Italian cars in hot pursuit, but by the end of the first lap he began to fade. Felice Nazzaro in another Fiat then took over, followed closely by Louis Wagner's Darracq. A fierce duel developed between the two until Wagner's half-shaft broke on the final lap, allowing the Italians to romp home victorious with Nazzaro's winning Fiat followed by Maurice Fabry's Itala.

The *Targa Florio* was followed in June by the *Kaiserpreis*, Germany's debut as the host of an international race. Held in the Taunus forest near Frankfurt and attended by no less a personage than Kaiser Wilhelm II, the event had all the trappings of a state occasion. The race was run over two days, with two heats and a final determining the winner. It shaped up as another confrontation between French and Italian manufacturers, but like the *Targa* it was dominated by the Italian Fiat team. Lancia won the first heat, Nazzaro the second and the final. The Italians had finally won a race outside of their home country; perhaps they could finally put an end to the Gallic stranglehold on international competition.

So it was that as the international racing circus came to Dieppe for the French *Grand Prix* in July, the battle lines were drawn, with the French manufacturers determined to reestablish the dominance of their racing teams. As if to heighten the nationalistic aspect of the competition, national colors, abandoned since the days of the Gordon Bennett Cup, were again adopted. The colors were the same as under the Gordon Bennett Cup rules with one notable exception — red, originally assigned to the United States, was now the official color for Italy. The color that would grace Italian cars throughout the rest of the century, from the famed Alfa Romeo P-2s and P-3s of the inter-war years to the Ferraris of today, had been adopted.

Arthur Duray, the winner of the 1906 *Circuit des Ardennes*, led more than half the race in his Lorraine-Dietrich, stretching out a seemingly insurmountable lead until transmission problems struck. With Duray's retirement, Nazzaro's Fiat and the Renault of Ferenc Szisz waged a fierce battle for the lead. In the end, French machines would take four of the first five places, but as at Athy in the 1903 Gordon Bennett Cup, the top spot would elude them, with Nazzaro's Fiat finishing seven minutes in front of Szisz.

There had been only a single American entry in the race—another of J. Walter Christie's designs. Like every Christie ever built, it was radical. It was the lightest of the thirty-seven cars entered, was powered by the largest engine ever to contest a *grand prix*— a transversely mounted V-4 displacing just under 20 liters—and featured front-wheel drive. Unfortunately, the powerful but ill-handling machine proved to be slow and unreliable, retiring on the fifth lap. To his dying day, Christie suspected sabotage.

Elsewhere, 1907 also saw the completion of the world's first purpose-built racing facility at Brooklands in England, featuring a high-banked oval 2.75 miles in circumference. Unfortunately, no race of international significance would be held there until the eve of World War II.

In the United States, twenty-four-hour races were proliferating, held at horse tracks like Brighton Beach on Long Island and Point Breeze, outside Philadelphia. Other locales, perceiving a chance to woo the Vanderbilt Cup away from its Long Island home, bid for the revival of the race in 1907, all promising a race held under conditions of absolute safety to participants and spectators. Understandably, their bids were rejected by Willie K. and the Vanderbilt Cup Commission, who were wed to their Motor Parkway project. But the cancellation of the Vanderbilt Cup, while leaving international racing in America in hibernation in 1907, also spurred locales such as Savannah, Ga., Briarcliff, N.Y., Lowell, Mass., and Philadelphia, Pa., to establish races of their own. The Vanderbilt Cup would reemerge in 1908, but it would never again hold its singular position as the preeminent American race.

6

Once a Year I See the Sun Rise

With the 1908 model year, an American automobile manufacturer unveiled the car that would put the nation on wheels. At its inception, Henry Ford's Model T was not the revolutionary machine that we now think of—the assembly line and mass production still lay five years in the future. Nevertheless, the car was the first to be designed and built with the average man in mind, both in price and in durability. Within a year of its introduction, 10,000 Model T's had been sold. The automobile was no longer merely a plaything for the rich, it was transportation for everyone. The age of the automobile had arrived with its horn blaring.

In the world of sports the unthinkable happened. A black man won the heavyweight championship of the world, shattering previously unshakable notions of white supremacy. It didn't matter that Jack Johnson was not only a consummate boxer, but also a connoisseur of classical music, a collector of fine cars, and a man familiar with the works of Shakespeare. He was simply the wrong color. The press belittled his fourteenth round victory over Tommy Burns, calling it a fluke, and began a search for a "great white hope" to regain the title. Despite white America's best efforts to unseat him, both inside and outside of the ring, including a conviction on a trumped-up morals charge, he would hold the crown until 1915.

In Switzerland, a chemist named Jacques Brandenberger applied a coat of liquid cellulose to a tablecloth in an attempt to create a stain-resistant fabric. The experiment was a failure. When dry, the cellulose failed to adhere to the cloth, peeling off in a transparent sheet. But while Brandenberger's experiment did nothing for fabrics, the canny chemist realized he had stumbled onto a totally new material. He called it cellophane. It would revolutionize food packaging.

Meanwhile, in Persia, the nation was in open revolt against the Shah, who refused to be bound by a constitution or to share power with an elected national assembly. And in the Balkans, the states of Bosnia and Hercegovina gained independence from the crumbling Ottoman Empire, only to be gobbled up by the Austro-Hungarian Empire. As things changed, so they would stay the same—ninety

75

years later, Persia, now Iran, and the Balkan states would remain among the world's trouble spots.

❖ ❖ ❖

In the world of motor racing, much was changing, and yet remaining the same as well. The ACF held its third *Grand Prix* at Dieppe in June, run under a new racing formula. Gone was the old 1,000 kilogram (2,204 lbs.) maximum weight. In its place was a formula imposing a minimum weight of 1,100 kilograms (2,425 lbs.) and establishing a maximum cylinder bore for four- and six-cylinder engines. The Dieppe circuit also featured the first pits, a five-foot-deep trench along the front straight for the storage of spare parts and support crews, designed to enable ground-level spectators to have an unobstructed view of the track.

If 1907 had shown that the Italian marques, most notably Fiat, could win in the face of French factory competition, the 1908 *Grand Prix* demonstrated that the previously unbeatable French marques had been surpassed — and not just by the Italians. In the race, Otto Salzer's Mercedes took the early lead. When he began to fade, the lead changed hands between the Fiats of Felice Nazzaro and Louis Wagner and the Benz of Victor Hemery. Then, at half distance, Christian Lautenschlager's Mercedes took over, holding the lead

Christian Lautenschlager's Mercedes awaits the start in the 1908 French *Grand Prix*. He would go on to win, with Benz teammates Victor Hemery and Réne Hanriot finishing second and third. The German sweep would cause the cancellation of the *Grand Prix* and a moratorium on big-time racing in Europe until 1912 (IMS Photo).

to the end. Benz pilots Victor Hemery and René Hanriot were second and third, giving Germany a sweep of the top positions. More significantly, no French machine had been in the hunt all day.

French reaction to the loss was worse than even the 1902 and 1903 Gordon Bennett Cup disasters — at least in the Gordon Bennett Cup they had been able to hold up the rules as an excuse. But to be beaten first by the Italians and then by the hated Germans in their own *Grand Prix*— a race they had designed to maximize their automotive dominance — was too terrible to contemplate. Such blows to Gallic pride could not be allowed to continue. By year's end, the French manufacturers had banded together to withdraw all support from *grand prix* racing, and the French *Grand Prix* had been cancelled. Top flight motor racing in Europe would go into hibernation until 1912.

If night was descending on racing in Europe, a new dawn had arisen for the sport in America. Jealous of the AAA's success with the Vanderbilt Cup, the ACA had been seeking a site to put on its own international competition. The city of Savannah obliged, building a 25.13-mile course and inviting both sanctioning bodies to hold races there. The ACA accepted and scheduled their Grand Prize for November. The AAA and the Vanderbilt Cup Commission declined, not wanting to leave the society atmosphere of New York and still confident that their Motor Parkway Course would be a success. Unfortunately, by October only nine miles of the roadway were open, from the Westbury area to Bethpage. A planned thirty-mile circuit at Riverhead had never been built. It would still be necessary to use public roads for part of the circuit.

The new Motor Parkway Course was located south and east of the site used in 1905 and 1906, centered around the towns of Bethpage, Plainview, Locust Grove and Jericho. It used virtually all of the Motor Parkway that had been built plus fourteen miles of public roads, including the old Jericho Turnpike. The section of the course along the Motor Parkway was first-rate. A new covered grandstand provided seats for 8,000. Pits like those

A view looking down the Long Island Motor Parkway toward the main grandstand during the running of the Vanderbilt Cup (image courtesy Smithtown [N.Y.] Library, Long Island Room).

at the French *grand prix* had running water and other amenities for the teams. Opposite the pits was a three-tiered pavilion for timers, press and scoreboard, and surrounding everything were vast parking areas and food and drink stands.

The new course was slightly shorter than its predecessors, at 23.46 miles around. To maintain a race distance similar to that of earlier Vanderbilt Cups, the race was increased to eleven laps. In an effort to keep the crowd in check and avoid a replay of 1906, the Motor Parkway portion of the course was surrounded by wire fencing. To maintain order on the public road sections, 1,300 security personnel were retained, including Thomas Francis Meaghers' Irish Brigade, a volunteer outfit allegedly composed of athletes and Spanish-American War veterans. Also returning for duty were the Pinkertons and special constables who had been ineffective in 1906. To augment this force, it was rumored that National Guard troops would be available, if necessary.

If the course had again changed, so too had the nature of the competition. Gone were the European factory teams, unwilling to make two trips to America for races a month apart or to build new cars for the old 1,000 kilogram formula — the Vanderbilt Cup had seen no need to adopt the new *grand prix* rules laid down by the ACF. In their place was the cream of American factory teams together with some of the best privately owned European racers.

Locomobile was back with two of its 1906 Vanderbilt Cup cars, but their driver, Joe Tracy, had retired from driving and taken a position as team manager at Matheson. To take his place, Andrew Riker had hired George Robertson, but not without some trepidation. The handsome, blond, twenty-three year-old New York native was certainly fast and seemed level-headed when talking race strategy. But sometimes it all just went wrong. Everyone remembered his crash in the Apperson in 1906. At the Savannah Challenge Cup in March, he had been disqualified for rough driving. Driving a Simplex at the Brighton Beach twenty-four-hour race in early October, Robertson had run down a race official who attempted to cross the track as Robertson came flying down the front straight locked in a battle with a Stearns. He was temporarily put under arrest until the police determined that the accident had been unavoidable. In fact, Robertson had tried so hard to stop that the Stearns had hit his Simplex from behind, shattering the Stearns' headlights and twisting its frame. Despite the incident, Robertson and co-driver Frank Lescault had gone on to win the race, establishing a record distance of 1,177 miles in the process. Only two weeks before the Vanderbilt Cup, Robertson had piloted a stock-chassis Locomobile to a crushing victory in the inaugural Fairmount Park race in Philadelphia, finishing over a lap ahead of the second-place Acme of Cyrus Patschke. Teamed with Robertson for the Vanderbilt Cup was Jim Florida, who had been running a close second at Fairmount Park when his Locomobile broke a water line two laps from the finish.

Thomas was back as well, with two of their 1906 cars for George Salzman and H. Gill. Although still rated at 115 horsepower, they had been updated and modified. B.L.M. returned with one of its 85-horsepower cars, but as in 1906, it would be withdrawn prior to the start. In addition, a whole host of American newcomers made their Vanderbilt Cup debut — two Knoxes for Dennison and Borque; two Mathesons for Louis Chevrolet and James Ryall; an Acme piloted by Cy Patschke. But perhaps the most interesting of the Americans was the 90-horsepower Chadwick driven by hillclimb star Willie Haupt. The huge six-cylinder machine sported an engine displacing only 11.6 liters (707 cubic inches), but it also packed a supercharger, the first to be used in a race car.

Arrayed against this American might was a strong field of European cars, including three *grand prix* machines. Emil Stricker, the only European driver in the race, was entered in Robert Graves' 14.4-liter, 120-horsepower, *grand prix* Mercedes. Foxhall Keene was also back with his 14.0-liter, 120-horsepower Mercedes, the ill-fated veteran that had crashed in 1905 and blown its engine in practice in 1906. And Willie K. Vanderbilt had entered his own 12-liter, 90-horsepower speed-record car, to be driven by W. C. Luttgen. The French entries consisted of a 16.3-liter, 130-horsepower Hotchkiss *grand prix* car driven by E. J. Kilpatrick, a 12-liter (732 cubic inch), 110-horsepower Richard-Brasier for Léon Pouget (which would fail to make the start), and a 12.1-liter (738 cubic inch), 105-horsepower Renault *grand prix* car for Lewis Strang. Strang was J. Walter Christie's nephew and a veteran of the 1907 and 1908 French *Grands Prix*. In 1907, he had been Christie's riding mechanic. In 1908, he had driven a Thomas, but had retired after only four laps after losing both first and second gears. Rounding out the field was a single Italian machine, a stock-chassis, 7.9-liter (482 cubic inch), 50-horsepower Isotta-Fraschini, driven by veteran Herbert Lytle.

Robertson's Locomobile was fastest in practice and a clear crowd favorite, but many of the experts ignored its chances in favor of Stricker's Mercedes or Strang's Renault. They remembered the car from 1906, when Joe Tracy had looked fast in practice, but could only muster a single fast lap in the race. Then too, experts tend to be conservative in their judgment, basing their opinions on past performance. Given the European dominance of both the Vanderbilt Cup and racing in general, it was tough for them to believe that a relic from 1906, and one which had disappointed them in its first outing, could possibly be faster than the newer French and German machines. They were in for a surprise.

Friday night brought rain that continued through Saturday morning, soaking the spectators as they made their way to the track in the pre-dawn darkness. Still, by 5 a.m., the new grandstand was filled to capacity. The rest of the course was no less crowded. Despite the miserable conditions, a crowd estimated at 250,000 lined every inch of it. Clearly, rain or no rain, the Vanderbilt Cup had its followers. For many, the race had become a tradition. As one woman bundled in a fur coat confided to her escort, "There is only one day a year when I see the sun rise, and that is when the Vanderbilt Cup race is run."[1]

But she would see no sunrise today. As the starting time approached, the sky remained dark. The rain tapered off to a drizzle, soaking the drivers as they waited. Visibility was so poor that the start was delayed half an hour. For the first time a Vanderbilt Cup would be run over muddy roads. Those remembering Tracy's performance in the soft conditions of 1906 had even more reason to doubt the Locomobile's chances.

By 6:30 the sky was lightening and the decision was made to go. First up was Florida's Locomobile, followed by Dennison's Knox and Stricker's Mercedes. One by one they came to the line, looked to starter Fred Wagner, and were gone. All except Lewis Strang — maybe it was his uncle's genes, or some curse on the family, or perhaps just racing luck. Whatever the cause, when Strang came to the line, his Renault stalled and refused to restart. He would get away twenty-eight minutes late and last only three laps, retiring with a burned-out clutch.

With the course greasy from the rain, the first lap was treacherous for many. Cy Patschke in the Acme skidded wildly at the Jericho turn, missing the outside fence by just inches, and throwing sheets of mud on the spectators, sending them scrambling. By comparison, George Robertson looked to be in complete control, setting up his Locomobile in a drift far in advance of the turn, then power sliding down to the apex, scrubbing off speed until the tires got traction, then blasting out of the corner and down the next straight.

Ill fortune continued to haunt society favorite Foxhall Keene. On the opening lap, his Mercedes caught fire. Keene succeeded in putting it out and managed to get back to his pits, but the nose of his car was scorched cinder-black. A lengthy pit stop to repair the damage put him out of contention, but the millionaire sportsman still soldiered on gamely. His luck hadn't changed, though. The car burst into flames again on lap five, this time burning off half of Keene's mustache and putting him out of the race for good.

At the end of lap one, Robertson's gray Locomobile, wearing the number 16, held a one-minute lead over Lytle's little Isotta-Fraschini and Haupt's massive Chadwick, which were within one second of each other. But the Locomobile's lead wouldn't last. Just after crossing the line, Robertson dived into the pits to take on water, giving back two minutes in the process. In the pits, the stop nearly turned to disaster when a crewman inadvertently picked up a gas can instead of the water hose. Catching sight of the error, Robertson's voice could be heard over his racer's booming exhaust, threatening the crewman with bodily harm.

Charging back through the pack of cars he had passed on lap one, Robertson again took the lead at the end of lap two, but this time by a scant fifteen seconds over Haupt, who had gotten by Lytle to take second place by a four-second margin. Back in the pack, the attrition was taking its toll. Chevrolet's Matheson, Gill's Thomas, both Knoxes and Kilpatrick's Hotchkiss were already out of contention, suffering from a variety of mechanical problems. Kilpatrick's retirement signaled the death knell for French hopes after three years of complete domination.

On lap three, Robertson scorched the course at a record-shattering pace, opening up his lead over Haupt to a minute and a half. Haupt, in turn, stretched his lead over Lytle's Isotta-Fraschini to nearly half a minute, with Stricker's Mercedes and Florida's Locomobile each one minute further back. To the experts, the performance of Lytle's Isotta was nothing short of miraculous. Giving up forty horsepower or more to the Locomobiles, Mercedes and Chadwick, the little red Italian machine that had dominated the stock-chassis races of 1908 proved more than able to hold its own.

Tires cost Robertson five minutes on lap four, dropping him back to fourth place, thirty seconds behind Stricker's Mercedes. Haupt took over the lead, his supercharged Chadwick finally able to open the gap over Lytle to nearly a minute. Further back, as Ryall's Matheson approached the grandstand, fire began pouring from its gearbox. Before the machine could be brought to a stop, flames enveloped its hood. As Ryall and his mechanic made hasty exits from the racer, a quick-thinking spectator grabbed a fire extinguisher and played it on the flames, preventing the car from burning completely, but Ryall's day was over.

On lap five Haupt continued to stretch the Chadwick's lead. Leaves plastered in its massive radiator, the huge machine kicked up a wake of stones and dirt like a dreadnought as it roared around the course. One minute back, Stricker finally got by the pesky Isotta for second. Robertson, in fourth, stopped to pick up two spares to replace the ones he had used on lap four. Still, the first four cars remained within four minutes of each other. It was anybody's race.

His tire problems remedied, Robertson again showed the crowd what his racer could do. Thundering through Cemetery Turn in a fearsome opposite-lock drift, cresting the Westbury Bridge airborne at 100 mph, Robertson blasted the big gray Locomobile around the course on another twenty-minute lap. He vaulted past Stricker and Lytle. At the end of lap six, only thirteen seconds separated him from the leader. Haupt searched for more power to keep the charging Locomobile at bay, but the supercharged Chadwick was slowing. At Bethpage on lap seven it ground to a halt, both magnetos out of action. Robertson sped past and into the lead, now two minutes up on Lytle, who had again wrested second place from Stricker. Further back, George Salzman's Thomas took over fourth, but no sooner had Salzman begun to move up than the engine of his racer went sour, dropping him back.

As Salzman faded, Luttgen in Willie K.'s Mercedes put on speed, taking over fourth. Nearer the front, Lytle and Stricker continued to battle, the German carving thirty seconds off his deficit, while Robertson stretched his lead to three and a half minutes. With eight laps completed, the race was shaping up as a classic international duel — American Locomobiles lying first and fifth, German Mercedes running third and fourth, and a lone Italian Isotta-Fraschini grimly hanging on to second.

For eight laps, Robertson had been the class of the field, cranking off twenty-minute laps whenever his machine was healthy. Only the stops for water and tires had kept him from running away with the race. Despite being down on power to the Mercedes and Thomas racers, the combination of Robertson and Locomobile was untouchable. No other car in the field, not even Jim Florida's sister machine, could turn in a lap under mid-twenty-ones over the fast, slick course. But on lap nine, the gray racer inexplicably slowed. Lytle, in second, cut the margin to under three minutes. Unfortunately, Stricker could not take advantage of the Locomobile's apparent weakness. His Mercedes had problems of its own. The problems turned into a conflagration on lap ten, the German machine catching fire.

Meanwhile, the trouble that had slowed Robertson on lap nine seemed to vanish. The Locomobile again turned a twenty-minute lap, stretching the lead to four minutes. With one lap to go, it was a two-car race. Luttgen and Florida had faded, unable to keep up with the pace of the leaders. Holding a four-minute lead, Robertson seemed in command, but a single mistake could undo him. After nearly four hours in the thick of a nip and tuck battle at record speeds, could Robertson maintain his composure, or would fatigue and nerves push him over the edge?

The crowd got its answer at Plainview. The curve there was fast, but Robertson still overcooked it. The Locomobile's long slide was too long this time. Spectators scattered as the racer ran wide and left the road. Throwing a tire, it threatened to roll, but somehow Robertson kept it upright. The crowd all around the track groaned as race announcer Peter Prunty gave the word, "Number 16 has gone off the track at Plainview."[2] The chance for an American victory seemed gone just fifteen miles short of the finish. But except for the tire, the big gray machine wasn't damaged at all. The only thing lost was some time. Thinking quickly, Robertson's mechanic, Glenn Ethridge, hammered on a spare. Then Robertson jammed the car back into gear and dropped his right foot, determined not to let victory slip away. Peter Prunty informed the crowd, "Number 16 is going again — not over two minutes lost."[3] The stands erupted. Hopes that had vanished just a minute before were revived as though back from the dead. Minutes later, as the American machine

George Robertson and the Locomobile that would forever after be known as "Old 16" capture the 1908 Vanderbilt Cup for the United States (image courtesy Smithtown [N.Y.] Library, Long Island Room).

appeared in the distance far down the Motor Parkway, the crowd in the grandstands began yelling wildly. As Robertson crossed the line, his racer was mobbed. Finally, an American victory in America's greatest race.

Officially, Robertson's time was 4:00:48.2 seconds, his margin of victory just 1:48 over Lytle, his average speed of 64.38 mph a record. But the crowd didn't care about any of that, they just knew that their man, and their car, had won. A mass of humanity engulfed the main straight. As in years past, the race had to be flagged.

But no one had informed Jim Florida. Trying desperately to wrest third place from Luttgen's Mercedes, he screamed down the Motor Parkway flat out. A wall of humanity still blocked the start-finish line. Stabbing the brakes, he carefully wove his way through the throng, dodging from one side of the track to the other, only to have a touring car loom up in front of him. He could not prevent the collision. The car then plowed into a spectator, David Schuh, breaking his leg. Apart from Foxhall Keene's mustache, it was the day's only injury.

The celebration seemed to go on for hours, and it wasn't confined to the track, or even to Nassau County for that matter. Upon learning of Robertson's victory, Bridgeport, Connecticut, the home of Locomobile, went crazy. First the factory whistle at the Locomobile works near Sea Side Park blared in celebration. Then every other factory whistle in the city chimed in, then the whistles of the steamboats in the harbor. Both Bridgeport and the nation had a new hero. Two, actually, for both Robertson and the gray Locomobile, forever after known as "Old 16," would become celebrities. Today, Old 16 resides in the Henry Ford Museum, looking much as it did that long ago day on Long Island when America won its first race.

7

Showdown at Savannah

One month later, the European teams came to Savannah for the inaugural running for the Gold Cup, the ACA's International Grand Prize. Two factors had lured them to Savannah and away from the Vanderbilt Cup. First, the prize money was twice what the Vanderbilt Cup offered, with $4,000 to the winner. Second, the ACA, patterned after the French ACF from its inception, had had no difficulty in adopting rules conforming to the new formula laid down by the ACF for its new race. It had even gone so far as to consider calling its race a "*grand prix*," but the idea was discarded as "too Frenchified."[1] Even with the English spelling, the race was every bit a *grand prix* as we use the term today.

The European factory teams had shown up in force with their *grand prix* machines. Owing to the new formula, they sported engines reduced in size from the largest of the 1,000-kilogram monsters, but these new engines were even more powerful than their older brethren. France was represented by a two-car team of 13.9-liter (852 cubic inch), 135-horsepower cars from Clément-Bayard for drivers Victor Rigal and Lucien Hautvast, a lone 13.6-liter (829 cubic inch), 130-horsepower De Dietrich for Arthur Duray, and a pair of 12.1-liter (737 cubic inch), 115-horsepower Renaults for the 1906 *Grand Prix* winner, Ferenc Szisz, and the American stock-chassis champion, Lewis Strang. Germany was represented by a three-car team of 12.5-liter (760 cubic inch), 120-horsepower Benz racers for René Hanriot, Fritz Erle, and 1905 Vanderbilt Cup-winner Victor Hemery. But the class of the field came from Italy, with three-car teams of 12.1-liter (737 cubic inch), 120-horsepower racers from both Itala and Fiat. Itala's drivers were a solid trio, 1906 *Targa Florio* winner Alessandro Cagno, veteran Henri Fournier, and Emilio Piacenza. But Fiat featured one of the strongest teams of drivers yet seen in the sport—1907 *Grand Prix* winner Felice Nazzaro, teamed with 1906 Vanderbilt Cup winner Louis Wagner. Vincenzo Lancia, the uncrowned king of the Vanderbilt Cups and a great American favorite, had retired from racing to found the car company that would bear his name. In his place on the team was the Brooklyn Italian who had seen his first car race just four years before.

Ralph DePalma was still a relative unknown to the American crowd. His racing career had had a rather checkered start, but in 1907 and 1908 he had begun to win races, most notably a victory in Readville, Massachusetts, over that king of the fairgrounds circuit, Barney Oldfield. That race not only brought DePalma his first public acclaim, it began the notorious feud between DePalma and Oldfield that would simmer and flame for the next decade.

If the European teams were a pack of wolves, the Americans were a flock of sheep with "Eat Me" stenciled on their backs. Missing from the race were Locomobile and Thomas, the cream of the American teams. Locomobile had retired Old 16 in the wake of its Vanderbilt Cup victory, feeling the racer had nothing left to prove. Even if they had wanted to run in the Grand Prize, their driver was unavailable. On the evening of his Vanderbilt Cup win, George Robertson had driven into New York to have dinner with famed restaurateur Jim Churchill. Parking his little Locomobile production car on a side street near Broadway, Robertson stepped out of the car and slipped on a manhole cover, breaking his ankle.

Among the Vanderbilt Cup cars, only Willie Haupt's supercharged Chadwick would contest the Grand Prize. Four of the other five American entries, an 8.9-liter (545 cubic inch), 50-horsepower Lozier for Ralph Mulford, an 11-liter (672 cubic inch), 90-horsepower Simplex for Joe Seymour, a 10.6-liter (645 cubic inch), 60-horsepower Acme six-cylinder for Len Zengle, and a 9.7-liter (589 cubic inch), 60-horsepower National six for English millionaire Hugh Harding, were basically stripped-down production cars. Only Bob Burman's 9.7-liter (589 cubic inch), 50-horsepower Buick was a true racing chassis, and it was hopelessly under-powered. It was the same story as the early years of the Vanderbilt Cup, the Americans showing up with machinery that was completely outclassed. They couldn't hope to compete with the European machines, especially over a course like Savannah.

After being rejected by the Vanderbilt Cup Commission, Savannah was determined to put on an impressive and trouble-free event. They had gone all out in building their track. Convict labor had been used to cut the course through the forest. The result was an immaculate 25.13-mile course that wound through fields and then plunged into tunnels formed by huge live oaks. It was paved with oiled gravel which was reputed to be virtually dust-free. Its roadway was between thirty and sixty feet wide, with its turns, already bearing names like "Thunderbolt Curve" and "Skidaway," all "properly banked." To put it simply, it was a course built for speed. If the course was impressive, crowd control would be as well, handled by 16,000 troops of the Georgia militia.

Virtually everyone acknowledged that the sixteen-lap, 402-mile Grand Prize shaped up as an all-European show. Although the French had been swept from the podium at their *Grand Prix* in June, the team, and particularly the Clément-Bayards and Renaults, looked formidable indeed. Lewis Strang had been clocked at 111 mph on the La Roche straight. But the favorites in the eyes of the experts were the teams from Fiat and Benz. Within those teams, former Vanderbilt Cup winners Wagner and Hemery and 1907 *Grand Prix* winner Felice Nazzaro were expected to lead the way. For once, the experts would be right, but not before the kid from Brooklyn showed the crowd he could run with the masters.

As the racers assembled for the 9:00 a.m. start, a dense fog hung over the course. Wet weather had made the roads slippery, and many of the drivers opted for non-skid tires. Still, the inclement weather hadn't kept the crowd home—150,000 fans lined the course, many of them society swells from the Northeast who had come down by steamship or by train to see the new race. With visibility minimal, the start was postponed. At 9:45 a.m., the fog still had not lifted, but the decision was made to go on with the race. The first two laps would be run in a blinding mist.

Rigal in the Clément-Bayard was first away, followed by Mulford's Lozier and Seymour's Simplex. It took less than a lap for the foggy conditions to claim their first victim. Rigal, with no car to lead him, ran off course in the mist. He managed to keep his racer on its wheels, but would finish the lap one spot from the bottom. With Rigal gone, Mulford took over the lead on the track. Despite the pack of howling European machines behind him, he managed to keep them at bay, crossing the start-finish line on lap one still in front. The crowd cheered wildly at the sight of a hometown car leading the pack, but as the racers flashed by one by one, reality returned. Despite leading the race, Mulford's Lozier would only be credited with sixteenth. The fastest of the Europeans, among the last of the starters, had already opened up a three-minute lead.

But the crowd had a new man to cheer. Unthinkably, the fastest of the European entries was not Wagner, or Hemery, or Nazzaro. It was DePalma, the American, leading teammate Wagner by twelve seconds and Hanriot's Benz by twenty. Szisz, Erle, Nazzaro and Hemery were all further back. A lone American machine, Willie Haupt in the supercharged Chadwick, was running with the leaders, but even he was no higher than seventh. With all thought of an American victory gone after only one lap, the crowd took up DePalma as their own.

They had even more to cheer on lap two. With the course still wet and the fog just beginning to lift, DePalma attacked, his big red Fiat shooting gravel from beneath its wheels like a Gatling gun as it slid around the Montgomery turn, topping 100 mph on the four-mile stretch of White Bluff Road. His time for the lap was 21:36, an average speed of nearly 70 mph. On the day, only Wagner's Fiat and Hanriot's Benz would join DePalma in the 21-minute club, and neither of them would equal his time even with conditions improving. DePalma's lead stretched to a minute on Wagner, who still held second by a narrow margin over Hanriot and Szisz. The young man from Brooklyn looked simply uncatchable.

But it all came apart on lap three. Unable to stand up to the strain, the big Fiat's tires gave up. And not one or two — DePalma could replace one or two in just a few minutes — all four packed it in. By the time he limped back to his pit, he had lost a full lap to the leaders and was hopelessly out of contention. Still, he put on the best show he could for the crowd, equaling his lap record on the seventh go-round and ultimately finishing ninth.

DePalma's was not the only Fiat in trouble on lap three. Louis Wagner had problems of his own — mechanical problems. As he stopped at his pit, his mechanic dived under the car; fumes from exploding exhaust pulses burned his eyes and clogged his lungs as he made his repairs. In the meantime, Wagner grabbed a gas can with his right hand and an oil can with his left and refilled the tanks of the monster. Repairs finished, the mechanic climbed back in his seat, while Wagner traded the cans for two bottles of champagne. Handing one to his mechanic, they drank them both dry, then were off, losing only two minutes.

Wagner's stop handed the lead to René Hanriot's Benz, with Ferenc Szisz in the Renault running seven seconds back. The two had opened a gap of forty seconds over

Fritz Erle's Benz, with Cagno's Itala and Nazzaro's Fiat running together another minute back. Then, on lap four, the race began to take the shape predicted by the pundits. As Cagno stopped for tires, Fritz Erle pushed his Benz past Szisz to take over second, while the Fiats of Nazzaro and Wagner vaulted past the Hungarian to claim third and fourth. The race was so close that, despite a respectable lap (22:55), Szisz had fallen from second to fifth.

Although it seemed impossible, the race became even tighter on lap five. The leading Benz drivers both stopped for tires. Hanriot was able to maintain the lead, but Erle dropped to sixth in the process. Still, the top six positions were all within little more than a minute of each other, Hanriot holding a four-second lead over Wagner, thirty seconds over Nazzaro and Szisz (whose times were identical), fifty-two seconds over Hemery, and sixty-two seconds over Erle.

Szisz slowed on lap six. A front wheel bearing was showing signs of fatigue from the furious pace. It would burn out completely on lap seven, sidelining the Renault, and with it the French challenge. Meanwhile, Hemery was finally making his move to the front, storming past the Fiats of Wagner and Nazzaro to take over second. Once again, the Benz team held down first and second, with Fiats third and fourth. And Fritz Erle had climbed back to fifth in his Benz. From here on out, it would be a two-team race. Still, Hanriot continued to show the way to the more illustrious drivers behind him, turning in a lap of 21:52, the only Benz driver to crack the twenty-two-minute barrier.

Hanriot stretched his lead to nearly two minutes on lap seven as Hemery, Nazzaro, Wagner and Erle made pit stops, most of them switching to smooth-tread tires in the drying conditions. On lap eight it would be Hanriot's turn to pit, but his tires were too worn to make it back around. A series of punctures would cost him twelve minutes. It was time he would never make up.

With Hanriot slowed by his tire problems, Wagner stormed to the front on lap eight with a sub-twenty-two-minute lap of his own (21:50), opening up a thirty-second gap on Hemery. For the first time since lap two a Fiat was leading, but the lead wouldn't last. Hemery took over as Wagner made a quick stop for tires. One lap past half-distance, 225 miles into the race, the top three, Hemery, Nazzaro and Wagner, were all within forty-eight seconds, with Fritz Erle's Benz only ninety seconds further back. Two Benz cars running first and fourth, two Fiats running second and third: if either team held an advantage, it hadn't shown up yet.

Wagner closed to within nine seconds of Hemery on lap ten, with Nazzaro a further forty-four seconds in arrears, and Erle another fifty seconds back and rapidly closing. But unlike the racers in front of him, Erle had chosen to stay with the non-skids. As he hurried his Benz around the circuit in an effort to catch the lead trio the decision would come back to haunt him.

By later estimates, the big Benz was doing at least 90 mph down White Bluff Road when its right rear tire exploded. One end of the steel-studded tread struck Erle in the back of his head, stunning him and knocking his hands from the wheel. The Benz, now out of control, bounded into a ditch, struck a rock, became airborne and rolled, ejecting both Erle and his mechanic. Initial reports were that Erle had been killed, but he somehow escaped with nothing more serious than a broken nose and broken jaw — and presumably a terrible headache. He even managed to walk some distance to the car that took him to Savannah Hospital. His mechanic was even more fortunate, with no injuries more serious than cuts and bruises.

With Erle out, the pendulum finally looked like it was swinging in Fiat's direction. Further evidence was not long in coming — Wagner re-took the lead from Hemery on lap eleven. On lap twelve, Nazzaro, first past the pits by virtue of his earlier start, stayed out. Hemery, now without a running mate, made a calculated gamble. He dived into the pits for fresh tires to see him through to the end. Wagner followed. Ferro, his mechanic, had just shouted that they had lost the oil tank. An instant later, two tires had shredded. Wagner hammered on the new wheels while Ferro grabbed an oil can and rubber tube to jury-rig an oil tank for the racer. For the remainder of the race, Ferro would sit holding the oil can between his legs.

Hemery emerged two minutes behind the new leader, with Wagner just thirteen seconds back. Nazzaro, now the rabbit, stretched his lead to three minutes as the other two got back up to speed. As Nazzaro slowed to conserve his worn tires, last changed on lap seven, Hemery, playing the part of the fox, began to tear large chunks from his lead, fifty-two seconds on lap fourteen, thirty-five seconds on lap fifteen, all the while with Wagner, in the role of the hound, giving chase just seconds behind. Still, it would not be enough. As the lead trio began the final lap, Nazzaro still held nearly two minutes in hand over Hemery, with Wagner only two seconds further back. If Nazzaro's tires could just last one more lap, he would win.

They wouldn't. Approaching the Montgomery turn, the Italian heard the report and felt the jolt of a tire gone — and with it his chances of victory. Before he could even get it changed, Hemery's Benz flashed by, a streak of white noise in the stillness. The fox had just run down the rabbit. Minutes later, as Nazzaro was about to get moving again, Wagner's red machine roared past. Both of them now knew it was a two-man race — less than one lap to take home all the marbles.

Hemery's Benz flashed across the finish line first. As the checkered flag flew, the crowd cheered wildly, many presuming him victorious. Hemery's mechanic danced in his seat, jubilant. But Wagner still had six minutes in hand by virtue of his later starting time. Hemery's Benz hadn't turned a lap under twenty-two minutes. Wagner's Fiat had, but could the red machine turn in one now, after 375 miles of racing and with Ferro holding that jury-rigged oil tank between his legs? That was the question that ran through the grandstand like a dirty rumor as the crowd waited. The answer was not long in coming. Summoning speed he had not shown since going to the lead on lap eight, Wagner cranked out a lap that Hemery just could not match, 21:52, and with it the laurels of the victor. Hemery, the fox, may have caught the rabbit, but in the end Wagner, the hound, had still chased him down.

Wagner's margin of victory was just fifty-six seconds, the closest in any American race. To top that off, his average speed was 65.1 mph, an American record, beating out George Robertson's showing in the Vanderbilt Cup only one month before. And if further spectacle was needed, it was supplied by René Hanriot. The Benz pilot, whose chances went south in a welter of punctures and pit stops, cemented fourth place only after running out of gas coming down the home straight, his Benz crawling silently across the line as he and his mechanic rocked forward and back in their seats, urging it on with their own momentum. Hanriot's teammates carried him from the car on their shoulders.

A huge throng descended to the start-finish line where Wagner was presented with the Gold Cup and formally congratulated. After two heartbreaking losses in the 1905 and 1906 Vanderbilt Cups, Fiat's American distributor, Mr. Hollander, was unable to restrain

The Grand Prize of the Automobile Club of America, also called "the Gold Cup," would be the most coveted trophy in American motorsport between 1908 and 1911 (image courtesy Smithtown [N.Y.] Library, Long Island Room).

his elation. In a scene that would be revisited some sixty years later by Andy Granatelli and Mario Andretti, he ran up to Wagner and planted a kiss on his cheek. A limping George Robertson offered his congratulations. Amid the tumult and shouting, some of the news photographers sought out Hemery to congratulate him on a fine drive. Always irritable, the Frenchman refused to be interviewed, saying that since the victory was Wagner's, he should not be asked to horn in. He sat sullenly on the edge of his pit. When a group of photographers tried to take his picture, he turned his back on them.

But if Hemery felt snake-bitten in the wake of the race, he had nothing on his teammate, René Hanriot, whose long day of troubles was not over yet. After pushing his big Benz down to his pit and re-fueling it, he wanted to take part in the celebration. He jumped back in his racer and reversed it back toward the start-finish line where the crowd was assembled. Almost instantly, a member of the Georgia militia ordered him to stop. Apparently, Hanriot didn't move quickly enough. Before he could bring the Benz to a halt, the soldier shot out its rear tires.

The top finishing American machine was Joe Seymour's Simplex in eleventh place, two laps back. "Wild" Bob Burman's Buick had lasted only two laps, Haupt's Chadwick only four. The only other Yank still running at the end was Ralph Mulford, his Lozier six laps in arrears. But the crowd didn't care about any of that. They had found a new American hero in Ralph DePalma. More importantly, they had just witnessed one of the great races of all time. Savannah, indeed, had put on a show. It would not be its last.

8

The Predictions of an Invisible Man

On the night of January 23, 1909, the White Star liner *Republic* was rammed by the steamship *Florida* in the fog-shrouded waters off Nantucket. In the wake of the collision, wireless operator Jack Binns of the *Republic* became the first man in history to send out the distress call, CQD. Binns spent hours in the frigid wireless room of the crippled and sinking ship, transmitting messages with cold and club-like fingers to any and all who could render assistance. Finally, he was able to direct the liner *Baltic* through the fog to the *Republic*'s position. The 1,500 passengers on the *Republic* were saved. There had been no loss of life other than the few who had been killed in the collision itself. Binns was hailed as a hero. Songs describing his deeds were composed. The Vitagraph Company dramatized the event on film. The infant technology of radio was already proving its worth. Unfortunately, Binns' efforts to obtain government regulations improving shipboard wireless, such as a requirement that the post be manned around the clock, fell on deaf ears. After all, his heroism and the then-current system had been sufficient to save every possible passenger. It would take a greater tragedy some years hence to make people listen.

In April, Teddy Roosevelt, after turning the presidency over to his hand-picked successor, William Howard Taft, arrived in Mombasa, in what was then British East Africa, accompanied by his son Kermit and several prominent naturalists. It was the beginning of his famous African expedition, one that would collect countless specimens for the Smithsonian Institution. Roosevelt's expedition marked him as one of the first Americans to venture into the interior of what was still by-and-large "the Dark Continent." It also signaled the beginning of the great era of African safari, opening the continent to those of means and providing an alternative to the "Grand Tour" of Europe as a rite of passage for the wealthy.

Other expeditions and feats were everywhere on the horizon in 1909. The largest of headlines were for Robert E. Peary, who reached the North Pole on his third expedition, after two failed attempts had claimed eight of his toes, and for Louis Blériot, who became the first man to pilot an airplane across the English Channel, using a monoplane of his own design with a top speed of 40 mph. But other stories would have even greater impact on the century to come.

In what was then Persia, now Iran, English adventurer William Knox D'Arcy struck oil. The find would mean billions of dollars, first for the Anglo-Persian Oil Company, then for its successors, BP and the British government, and finally for the independent states of the Middle East. It would play a major part in the outcome of two world wars and would embroil both the United States and Europe in a whole host of lesser conflicts in the region for the rest of the century.

In the United States, Belgian-born chemist Leo Baekeland invented the first plastic — Bakelite. Soon everything from billiard balls to handbags to electrical insulators would be made from the inexpensive, durable new substance. It would be touted as "the material of a thousand uses." Perhaps more significantly, it would spur scientists around the world to develop more new materials. The age of plastics had arrived.

Outside the world of adventure, big oil and invention, Frank Lloyd Wright completed construction of the Robie House, perhaps the finest of his "prairie" designs; the Kewpie doll became an international fad; and the Lincoln penny ended the fifty-year reign of the Indian-head.

❖ ❖ ❖

In the world of auto racing there were whispers of change in the wind as well, but the words in the whispers were largely disturbing to the American road-racing fraternity. With the French manufacturers' boycott in the wake of the 1908 *Grand Prix*, racing in Europe was largely moribund. In August, the first dedicated racing facility in the United States, the brain-child of Carl G. Fisher, James A. Allison, Arthur C. Newby, and Frank H. Wheeler, opened in Indianapolis, Indiana. That facility, called the Indianapolis Motor Speedway, was a 2.5-mile oval paved with crushed stone and asphalt. Immediately after its opening, the track surface began to disintegrate under racing conditions. Within a month the track would be re-paved with brick, and by 1911 an annual 500-mile race would be scheduled. Indianapolis and the ovals that would follow it would ultimately signal the demise of road-racing in America.

To make matters worse, a backlash against all-out racing machines had been gathering momentum as well. Many in the motoring press howled that such machines were "freaks" that bore no relationship to ordinary production cars and that the appropriation of public roads for races between them was "ill-advised, unconstitutional, useless, and dangerous."[1] Of course, such criticism had been going on for years and had routinely been ignored by the Vanderbilt Cup organizers. But 1909 was different. The abandonment of the Vanderbilt Cup by the European teams in 1908 had not only shaken them awake, it had changed the very nature of their race. More importantly, Henry Ford's Model T had put cars in the hands of the masses. With more manufacturers selling more cars, and more people driving them, the clamor for an abandonment of all-out racing machines in favor of "stock chassis" racers was no longer confined to a few mouthy journalists. It now had the support of both the manufacturers and a substantial segment of the motoring public.

So it was that in planning the 1909 Vanderbilt Cup, its organizers faced a dilemma. The old 1,000-kilogram formula clearly needed changing. Abandoned by the Europeans, difficult for newer racers to comply with, and coming under increasing criticism, it had outlived its usefulness. But the new formula adopted by the ACF in 1908 did not recommend itself either. After all, the body that had established that formula was now, for all intents and purposes, out of the racing business. And there was no reason to believe that when European racing came back, if it came back at all, it would still adhere to the ACF's 1908 formula.

Matters were further complicated by preliminary discussions between the AAA and the ACA regarding the merger of racing operations for the Vanderbilt Cup and Grand Prize. Obviously, neither body had any interest in seeing their race become a mirror image of the other. This was particularly true for the Vanderbilt Cup. With its earlier date on the calendar, its smaller prize money, and its shorter race distance, it was likely to be viewed as the lesser event of the two, a totally unacceptable proposition. Moreover, it was unlikely that the Europeans could be enticed to sail to America twice in one season, meaning that the two races would have to be run in conjunction with each other. Otherwise, the Vanderbilt Cup would run the risk of finding itself without European entrants even if it did adopt rules to suit them. There didn't seem to be any suitable answer.

Faced with these competing concerns, the organizers caved in to public opinion and pressure from the Manufacturers Contest Association. For the past two years, "stock chassis" races had been proliferating on the AAA schedule. Most of the twenty-four-hour races at places like Point Breeze and Brighton Beach were of the "stock chassis" variety. Since 1908, "stock chassis" races had been held at Fairmount Park in Philadelphia and at the Merrimac Valley course near Lowell, Massachusetts. A "stock chassis" race would free the Vanderbilt Cup from the vagaries of European rule-makers and manufacturers, would cater to public opinion, and would return the race to its roots as a proving ground for the American automobile industry. And so it was settled — for 1909 the Vanderbilt Cup would be a "stock chassis" race. On paper, the decision looked good. Then again, races aren't run on paper.

With its October date, the Vanderbilt Cup was the final event on the calendar of American racing. (The temporary truce between the AAA and ACA had led to an eleventh-hour agreement that all future Grand Prize races would be run over the Vanderbilt Cup course rather than at Savannah, effectively scuttling the Grand Prize for 1909). For most of the summer, George Robertson had been the man to beat. Now driving for Simplex, he had won the Brighton Beach Twenty-Four Hours in July, this time teamed with Al Poole, the duo finishing fifty miles ahead of their nearest competitor. In September, he had won the 300-mile race at Lowell, Massachusetts, his Simplex finishing over twenty minutes ahead of Poole's Isotta-Fraschini. In early October at Fairmount Park, he had cruised to an easy victory over Bert Dingley's Chalmers-Detroit. No less an authority than *The New York Times* had proclaimed the twenty-four-year-old Robertson "America's premier racing driver."[2] Unfortunately, Robertson would go missing from the Vanderbilt Cup, as would Ralph DePalma and Herbert Lytle. Their absences would be noted.

With its change to a stock chassis format, the Vanderbilt Cup, in actuality, became three races in one. The Cup, itself, was reserved for competition between cars of Classes 1 and 2 as defined by the AAA: cars with engines displacing between 451 and 600 cubic inches and a minimum weight of 2,400 lbs., and cars with engines displacing between 301 and 450 cubic inches and weighing a minimum of 2,100 lbs. Concurrently with the running of the Vanderbilt Cup would be races for the Wheatley Hills Sweepstakes and the Massapequa Sweepstakes. The Wheatley Hills Sweepstakes was open to cars with engines between 231 and 300 cubic inches and a minimum weight of 1,800 lbs., the Massapequa Sweepstakes to cars of 161 to 230 cubic inch displacement and a minimum weight of 1,500 lbs.

The course, itself, was also new — now seemingly an annual event. For 1909 it had been shortened substantially. It was now a 12.64-mile triangle running between Hicksville, Westbury and Central Park. The Vanderbilt Cup would cover twenty-two laps of the circuit, now known as the Hempstead Plains course, with the Wheatley Hills Sweepstakes being fifteen laps in length and the Massapequa Stakes only ten. The plan was to start the cars at fifteen-second intervals beginning at 9:00 a.m., instead of the traditional daybreak, with the Massapequa Stakes cars going first, followed by the Wheatley Hills cars, and finally the Vanderbilt Cup cars.

Despite the change to stock chassis machines, the organizers remained hopeful that the race would capture public attention in the way that its predecessors had. One way to accomplish that goal was with a speed record, and the new Hempstead Plains course was designed with that factor in mind. It was completely free of hills, had only six real turns, and nearly 5.2 miles of its length was composed of the concrete-paved Long Island Motor Parkway. Practice times from early in the week before the race demonstrated that the course would be fast. Despite giving up a minimum of thirty horsepower to the all-out racing machines that had contested the race in prior years, many of the cars were lapping at similar speeds. Johnny Aitken's 380-cubic inch National was fastest at nearly 70 mph. Bert Dingley's 368-cubic inch Chalmers-Detroit had turned in a time of eleven minutes flat. Hugh Harding in a 600-cubic inch Apperson and Edward Parker in a 445-cubic inch Fiat had engaged in a furious speed duel, racing side by side for more than five miles at speeds over 70 mph. Passing the grandstand together, both clocked speeds of over 68 mph. Likewise, Lee Lorimer's Chalmers-Detroit and Harry Stillman's 316-cubic inch Marmon were turning laps at well over 60 mph.

Many of the drivers were predicting a record, much to the organizers' delight. One who was not was Harry Grant. The burly thirty-two-year-old from Boston, where he worked as a salesman for Alco when not driving for the company, had begun his racing career in 1907. While he had yet to garner any major victories, he had been leading Robertson by five minutes at Lowell when a blown tire tangled in his Alco's chain had put him out of the running. He was also gaining a reputation as a superb race tactician. When asked his prediction for the upcoming race, Grant minced no words — the winner would average 62 mph.

But Harry Grant's voice was just one among many and was largely ignored, especially since the race organizers were more than a little interested in promoting this version of the Vanderbilt Cup as a speed duel *non pareil*. In a speech at the Garden City Hotel on the Wednesday before the race, William K. Vanderbilt, Jr., told a gathering of journalists that he expected a new record time for the race, despite its change in format. He went on to say that the racing of stock chassis machines was of vital importance to the automobile industry in improving the quality of road cars, and to issue an apology for the 1908 race, saying that it had not been up to normal Vanderbilt Cup standards due to misunderstandings between the organizations governing racing. In closing, he announced the formation of the Motor Cups Holding Company to handle the future running of both the Vanderbilt Cup and the Grand Prize.

Despite the absence of European factory teams and some of America's superstar drivers, the race nevertheless shaped up as an interesting one. The race would pit heavier, larger-engined, and more traditional Eastern-based racers like Leland Mitchell's 597-cubic inch Simplex and Harry Grant's 565-cubic inch Alco 6-cylinder against lighter, smaller-engined cars from Midwestern manufacturers like the Chalmers-Detroits and Louis Chevrolet's 316-cubic inch Buick. In competition, the smaller cars were looking more and more like the equals of their larger brethren. There was also a Europe vs. America angle. Five privately owned European cars were entered — 470-cubic inch Fiats for Lewis Strang and Eddie Hearne, as well as Edward Parker's 445-cubic inch, a 475-cubic inch Isotta-Fraschini for Joe Seymour, and a 580-cubic inch Mercedes for racing newcomer Spencer Wishart — to put the American machinery to the test.

The Chalmers-Detroit team, among the fastest of the light cars in practice, suffered a setback on the Thursday prior to the race. At the first bridge on the motor parkway, Bert Dingley crashed at over 60 mph. His racer left the road and rolled twice, finally coming to rest in a ditch. Both Dingley and Harry Richard, his mechanic, were thrown out, but Richard was thrown in the path of the car, which landed on him, crushing three of his ribs. He would survive, but race day would be spent in the hospital. Dingley was luckier, but still suffered a shoulder injury that would sideline him for the race. With their top driver out, Chalmers-Detroit pulled Billy Knipper from one of their Massapequa Sweepstakes cars and put him in for Dingley, but no one supposed the relative unknown from out west could lead the team as Dingley had. They were in for a surprise.

In the days leading up to the race, Long Island filled up as it had in years past. Every hotel room in Nassau County was booked. The society set opened their country houses to family and friends. All rooms at the Meadow Brook and Rockaway hunt clubs were filled by out-of-town members and their guests. The clubs had even scheduled foxhunts to add to the racing festivities. As late as the day before the race, a crowd of 250,000 was predicted. But that was before the cold front blew in.

As Saturday approached, the experts were giving the nod to Lewis Strang as the pre-race favorite. Strang's Fiat had set fastest time in Friday's practice. And, after all, hadn't Fiat been a dominant force in racing for the past two years? With Bert Dingley sidelined, those looking for an American machine to cheer looked to Louis Chevrolet's Buick. It was beyond question that Chevrolet would be fast — he always was. The question was whether he could keep the machinery together. His spectacular 1905 crash at the Guinea Road S-curve was legendary. In 1908, he had lasted one lap before his Matheson blew up. And since coming to Buick, he had led the opening laps at Lowell and Fairmount Park, only to have a broken frame and another blown engine put him out of each race. To put it simply, big Louis was tough on the equipment.

Saturday dawned clear and bright, but the sun had no heat. Overnight, the temperature had plummeted, making the day feel more like mid-winter than autumn. To make matters worse, a bitterly cold wind blew out of the west. It was a day to curl up in front of a fire, not one to be sitting for hours outdoors. Much of the expected crowd failed to show up. The society set, so long a mainstay of the race, stayed home in droves. Even Virginia Vanderbilt, the head cheerleader at previous events, was missing. By 9:00 a.m., the crowd numbered no more than 75,000. It would dwindle still further as the day wore on.

Nearly alone among the rich and famous at the race was heavyweight champion Jack Johnson. His presence would not go unnoticed, nor would the newspapers refrain from another opportunity to slam the champ. One journal, which went on record as decrying the absence of all-night parties at this running of the race owing to its later starting time, noted with derision that Johnson and his entourage of twenty-five "colored sports" had "several times twenty-five bottles of wine in their cars," while Johnson himself "wandered around the stand with a quart in each outer pocket and a pint or two in an inner coat."[3] In prior years, this same journal had heartily approved of society swells knocking back shots of single-malt scotch at 6:00 a.m., but when it came to Jack Johnson this same type of conduct was panned.

As the clock reached 9:00 a.m., starter Fred Wagner dispatched the Massapequa and Wheatley Hills cars one by one. Just over two minutes later, it was the Vanderbilt Cup cars' turn to go off. Lewis Strang in the favored Fiat was first away, followed by Leland Mitchell's Simplex, Eddie Hearne's Fiat and the rest. Strang wouldn't last one lap. As he sped along the course, a stone either dislodged or thrown from an embankment intersected his Fiat's trajectory perfectly, bounding in front of the machine and torpedoing its radiator. The favorite was finished.

As the racers came around at the end of lap one, the crowd was in for another surprise. The other pre-race favorite, Louis Chevrolet, was indeed near the lead, lying second, but the man at the front was Spencer Wishart, a complete unknown. The nineteen-year-old Wishart was the son of a millionaire New York banker, an amateur in the Foxhall Keene tradition. But Keene had never led the Vanderbilt Cup. It was a shame the society crowd had stayed home: one of their own was finally in front.

Beginning with the 1909 Vanderbilt Cup, Spencer Wishart's white Mercedes was a fixture at every Vanderbilt Cup, Grand Prize and Indianapolis 500 until Wishart joined the Mercer team in the summer of 1912 (IMS Photo).

By the next time around, both Chevrolet's Buick and Billy Knipper's Chalmers-Detroit had gotten by Wishart's Mercedes. Still, the teenager clung to third place, only three seconds back of the leader. By lap three, Wishart had climbed back to second as a slow lap slid Knipper to fourth behind Joe Seymour's Isotta-Fraschini. Chevrolet had had enough. With the Mercedes still hot on his heels (Wishart had started just behind him), Louis turned in one of those laps for which he was rightly famous, determined to make the German machine fade. He blasted his Buick down the concrete ribbon of the motor parkway. He drifted it hard through the dangerous Westbury turn, its wheels throwing dirt at the crowd that ringed its outside edge, backing them away panic stricken. As he flashed over the line, the clock told the story — 9:47 for the lap — over 77 mph. He had opened up a gap of a minute on Wishart.

He had also destroyed his engine. On lap five it blew, handing the lead back to the teenager. But Chevrolet wasn't the only one having problems. Already the attrition was horrendous. Leland Mitchell's Simplex had snapped its crankshaft on lap three. Johnny Aitken's National lost a wheel and nearly rolled. Eddie Hearne's Fiat put a rod through the side of its engine. The race had not reached quarter distance and already a third of the racers were out. If this kept up no one would finish.

The carnage continued on lap six. Joe Seymour's Isotta-Fraschini, just thirty-five seconds behind Wishart at the start of the lap, coasted to a stop with its steering-gear broken, handing over second to Billy Knipper in the Chalmers-Detroit. The teenager and the stand-in were now at the front, much to the crowd's great surprise. In truth, nothing had been expected of either of them, but here they were leading the year's most prestigious race, with Wishart holding a lead of one minute and change over Knipper.

But the teenager's luck wouldn't last. Lap seven saw the Mercedes fall to fifth, over five minutes back of Knipper, the new leader. A series of tire and mechanical problems would put Wishart many laps down, though he soldiered on gamely to the finish. And still, the attrition continued. Harry Stillman's Marmon holed its radiator, reducing the number of competitors to nine. Through the first quarter of the race, the pace had been furious. Wishart had averaged over 67 mph for the first six laps. Such speeds were nearly unheard of, even with *grand prix* machines. For stock chassis cars to maintain such a pace was unthinkable. Unfortunately, it was grinding them into powder.

As the race approached middle distance, the lightweight Chalmers-Detroit Bluebirds took control, with Billy Knipper leading teammate Lee Lorimer by thirty-five seconds, the pair enjoying a five-minute lead over Hugh Harding's Apperson in third, with Charlie Merz' National another thirty seconds back. Still further back in fifth was Harry Grant's Alco, now running ten minutes behind the leader. But nobody was paying attention to the Boston car salesman. Not yet.

In fact, so little attention was being paid to Grant and his Alco that the official scorers missed him completely on lap ten. As he completed his eleventh round, the scorers posted a tenth lap of twenty-two minutes, putting Grant back of Ed Parker's Fiat in sixth. Alco race manager Arthur Jervis was off to the scorer's tent like a shot. He claimed that the scorers had missed Grant's tenth lap — that the twenty-two-minute lap ten should really be two eleven-minute laps. Fortunately, a number of other scorers and journalists nearby confirmed Jervis' version of events. But that did not put an end to the matter. The question now was, who to rely on: the official scorers, whose word was supposed to be "official," or the unofficial scorers who uniformly had Grant listed for two laps, instead of one. There was nothing to do but to put the matter to the race referee, Willie K. Vanderbilt.

As the discussion continued, the laps continued to fall. So did the racers. On lap eleven, Hugh Harding rolled his third-place Apperson after its steering knuckle broke. Fortunately, neither Harding nor his mechanic were injured. Grant was now an unofficial fourth, but still twelve minutes back of the lead duo of Chalmers-Detroits. By lap twelve, he was an unofficial third after getting by Charlie Merz' fading National (its engine would blow on lap thirteen). On lap thirteen, the unofficial third became second when Lee Lorimer's second-place Chalmers blew up. Only five of the Vanderbilt Cup cars now remained, and Wishart's Mercedes and Elmer Knox's Atlas were many laps in arrears. The race had come down to one between Billy Knipper in the lightweight Chalmers-Detroit, Harry Grant in the heavyweight Alco, and Edward Parker in the Italian Fiat.

As the laps wound down, no answer to the scoring dilemma was forthcoming. The westerner in the lightweight continued to lead, but the gap inexorably eroded. A pit stop on lap sixteen brought Grant to within nine minutes, still unofficially. Two conservative car-saving laps by Knipper, an attempt to cool the Chalmers-Detroit's overheating engine, cut his lead to seven minutes. A pit stop for gas, water and tires on lap nineteen cut it to three.

Then, on lap twenty, the Chalmers didn't come around. Its cooked engine had finally sidelined it. The race was now between Parker and Grant, and still the officials were unsure of who was in front. By this time, Grant's Alco either had three minutes in hand, or was eight minutes behind, but the scoreboard still said Parker was leading. As the cars completed lap twenty-one the gap remained constant. Starter Fred Wagner walked out

Harry Grant's six-cylinder Alco crosses the finish line in the 1909 running of the Vanderbilt Cup (image courtesy Smithtown [N.Y.] Library, Long Island Room).

onto the track at the start-finish line, checkered flag in hand, ready to flag down the winner. Still the scoreboard had the Fiat in front. Grant whizzed by in the Alco. Wagner never budged. Six minutes later, Parker took the flag. Then all hell broke loose.

In the end, Vanderbilt did the right thing and awarded the victory to Grant and the Alco. The evidence from the other scorers and journalists was overwhelming. It was clear that the official scorers had simply missed the car as it came around for its tenth lap. But lost in all the confusion was the damage done to Parker's Fiat team by the belated decision. On lap nineteen, Knipper's last lap, less than two minutes had separated the leaders. Over the final three laps, Parker, believing his Fiat to be in the lead, had coasted, giving up a further three minutes to Grant. Had the Fiat driver realized his situation, he might have chased down the front-running Alco. He certainly could have tried, but he never had the chance.

Still, Vanderbilt's pronouncement made the whole thing official — Harry Grant and Alco were the winners. And Grant had one more feather he could add to his cap — the man nobody noticed had not only won the race, he had done so just as he predicted. His average speed was 62.8 mph.

If the Vanderbilt Cup race, itself, had been less than was hoped for, the Wheatley Hills and Massapequa Sweepstakes races did nothing to improve on the day. In the Wheatley Hills sweepstakes, the attrition had been even worse. Of the four cars that started there was only one finisher, Ray Harroun in a Marmon. And while Harroun and Marmon would go on to gain fame at Indianapolis in 1911, his performance on this day was largely ignored. So too were the results of the Massapequa Sweepstakes, where Joe Matson's Chalmers-Detroit had cruised to victory with a twenty-minute lead over the Maxwells of Martin Dooley and Arthur See.

In the final analysis, the race was a dud. Although it would remain a jewel in the crown of American racing until its demise in 1916, the Vanderbilt Cup would never again play host to international competition at the very highest level. The New York newspapers were less than gentle in reporting the lackluster crowd, the rate of attrition that left only two cars in contention, and the inept scoring that resulted in the flag being thrown to the wrong car. The organizers were chastised for holding the race so late in the year, for poor crowd control at the Westbury turn, for everything associated with the race. Clearly, changes were necessary. They would come, but they would not all be for the better, especially in the eyes of New Yorkers who looked on the Vanderbilt Cup as their own.

9

Last Dance on Long Island

While few of the wealthy New Yorkers who regularly patronized the Vanderbilt Cup attended in 1909, one who did was the twenty-two-year-old David Bruce-Brown. Tall, blond, handsome and charming, the young Bruce-Brown seemingly had everything a man of his age could want. But what he wanted more than anything was to drive a race car in events like the Vanderbilt Cup and Grand Prize. His passion for the sport was all-consuming.

He had begun his racing career in 1907, entering a car that was owned by his mother. In 1908, he had run away from Harstrom's School in Norfolk, Virginia, to go to Daytona, Florida, for the race meeting there. He talked his way onto the Fiat team as an apprentice mechanic. He hit it off with the team almost instantly and was taken under the wing of team manager Emanuele Cedrino, who would become his mentor. Cedrino allowed Bruce-Brown to ride with him in practice and testing. Then, when the professional races were over, the man they now called "Cedrino's millionaire mechanic"[1] was permitted to take out one of the Fiats for the amateur one-mile straightaway event. Bruce-Brown won with a time of 33.6 seconds (107.14 mph), breaking the record set by William K. Vanderbilt, Jr., in 1904.

This first taste of serious competition was followed by an amateur-class victory at the Yale-sponsored Shingle Club Hillclimb. Bruce-Brown then went out and got himself a front-line race car, one of the Benz *grand prix* cars that had raced at Savannah (it is unclear whether the car was Hemery's or Hanriot's). He campaigned this car throughout 1909, again winning the Shingle Club Hillclimb and setting new records at Daytona.

But there in the grandstand on that cold October day with the 1909 racing season just ended, the wealthy young man with the promising talent and the young Robert Redford looks had an important decision to make — whether to remain an amateur or turn professional in order to drive for the best teams and have the best equipment. Ultimately, his decision would make headlines and history. It would also cost him his life.

❖ ❖ ❖

As the first decade of the century came to a close, Flo Ziegfeld's Follies, featuring Fanny Brice, was the talk of New York. The first neon signs began to appear, giving the streets of the city an electrified glow that belonged to the new century, not the last. In Russia, Wassily Kandinsky completed the first abstract painting, *Improvisation XIV*, using colors and shapes like musical notes to express ideas and emotions.

On the automotive front, 1910 was a year when speed caught the American public's attention in a way that it never had before. At Daytona, Barney Oldfield, piloting the 200-horsepower "Blitzen" Benz, set a new world speed record of 131.724 mph — more than two miles per minute. The feat was earth-shattering. Very simply, it was the fastest that man had ever gone, whether on land, over water, or through the air — the fastest thing on the planet. As Oldfield characterized it, the record was "as near to the absolute limit of speed as humanity will ever travel."[2] Was Oldfield's statement rank hyperbole and bald self-promotion? Sure. But to put the feat in perspective today, imagine a car driven, not at two miles a minute, not even at the speed of sound — but faster than the speed of the space shuttle or a Saturn booster. That is the way folks in 1910 looked on Oldfield's feat.

While Oldfield garnered the headlines, in back rooms and boardrooms across the country events were taking shape that would impact the American racing scene for much of the century's second decade and would become legend in the minds of later generations. In Trenton, New Jersey, the Roebling family, along with brothers John and Anthony Kuser, began production of the first Mercer Raceabout. In Indianapolis, Indiana, an engineer named Harry Stutz left the Marion Motor Car Company to form the Stutz Motor Car Parts Company with the help of his friend Henry Campbell. By 1911, Stutz would join Mercer in producing the first American sports cars, fueling the public's infatuation with speed.

To imagine the impact that these cars — the Mercer Raceabout and the Stutz Bearcat — generated in their day, those of us who remember the early 1960s need only hearken back to the introduction of the Jaguar E-Type and the Corvette Stingray, cars that left young boys slack-jawed and wide-eyed, and whose rivalry was so legendary that it became the basis for Jan & Dean's rock-and-roll hit "Deadman's Curve." Like the XK-E and the Vette, the Mercer and the Stutz each had their own unique strengths and their own clientele. The Raceabout, like the XK-E, with its unmatched handling and its low, lithe silhouette that seemed to crouch between its wheels, endeared itself to the eastern contingent of gentlemen racers. The Bearcat, like the Stingray, relied on its larger engine and faster straight-line speed to become the overwhelming choice in the wide open spaces of the Midwest. But the rivalry wouldn't be confined to the roads of America — they would do battle on the racetrack as well.

❖ ❖ ❖

Determined to remedy the problems that had beset the 1909 race, the Vanderbilt Cup organizers again set about making changes to the *grande dame* of American racing. Listening to the critics, they moved the date from the last Saturday in October to the first. The starting time was also returned to its traditional 6:00 a.m., perhaps in the hope that a revival of the all-night pre-race parties that were features of earlier races would mellow the mood of the racing journalists who had bashed the 1909 race so mercilessly. While maintaining a stock chassis format, the rules were expanded to allow for more modifications in the hopes of improving reliability. No one was anxious to see a repeat of the attrition the race had faced the previous year. As an added hedge, the organizers restructured the start of the light car races, with the Wheatley Hills Sweepstakes going off when the Vanderbilt Cup cars had been running one hour and the Massapequa Sweepstakes starting thirty minutes later. With these later starting times, it was hoped that even if attrition in the Vanderbilt Cup ran high the light cars would be there to watch at the end. But perhaps the most shocking change from previous Vanderbilt Cups was actually no change at all. For the first time in history, the course stayed the same as the year before.

With the public attention now focused on speed, the careful massaging of the rules of the race, and the additional year for teams to prepare and sort out their cars, the 1910 race shaped up to be everything the 1909 race had not been. The entry list was long, a record thirty-one cars for the Vanderbilt Cup alone, and composed of many powerful teams. National, among the fastest of the cars in 1909, fielded a three-car team of 447-cubic inch cars for Johnny Aitken, Louis Disbrow and Al Livingston. Buick fielded its own three-car team, utilizing a lightweight Marquette chassis designed by Louis Chevrolet and powered by a 594-cubic inch engine. Big Louis would also pilot one of the cars. The other two spots would be taken by his younger brother, Arthur, and "Wild" Bob Burman. Marmon, stepping up from the lightweight classes, fielded a two-car team, with Ray Harroun piloting a 413-cubic inch machine and Joe Dawson a little 318-cubic-incher. Even German powerhouse Benz would be there, with a three-car team of 471-cubic inch cars driven by 1908 Vanderbilt Cup winner George Robertson, Eddie Hearne, and newly-turned-pro David Bruce-Brown. Simplex fielded a two-car team of 597-cubic inch racers for Ralph Beardsley and Leland Mitchell, although the team had met with diminished success since Robertson's departure. Alco returned with its 1909 winner, again piloted by Harry Grant, but this year painted an eye-catching jet black, perhaps in hopes that the scorers would notice it. Spencer Wishart, the teenage phenomenon of the 1909 race, was back with his Mercedes. Filling out the field of front-line cars was a single 544-cubic inch Lozier driven by Ralph Mulford.

While Mulford had competed only once before in either the Vanderbilt Cup or the Grand Prize, and that in the 1908 Grand Prize where his stock-chassis Lozier was simply no match for the Benzes and Fiats, he was well known to race fans of the day. The gangly twenty-five-year-old native of New Jersey, with the prominent ears, the big toothy grin, and the congenial personality that had earned him the nickname "Smilin' Ralph" (a nickname sometimes also applied to DePalma), had gotten his start with Lozier at age sixteen, working in the boat-engine factory at Plattsburgh, New York, as a marine engineer. Mulford was a natural around mechanical things, and when Lozier went into the car-making business in 1905, Mulford went with it. When the company decided to go racing in 1907, Mulford was pulled out of the shop along with several other young men and told that they were the racing team.

Success was not long in coming. At Point Breeze, just outside Philadelphia, in June 1907, Mulford and co-driver Harry Michener won one of the most brutal twenty-four-hour races ever. Nine hours into the race, the rains came. By the twelfth hour, it was a deluge. The dirt horse track became a quagmire. Competitors were forced to fit chains to all four wheels to develop any traction at all. Goggles caked with mud and had to be abandoned. Flying stones pelted the drivers' faces. By the twenty-second hour, five members of the Frayer-Miller team, which had been leading the race for most of the way, were stretched out on cots in the team's pit area with open lacerations, eyes swollen shut, and faces looking like tenderized liver. Driving through this maelstrom, Mulford and

Michener made up a thirty-mile deficit in the last six hours and won the race convincingly.

In September 1908, Mulford and co-driver Harry Cobe set a world's distance record of 1,107 miles at the twenty-four-hour race at Brighton Beach, a record that would be beaten by George Robertson and Frank Lescault in a Simplex less than a month later. But Mulford's prowess was not confined merely to long-distance events. Just a month before the 1910 Vanderbilt Cup, he won the prestigious Elgin Trophy, the "stock chassis road race championship of America," at Elgin, Illinois. Covering the 305-mile race distance at an average speed of 62.5 mph, Mulford finished nearly thirteen miles ahead of Al Livingston's second-place National. In the process, he demonstrated the skills for which he would become famous — an exceptionally smooth driving style, and an engineer's meticulous preparation and feel for the machinery. At Elgin, those talents allowed him to run the entire race on only one pit stop.

Unlike Louis Chevrolet, Spencer Wishart, or even George Robertson, Mulford was not one to turn in a simply impossible, terrifyingly fast lap, with the crowd backing away from the fences in fear for their lives, expecting a crash at any second. Like Harry Grant, he was a master tactician, but if anything Mulford was faster and smoother. Very simply, if he had the machinery, and his engineering prowess meant he often did, he would be there at the end when it counted.

❖ ❖ ❖

Events that would impact the Vanderbilt Cup race itself began earlier than usual in 1910. In the weeks leading up to the race, the Benz team looked like a strong favorite. The German marque's machines were always fast, whether competing in a *grand prix* or a stock-chassis event, and this year the team had George Robertson, "America's premier racing driver," the winner of the 1908 Vanderbilt Cup and a whole host of other races, as their lead driver. Teamed with relative newcomers, Eddie Hearne, an heir to a gold-mining fortune who had begun racing in 1909, and Vanderbilt Cup rookie David Bruce-Brown, it was hoped that Robertson's experience, as well as his talent for speed, would rub off on his teammates.

Unfortunately, the whole thing went wrong. A sportswriter wanted a story and persuaded Robertson to take him out for a demonstration ride. As the big Benz boomed through the Massapequa turn, it caught a rut. The terrified journalist grabbed Robertson's arm and he lost control. The Benz did a full barrel roll in the air at 70 mph before rolling again and then coming to rest back on its wheels. Robertson and the scribe were flung from the car. Robertson's arm was crushed beneath the weight of the machine. The initial report on his condition was that he was "considerably bruised and scratched," but that no bones were broken. He was expected to be fit to drive in the race. Unfortunately, the report was wrong. Although he had sustained no fractures, Robertson's arm was a mess. Without modern technology, we cannot say specifically what damage had been done, but it was definitely serious. In the parlance of the day, his arm had been "maimed." It would never heal properly. Although no one knew it as yet, the career of "America's premier racing driver" was over. As for the unnamed sportswriter, as Robertson would later tell it, "his derby wasn't even dented."[3]

Robertson's injury left the Benz team leaderless. At first, the team, believing the doctor's reports, expected Robertson to return. But as the days went by without improvement in his condition, it became obvious a replacement was necessary. German Franz Heim was designated to fill in, but he not only lacked Robertson's experience and talent, he couldn't speak a word of English. Hearne and Bruce-Brown would just have to fend for themselves.

Robertson's accident left David Bruce-Brown in a particularly touchy situation. His family, particularly his mother, had never completely approved of his racing career. In the wake of Robertson's crash, the family became even more adamant that he give up the sport. His mother threatened to disown him — not an idle threat when it meant an inheritance of millions of dollars. Bruce-Brown refused to succumb to the pressure, but it was the last thing he needed in the days leading up to the race.

❖ ❖ ❖

Intermittent rains during the week of practice made it difficult to gauge the relative speed of the racers. It also left the portion of the course between Hicksville and Westbury rutted, lumpy and dangerous. Many of the drivers were nervous. As David Bruce-Brown said in an interview, "It's going to be difficult to make a fast time. The track will not permit it."[4] Johnny Aitken echoed similar sentiments, saying he expected a lot of difficulty in passing, especially with the number of cars on the course. Virtually all of the racers hinted that they wouldn't be surprised by slow lap times and a number of accidents. Once again, Harry Grant disagreed, at least about the speed. Despite driving the same car as in 1909, he predicted a much faster race. "Sixty-five miles per hour," he said.[5] This time people noticed.

❖ ❖ ❖

With the absence of much meaningful information from practice, pre-race attention focused on Grant, lap-record holder Louis Chevrolet, and Franz Heim in Robertson's Benz, but there was no clear favorite. Even Aztec Indian Tobin de Hymel, who would be competing in his first Vanderbilt Cup in a Stoddard-Dayton, had his supporters.

As in years past, the crowd began pouring in on the evening before the race. By 9:00 p.m. the parking lot of the Garden City Hotel was packed with cars, the female motorists wearing heavy coats and veils, the men sporting goggles and fur ulsters. The night trains on the Long Island Railroad were filled to

Harry Grant became the first two-time winner of the Vanderbilt Cup by driving his stock chassis, six-cylinder Alco to victory in 1909 and 1910. A master race tactician, he predicted his winning speed on each occasion to within one mph (IMS Photo).

overflowing with race-goers exiting the trains at Hicksville. Among the motorists headed out to the course on Friday night was Ferdinand D'Viuva, the sales manager for Pope-Hartford automobiles in New York City. He was taking his wife and six of their friends to see John Fleming and Bert Dingley campaign two 389-cubic inch Pope-Hartfords in the big race. As D'Viuva motored quickly down a steep, dimly lit hill, his overloaded car's brakes failed. D'Viuva lost control. The car shot sideways into a ditch and rolled over, spilling people everywhere and pinning D'Viuva and his wife underneath. Their friends got away with minor injuries, but Mr. and Mrs. D'Viuva weren't so lucky. Her leg was broken. He was dead — and while the accident was presumably no fault of the Vanderbilt Cup or its organizers, when the tally of dead and injured was compiled on Saturday evening, the D'Viuvas and their friends would be counted with the others. The number would be alarmingly high.

By 2:00 a.m. the scene at the course revealed hundreds of bonfires blazing in the adjacent fields, while streams of headlights cut through the darkness. Odors of coffee, gasoline and frankfurters wafted through the air as men and women slept huddled in the tonneaus of their cars, their chauffeurs watching over them or catching naps themselves. As the crowd slept, the racers formed up in the pits and performed final tuning and preparation on their cars. By 6:00 a.m. the crowd numbered in excess of 275,000 despite a pre-dawn drizzle. The weather on the day would reward their loyalty. By 6:30 the sun would break through the clouds, and the day would warm to near-summer temperatures.

As the signal to start engines was given, the machines burst into life, spitting tongues of blue flame and black smoke. The noise was deafening, like a volley of massed Gatling guns. The smoke got so thick in the cold, damp, early-morning air that the far side of the track was nearly obscured. Through this haze, starter Fred Wagner gave the signal to Al Livingston's National. Fifteen seconds later, it was the white Lozier of Ralph Mulford, he and his mechanic both clad in spotless white coveralls and hoods. Then Arthur Chevrolet's Marquette-Buick, then Spencer Wishart's Mercedes, off they went one by one in rapid succession.

Harold Stone started twelfth. The young Columbia pilot from California was on his honeymoon. His wife of one month waved from the grandstand as he moved to the line. He waved back as he shot off down the straight, while she watched on tiptoes until he was out of sight. Still more racers came to the line: Bruce-Brown's Benz, Grant's Alco, Harroun's Marmon, Dingley's Pope-Hartford, Dawson's Marmon, Burman's Buick, Louis Chevrolet's Buick, each blasting away in a rumble of dirty thunder. Eight minutes later it grew quiet as the last car disappeared in the distance.

Young Harold Stone would not make one lap. Crossing the hump-backed span called New Bridge at the western end of the Motor Parkway, the honeymooner's Columbia blew its left rear tire. The racer swerved drunkenly as it crested the span, then veered sharply right, crashed through the guard rail and shot off the embankment, crashing to the ground upside-down some distance below. Stone's mechanic, Matthew Bacon, was caught under the wreckage and crushed. Stone's right leg was mangled. Despite an emergency amputation, his injuries were too serious, his blood loss too great. The young driver would make his young wife a young widow.

As the racers finished the first lap, the scoreboard showed the Marquette-Buick team dominating. Louis Chevrolet was leading, while brother Arthur and Bob Burman were tied for third with identical times. Only Belcher's Knox broke the Buick stranglehold at the front. On lap two, Louis solidified his hold on the lead, stretching it out to well over a minute, but brother Arthur began having problems, falling back from the leaders. By lap seven, his race would be over.

Further back, it was not a good day for the rich kids. Spencer Wishart lost five minutes to the leaders on lap two. The Mercedes pilot who had chased Chevrolet so doggedly through the opening laps in 1909 would never be a factor, losing more time on lap four, then slowing with mechanical ills on lap ten. He would finish five laps in arrears. Likewise, David Bruce-Brown lost seven minutes on lap two. It was time the young Benz driver could never make up, ultimately finishing twelfth, one lap back.

By lap three, "Wild Bob" had joined "Big Louis" at the top of the leaderboard, the two Buicks a minute apart, and nearly a minute in front of Joe Dawson's Marmon. They continued to inch away on laps four and five, opening the gap by a further fifteen seconds each lap. Back in the pack, the powerful Benz team had suffered more setbacks. On lap five, Franz Heim's racer caught fire and was finished for the day. Two laps later, Eddie Hearne would join the list of casualties when tire problems cost him nine minutes. Like Bruce-Brown, he would soldier on to the end, finishing eighth, but he would never be a factor.

Through laps six, seven and eight, the Buick tandem continued to outpace the field, turning laps at nearly 75 mph. Despite a quick stop by Burman for tires on lap seven, the pair held a comfortable lead over Dawson and Mulford as the first round of pit stops approached. Chevrolet and Mulford dived into the pits on lap nine. The Lozier stop cost Mulford four minutes, but by comparison to the Buick's, it was ballet at light speed. A cranky carburetor took nine minutes to remedy, dropping Chevrolet to seventh, six minutes back of his teammate.

With Chevrolet now out of the lead and Mulford no longer putting on pressure from behind, Joe Dawson chose lap ten to make his move on Burman, who had passed Dawson on lap three and now lay just over a minute in front on the track. He needn't have bothered. As Dawson cut four seconds off his little, yellow Marmon's previous best, Burman's Buick blew up, handing him the lead on a platter. Dawson's lead on the now-disorganized field was nearly four minutes, but the man now lying second might be cause for concern nonetheless. Just as in 1909, Harry Grant was beginning to make his presence felt. Looking further down the leaderboard, things didn't look any better. Louis Chevrolet had clawed his way back into third, just a minute behind Grant, with Ralph Mulford hot on his heels in fourth. Dawson might have four minutes in hand, but he had yet to pit. When he did, he would be in a dogfight with three of the best in the business.

Dawson got some relief on lap eleven. Grant pitted, opening the Marmon's lead to five minutes over Chevrolet—enough time for Dawson to pit and still stay in front. He didn't dare wait any longer. On lap twelve, he came in. Four minutes later he was back on the track with a full load of fuel and fresh tires. More importantly, he still held a minute in hand over Chevrolet's Buick.

By this time, the course was deteriorating badly. The Westbury turn looked more like a plowed field than a road, with ruts over a foot deep and more than fourteen feet long. The Hicksville turn was nearly impassable. In the corners, the racers fought for control of their machines as the ruts tore the wheel from their hands. As conditions deteriorated, so did the decorum of the crowd, with spectators inching out onto the track in the worst of the spots, or foolishly trying to cross the track to get a better vantage point on the other side. The combination was a recipe for disaster.

As Dawson fought gamely to retain his lead, Chevrolet began to chew it away in large chunks. Fifteen seconds evaporated on lap thirteen. By the end of lap fourteen, the Buick was back in the lead, shaving nearly a minute from the little Marmon's time on that lap alone. But once again, Chevrolet's lead wouldn't last. His racer's balky carburetor again gave him trouble, forcing him to pit. As he did so, the accidents started.

Billy Knipper's Lancia was entered in the Massapequa Sweepstakes. Starting ninety minutes after the big cars, the westerner in the little Italian machine had just completed his sixth lap and was lying second when he lost control on the torn up dirt roadway. The crowd, now standing out on the road itself, left Knipper no room. As they fled from the skidding machine, one of their number, Morris Levinson, was not fast enough. The Lancia hit him, shattering his leg and finishing Knipper's day.

Louis Chevrolet was a fast and talented driver, but in the end he probably earned more notoriety for his spectacular crashes and broken equipment than he did for actual race results. His frightful crash in the 1910 Vanderbilt Cup, which resulted in the death of his mechanic, Charles Miller, and injuries to three female spectators, was one of the factors responsible for the Vanderbilt Cup's banishment from Long Island (IMS Photo).

As Louis Chevrolet pulled back on the track, he knew nothing of Billy Knipper's crash. What he did know was that he was now lying fourth, nearly six minutes behind Dawson's Marmon. With seven laps to go, it was time for him to put on one of those patented flying laps for which he was rightly famous. He slammed the big Marquette-Buick down the Motor Parkway, then blasted through the Hicksville turn in a long, lurid power slide, his machine dancing over the ruts as he fought for control. Then it was off down the straight toward Westbury, his foot to the floor. But the strain was too much for the Buick, a rut caught a wheel, its steering link snapped. The car left the road at a hideous speed, later estimated at better than 70 mph. It smashed into a spectator's car occupied by three women, demolishing it and injuring them. Without losing speed, the Buick then tore through a fence and uprooted a cedar tree. Its energy still not yet spent, the big racer stood on its nose and rolled end-over-end, throwing Chevrolet twenty feet from the wreck and grinding the now-lifeless body of mechanic Charles Miller beneath it. The racer finally came to a halt at the edge of a farmhouse porch. Chevrolet's shoulder was broken. Upon learning of Miller's death, he collapsed. Still, the carnage was a long way from over.

With Chevrolet now out of the race, Dawson's lead once again looked secure. Mulford had been forced to pit on lap thirteen, putting him eleven minutes back. That left Harry Grant to contend with. As the racers completed lap sixteen, Grant was running second, his black Alco two minutes back of the Marmon. It was the largest lead Dawson had had since his pit stop, but certainly not enough to feel comfortable. Unlike Chevrolet, who could not abide having another car in the lead, the chess-player Grant would bide his time, waiting for his opportunity.

On lap seventeen, Grant made a pit stop for gas, tires and oil, giving Dawson another two minutes in hand. Still, Dawson knew it would not be enough if he ran into trouble. On lap eighteen he did — and trouble's name was Henry Hagedorn. Hagedorn, a spectator, tried to cross the course at the Hicksville turn just as Dawson came barreling around it, his yellow racer fighting for traction. There was no way for Dawson to miss him. Hagedorn was thrown forty feet by the impact, both of his legs broken. Dawson was uninjured, but he stopped to check on Hagedorn's condition. Then he noticed that one of the Marmon's wheels was damaged. The pit stop to change it would cost Dawson eight minutes and the lead.

While Dawson and Hagedorn were meeting so painfully at Hicksville, John Fleming was having a similar experience at Westbury. The Pope-Hartford driver came around the deeply rutted turn to find spectator Thomas Muller choosing just that moment to cross the track. Muller was luckier than Hagedorn; only one of his legs was broken.

Driver of Car No. 6

Pope-Hartford entered cars for John Fleming and Bert Dingley in the 1910 Vanderbilt Cup. Fleming would be placed as high as fourth before running into spectator Thomas Muller, who was attempting to cross the track just as Fleming's machine came around the Westbury turn (image courtesy of the Smithtown (N.Y.) Library, Long Island Room).

Harry Grant's *Bête Noire* Alco, seen here in its 1911 Indianapolis livery, was the first car to win back-to-back Vanderbilt Cup races (IMS Photo).

With eighteen laps gone, Grant finally had the lead, a cushion of three and one-half minutes over Johnny Aitken's National and four over Dawson. It looked like the master tactician was poised to wrap up the victory just as he had done the year before. Dawson gave chase, but the lead looked secure. With the course nearly impassable, a fast lap was out of the question. Yet Dawson continued to carve at it, clipping over a minute on lap nineteen, and shaving another thirty seconds on lap twenty to take second from Aitken. Still, Grant's lead looked too great; with just two laps to go, the *Bête Noire* had two minutes in hand on the little yellow flyer.

But the fickle gods of racing were still not quite finished. As the big Alco came past the start-finish line to take the green flag meaning one lap to go, its left front tire exploded. Grant wheeled immediately into his pit. An army of mechanics swarmed over the machine. Grant sat stoically as the seconds ticked by, and with them his lead. One minute later, a new tire was back on his racer and he shot from the pit just as the small form of Joe Dawson's Marmon took shape in the distance.

Turning laps a full thirty seconds faster than Grant's, Dawson had cut the lead to forty-three seconds. On the final lap, he'd slice another eighteen from the Alco's lead, but that was as close as he could come. For his part, Grant raced according to plan — "laps in from 11:15 to 11:30."[6] For the second year in a row the plan was simply perfect, Harry Grant and his Alco were winners — his winning speed 65.2 mph, just as he'd predicted.

As word of the victory spread to Providence, Rhode Island, where Alco was head-quartered and a celebration began, the mood at the race track remained somber. The race had been thrilling and the public address system had said little of the accidents and nothing of the injuries and deaths, but word had somehow spread through the crowd. It cast a pall over the proceedings. By Sunday morning, the newspapers would announce the final tally of killed and injured, taking care to include every casualty even remotely related to the race. *The New York Times* headline read, "4 Dead, 20 Hurt."[7] Nothing more needed saying. Such carnage was plainly intolerable, particularly with so many spectators among the casualties. The Vanderbilt Cup would be banished for good, never to return to Long Island until its re-incarnation in the late 1930s.

10

The Young Master

Originally, the Grand Prize had been scheduled to take place two weeks after the Vanderbilt Cup on the Hempstead Plains course (Fairmount Park had priority to the second Saturday in October), but it was not to be. In the wake of the deaths and injuries surrounding the Vanderbilt Cup, the authorities were adamant — racing on the public roads of Nassau County was out of the question. Scrambling to find a suitable location, the organizers considered a number of potential sites, including Fairmount Park, which had a spotless reputation for safety. In the end, the Motor Cups Holding Company decided to return to Savannah. The Grand Prize was re-scheduled for November 12.

For 1910, the Savannah circuit had been shortened to 17.3 miles. The Grand Prize would cover twenty-four laps of the circuit, a total distance of 415.2 miles. As in 1908, special provisions were made for the Northeastern press and its well-to-do race fans. Express trains and excursion steamships ferried the wealthy. New York newspapermen had a special train to themselves that they used as a base of operations once in Savannah. Governor Brown ate with them in the train's dining car after the races and used the opportunity to promote Georgia as a center for motor racing.

If the provisions for transportation to Savannah were once again first rate, so too was the track itself. A gang of about one hundred Negro convicts was employed to get the course in shape. As a reward for their labors, they were allowed to watch the races from a corral near the judge's stand where their rifle-toting jailers could keep a close watch on them. *The New York Times* reported that they saw the whole show "without the slightest inconvenience to themselves, except perhaps their striped clothing and leg chains."[1] Remembering the close finish of its first Grand Prize, which had required the official timers to confer and compare their results before announcing the winner, the Savannah organizers also took the precaution of engaging Charles H. Warner to provide them with electrical timing equipment. They would need it.

With France now completely boycotting international racing, only the German and Italian manufacturers fielded teams for the Grand Prize. The engine-size formula adopted by the ACA for the Grand Prize in 1908 had by now been dispensed with. Engines were unrestricted. Italy was represented by a trio of 616-cubic inch Fiats. As in 1908, their drivers would be Louis Wagner, Felice Nazzaro, and Ralph DePalma. Germany was represented by a trio of racers from Benz, two massive 920-cubic inch machines for Victor Hemery and David Bruce-Brown, and a 736-cubic incher for hillclimb specialist Willie Haupt.

Against these two teams that had dominated the Grand Prize in its first running, the United States' entries looked more competitive than usual. Originally, seventeen American-made cars had been entered, but the entries from Stoddard-Dayton and American were later withdrawn, and the two-car team from National never arrived, reducing the entries to thirteen. That number was further reduced in practice when Joe Matson's Simplex and Hughie Hughes' Marquette-Buick succumbed to mechanical problems. Washington A. Roebling II, son of the president of Mercer and influential backer of its racing program, blew up his specially built Roebling-Planche, while fellow Trenton-based manufacturer William Sharp crashed in his Sharp Arrow, killing both himself and his mechanic.

Despite the pre-race attrition, the remaining nine entries, if still being by-and-large production-based and not packing engines as large as the Europeans, represented the best of the lot, most being Vanderbilt Cup cars. Two 594-cubic inch Marquette-Buicks were fielded for Bob Burman and Arthur Chevrolet. Two Loziers were entered, a 544-cubic inch car for Ralph Mulford and a 370-cubic inch, 6-cylinder for Joe Horan. Marmon brought its little 318-cubic inch racer for Ray Harroun and a 382-cubic inch car for Joe Dawson. Pope-Hartford fielded two 390-cubic inch cars for Louis Disbrow and Charles Basle. And Alco had Harry Grant in its 565-cubic inch 6-cylinder, the two-time Vanderbilt Cup winner.

Like the Vanderbilt Cup, the 1910 Grand Prize featured light car races in addition to the main event. But unlike the Vanderbilt Cup format, the light cars would not run concurrently with the big machines. Instead, the Savannah Trophy for 231- to 300-cubic inch cars and the Tiedeman Trophy for 161- to 230-cubic inch cars were held the day prior to the Grand Prize. Joe Dawson won the Savannah Trophy in a Marmon, followed by Washington A. Roebling II in a Mercer and Englishman Hughie Hughes in an F.A.L. Billy Knipper's Lancia won the Tiedeman Trophy, followed by F. A. Witt in an E.M.F. and Thomas Costello in a Maxwell.

Race day for the Grand Prize dawned sunny and bright, excellent racing conditions. Only a 20-mph wind kept the day from being perfect. At 9:00 a.m. sharp, starter Fred Wagner sent the first car away, Arthur Chevrolet's Marquette-Buick. The rest of the field followed at thirty-second intervals — Mulford's Lozier, Basle's Pope, Grant's Alco, Dawson's Marmon. As in 1908, the Europeans started toward the back of the field. Seven minutes later, Ralph DePalma's Fiat was the last car away.

The crowd didn't have long to wait for the return of their heroes. Just over seven minutes later, the leading cars came back around. First across the stripe was Chevrolet's Marquette-Buick, much to the delight of the American crowd. But the knowledgeable in the grandstands kept quiet. They remembered the cheer that had accompanied Mulford's Lozier in 1908, and the fact that although first across the line he had been nowhere near the lead. They weren't about to embarrass themselves again by cheering wildly for nothing. But as the racers flashed by and the scoreboard told its story, they were sorry they had sat on their hands. The only car faster was Hemery's Benz — and that by only one second.

Behind Chevrolet, the might of Europe rolled — Wagner's Fiat, Bruce-Brown's Benz, Haupt's Benz, Nazzaro's Fiat. Besides Chevrolet, only Joe Dawson had cracked the European stranglehold at the top, running in seventh just ahead of DePalma. It seemed sure that the Benz and Fiat pilots would force their way past on lap two, but the Yanks held on grimly. Wagner got by Chevrolet for second, but the Buick still held the Benzes at bay, while Dawson maintained his lead over DePalma. The pair clung to their precarious positions on lap three, as Wagner put on a display of Fiat power for the crowd.

Following Grant's black Alco out of the final turn by 70 yards, the quiet Alsatian poured on the power down the straight, his big Fiat simply blowing by the Alco as the two passed the grandstands. In just three laps, he had made up over four and one-half minutes on the Vanderbilt Cup winner. Undoubtedly, Grant was playing his waiting game, running at a pace he thought would win. But that tactic didn't look promising in the face of the power and speed of the Fiat.

Often overshadowed by brother Louis, Arthur Chevrolet could be a fast and talented driver when given the right machinery, as he demonstrated during the opening laps of the 1910 Grand Prize. Chevrolet in a Marquette-Buick held off challenges from David Bruce-Brown's Benz and Felice Nazzaro's Fiat for nearly an hour before falling back due to tire trouble and a botched pit stop (IMS Photo).

On lap four, the American challenge, that had captivated the crowd for most of an hour, began to evaporate. Tire troubles dropped Chevrolet's Marquette-Buick to tenth, a slipping jack costing him nearly four minutes in the pits. Wagner, still in second, continued his assault on the lead, passing the Benz of David Bruce-Brown that had started thirty seconds in front. But Bruce-Brown, now in third with Chevrolet's departure, fought back. The two came around the final turn side by side, with the Fiat leading slightly. As they passed the pits, the big Benz forged ahead. The crowd cheered wildly for the man they still thought of as "the young amateur." The handsome, blond millionaire, his face now obscured by a mask and goggles, waved back in acknowledgement.

Wagner and Bruce-Brown continued their battle on lap five, the Fiat and the Benz never more than a few yards apart. As they did so, Felice Nazzaro attacked, turning in a lap at over 75 mph. In doing so, he wrested third place from Bruce-Brown on the leaderboard. Further back, the last of the American threat died when Joe Dawson's Marmon coasted silently to a halt, its crankshaft in pieces. The order then was Hemery's Benz in first, followed by the Fiats of Wagner and Nazzaro, with Bruce-Brown's Benz, Haupt's Benz and DePalma's Fiat rounding out the top six. The Europeans were in total control, the best-placed American being Harry Grant's Alco in seventh.

As the laps unwound toward one-third distance, the duel between Wagner and Bruce-Brown continued, each of them seeming content to follow for a time, only to jump to the lead when they saw an opportunity. With a clear track in front of him, Nazzaro continued his run of quick laps, displacing Wagner for second place on lap six and whittling away at Hemery's lead, lowering the lap record to 13:42 on lap eight.

On lap nine, Hemery came into his pit for rear tires, relinquishing the lead to Nazzaro. But the Italian wouldn't even last a lap at the top. Still blasting around the course on his record pace, Nazzaro's Fiat skidded wildly at Burnside Ave., slamming into a ditch. The Fiat's rear axle was bent, but Nazzaro never stopped, guiding his crippled racer around in 14:01. Still, in the nip-and-tuck battle at the front, the delay was enough to put Wagner in the lead as the leaders crossed the stripe on lap nine. Nazzaro and Bruce-Brown were tied for second with identical times, followed by Hemery, Haupt and DePalma.

Among the Americans, Grant's Alco continued its steady pacing in seventh. Just behind came Bob Burman's Marquette-Buick. Burman, demonstrating the reason for his nickname, "Wild Bob," was driving the wheels off his racer — literally. So far, his drive had been marked by flat-out sprints punctuated by no less than three pit stops to replace his shredded tires. Arthur Chevrolet's valiant, if doomed, attempt to climb back among the leaders had ended on lap nine, his Marquette-Buick snapping its crankshaft.

A slow lap ten dropped Hemery to fifth, while Nazzaro pushed his crippled racer quickly enough to cement second ahead of the Benz of Bruce-Brown. The leader-board now showed the Fiats of Wagner and Nazzaro in front, followed by the Benzes of Bruce-Brown and Haupt, the quartet within seventy seconds of each other. DePalma in the remaining Fiat continued to cruise in sixth.

With their European star mired back in fifth and Fiat controlling the top two positions, the Benz pit signaled their American duo to charge. Willie Haupt poured on the gas, but Bruce-Brown could not. Like Hemery, he needed tires, and the stop dropped him to sixth, behind even DePalma. Still, Haupt's move to chase down the Fiats was successful more quickly than even he could have imagined. Nazzaro was flagged in for inspection of his axle, while Wagner pitted for water, gas and oil. Nazzaro emerged eleven seconds behind the lead Benz, with Wagner in third nearly four minutes back. Behind the six European machines, the American favorite's day ended. Harry Grant's black Alco stripped its gearbox and rolled to a stop.

On lap twelve, Haupt pitted for oil and water. Nazzaro did likewise for water and gas. The quick stops allowed the pair to hold their positions at the top, but their cushion over Wagner and the rest was a memory. Haupt pushed his Benz even harder, trying desperately to keep the Fiats at bay. At the turn past the grandstand, he lost it: the big Benz left the road, clipped a tree and rolled over, spilling Haupt and mechanic Horace Feyhe into some bushes. The shrubbery cushioned their landings and neither was seriously hurt, but the hillclimb ace's vision of victory in the Grand Prize had become just a daydream.

With Haupt out, Nazzaro took over the lead. Meanwhile, DePalma, now in the thick of things after the pit stops by the others, finally got the "Go!" sign from his pit.

He wasted no time, passing Hemery for fourth on lap twelve, vaulting past Wagner into second on lap thirteen. Again, a pair of Fiats were at the front, but the third of the trio, Wagner, was beginning to fade. A broken chain dropped him to fourth, behind Bruce-Brown's speeding Benz. Still, all of the top five remained within 1:45 of each other.

Hemery got by the fading Fiat on lap fourteen, as Wagner was forced to pit with a broken spring clip. The stop dropped him out of contention, behind even the Marquette-Buick of Bob Burman, who was still pursuing his run-till-it-breaks race strategy. At the front, the Fiats of Nazzaro and DePalma continued to lead, with the Benzes of Bruce-Brown and Hemery chasing hard. For two more laps the quartet stayed the same, the *Grand Prix* winner and the Brooklyn immigrant flogging their speeding Fiats for all they were worth, trying desperately to maintain their lead over the pair of big Benzes piloted by the young millionaire and the Vanderbilt Cup winner.

Then, on lap seventeen, the race changed complexion again. The bent axle on Nazzaro's leading Fiat finally began to slow the speeding Italian; he fell back to second, handing the lead to DePalma. On lap eighteen he dropped behind Bruce-Brown and Hemery. On lap nineteen the Fiat was out, its drive chains finally snapping from the stress. It was now DePalma all alone at the front, with the Benz of Bruce-Brown just one minute back and Hemery another minute behind.

Louis Wagner had no hope of catching the leaders. Twenty-five minutes in the pits had dropped him to ninth, behind not only Burman, but also the Loziers and Ray Harroun's Marmon, which Joe Dawson had taken over on lap fourteen. To make matters worse, the broken spring clip on his Fiat was irreparable, meaning Wagner was driving a car that was all but unmanageable. Nevertheless, the Alsatian had gotten permission from his pit to make up as much time as he could, and he was making the most of it. But on lap seventeen, he tried to swerve around a rut. His crippled racer simply wasn't up to the task. It somersaulted off the road, throwing Wagner and mechanic Ferro into the weeds. Ferro was unhurt, but Louis had two broken ribs. It was the worst crash he would suffer in a racing career spanning twenty-six years.

As the final laps unwound, DePalma turned in successive laps at record or near-record speed, grimly trying to open the gap between his flying Fiat and Bruce-Brown's big Benz. But the young millionaire was nearly his equal, turning in near-record laps of his own. Still, DePalma managed to widen the gap — to ninety seconds on lap twenty, to nearly two minutes as the leaders approached the last turn on lap twenty-one. By virtue of his later starting time, DePalma's Fiat was close on the tail of Bruce-Brown's Benz as the two reached the turn onto the main straight. Snatching the inside line, DePalma drew his Fiat even with the Benz as the two exited the corner. The crowd was on its feet as the pair passed the grandstands, enthralled by the display that the two young Americans were putting on. DePalma tried valiantly to find a way by, but the pure, straight-line speed of the Benz was too much. As the two sped into the distance, the German machine nosed ahead.

Minutes later, they were back. This time, Bruce-Brown had a slight lead on the Fiat, but DePalma still led overall. The crowd stood and cheered both their boys as they flashed by the grandstand. It was the last they would see of DePalma. His record pace had run down his rival, but it was simply too much for the Fiat's machinery. On lap twenty-three, a cylinder cracked. For the second time in two runnings of the Grand Prize, DePalma had led the race and captivated the crowd, only to be betrayed by the frailties of his mount.

"The young master," David Bruce-Brown, won the Grand Prize for Benz in 1910 and Fiat in 1911. Sadly, he would be fatally injured in practice for the 1912 race when his Fiat blew a tire and rolled end-over-end. He was just twenty-five years old (IMS Photo).

As DePalma's Fiat slowed, Bruce-Brown did likewise. With little more than a lap to run and Hemery over a minute back, his victory seemed assured. But the surly Frenchman with the scraggly mustache hadn't given up. Still over one minute ahead of Bruce-Brown by virtue of his earlier start, Hemery was blasting the big Benz around the course in a last desperate bid to avenge the disappointment of 1908. As the two crossed the line on lap twenty-three the gap stood at 1:19, too much ground to make up. Still Hemery tried valiantly, turning in a last lap of 13:54 with his tired machine. As his Benz took the checker this year, there were no shouts of victory. Most in the crowd thought the race was Bruce-Brown's in a walk, and Hemery knew, at best, he had made it a nail-biter that could go either way. He couldn't do more.

The crowd sat impatiently, waiting for their hero, but the gap on the track between Bruce-Brown and Hemery seemed to have grown. The time was now two minutes and counting and still there was no sign of the second Benz. Those with stop watches saw the time drain slowly away. The track announcer began to toll off the seconds. As the numbers became single digits the big Benz came around the last corner and onto the straight. When Bruce-Brown crossed the line it was too close to call, except for the electrical timer.

It alone told the story — Bruce-Brown was the winner by 1.42 seconds, the closest race finish in history.

Behind Hemery came Burman in his Marquette-Buick, eighteen minutes back, his final pit stop count at fifteen. Rounding out the six finishers were the Loziers of Mulford and Horan, and the Harroun/Dawson Marmon. But the cheers on this day were reserved for the young millionaire, the first American to win a *grand prix*. Before he could even climb down from his seat, his mother rushed onto the track to plant a kiss on his grimy cheek, all thoughts of disowning him apparently forgotten. Even the bad-tempered Hemery got caught up in the celebration. While clearly disappointed at the outcome — confiding to a friend, "I wouldn't have minded one minute, but one second *is* hard luck"[2] — he was among the first to congratulate his teammate, pouring a bottle of champagne over Bruce-Brown's head and pronouncing him "the young master."[3] Without realizing it, he had started a victory tradition that survives to this day.

Savannah's second Grand Prize, like its first, had been an impeccably orchestrated and highly entertaining race, with exciting duels throughout and a finish that had the fans on the edge of their seats. It would be hard to imagine a better race than this one, but for Savannah the best was still yet to come.

11

Mr. Harroun Was a Fine Gentleman

As the new century entered its second decade, old troubles boiled over while new ideas appeared on the horizon. Morocco, the focal point of the *Entente Cordiale* between France and Britain seven years before, again became a world hot spot when Kaiser Wilhelm II ordered the German battleship *Panther* to the port city of Agadir, ostensibly to "protect German lives and property." The true motive was to disrupt French rule in the area and to open a wedge in the alliance between Britain and France. For 151 days the kaiser rattled his saber, letting the world believe that further naval action by Germany was imminent, all the while making outrageous and conflicting territorial demands. The Second Moroccan Crisis, as it came to be called, was finally settled with German agreement to accept 100,000 square miles of Congo hinterland from France and to relinquish any further claims on Morocco. More significantly, instead of dividing France and Britain, the crisis put them on a war footing with increasingly formalized arrangements for their mutual defense. It also left the kaiser's Germany even more isolated and complaining more stridently than ever of hostile "encirclement." The clock counting down to World War I was now ticking loudly.

Half a world away, the Chinese Revolution, led by Sun Yat-sen, toppled the corrupt Qing Dynasty that had ruled since 1644. The revolution brought about the abdication of China's last emperor, Pu Yi, and the institution of a fledgling republican government that would last less than half a century. But imperialism was not on the wane everywhere in Asia. Just across the Himalayas, Britain's King George V made the first royal visit to India to be formally crowned its new emperor.

On the scientific front, British physicist Ernest Rutherford proved that atoms were not solid, as most scientists thought. Instead, he theorized that atoms were composed of a central nucleus surrounded by orbiting electrons. In doing so, he provided the structure of the atom that most of us recognize today and laid the groundwork for the understanding of nuclear energy. In other discoveries, Norwegian Roald Amundsen became the first man to reach the South Pole, and Yale University professor Hiram Bingham discovered the "lost city" of the Incas at Machu Picchu.

Closer to home, a tragic fire at the Triangle Shirtwaist factory in New York resulted in the deaths of 146 people, mostly immigrant seamstresses who had been trapped inside behind locked doors. The fire highlighted the sweatshop conditions that still existed throughout many industries and brought about a move for better fire-safety and labor laws.

On a happier note, a young New York songwriter originally named Israel Baline had his first big hit — though by this time he had changed his name to the more familiar Irving Berlin. *Alexander's Ragtime Band* was not only a sensation that sold over a million copies, it was a breakthrough that redefined American popular music. It also provided the foundation for a career that would span seven decades and see Berlin publish over 1,000 songs, including the all-time bestseller *White Christmas*.

❖ ❖ ❖

Old and new intertwined in the world of motor racing as well in 1911. On April 23, Bob Burman used Barney Oldfield's old "Blitzen" Benz to set a new speed record of 141.732 mph at Daytona. It was twice as fast as any airplane had flown — the fastest that man had ever traveled.

Bob Burman in the "Blitzen" Benz at Daytona. The car was a mix of old and new technology: The older technology of chain drive, but more advanced wire wheels instead of the wooden spoke variety, and a beak at the top of the radiator — a primitive attempt at streamlining (IMS Photo).

Bob Burman poses with his crown as "World Speed King" after driving the "Blitzen" Benz to a world speed record of 141.732 mph on April 23, 1911 (IMS Photo).

On Memorial Day, then known as Decoration Day, the two-year-old oval at Indianapolis staged a new race calculated to make both the city and the speedway the Mecca of motor racing in America. The 500-mile International Sweepstakes, as the race was called, was designed to supplant the Vanderbilt Cup and Grand Prize as America's preeminent race. First, it was longer than either of the road races. In fact, the organizers settled on the 500-mile distance because it was the longest distance that would allow the race to be completed in one day and still permit spectators to drive to and from the track in daylight. More significantly, the purse was a whopping $25,000, with $10,000 to the winner. Both figures were more than twice the amount paid by the Grand Prize, its closest competitor. Adopting the AAA's formula, the race was limited to cars of 600 cubic inches or less. The rule eliminated the largest of the European *grand prix* machines and allowed the American entries to compete on a more equal footing.

The European factory teams, unable to employ their fastest cars and unwilling to make two trips across the Atlantic in one season, stayed home, awaiting the Grand Prize in November. But that is not to say the first Indianapolis 500 was an all-American contest. Benz came the closest to fielding a team, with two cars entered by E. A. Moross for Billy Knipper and Bob Burman. The remainder of the European entries were privately owned cars for the rich kids. Spencer Wishart was back with his Mercedes. David Bruce-Brown, who had left Benz and returned to his old home at Fiat, replacing Ralph DePalma as their American ace, was entered in one of their machines owned by E. E. Hewlett. Gold-mining heir Eddie Hearne had a Fiat of his own. A third was entered by a newcomer to the big time, Caleb Bragg.

Caleb Smith Bragg was a Yale graduate and the son of a wealthy Cincinnati publisher. Small and slightly built, weighing only 127 lbs., he looked nothing like the typical race driver of the time, either in his stature or in his dress. Always attired in expensively tailored suits, a habit that would lead journalists to dub him the "Chesterfield of the racing crowd," the twenty-three-year-old Bragg often raced in a dress shirt and tie, like his friend Ralph DePalma. Bragg may not have looked the part of a race driver, but beneath his dapper dress and wiry frame lurked the soul of a gunfighter.

His first involvement in racing was as a replacement for DePalma in a match race

Top: "Speed King" Bob Burman's Benz leads Ray Harroun in the Marmon Wasp at Indianapolis, 1911 (IMS Photo). *Bottom*: Spencer Wishart wheels his white Mercedes past the grandstands on his way to fourth place in the 1911 Indianapolis 500 (IMS Photo).

with Barney Oldfield at the opening of the world's first board track at Playa Del Rey, California, in April 1910. Scheduled as part of the inaugural festivities, the race was originally to have been a three-way affair, with DePalma in his 200-horsepower Fiat "Mephistopheles," Oldfield in the "Blitzen" Benz, and George Robertson in the 90-horsepower Simplex "Zip," a track special that had just set the 10-mile speed record at 91 mph. Unfortunately, Robertson was hospitalized with an ear infection prior to the race and had to cancel. Then, on the day of the race, DePalma's temperamental Fiat cracked a cylinder on its way to the starting line. Just when it looked like the race would have to be cancelled entirely, the unknown Bragg stepped forward, challenging Oldfield to a match race between his "Blitzen" Benz and Bragg's hot-rodded Fiat 90—best of three two-lap sprints around the one-mile bowl. When Oldfield balked, Bragg even offered to put up the $2,000 prize money. The "unknown" then proceeded to go out and beat Oldfield twice in a row. While the victory probably earned Bragg the ire of Oldfield, who had no particular affection for DePalma and routinely derided his nationality, referring to him as "the Barber," it cemented a friendship with DePalma that would see the older Italian-born pro take time out to school the young amateur in the tricks of the racing profession. It would also survive an episode of triumph and tragedy, tarnishing the luster of Bragg's greatest victory, and would ultimately see Bragg become DePalma's handpicked teammate.

Arrayed against this handful of European machines were no less than forty American entries, although only thirty-four would make it to the start. Many of the teams had previous Vanderbilt Cup or Grand Prize experience. Alco entered its Vanderbilt Cup winner, as always piloted by Harry Grant. Buick fielded cars for Arthur Chevrolet and Charles Basle. Simplex entered a two-car team for Ralph DePalma and Ralph Beardsley. National fielded cars for Johnny Aitken, Charlie Merz and Indianapolis resident Howard "Howdy" Wilcox, who had gotten his start in racing as Johnny Aitken's riding mechanic. Marmon had a two-car team, one machine a single-seater designed by veteran Ray Harroun, who had come out of retirement to drive it, the other a conventional two-seater for Joe Dawson. Lozier fielded cars for Ralph Mulford and Californian Teddy Tetzlaff. The Lozier pair could not have been more dissimilar. While "Smilin' Ralph" was a gentleman whose religious beliefs were so strongly held that he

The "fine gentleman" himself, Ray Harroun, came out of retirement to design, build and drive the Marmon Wasp to victory in the inaugural Indianapolis 500 (IMS Photo).

The drivers for the Lozier team at the inaugural Indianapolis 500 were an odd couple at best. While Ralph Mulford was a devout Christian with a personality that earned him the nickname "Smilin' Ralph," a meticulous engineer and a driver who was renowned for taking care of his equipment, Teddy Tetzlaff, pictured here, was a hard-charging driver with a win-or-break attitude and a personality that had earned him the nickname "Terrible Teddy" for his ill-tempered behavior, both on track and off (IMS Photo).

refused to race on Sunday, a meticulous engineer and a driver renowned for his smooth driving style, much in the manner of a Harry Grant, Tetzlaff— known as "Terrible Teddy" for his wild, sometimes ill-tempered, nature — was a charger in the Bob Burman or Louis Chevrolet idiom who had little regard for the machinery.

In addition to the veteran manufacturers, many newcomers to automobile manufacture, or to big-time motor racing, made Indianapolis their debut. The reasoning was simple. As Harry Stutz confided to his friend Henry Campbell, upon deciding to enter his new Stutz at Indy, "This is just the time and place to launch the car. If it stands up, more people are going to know about it than could ever be reached through a costly advertising campaign." When Campbell asked, "What if it doesn't?," Stutz responded, "Then it'll get lost in the shuffle, but at least we'll have learned more in that one race than we ever could from ten thousand miles of road testing."[1] Gil Anderson would drive the new and untried machine.

Of a similar mind was Merrill Meigs, head of the one-year-old automobile division of the J. I. Case Threshing Machine Co. Meigs hired Lewis Strang, Will Jones and "the

Flying Dutchman," Joe Jagersberger, to drive a team of Case cars at Indy. In fact, Meigs was so taken with the idea of using racing to promote the Case name that the company was the first to formally enter a car for the 500.

Stepping up in class was Mercer, with two of their little 300-cubic inch Raceabouts entered for Hughie Hughes and Charles Bigelow. Until now, Mercer had contented itself with competing in, and often dominating, light car races like the Wheatley Hills and Savannah trophies, but the allure of Indianapolis enticed the team into competition with the big boys.

Officially, the race was won by Ray Harroun in the single-seat Marmon Wasp, famous for being the first racer, and some claim the first car, to use a rear-view mirror. It is Ray Harroun's face on the Borg-Warner Trophy; it was Ray Harroun who walked away with the $10,000. But in fact, no one living or dead really knows who won that first Indy 500 on that long-ago Decoration Day in 1911. After 500 miles, it was not Harroun's "32" at the top of the scoreboard; it was "33," the number of Ralph Mulford's Lozier.

The problem arose from the timing and scoring system used in the race. Indianapolis, taking a cue from the electrical scoring system used at Savannah, employed a sophisticated system of its own. The system utilized four Burroughs adding machines, two

The site some commentators have claimed is the scene of the crime — the timing booth for the 1911 Indianapolis 500 (IMS Photo).

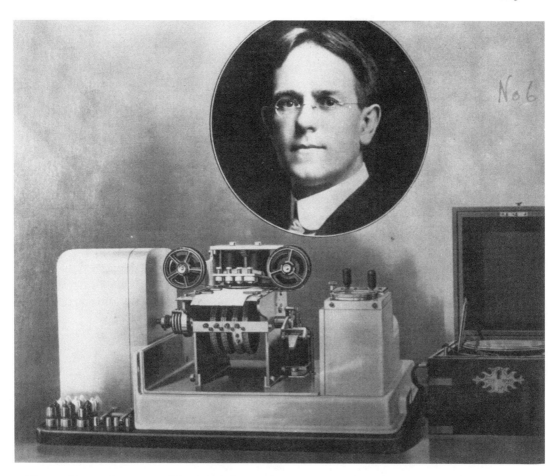

The machine at the center of the 1911 Indianapolis controversy, the Warner Harograph timer, and its inventor (IMS Photo).

Columbia Dictaphones, a Warner Harograph, and a Teleautograph to record the cars' lap times and positions and transmit that information to four scoreboards around the track. The system was manned by one hundred workers. Unfortunately, the heart of the system, the Harograph, a machine that mechanically recorded the precise time when each competitor's wheels hit a wire at the end of each lap, failed at least twice during the race — once being out of commission for as long as an hour. That left the matter of scoring to the human element. Here again, the system failed. Many of the men assigned the job had no experience in timing races. Most of them were picked from the society set of Indianapolis. To make matters worse, two hundred men were originally selected for the hundred positions, causing further confusion and turmoil.

Despite all of those failings, the system just might have worked, except for an incident involving Joe Jagersberger and Harry Knight. At about the 220-mile mark (no one can be sure), the Flying Dutchman's Case broke a steering knuckle as it sped down the front straight. The uncontrollable car, its front wheels splayed, came grinding to a halt directly opposite the pits, but before it could stop completely, John Wood, Jagersberger's mechanic, either jumped or was thrown out. Next on the scene was Harry Knight's Westcott. In attempting to avoid both the sprawling Wood and the crippled Case, Knight lost

Herbert Lytle's Apperson lies overturned after being hit by Harry Knight's Westcott in the multi-car crash that some commentators believe cost Ralph Mulford the victory in the 1911 Indianapolis 500 (IMS Photo).

control. The Westcott headed straight for that portion of pit row immediately adjacent to the timing stand. It slammed into Herbert Lytle's parked Apperson, throwing Knight and mechanic John Glover from their machine. The Apperson then overturned and smashed into Eddie Hearne's Fiat. The chain reaction left stunned drivers and mechanics and broken racers everywhere. It was all too much for the contingent in the timing stand. A mass exodus ensued, with nearly everyone abandoning their posts.

Ralph Mulford and David Bruce-Brown were among the next group of racers to arrive. The duo, who had been battling at or near the front for most of the day, were confronted with a track obstructed by wrecked cars and knots of people. Somehow, they found a way through, but the scoring stand was empty — its occupants either recovering from their close call, or offering their assistance with accident clean up. To make matters worse, at about this same time Ray Harroun's Marmon Wasp came into the pits. Cy Patschke had taken over the driving chores earlier and was now handing the wheel back to Harroun.

The remainder of the race was incident-free, with Mulford, Bruce-Brown and Harroun at the front. As the trio took the green flag, indicating one lap to go, the Lozier was

Top: In the wake of the multi-car crash involving Joe Jagersberger's Case and Harry Knight's Westcott, Eddie Hearne's Fiat (18) lies bent and broken after being hit by Herbert Lytle's Apperson (overturned in background). For his part, Lytle was also a victim of circumstance, being struck by the Westcott while sitting in the pits, then careening into the Fiat (IMS Photo). *Bottom*: Ralph Mulford's Lozier speeds past the timing and scoring stands during the 1911 Indianapolis 500 (IMS Photo).

The solitary figure of Ray Harroun pilots his Marmon Wasp toward victory in the 1911 500 (IMS Photo).

in front, followed, in order, by the Fiat and the Marmon. The scoreboard confirmed their positions. A broken spark lever sidelined Bruce-Brown on the final lap and his Fiat limped home behind the lead duo, but at the checker it was Mulford again first past the stripe with Harroun trailing behind. Lozier team orders instructed Mulford to take three "safety" laps, a precaution in the event of a scoring error. But by the time he was done, Harroun and the Marmon were already being celebrated as the winners.

A howl led by Charles Emise arose from the Lozier camp. He pointed out that the scoreboard had Mulford in the lead. The judges claimed that it was inaccurate. The matter was submitted to the race referee, the seemingly ubiquitous Arthur R. Pardington. Pardington, undoubtedly remembering the Vanderbilt Cup fiasco of 1909, announced that the race results would not be official until the next morning. Privately, he said that every position in the race was under scrutiny, *except* for the winner.

That night at the Claypool Hotel, the race officials assembled. The next morning, they announced their "official" results with Harroun declared the winner, Mulford second, and Bruce-Brown third. When the results were published, more protests were filed. Bruce-Brown's team claimed that he had finished second. Mulford and Emise re-asserted Lozier's claim to first. The officials reconvened. Testimony from drivers and team managers was heard. They complained that the scoreboards were not recording their laps, that the judge's stand was empty every time something happened, that racers who took "safety" laps were penalized in the standings. Then, after conferring among themselves, the race officials published a new set of "official" results. The top three remained the same, although Harroun's margin of victory was reduced from 5:38 to 1:43. Further back, some positions were shuffled. In the most remarkable alteration, Joe Dawson's Marmon, which had not even been listed in the top ten originally, was placed fifth. To make the final results more disturbing, no one could agree on when Harroun had passed Mulford for the lead. The official report showed Mulford in the lead from lap 177 to lap 181, when Harroun took over. In contrast, the newspaper accounts uniformly claimed that Harroun led from at least lap 100 to the end, but none contained an account of the pass that put the Marmon in front.

Despite the controversy surrounding the race, little of it made the newspapers. *The New York Times* merely mentioned that some of the finishing positions in the race had been changed. Only the *Indianapolis News* gave it significant coverage. Moreover, to insure that the final results would not be the subject of further scrutiny, Pardington ordered all of the timing and scoring sheets destroyed. He tried to pass off the order as one to protect the reputations of the cars that had fallen out, saying that "lap positions and lap times will never be divulged on those cars forced from the race. We consider it unfair to such as the Apperson which was withdrawn through no fault of its own."[2] Still, the excuse rang hollow, especially coming from the man who so skillfully talked Long Island farmers out of their land just so Willie K. Vanderbilt could have his pet highway.

So who really won? There are those who claim Harroun and Marmon were the beneficiaries of hometown judging. Marmon was an Indianapolis-based manufacturer and Howard Marmon was a pillar of the local business community. In contrast, Lozier was based in Plattsburgh, New York, and Mulford hailed from New Jersey. But the truth is that no one really knows, not even Ralph Mulford. When asked almost fifty years later to give his version of the story, "Smilin' Ralph" declined to re-open the controversy. "Mr. Harroun was a fine gentleman," he said, "a champion driver and a very great development engineer.... I wouldn't want him to suffer any embarrassment, nor the Indianapolis Motor Speedway. They have publicly credited me with leading the race and each year send me something as a remembrance ... to let me know I have not been forgotten."[3]

12

You Would Have Weeped Today

The remainder of 1911 was little kinder to Ralph Mulford than Indianapolis had been. In August, at the National Trophy Race at Elgin, Illinois, his Lozier failed to finish the race it had won the year before. At Fairmount Park in October, he finished second once again, this time after a race-long battle with Spencer Wishart's Mercedes and the eventual winner, wealthy Philadelphia amateur Erwin Bergdoll in a 731-cubic inch Benz.

The loss at Fairmount Park was particularly disappointing because Mulford had come so close to pulling out the victory, despite being saddled with a car that had nowhere near the power of either the Mercedes or the big Benz. Mulford had managed to stay within two minutes of the big black German machine through the first thirteen laps, all the while being engaged in a nip and tuck battle with Wishart's white Mercedes. On lap fourteen, a tire stop by Bergdoll allowed Mulford to creep within forty seconds and to pass the Benz on the track, but as the two racers sped wheel to wheel down West River Drive the Benz re-took the lead. At the tunnel turn, a tight left, Mulford put on a display of driving that brought the crowd to their feet. Outbraking the Benz as the cars approached the corner, he slashed to the inside line and alongside the powerful German machine. The two cars exited the tunnel side by side, with Mulford on the outside through the notorious "Dip of Death," an off-camber downhill right-hander followed immediately by an uphill straight. Still, Mulford kept the power on and stayed even with the Benz as his Lozier danced toward the edge of the road. At the bottom of the dip, the Lozier, still wheel to wheel with the Benz, got traction and bolted up the hill, now on the preferred inside line for the next curve. But it was all too much for Mulford's mechanic, Billy Chandler. As the Lozier's tires skidded and then grabbed hold in the off-camber dip, the force jarred him out of his seat and onto the soft turf at the roadside. He landed on his hands and knees, unhurt. Mulford stopped instantly and ran back to check on his teammate, who was just then getting to his feet. The two then rushed back to their machine and sped off, but the delay had cost Mulford a full two minutes.

Bergdoll would again have tire problems later in the race, as would Wishart, but Mulford would have tire troubles of his own, preventing him from taking advantage of

128

his competitors' stops. In the end both Bergdoll's Benz and Wishart's Mercedes would finish in front of the Lozier. But in an ironic twist of fate, Wishart would be disqualified for losing his mechanic, Bob Willoughby, on lap twenty-two in an incident similar to Mulford's and Chandler's. Unlike Mulford, Wishart hadn't stopped to pick up Willoughby, driving the remainder of the lap solo before stopping to pick up a replacement at his pit. Wishart's failure to stop was deemed a violation of the rule requiring each car to have a mechanic on board at all times.

So it was that as the racing fraternity came to Savannah for the Vanderbilt Cup and the Grand Prize, "Smilin' Ralph" was surely hoping that November would finally bring him something to smile about. For the first time, the Vanderbilt Cup and Grand Prize would actually be run over the same course within days of each other, a move that had been in the works since 1909. In the wake of the carnage of the 1910 Vanderbilt Cup, the AAA had all but anointed Savannah as Long Island's successor, announcing early in the year that it would sanction no site for the Vanderbilt Cup that could not provide a security force composed of local militia. While the move from Long Island deprived the race of some of the luster provided in years past by "the smart set, Gotham's Four Hundred and the polo field" fraternity,[1] there was no question that Savannah had become the pre-eminent road racing venue in America. No less an authority than Fred Wagner, the perennial starter for the Vanderbilt Cup, pronounced Savannah "the finest road course in the world."[2] In fact, in 1910, when the Fiat and Benz teams, already in America, were told that the Grand Prize would be held at Savannah instead of Long Island, the news was warmly received. Fiat driver Louis Wagner exclaimed, "I'm ready to go tonight!" It was not just the crowd control issue that made Savannah a favorite. The course "had a particular charm" and the race organizers went out of their way to make the drivers and teams feel welcome, arranging lavish dinners, taking them on fishing expeditions. As Louis Wagner said about Savannah years later, "It was a wonderful life. We hated to leave."[3]

For 1911, the course had again been improved. It had been straightened and widened in areas, some of the turns had been eased, and the final turn leading onto the front straight, the site of so much action in 1910, had been banked. The result of all these improvements was a minor reduction in the length of the course to 17.14 miles. The Vanderbilt Cup would make seventeen laps of the circuit, a race length of just over 291 miles.

But if Savannah was a suitable replacement for Long Island as the site for the Vanderbilt Cup, all was not otherwise rosy for America's grand old race. To begin with, entries were down — from thirty in 1910 to just fourteen a year later — and the schedule of events called for the Vanderbilt Cup to be run on the same day as the Savannah Challenge and Tiedeman Trophy light car races. As Fred Wagner lamented, "You would have weeped today to see the dear old race being treated as a sort of side show."[4]

In truth, the limited number of entrants was not a reflection of the Vanderbilt Cup's loss of stature. Among American competitors in the Grand Prize, only Buick held its cars out of the Vanderbilt Cup. The simple fact was that the number of entrants had been down at most of the year's races. The reasons were varied, but many of the old guard of American manufacturers were curtailing their commitment to racing. Simplex, a Vanderbilt Cup entrant as far back as 1904, confined its efforts to track racing with its Simplex "Zip." National did likewise. Two-time winner Alco withdrew from racing altogether. The American Locomotive Company was already beginning to experience the economic stresses that would cause it to abandon its automotive venture in 1913. More significantly, the Vanderbilt Cup's expanded rules for 1911, allowing virtually any machine of 600 cubic inches or less so long as it came from a manufacturer which had produced fifty or more cars during the preceding twelve months, convinced Alco's decision-makers that Grant's stock-chassis Alco-6, the winner of the 1909 and 1910 races, would be at a competitive disadvantage. Unwilling to build a new car and unsure of victory with its old one, Alco declined to defend its crown.

Still, if the field lacked the front-line *grand prix* machines of the early Vanderbilt Cup years or the outright numbers of more recent ones, it was nevertheless a fast and competitive contingent that assembled for the 1911 race. Among the Americans, Lozier fielded two of its 544-cubic inch machines for Ralph Mulford and Harry Grant. Indianapolis winner Marmon had 496-cubic inch cars for Bob Burman and Cy Patschke. Abbott-Detroit entered 349-cubic inch cars for Leland Mitchell and Carl Limberg. Single cars were entered by Jackson, a 430-cubic inch machine for Harry Cobe, and Pope-Hartford, a 389-cubic-incher for Louis Disbrow. Rounding out the American entries was Savannah Challenge winner Mercer, with one of its little 300-cubic inch machines for Hughie Hughes.

Among the Europeans, only Fiat had a factory team. These were their 1910 Grand Prize machines with engines sleeved down to 589 cubic inches. Three of the big brutes were entered for David Bruce-Brown, Ed Parker, and Joe Matson. Rounding out the field were two privately owned Mercedes, both modified versions of 1908 *grand prix* machines. One was Spencer Wishart's familiar white racer. The other, painted a battleship gray and quickly dubbed "the Grey Ghost," was owned by Ernest Schroeder, a New Jersey lamp

manufacturer. It would be driven by Ralph DePalma. It was the beginning of a partnership between car and driver that would rival any in racing history. Before DePalma and the Grey Ghost completed their long career together, the car would break its driver's heart, nearly kill him, spur him to his greatest triumph, and make both of them more famous in defeat than in any victory of their long and storied careers.

In practice the Fiats looked fastest, with Joe Matson turning in a lap of 13:17. The fastest of the Mercedes was Wishart's at 13:25. DePalma had been unable to get the Grey Ghost under fourteen minutes. Among the American contingent, the

Since first bursting onto the scene at the 1908 Grand Prize, Ralph DePalma had shown that he was a talented driver. But talent alone was not enough, as evidenced by the 1911 Vanderbilt Cup, where Ralph Mulford's Lozier bested DePalma's faster Mercedes because Mulford drove a nearly perfect tactical race (IMS Photo).

Loziers were the class of the field, with both Mulford and Grant turning in laps in the 13:30 range. Despite the lap times, the bettors were putting their money on DePalma and Mercedes. Those with a hometown bias, perhaps remembering the outcome at Indianapolis, seemed to favor the Marmon and Lozier teams in about equal numbers.

Harry Grant, now vested with an ability approaching clairvoyance in the minds of many due to his accurate predictions in the 1909 and 1910 Vanderbilt Cups, said no matter who won, he didn't expect the winning speed to exceed the mark of 74.7 mph set at Santa Monica a few weeks earlier.[5] For once, Grant's prediction was based on something more substantial than his own uncanny ability to foretell the outcome of a race. The speed of the cars was now surpassing the capabilities of their tires. At speeds in excess of 75 mph, the tires would come apart after only a few laps. It would be a major factor in the race.

Race day dawned cold, with a heavy fog that delayed the start of the Savannah Challenge and Tiedeman Trophy races from 7:30 to 8:00 a.m. The chilly temperatures kept the crowd home as well. Only 25,000 witnessed Hughie Hughes' victory for Mercer over the Marmons of Louis Heineman and Joe Nikrent. But by the start of the Vanderbilt Cup at 11:47 a.m., delayed from its scheduled 10:30 a.m. starting time by the late-running light car races, conditions were nearly ideal. A bright sun had burned off the early morning chill and only a healthy breeze kept temperatures from being downright balmy. As it was, the crowd of 100,000 which now filled the two grandstands and lined the course discarded the fur wraps and heavy coats that had been the order of the day for the early races.

As the big cars took their places two-by-two on the starting grid, awaiting Fred Wagner's instructions, they formed a kaleidoscope of color. Harry Grant's white Lozier was flagged away first, followed at thirty-second intervals by Bob Burman's yellow and black, long-nosed Marmon; Louis Disbrow's vermilion Pope-Hartford; Spencer Wishart's white Mercedes; Harry Cobe's red Jackson; Hughie Hughes in the chrome yellow Mercer; Carl Limberg's blue Abbott-Detroit; Ralph Mulford and mechanic Billy Chandler, clad in spotless white hoods and sweaters with "Lozier" emblazoned across the front, in their equally spotless white Lozier; Leland Mitchell in the second blue Abbott-Detroit; Ralph DePalma in the Grey Ghost Mercedes; and the trio of red Fiats for Ed Parker, David Bruce-Brown and Joe Matson, the flood of crimson at the tail of the procession broken only by Cy Patschke's yellow and black Marmon.

At the end of the first lap, Grant's Lozier was first across the stripe, but the field

Ralph Mulford demonstrates the reason for his nickname, "Smilin' Ralph." The 1911 Vanderbilt Cup winner was a meticulous engineer and a brilliant tactical driver (IMS Photo).

had bunched up sharply behind him. When the racers had all crossed the line, the leader-board had DePalma in front, eight seconds ahead of Patschke's Marmon. Wishart in the second Mercedes was third, three seconds further back, followed by Mulford four seconds in arrears, and the Fiats of Matson and Parker filling out the top six. Only twenty-four seconds separated DePalma from Parker. On lap two, DePalma kept his foot to the floor, trying to separate the Grey Ghost from the pack. In the process, he set the lap record at 13:14, nearly 78 mph. Still the pack held on grimly. Matson was forced to pit for water; a broken radiator would sideline him on lap five. His stop cut the lead group to five, but little more than a minute separated them.

On lap three, it was Parker's turn to stop, cutting the lead group to four. DePalma continued to extend his lead, setting a pace none of the others could match. He managed to open a gap of fifty-one seconds on Patschke's Marmon, but the rest of the gang of four, Wishart and Mulford, trailed by mere seconds. By lap four, DePalma had a minute in hand as Patschke became the third of the lead group to fade. Wishart and Mulford, now just one second apart, lay one minute behind DePalma, one minute ahead of Burman, Bruce-Brown and the rest.

As usual, the opening laps had shown DePalma's remarkable talent for speed. And as usual, that speed had a price. On lap five, it was time for payment. The gray Mercedes blew two tires on the back straight, costing DePalma two minutes. A stop at his pit for replacements and a carburetor adjustment on the next lap cost two minutes more. Meanwhile, Wishart had problems of his own, pulling into his pit on lap five with his tire treads shredded and flapping. Sloppy pit work cost him even more time when the white Mercedes toppled off the jack. When it had all shaken out, the Mercedes duo, so strong in the early going, were now lying third and fifth. Mulford's Lozier led by more than a minute over Burman's Marmon. DePalma in the Grey Ghost was another minute back, followed by David Bruce-Brown's Fiat and Wishart's Mercedes.

David Bruce-Brown at the wheel of his Fiat in the 1911 Vanderbilt Cup (IMS Photo).

Bruce-Brown no sooner broke into the top five than his machine broke under him. A wheel on his Fiat collapsed. His retirement lifted Wishart to fourth, but neither of the Mercedes pilots could make up any time on the front-running Lozier. Mulford continued his metronome-like laps, ticking them off with precision. Behind him, Bob Burman, his closest pursuer, fell out on lap eight. Unbeknownst to Wild Bob or his mechanic, a stone had holed the Marmon's gas tank. It sputtered to a stop on the course, its day over. Another tire stop by DePalma handed second to Wishart, but Mulford still had three minutes in hand on the white Mercedes.

As the race passed half distance, Smilin' Ralph and the Lozier continued to motor while the Mercedes duo gave chase. DePalma, now in third, chopped seconds off Mulford's lead lap by lap, but his time in the pits had been measured in minutes, not seconds. It was simply too much to make up. Wishart in the second-place Mercedes could match the speed of the big Lozier, but couldn't make up ground. Then, on lap eleven, more problems cost him nearly nine minutes, relegating him to sixth. It was now a two-man race, with the Lozier leading the gray Mercedes by five minutes. DePalma would clearly need help from Lady Luck to make up the gap.

On lap thirteen the white Lozier finally pitted for gas, water and tires. A slow stop might give DePalma a chance at the win, but the Lozier crew was perfect. The stop timed out at 1:06, the fastest of the day. Still, the stop had cut DePalma's deficit to less than four minutes; with a little more help he might make it a race. He continued to whittle at the white Lozier's lead while Wishart blazed back up to third, passing Parker's lone remaining Fiat, Disbrow's Pope-Hartford, and Grant's Lozier.

On lap fifteen the Lozier was back in the pits — a tire had let go. But again, the stop was a picture of precision and Mulford was rolling in little more than a minute. The margin on DePalma was down to two minutes, but with two laps to go and fresh tires on the Lozier, two minutes was more than enough. Mulford cruised to the checker, winning by a margin of 2:11. Behind DePalma, Wishart's Mercedes took third, ten minutes back of the leader; Grant's Lozier was fourth, another four minutes back; Parker's Fiat was fifth, five minutes more in arrears; and Disbrow's Pope-Hartford rounded out the finishers, another five minutes behind.

Seemingly, the race had been less than spectacular, with Mulford in control from the fifth lap on. Still, the fans cheered wildly at the finish, the American crowd full of hometown pride. An American machine, and a basically stock one at that, had finally taken on the European specials and bested them — and not from attrition, but from pure, raw speed. It was something that couldn't be said of any of the previous American victories in the Vanderbilt Cup.

If the result was a cause for celebration to those who witnessed it, it became something more for those who looked at it in depth in the weeks, months and years that followed. Looking back, it must be said that Ralph Mulford drove a nearly perfect race. Faced with the vastly more powerful Mercedes and Fiat contingents, Mulford was nevertheless able to keep his Lozier in contention during the early stages of the race, while still preserving its tires. Upon taking the lead, he kept his pursuers at bay without straining his machine or overtaxing his tires. His scheduled pit stop on lap thirteen was a picture of perfection, the fastest of the day. All in all, it was a remarkable performance. Two seemingly anomalous statistics perhaps better than any others put Mulford's drive into perspective. On eleven of the seventeen laps of the race, DePalma was faster than

Mulford — and on three of the six where Mulford was faster, DePalma had stopped for tires. Nevertheless, Mulford's race average was 74.07 mph, the fastest yet recorded at Savannah and within a few tenths of a mile per hour of the world record. It is amazing that Mulford could seem to run so slow and still finish so fast. It was a lesson in race driving and strategy that wouldn't be lost on the other Ralph — the one named DePalma.

13

Oh Boy! Let Her Ride

In the wake of the Vanderbilt Cup, Ralph Mulford and the Lozier team came in for a good bit of attention. How had Lozier taken a basically stock car, one that had been nowhere near as fast as the Europeans the previous season, and turned it into the giant-killer that it had become? Mulford provided the answer in just one sentence—"preparation, practice, pit work and hard driving."[1] But in that single sentence lay years of experience and months of effort. The car had been taken from the production line, completely disassembled, minutely inspected and painstakingly reassembled by Mulford and his crew. The engine had then been run at full power for twenty-four hours and once again inspected. If any part showed wear, it was replaced and the test run again until everything was perfect. The chassis was then road tested. At the race site, a camp was selected giving Mulford and his crew easy access to the course and a vantage point for timing their competitors. In practice, Mulford would memorize the course and make careful adjustments to the engine and chassis, always in search of the racer's best lap time. Three days before the race, the engine would again be disassembled and inspected, then a couple of break-in laps and a final few fast laps would be driven to get the racer ready. All the while, the pit crew would be busy keeping everything spotless and conducting repeated pit stop drills. Viewed from a vantage point ninety years on, the time and effort put into this preparation and practice does not seem extraordinary, but in 1911 it was. It was a model that would be emulated throughout the racing fraternity due to the result it achieved—a 51-horsepower, stock-chassis Lozier that could run with the big boys and beat them.

❖ ❖ ❖

The 1911 Grand Prize ranks among those races which, at the time, are anointed with the appellation "Greatest Race Ever Run." Nearly unknown today, the Grand Prize did not produce the split-second finish of the 1910 race, or of later races like the Indianapolis 500s of 1982 with Gordon Johncock and Rick Mears, or 1992 with Al Unser, Jr., and Scott Goodyear. Nor did it feature a masterpiece of supreme driving skill like Vincenzo

Lancia's doomed runaway in the 1905 Vanderbilt Cup, or Tazio Nuvolari's win for Alfa-Romeo in the 1935 German *Grand Prix*, where he outdistanced the massed hordes from Mercedes-Benz and Auto Union, or Juan Fangio's win in the same race in 1957, where his consummate skill in the Maserati 250-F vanquished the faster Ferraris of Mike Hawthorn and Peter Collins. Nevertheless, for thrilling action from wire to wire, a whole host of potential winners in a variety of cars, a dose of hard racing luck, and an outcome in doubt until nearly the end, the 1911 Grand Prize can wear its mantle proudly.

The race, twenty-four laps of the 17.14-mile Savannah circuit, a total distance of 411.36 miles, was run on Thanksgiving Day, three days after the Vanderbilt Cup. If the Vanderbilt Cup field had been a competitive one, the field for the Grand Prize looked even stronger. For the Europeans, Ralph DePalma and Spencer Wishart were back with their 597-cubic inch Mercedes, now rated at 140 horsepower. Full factory teams were fielded by Benz and Fiat. Benz brought three of its powerful 928-cubic inch machines, teaming Victor Hemery with Americans Eddie Hearne and Erwin Bergdoll. Fiat fielded three of the 863-cubic inch S-74s designed for the stillborn 1911 French *Grand Prix*. With Felice Nazzaro, like Lancia before him, now retired from racing to build his own car, Fiat tapped Louis Wagner as its European ace and teamed him with Americans David Bruce-Brown and Caleb Bragg.

The American entries were much the same as in the Vanderbilt Cup. Lozier entered a single car for Ralph Mulford. Marmon returned with cars for Bob Burman and Cy Patschke. Abbott-Detroit fielded two of its little blue machines for Leland Mitchell and Carl Limberg. Louis Disbrow would again be at the wheel of the Pope-Hartford, and rounding out the field were the pair of 593-cubic inch Marquette-Buicks that had been held out of the Vanderbilt Cup. Now rated at 100 horsepower, these modified versions of the machines made famous by Louis Chevrolet and Bob Burman would be driven by Charlie Basle and Harry Cobe.

Many fans of Indy-car or *grand prix* racing today complain that all the cars look alike. Shaped in the wind tunnel and sprouting wings on nose and tail, the cars can often be distinguished only by their paint jobs. Those fans should have been in Savannah in 1911 to witness the varied body shapes and sizes of the racers of that era. Most impressive in size were the Fiats, huge red monsters with barn-like radiators and hoods towering nearly to eye level. They dwarfed many of the American entries. Then there were the Benzes, massive white machines, all Teutonic might, their flat, round-topped radiators with the signature six-section grill recognizable to any Mercedes-Benz owner today. But if the Fiats and Benzes were behemoths, the Mercedes were elegance at speed. With their beautiful proportions, dropped frames and distinctive, swept back, V-shaped radiators, they looked fast even standing still.

The American machines, if lacking the gargantuan size and brutish proportions of the Fiats and Benzes, each had a look all their own. The Marquette-Buicks were embodiments of power, with angular radiators and four huge exhaust pipes protruding out the left side of their engine compartments. Mulford's Lozier was all business, gleaming white with its trademark square radiator and flat-topped hood. By comparison, the Marmons were low and sleek, with long, tapered, aardvark-like noses. Rounding out the field were Disbrow's Pope-Hartford and the little Abbott-Detroits; with their low streamlined shapes and rounded engine covers, they seemed to crouch between their wheels like big cats.

In practice, Eddie Hearne's big Benz was fastest, with a lap at over 80 mph. Among the rest of the entrants only Louis Wagner's Fiat joined Hearne in the 80-mph club. So the battle again looked like a shootout between Benz and Fiat as the two previous Grand Prizes had been. Mercer ace Hughie Hughes, filling in for Harry Grant as pre-race pundit, predicted a race average of 74 mph, a victory for Hemery's Benz, second place to Wagner's Fiat, and a third-place dogfight between Mulford and DePalma. The oddsmakers disagreed, but only slightly, listing Hemery and Wagner as co-favorites at 3 to 1; Bruce-Brown at 4 to 1; Mulford, Hearne and Bergdoll at 5 to 1; Bragg at 6 to 1; and DePalma at 8 to 1. The rest of the field weren't given much chance, carrying odds ranging from 30 to 1 to 100 to 1, the little Abbott-Detroits of Mitchell and Limberg in the latter category.

On Wednesday it rained, discouraging practice. Still the Benz team, the Buicks and Bruce-Brown spent time checking the course, looking for changes brought about by the rain or by Monday's races. Other teams spent the day going over their cars one last time, making sure all was in readiness. Race day dawned clear and cold. The fans in the stands were bundled in furs and heavy coats to ward off the chill. Still, the weather hadn't kept anyone home. The grandstands were packed to capacity and it was standing-room only around the course.

Wagner's Fiat was first away, with the remaining fifteen racers following at thirty-second intervals. As the racers came back around, the Alsatian co-favorite was still in front, blowing on his hands to ward off the cold as he flashed down the main straight. But the leader was his American teammate, Caleb Bragg. In fact, both Americans on the Fiat team were leading the European pro, with Bruce-Brown six seconds back in second position, five seconds ahead of the third-place Wagner. Behind the trio of big Fiats, no less than eleven of the sixteen starters were still within a minute of the lead. DePalma was fourth, just two seconds behind Wagner, then two seconds further back came Hemery in the Benz, then Bergdoll and Wishart twenty seconds astern, followed by Hearne's Benz, Mulford's Lozier, and the Marmons of Patschke and Burman.

On lap two, Hemery got by DePalma for fourth, Hearne climbed two places to sixth, and Bergdoll pulled five seconds clear of Wishart to take over seventh alone. But despite the vast power of the Benzes, now lying fourth, sixth, and seventh, the Fiats were still in control. Their pace, like that of all of the leaders, was simply sensational, with Bragg lapping within a whisker of 80 mph. On lap three his pace never slowed, yet Bruce-Brown crept to within one second at the stripe. Behind them, their teammate dropped back, the first victim of the tire wear that would plague the big Fiats all day. Further back, Wishart's Mercedes began to fade as well; a cracked cylinder would finally end its day on lap ten.

On lap four the tire gremlin visited the Fiats of both Bragg and Bruce-Brown. Hemery had problems of his own: his engine had gone sour. The problem would later be traced to defective exhaust valves, but by then the surly Frenchman would be miles behind and hopelessly out of contention. With all of the top trio in trouble, DePalma took the lead, his Mercedes twenty seconds up on Bruce-Brown's slowing Fiat. Ten seconds behind was Hearne's Benz followed by his teammate Bergdoll, now just over a minute back of the lead. At the same time, the Marmons of Burman and Patschke were making their move. Burman had passed Mulford on lap three and now passed the pitted Fiat of Bragg to take over fifth by one second. Patschke followed two places back, with the smoothly cruising Mulford rounding out the top eight, and Wagner still striving to get back in contention.

On lap five the positions reshuffled again. DePalma dropped to fifth, slowed by a leaking gas line. Bruce-Brown made his pit stop for tires, falling to eighth with a six-minute stop, the result of cold limbs, hands and fingers (unlike the Vanderbilt Cup, the Grand Prize, adopting the rules of the French *Grand Prix*, required that all repairs be performed by the driver and riding mechanic only). With the top two in trouble, Eddie Hearne took the lead for the Benz team, but behind him all was not well. His teammate Bergdoll was beginning to fade. A cracked cylinder would end his day on lap eight. And just behind Bergdoll, Bob Burman's magneto gave up. The retirements vaulted Bragg's Fiat back to second, thirty seconds behind Hearne, with Mulford's Lozier in third another forty-five seconds back, and Patschke's Marmon in fourth just four seconds behind Mulford.

On lap six Hearne continued to lead, but Bragg, his pursuer, again ravaged his tires, requiring another visit to his pit. The stop dropped him to fifth. Meanwhile, Cy Patschke continued to flog his little Marmon for all it was worth, passing Mulford and closing the gap on the leader. Behind Patschke, Wagner had the bit in his teeth as well, charging back up through the pack in his brute of a Fiat to take over third. Mulford cruised in fourth, trying to maintain the pace that had brought him the Vanderbilt Cup just three days before, while DePalma again dived into his pit for repairs.

Lap seven saw Hearne and Wagner stop for tires. The record pace, still nearly 77 mph, was tearing up tires for everybody, but the Fiats were particularly prone to the malady. Hearne's stop handed the lead to Cy Patschke, but the stop was a quick one and Eddie managed to hang onto second, seven seconds in front of Mulford, eight in front of Bragg. Wagner's stop dropped him to fifth, another minute back, with Bruce-Brown a further two minutes behind and DePalma bringing up the rear of the lead pack.

When the scoreboard showed Patschke as the leader the big crowd went crazy. It was the first time an American car had led a *grand prix*. Was it possible that the little long-nosed Marmon could repeat its Indianapolis feat? Over the eighth circuit Patschke pushed his little machine to its limit, determined to hold onto his lead. Nevertheless, Hearne's big Benz shaved twelve seconds off the gap. Then on lap nine it all came apart for the little yellow and black racer — literally. The Marmon coasted to a stop out on the circuit. From the terrible pounding of the record-setting pace, the machine had beaten itself to bits. Its engine mounts had failed, and the engine was flailing around loose in the chassis. Patschke had literally driven his machine to pieces.

With the Marmon out, Hearne reassumed the lead. But Wagner was now on a tear, vaulting past Mulford into second and halving the gap between his Fiat and Hearne's leading Benz — the margin now just twenty-three seconds. Unfortunately, the Fiats had once again shredded their tires. Wagner, Bragg and Bruce-Brown, lying second, third and fourth on lap ten and all within striking distance, were each forced to pit. Their three-minute lead over DePalma and Mulford allowed Wagner and Bruce-Brown to hold their positions, but they were now nearly four minutes behind Hearne. Bragg's stop, on the other hand, was a disaster. Cold hands, tired limbs, and recalcitrant machinery conspired to cost the Fiat driver fifteen minutes, leaving him twelve minutes behind Mulford at the tail of the lead pack. With one bad pit stop, he had ceased to be a factor.

In counterpoint to Bragg's fiasco, Mulford's stop on lap ten, his first of the race, was a model of efficiency. The Lozier took on gas, water and tires and was back in the race in less than four minutes. It emerged from the pits just one second behind DePalma's

Mercedes in fifth. Also emerging from the pits after a stop of over an hour was Hemery's Benz. He was just on his fourth lap, while the leaders were completing their tenth, but he had promised the crowd a lap record and he was going to deliver. One lap to get back up to speed, then he put the boot to the Benz. The big machine bellowed as it roared off in blazing acceleration. Boring holes through the traffic, broad-sliding the Beaulieu hairpin, flashing down Ferguson Avenue like a big, white blur, Hemery finally reappeared at the top of the main straight, locked in a vicious slide around the banked final corner. As he flashed across the line the clock told the story — 12:36, 81.6 mph, a new record. The crowd cheered their speed king, the surly little Frenchman of whom they had grown so fond in the wake of his heart-breaking losses. Hemery acknowledged their cheers with a wave, did a couple of cool-down laps and pulled in, his day over.

As the race passed half-distance, Hearne's lead looked secure with three minutes in hand. Over the next two laps, the Fiats of Wagner and Bruce-Brown took turns trying to run down the big Benz, but neither could crack the three-minute barrier that separated them from the leader. Then on lap fourteen it was Hearne's turn for tires. With his three-minute lead, he stayed at the front, but his safety margin was gone. Wagner was just sixteen seconds back, but the second member of the Fiat tandem had again torched his tires. Another pit stop dropped Bruce-Brown to fifth, thirty seconds behind Mulford's Lozier.

With Hearne's white machine now just seconds ahead, Wagner spurred his huge Fiat for all it was worth, determined to take the lead, a position that had eluded him all day. But in an uncharacteristic lapse, he overran a turn. The monster machine caught an overhanging tree limb, wrenching its rear axle and damaging the steering. The retirement left just four at the front — Hearne's Benz leading by a minute over DePalma's Mercedes, with Mulford in the Lozier twenty-eight seconds back, and Bruce-Brown's Fiat just three seconds further astern. Over 250 miles into the race, little more than ninety seconds separated the leaders.

On lap sixteen Bruce-Brown charged as DePalma stopped for tires. Still the Fiat was unable to make up any ground. All the hot lap had done was destroy another tire. On lap seventeen Bruce-Brown pitted, handing second place to the smooth-driving Mulford, who was still holding position ninety seconds astern of the leader. On lap eighteen Mulford nibbled away seconds on the leader as Hearne, now fatigued from leading the race for ten laps and fending off challenges from Patschke, Wagner, Bruce-Brown and DePalma, began to fade. Behind Mulford, Bruce-Brown again came roaring up, chopping nearly thirty seconds off the gap separating him from second. Then Hearne was in the pits for a tire of his own, and again his cushion vanished. He got out with the lead, but the Lozier was now hot on his heels, and Bruce-Brown in the Fiat was still closing fast. Within one lap the order of the top three reversed itself completely, with the charging Fiat of Bruce-Brown taking control, Mulford's Lozier just fourteen seconds behind, and a tired Eddie Hearne now clinging to third, his Benz another seventeen seconds back. The fourth of the group, DePalma, stopped again on lap nineteen. His Mercedes was now four minutes down on the leaders. It was a three-man race to the finish.

Now nearly five hours into the race, an exhausted Eddie Hearne got a shot of adrenaline. Fatigue may have enabled Bruce-Brown and Mulford to catch him, but his race wasn't over — not yet. Finding more speed than he had shown all day, he passed Mulford's Lozier for second and set off in search of Bruce-Brown. Then, on lap twenty-two,

Eddie Hearne, pictured here in the Fiat sweater he wore at Indianapolis, was heir to a gold-mining fortune, but he was no mere dilettante as a driver. As a member of the Benz team in the 1911 Grand Prize he held the lead through twenty-two of the race's twenty-four laps, fending off repeated attacks by Ralph DePalma's Mercedes, 1910 Grand Prize winner David Bruce-Brown's Fiat, and Vanderbilt Cup winner Ralph Mulford's Lozier, before tire problems just twenty-five miles from the finish relegated him to second place, behind Bruce-Brown (IMS Photo).

with just two laps remaining, all three of the leaders came into the pits. Bruce-Brown arrived first, to the cheers of the society contingent and those looking for a repeat of last year. He was followed only seconds later by Mulford, who was greeted by an ovation of his own. Many in the crowd were pulling for the result that had, until now, been unthinkable — a Lozier sweep of the Vanderbilt Cup and Grand Prize. Then in came Hearne to another rousing cheer. The crowd sat in tense silence as the drivers and mechanics worked furiously on their machines. Mulford was first away — gas only — just thrity-six seconds — another perfectly orchestrated stop by the Lozier team. Bruce-Brown was just seconds behind. A left rear tire had taken just 1:06 to change. Hearne followed after what seemed an eternity, but in truth his own tire change had taken just over a minute. As the big Benz disappeared in the distance, the scoreboard told the story. Hearne held the lead by a scant twenty-six seconds over Mulford, with Bruce-Brown just sixteen seconds further astern — forty-two seconds between them with thirty-four miles to go.

Mulford, the leader on the track, had spent the whole race maintaining his pace. While others like Wagner and Bruce-Brown had flashed to the front, only to fall back in a welter of tire stops, Mulford had marched to his own racing rhythm, keeping to his pace whether second or sixth, whether two seconds back or two minutes. As proof of this fact, his time for the first seventeen laps was just fifteen seconds faster than his Vanderbilt Cup time, despite a race whose pace had been far faster throughout. The strategy was working to perfection: with two laps to go he was second and just twenty-six seconds behind Hearne. Yet time was running out, the laps were unwinding, it seemed time to push for the lead. With that thought in his mind, Mulford departed from the rhythm he had held the whole race. As he would say later, "Just keep the front wheels in the road and let the rear do the pushing regardless of angle. Oh Boy!, let her ride."[2] The immaculate white Lozier, now streaked with grime from five hours of racing, was simply flying as it approached the dangerous railroad crossing. At the grade the car became airborne, flying some fifty feet through the air as it had twenty-two times before on this day. But this time Mulford kept his foot to the floor as the wheels left the ground, searching for every ounce of speed. The unloaded engine screamed, then the Lozier crashed to earth.

With a sickening sound the driveshaft snapped. Smilin' Ralph, so close to victory, would be left to walk back to his pit in defeat.

Behind Mulford, Bruce-Brown was flying as well, turning in a time on lap twenty-three that was nearly as fast as his second, his fastest of the race. But as it turned out, the charge to the lead wasn't needed. Just twenty-five miles from the finish Hearne had another tire go. The two-minute stop for replacement gave the victory to Bruce-Brown in a walk. Hearne salvaged second, some two minutes back, with DePalma in third another minute astern and Bragg fourth, fully twenty minutes behind the leader. Louis Disbrow got fifth in the little Pope-Hartford, the only American entry to finish. The American victory that had seemed so near now lay in ashes beneath the slowly cooling hulk of a broken white Lozier. It would be some time before the Yanks would be this close again.

The crowd, while deprived of an American victory, nevertheless had much to cheer. The race had been won at a record speed, 74.45 mph, and Bruce-Brown's win was a popular one with the fans. Moreover, since this was his second Grand Prize victory, it made history on a number of counts: he became the first man to win the race twice in succession, the first two-time winner of any *grand prix* event, and the first to win two *grands prix*. As his mother climbed down from her box and charged across the track to embrace her son with the hug and motherly kisses that had become the signature finale to a Bruce-Brown victory, the crowd cheered wildly. For the third time Savannah had put on a show. Little did anyone know that it would be its last.

14

Dago Luck (Part One)

April 15, 1912, produced the news story of the century. The tale of the sinking of the "unsinkable" ocean liner R.M.S. *Titanic* on its maiden voyage is one that has rung through the years like the haunting reverberations of some huge bell, tolling its warning to mankind. Made famous to successive generations by Walter Lord's classic *A Night to Remember*, and by James Cameron's Oscar-winning film *Titanic*, the event has taken on a significance all out of proportion to the actual size of the tragedy. Many Baby Boomers or Generation X'ers who know every detail of the stories of Benjamin Guggenheim, John Jacob Astor, Isidor and Ida Straus, and many of the other 1,513 souls who lost their lives on that fateful night in 1912, would be hard pressed to find Verdun on a map, let alone relate a single story from the epic battle that took place there just four years later — a battle that ground up the young men of Germany and France by the millions and scarred the psyche of Europe for a generation, compelling Gertrude Stein to call the surviving youth of World War I "the Lost Generation."

More than a few scholars have spent a good part of their professional careers documenting in detail the tragedy of the *Titanic* or providing explanations for its exceptional significance to later generations. I will not do so here. But one *Titanic* story has been omitted from virtually every published account — and it is one that directly impacts our story. Among the millionaires who died in the frigid waters of the North Atlantic on that fateful night was the thirty-one-year-old Washington A. Roebling II, the mainstay behind the ill-fated Roebling-Planche Grand Prize racer. More importantly, Roebling was the scion of the Mercer Automobile Company and the chief proponent of its racing program. The young Roebling's death, just as Mercer embarked upon its venture into big-time motor racing, would have a profound effect on the firm's decisions regarding its racing program in the years to come.

❖ ❖ ❖

Elsewhere in 1912, it was a bad year for science. In a gravel pit near the town of Piltdown, England, a British lawyer and amateur geologist named Charles Dawson claimed to have discovered the fossil remains of a prehistoric human skull with an ape-like jaw. Experts instantly declared *Evanthropus dawsoni*, or Piltdown Man, the find of the century — the "missing link" between apes and humans that had been posited by Charles Darwin in his *On the Origin of Species*. It would not be until 1953 that Piltdown Man would be discredited, not merely as something less than its original proponent proclaimed, but as an outright hoax. Radiocarbon dating proved that the skull, a woman's, was just six hundred years old, and the jawbone was from an Indonesian orangutan of similar vintage. No culprit was ever identified, but the scandal reached far beyond Dawson, even touching such notables as Arthur Conan Doyle.

In Germany, meteorologist and explorer Alfred Wegener, noting how the Atlantic coastlines of the Americas, Europe and Africa seem to fit like the pieces of a puzzle, and citing the existence of similar fossils and rocks in both Brazil and South Africa, proposed his theory of continental drift. He hypothesized that the planet's continents had all been joined together as one super-continent at some time in the past and had gradually drifted apart. Unfortunately, the bulk of the scientific community rejected the theory out of hand, one even going so far as to sneer that the model proposed by Wegener and his supporters was nothing more than "The delirious ravings of people with bad cases of moving crust disease and wandering pole plague."[1] It would not be until the 1960s that scientific discoveries would validate Wegener's theory, opening the door to the new field of plate tectonics, an underlying principle of modern geological theory.

In the world of sports there was triumph and tragedy. Native American Jim Thorpe won the pentathlon and decathlon at the Stockholm Olympic Games, the latter with a world-record score so remarkable that it still would have merited a silver medal nearly two generations later at the 1948 London Olympics. The incredible performance moved King Gustav V to tell Thorpe at the medal ceremony, "Sir, you are the greatest athlete in the world." In a response that has become famous, Thorpe merely replied, "Thanks, King."[2]

Unfortunately, within six months of Thorpe's stunning feat, a newspaper would reveal that he had earned $25 a week playing minor league baseball in North Carolina during his college vacations in 1909 and 1910. Under the rules of the day, Thorpe's receipt of money, even so small an amount, deprived him of his amateur status in all sports. The International Olympic Committee stripped Thorpe of his medals and offered them to the second-place finishers in each event. In a show of support for Thorpe, they declined them. Still, despite a poll of Associated Press sportswriters in 1950 declaring Thorpe the greatest athlete of the first half-century, his achievements would live under a cloud until 1982, nearly thirty years after his death, when the I.O.C. would finally restore his name to the record books and his medals to his children.

If the news from the North Atlantic and the sporting world was tragic, and men of science were chasing their tails, things were better at home. In Hollywood, Mack Sennett, a D. W. Griffith protégé, opened his Keystone studio. Over the next two decades he would make America laugh with the Keystone Kops and introduce audiences everywhere to an unknown English music-hall comic named Charlie Chaplin. Elsewhere, Nabisco introduced Oreo and Lorna Doone cookies, Cracker Jack began putting prizes in its boxes, and Hellmann's introduced its bottled mayonnaise. Finally, a tuna salad sandwich could be made without catching your own fish or mixing your own mayo.

❖ ❖ ❖

In the four years that Ralph DePalma had been involved in big-time motor racing, he had yet to win a major event. Ninth in the 1908 Grand Prize after setting the lap record and leading the opening laps; forced to settle for seventh in the 1910 race after his Fiat cracked a cylinder while leading, just two laps from the checker; no better than sixth in a Simplex in the inaugural Indianapolis 500; second to Mulford's Lozier in the 1911 Vanderbilt Cup despite leading the first four laps and being faster than the Lozier pilot throughout the race, this time a victim of tire troubles; third in the 1911 Grand Prize, his Mercedes betrayed by a leaking gas line, the list seemed to go on and on. True, many other drivers of note had yet to win a major race, but DePalma was so obviously talented and so often in the lead that it seemed Lady Luck was on a vendetta aimed particularly at him. If many race fans thought DePalma was snake-bit before the running of the 1912 Indianapolis 500, virtually no one would doubt it afterward. Yet the race would add more to the DePalma legend than any of the 2,000-plus victories in his long and storied career.

Early May had been good to the Italian from Brooklyn. Driving for Mercer in the 150-mile road race for light cars at Santa Monica, California, DePalma had won at a record speed for the class, beating out the Cases of Joe Nikrent and Louis Disbrow. On the following day at Los Angeles Speedway he had driven the little Mercer to new Class C speedway records at all distances between one and twenty miles, with a speed of 78.94 mph for the mile and 80.35 mph for the twenty-mile mark. But for Indianapolis, he would exchange his Mercer for his trusty mount from 1911, Ernest Schroeder's Grey Ghost Mercedes.

For 1912, Indianapolis again upped the ante for its 500-mile race, doubling the prize money to $50,000, with a record $20,000 of that to be paid to the winner. It was a staggering amount when compared to the relatively paltry prize money paid by the Vanderbilt Cup and Grand Prize. But despite the chance for a windfall, there was no interest from the European manufacturers. The only European cars in the field would be privately owned. They were the Grey Ghost Mercedes for DePalma, Spencer Wishart's white sister-machine, a 590-cubic inch Fiat for Teddy Tetzlaff, and a 437-cubic inch Opel for Indy newcomer Len Ormsby.

Arrayed against these four European entries would be no less than twenty American cars. National fielded a three-car team for David Bruce-Brown, Howdy Wilcox and Joe Dawson. Bruce-Brown and Wilcox would pilot big 589-cubic inch machines, while Dawson would handle a 490-cubic incher. Stutz, likewise, had a three-car team of 390-cubic inch racers for Gil Anderson, Charlie Merz, and Len Zengle. Case entered 448-cubic inch cars for Louis Disbrow and Eddie Hearne. Among the other notables, Mercer fielded a car for Hughie Hughes, as usual the smallest-engined car in the race at just 300 cubic inches, and Lozier stalwart Ralph Mulford would be driving a 597-cubic inch Knox. Like Locomobile and Alco before it, Lozier had retired from racing in the wake of its win in the Vanderbilt Cup.

In practice, the Nationals established themselves as the cars to beat, with David Bruce-Brown fastest qualifier at 88.45 mph. His teammates, Howdy Wilcox and Joe Dawson, were third and fourth fastest, with speeds of 87.20 and 86.13 mph. The only car to

Spencer Wishart in his privately owned Mercedes, pictured here in its 1912 Indianapolis livery (IMS Photo).

break the National stranglehold at the top was Ralph Mulford's Knox at 87.88 mph. As always, Mulford's car was meticulously prepared — and fast. Behind these four were the fastest of the European entries, DePalma's Mercedes at 86.02 mph, and Tetzlaff's Fiat at 84.24 mph. Unlike modern practice at the Speedway, starting position was not determined by lap time. Instead, as had been done in the inaugural 500, positions for the flying start were determined by date of entry. The result was that the fastest six qualifiers were inverted in the field. Bruce-Brown, a late entry, would start next-to-last in twenty-third place, Mulford in sixteenth, Dawson and Wilcox in seventh and eighth, and Tetzlaff and DePalma third and fourth.

As race day approached, Indianapolis was full to overflowing with race fans. Fred Wagner, who would be starting the race as he had all Vanderbilt Cups and Grand Prizes within recent memory, reported, "Tonight the Claypool resembles the Garden City Hotel on Long Island the night before a Vanderbilt Cup race. One can scarcely move about in the jammed corridors. Almost every residence in town is accommodating visitors."[3] The Indianapolis natives had learned from their Nassau County brethren, selling boxed "Speedway lunches"[4] to the throng that descended on the track. Two thousand people were waiting when the Speedway's gates opened at 4:00 a.m., many having stayed up all night to get the best seats for the big race.

A crowd of 90,000 witnessed the 10:00 a.m. start as Teddy Tetzlaff jumped to the

Top: Charlie Merz' Stutz speeds past the timing and scoring towers on its way to fourth place in the 1912 Indianapolis 500 (IMS Photo). *Bottom*: Hughie Hughes in his Mercer en route to third place in the 1912 Indianapolis 500 (IMS Photo).

Joe Dawson poses for photographers in the No. 8 National that would go on to win the 1912 running of the Indianapolis 500 (IMS Photo).

early lead. But by lap three DePalma had caught him and moved to the front. From then on the Grey Ghost just motored away. By the twenty-lap mark, fifty miles, David Bruce-Brown had fought his way through the pack into second, but DePalma already had a lap on the field. Six laps later, Bruce-Brown's National was out; a burned valve had finished its day. By the hundred-mile mark, DePalma's lead was two laps over Joe Dawson's National. Fifty miles further on it was three laps, as Wishart's Mercedes displaced Dawson for second.

Just past the two-hundred-mile mark, DePalma pulled in for tires, the Mercedes duo seemingly in complete control. No sooner had the Grey Ghost resumed the race than Wishart's white Mercedes was in with a broken water line, its race over. Still, DePalma looked uncatchable as Tetzlaff and Dawson fought it out for second. At three hundred miles, Dawson had taken over second by himself, but there was simply no chance to catch the flying gray Mercedes. Its lead was now four laps, and still it pulled away.

For most of the final two hundred miles the race was by and large a procession, with DePalma putting another two laps on the field. Dawson held second securely, with ten minutes and change on Teddy Tetzlaff's Fiat. Only the battle for fourth still raged between Hughie Hughes' Mercer and Charlie Merz' Stutz. Time and again, Hughes would power

Top: The teams ready for the start of the 1912 Indianapolis 500 (IMS Photo). *Bottom*: Ralph DePalma rumbles past the grandstand in the Grey Ghost Mercedes on his way to a seemingly sure victory in the 1912 Indianapolis 500 (IMS Photo).

his little machine away from the Stutz, sometimes even threatening Tetzlaff for third, only to be slowed with shredded tires. Fortunately, the Mercer was equipped with the new knock-off wheels that lessened his time in the pits.

With just ten miles to go, most in the crowd had already anointed DePalma their champion. His lead was six laps over Dawson with just four to go, and the Grey Ghost was running superbly. But then some in the crowd noticed something apparently wrong with the big gray machine. It had slowed noticeably, and from the sound of its engine it seemed to be running on just two or three cylinders. Still, DePalma could limp the Mercedes home from there if necessary. The ten-mile distance became seven, then five, and still the Grey Ghost motored on. Then, with two laps to go, the unthinkable happened: as the Mercedes rolled down the backstretch its engine went silent. A burned piston had finally disintegrated and its rod had let go. The car coasted silently through Turn Three and down the short chute to Turn Four. Using the last of its momentum, DePalma swung the Mercedes to the side of the track, then he and his hand-picked mechanic, Australian Rupert Jeffkins, began pushing their broken machine to the finish. Through Turn Four and onto the front straight they pushed as Dawson unwound the laps of their lead one by one. The crowd was on its feet, cheering itself hoarse at the valiant but vain effort of DePalma and Jeffkins, hoping against hope that somehow their remarkable tenacity could be rewarded. It was too much to ask. Making it back to their pit near exhaustion, the duo was greeted with the sight of Dawson's National taking the checkered flag and victory.

Ralph DePalma and mechanic Rupert Jeffkins push the silent "Grey Ghost" Mercedes home at the close of the 1912 Indianapolis 500. Leading by five laps with just two remaining when the Grey Ghost burned a piston, their valiant, but doomed, effort to push their crippled car to the finish line cemented the pair's place among the legends of American sports (IMS Photo).

Top: Joe Dawson's National speeds across the finish line to victory at the 1912 Indianapolis 500. It was the last time an American racer would win the 500 until after the suspension of racing with America's entry into World War I (IMS Photo). *Bottom*: Teddy Tetzlaff's Fiat (3) leads Gil Anderson's Stutz (1) on his way to a second-place finish in the 1912 Indianapolis 500 (IMS Photo).

Robbed of a seemingly sure Vanderbilt Cup victory in 1910 by the on-track wanderings of spectator Henry Hagedorn, Joe Dawson saw Lady Luck even things out at Indianapolis in 1912 when Ralph DePalma's Mercedes blew up while holding a five-lap lead with just two laps to go, handing the victory to Dawson's National (IMS Photo).

The finishing order behind Dawson was Tetzlaff second in the Fiat, Hughes' Mercer third, and Charlie Merz' Stutz fourth. Having failed to complete the full 500 miles, DePalma was not even listed as a finisher. At the victory celebration, DePalma congratulated Dawson; then he turned to the massed reporters. As always, he was the consummate sportsman. "It was Dago luck," he said. "That's all you can make out of it. It was a hard race to lose, but it's all in the game. I did my best, and since I've lost out, I'm for the man who picked the prize."[5]

When the press asked Joe Dawson, the man they called "Kid," how he felt about winning the race only because of DePalma's misfortune, he responded in kind. "I've been up against the same thing," he said. "The game's all luck."[6] He was probably remembering that October day in 1910 when fate in the form of the unlucky pedestrian Henry Hagedorn had conspired with Harry Grant to rob him of the win in the Vanderbilt Cup. Now Lady Luck had evened things up in America's richest race. Then Joe Dawson had one more quote for the scribes. "I've heard the call of the ranch," said the Indianapolis native. "I believe I will buy one."[7]

If winning the Indianapolis 500 bought Joe Dawson a ranch, losing it brought Ralph DePalma immortality. While relatively few race fans can remember the name of the man who won the 1912 race, the specter of the exhausted DePalma and Jeffkins heroically pushing their crippled racer toward the finish has become part of the legend of twentieth-century sport. It ranks with the greatest of them: Knute Rockne's "win one for the Gipper" halftime speech; Leigh-Mallory's doomed attempt at Mt. Everest "because it was there"; Bobby Jones' Grand Slam; Babe Ruth's called shot; Jesse Owens' four gold medals in the '36 Olympics; a dying Lou Gehrig's "luckiest man on the face of the earth" retirement speech; Joe Dimaggio's 56-game hitting streak; Bobby Thomson's "shot heard 'round the world"; Don Larsen's perfect game; the "miracle on ice" of the 1980 U.S. Olympic hockey team; the Ice Bowl; Secretariat's win in the Belmont Stakes; the Immaculate Reception; the Thrilla in Manila. They are events that transcend mere winning and losing, triumphs and tragedies so singularly moving or improbable that if they hadn't really happened no writer could invent them. Like the tale of the *Titanic*, they are legends that live in our memory, being told and retold to successive generations.

15

Dago Luck (Part Two)

After a four-year moratorium, the French *Grand Prix* resumed on June 25 and 26, 1912, at the Dieppe circuit, a monster 48 miles in length. The race, a two-day affair like its predecessors, covered 20 laps, 956 miles in all. Going into the race, the brutish 14.1-liter (862 cubic inch) S-74 Fiats were favored. These were essentially the same cars run in the 1911 Grand Prize. They were undeniably fast, but even by 1911 standards their chain-drive technology and their huge, slow-revving engines were becoming a bit long in the tooth. Three cars were entered for Louis Wagner, Ralph DePalma, and David Bruce-Brown, a testament to the high regard in which these American drivers were held.

The French effort was spearheaded by teams from Lorraine-Dietrich and Peugeot, but, owing to the French manufacturers' four-year absence from big-time racing, both were relatively unknown quantities. The 15-liter Lorraine-Dietrichs for Victor Hemery and René Hanriot at least relied on the proven technology of massive engine size; the three-car team of Peugeots for Georges Boillot, Jules Goux, and Paolo Zuccarelli were a completely radical and untried design. Called the L-76, these new Peugeot racers from the drafting table of Swiss designer Ernest Henry adapted principles learned in the light car, or *voiturette*, racing that had been going on in France during the boycott. They were smaller and lighter than anything that had ever been seen in a European *grand prix* before. They featured shaft drive instead of the traditional chains, and quick-change detachable wheels instead of the cumbersome detachable rims of the Fiats. But it was in the engine room where these new machines departed most completely from the norm. They displaced a mere 7.6 liters (464 cubic inches), barely half the size of the Fiats, and instead of having their valves in the block in an L-head or T-head arrangement, they had four over-head valves per cylinder driven by two overhead camshafts. The radical design allowed for unimpeded flow of the air-fuel mixture and featured hemispherical combustion chambers, the ideal shape for power production, and centrally located spark plugs. Although no one knew it as yet, the little L-76 would set the standard for racing-engine design that would be followed for the rest of the century.

In practice, Georges Boillot gave the assembled racers and fans a preview of the speed of the little blue machines, burning up the circuit in a sub-thirty-six-minute lap, over 80 mph. But the Fiats were by no means outgunned, especially in the hands of men like Wagner, Bruce-Brown and DePalma. While the Peugeots boasted a higher top speed, the Fiats, with their massive high-torque engines, displayed better acceleration out of the corners. In the race, Bruce-Brown led the opening lap over Boillot and Hemery. He continued to lead throughout the first day, finishing the tenth lap with a two-minute lead on the Peugeot. DePalma had been as high as fifth, but a broken fuel line in his S-74 necessitated a fuel stop out on the course, which, under the rules for the *grand prix,* was cause for disqualification.

Overnight rain left the course slick for day two, and much of the surface was breaking apart from the incessant pounding. In these difficult conditions, Boillot in the lighter, more agile Peugeot mounted a relentless charge on Bruce-Brown's Fiat. For 100 miles only seconds separated the little blue machine from the blood-red behemoth. Still, the big, blond American held off the French challenge. On lap thirteen, Boillot finally closed the gap on the Fiat, driving the Peugeot past the red car as the two screamed down the long St. Martin straight. Unfortunately, Boillot then turned in his seat to observe Bruce-Brown's reaction. In that moment's inattention, his Peugeot went off line, its left-side wheels rode up on the edge of a grassy bank and Boillot almost lost it, being forced to back off the throttle to save himself. In a flash, Bruce-Brown was back past the Peugeot. Try as he might, Boillot couldn't catch the big Fiat again until the cars reached the fork at Dieppe. Getting around the turn first, the American used the Fiat's superior acceleration to again pull away from the Peugeot.

At the end of thirteen laps, it looked like Bruce-Brown might add a French *Grand Prix* to his two Grand Prize wins. But on lap fourteen the Fiat slowed. Its fuel line had ruptured, just like DePalma's. Like DePalma, Bruce-Brown was forced to take on fuel, resulting in disqualification. At the urging of his team he soldiered on to an unofficial third, but the race records would show Boillot's Peugeot the winner, Wagner's Fiat in second, and the Sunbeams of Victor Rigal, Dario Resta, and Emil Medinger third, fourth and fifth. France had returned to the big time with a vengeance.

❖ ❖ ❖

As early as 1911, there were rumors that Savannah would not be the site of the 1912 Vanderbilt Cup and Grand Prize. Friction had arisen among the race organizers, and despite the course's beauty there were complaints regarding its length. It required huge numbers of men to police, and with the advent of shorter road courses and oval tracks spectators were becoming accustomed to seeing the cars at more frequent intervals. Some in the Savannah racing community favored abandoning the races altogether, while others advocated the establishment of a shorter course. The controversy prompted Fred Wagner to predict that Savannah had seen its last race, a sentiment echoed by the city's Mayor Tiedeman. The sponsoring Savannah Automobile Club announced that they would leave it up to the people of Savannah to decide the issue. With the cost of maintaining and policing the course, as well as the cost of putting on the races themselves, it is difficult to gauge whether the Vanderbilt Cup and Grand Prize were beneficial to the economy of Savannah or a drain on its resources. While no one would come out and say it, it seemed no one wanted to be responsible for a further expenditure of public funds to support the two races. In the end, Savannah sat on its hands while a prosperous group of brewers from

Milwaukee, Wisconsin, acting through the Milwaukee Automobile Dealers Association, was awarded the 1912 races. For the remaining years of their existence the Vanderbilt Cup and Grand Prize would wander the country with no permanent home.

❖ ❖ ❖

The course in the Milwaukee suburb of Wauwatosa was just 7.88 miles around. Worse yet, it was narrow. But if the track was small, so were the fields for the Vanderbilt Cup and Grand Prize; just eight for the former, thirteen for the latter. The success of the Indianapolis 500 had signaled a move toward oval track racing that was gathering momentum. In addition, the stock chassis movement that had started in 1908 was now all but dead. With the new AAA rules prescribing only engine displacement and allowing pure racing machines, the ante had again been increased if a manufacturer hoped to be competitive. Few were willing to expend the time or money on such programs, especially when faced with ever-stiffer competition for road-car sales from the giants, Ford and General Motors. Moreover, the first generation of manufacturers which had been willing to enter the fray, Simplex, Thomas, Locomobile, Alco, and Lozier, for example, had all had their successes and retired from the game. The new kids on the block, Mercer and Stutz, had racing programs that, even though successful, were still in the development stage. The result was that only four American machines were entered for the Vanderbilt Cup and Grand Prize. Mercer fielded one of its little 300-cubic inch machines for Hughie Hughes, while Stutz entered a 389-cubic-incher for Gil Anderson. Among the American manufacturers, only Knox sported an engine anywhere near the size of the Europeans,

with a 597-cubic inch racer for Ralph Mulford. In addition to the factory-backed machines, a privately owned car, an old 544-cubic inch Lozier, was entered in each event. Harry Nelson would drive it in the Vanderbilt Cup, Louis Fontaine in the Grand Prize.

The European entries were similar to those in prior years, with the exception that the focus was now placed primarily on the Grand Prize. The result was that the Vanderbilt Cup would be contested by only three privately owned

Englishman Hughie Hughes was a stalwart for the Mercer team in its early days. His little 300 cubic inch machine often gave racers with much larger engines all they could handle. A perfect example is his second-place finish to DePalma in the Grey Ghost Mercedes in the 1912 Vanderbilt Cup (IMS Photo).

Mercedes and a single Fiat. The Mercedes were Wishart's white machine, Schroeder's Grey Ghost for DePalma, and a third for newcomer George Clark. The Fiat was the 1911 Vanderbilt Cup car that Teddy Tetzlaff had been campaigning all season. But even in the Grand Prize nothing approaching true factory involvement was evident. The French again stayed home, basking in the glow of Boillot's victory for Peugeot in their *Grand Prix*. Three Fiat S-74s were entered, for David Bruce-Brown, Teddy Tetzlaff, and Caleb Bragg, but Bragg's was his personal machine, while the other two were entered by Fiat's American agent. Benz was represented by three of their 982-cubic inch racers, but Erwin Bergdoll's was owner-driven, while those for Bob Burman and Joe Horan were backed by wealthy sportsmen.

If the field in each race was small, however, the quality of the drivers was first rate. Some commentators have pointed to the absence of European pilots, like Hemery and Wagner, to claim that the 1912 races lacked the top-caliber competition of their predecessors. Not so. To the contrary, the wealth of driving talent in America had made the importation of European drivers unnecessary. The ability of the top Americans had been amply demonstrated by the performances of Bergdoll, Bragg, Bruce-Brown, DePalma, and Hearne in previous Grand Prizes. It had been proven beyond question by the drives of Bruce-Brown and DePalma at the French *Grand Prix*. In fact, with his two Grand Prize victories, third place at the inaugural Indianapolis 500, fastest practice time in its second running, and his masterful drive at the French *Grand Prix*, David Bruce-Brown was widely regarded as the world's best driver. There was simply no reason to incur the expense of importing foreign talent when the home-grown variety was as fast or faster.

In practice, Teddy Tetzlaff was fastest, his Vanderbilt Cup car covering the narrow circuit in 6:16 — 75.44 mph. That was no surprise; Tetzlaff had won the big-car race at Santa Monica in May with the same machine, establishing a road-racing speed record of 78.5 mph in the process. What was surprising was that Tetzlaff was slightly slower in his Grand Prize S-74, despite its additional 260 cubic inches. Even so, he and Bragg were tied for fastest time among the Grand Prize machines with times of 6:22. Among their competitors, the closest was DePalma with a 6:24, followed by Wishart and Bergdoll at 6:26. Everyone else was well off the pace. Among the less experienced drivers, this may have been due, in part, to "Terrible" Teddy's driving style in practice. George

No./9

Mercedes driver George Clark found himself completely unnerved in practice for the 1912 Vanderbilt Cup when he was nearly run off the road by "Terrible" Teddy Tetzlaff in his Fiat. After nearly rolling his machine, Clark was so shaken that his practice times thereafter were well off the pace (IMS Photo).

Clark nearly crashed when Tetzlaff's Fiat shot by him, missing Clark's Mercedes by inches. Clark swerved hard to avoid the expected collision, and his racer shot up on two wheels and nearly rolled, righting itself only when it ran into a ditch filled with soft sand that slowed it. Clark continued on without stopping, but his fastest time thereafter was nearly seven minutes. In fact, Tetzlaff ran up behind cars so closely that on one practice lap his goggles were hit by a stone, smashing the glass of the right lens, shards of which flew into his eye. Living up to his reputation for toughness, he never stopped until he got back to his pit. There he had the glass removed from his eye and then was quickly out for another lap.

Missing from the practice festivities, however, was David Bruce-Brown. After early trials, he had gone to New York with his manager, arriving back in Milwaukee around noon on October 1, the day before the Vanderbilt Cup. By the time he arrived at the Wauwatosa course, it was mid-afternoon. His mechanic, Tony Scudalari, quickly had the big S-74 ready, and in short order Bruce-Brown had shattered the lap record at 5:53.8 — over 80 mph. When word of the record was announced, Teddy Tetzlaff climbed back into his Fiat, determined to post fastest time for himself. Bruce-Brown followed, looking to lower his record still further, despite a warning from Fred Wagner that his tires were worn. The two blood-red behemoths boomed down the undulating backstretch along Fond du Lac Road, nearly nose-to-tail at 90 mph with Bruce-Brown closing on his rival, when the left rear tire of his S-74 blew. Bruce-Brown fought for control on the narrow roadway, but the car veered hard left and into a ditch. There the monster hit a rut and flipped high in the air and end-over-end across the track. Bruce-Brown and Scudalari were catapulted violently across the roadway and into a field. Both were badly injured and unconscious.

Deafened by the roar of his own machine, Tetzlaff was oblivious to the crash until he reached the Graveyard Turn at the end of the straight. When he slowed, he noticed that Bruce-Brown was missing. He quickly reported the absence to race officials, but still no one knew of the hideous crash. Moments later, George Clark came upon the scene of the wreck. Seeing the plight of the still-unconscious Bruce-Brown and Scudalari, he rendered what assistance he could, then telephoned for an ambulance from a nearby farmhouse.

The two stricken racers were taken to Trinity Hospital. There was clearly no hope for Scudalari. His skull had been crushed by the impact. As Bruce-Brown's close friends, Caleb Bragg and Ralph DePalma, waited outside in the hallway, doctors tried to save the young millionaire's life. His left leg was broken, and he had suffered internal injuries, but most seriously his skull, like Scudalari's, was fractured. Surgeons trephined the bone on both sides, trying to relieve the pressure on his brain, but it wasn't enough. Just three hours after the crash, the brawny young man with the infectious charm, the Robert Redford looks, the millions in the bank, and the world of driving talent was dead. He was just twenty-five years old.

Upon receiving the news, DePalma, Bragg, and even the "terrible one," Teddy Tetzlaff, stood crying openly in the hospital corridor. Later that evening, a visibly shaken Caleb Bragg announced his withdrawal from the Grand Prize, claiming that Bruce-Brown's death was attributable to the fact that the course was dangerously narrow. DePalma told reporters he was thinking of withdrawing as well. Such a state of affairs could not be allowed to continue. Race organizers quickly tapped their referee, once again that ubiquitous spindoctor, A. R. Pardington, to issue a statement. "The accident was unavoidable," he said, "and the track was in no wise to blame. It is in excellent condition. The casting of the tire would have upset any machine traveling at that speed no matter how excellent the course was."[1]

In the end, Bragg agreed to reconsider his withdrawal, as did DePalma, and little more would be said about the condition of the track, at least until after the last of the races. But Bruce-Brown's death cast a pall over the proceedings for the race teams and the knowledgeable among the fans in the stands. For the rest — the picnickers on an outing at the track, the brewery workers enjoying a day of vacation — the memory of the man whom Louis Wagner would call "the greatest road racer I have ever seen"[2] was already fading.

❖ ❖ ❖

No Vanderbilt Cup had been won from the front since George Robertson's meteoric tear through the field in Old 16 in 1908. In fact, the race had rarely been good to frontrunners since its inception. Witness George Teste's disastrous record-run in the opening laps of the inaugural event, or Vincenzo Lancia's doomed runaway in 1905, or Louis Chevrolet's ill-fated charges to the front in 1909 and 1910, or even Ralph DePalma's tire-shredding attack in 1911. Only in 1906 had Louis Wagner managed to win going wire-to-wire, and even that was a near thing when a last lap blow-out nearly cost him the race. At Milwaukee, moreover, the task would be even more difficult to accomplish, thirty-eight laps over a narrow and hazardous course (no matter what A. R. Pardington said).

But Teddy Tetzlaff had only one strategy — to go as fast as he could for as long as he could. Like Lancia and Chevrolet before him, he couldn't abide running second to anyone, at any time, for any reason. So, as the eight starters took their orders from Fred Wagner and departed in a thunder of noise, it was no surprise to the 60,000 fans in attendance that Tetzlaff would take the opening lap lead. He did. The only question was whether Italian engineering had designed and built a strong enough machine to withstand the thrashing that the Terrible One was sure to inflict.

Behind Tetzlaff, it was Mulford's Knox in second, uncharacteristically near the front so early in the race. He was followed by the trio of Mercedes led by the race's other renowned charger, Spencer Wishart. They were followed by the remaining American entries, with Hughie Hughes' Mercer drawing even with Clark's fifth-place Mercedes at the stripe. But as the field sorted itself out behind Tetzlaff over the opening laps, it was American engineering, not Italian, that showed its Achilles heel. Mulford, he of the meticulous preparation, began falling back. By lap three he was out, his Knox's magneto no longer throwing spark. Two laps later it was Nelson in the Lozier, his machine running poorly, suffering a variety of ills. By lap six he was hopelessly out of contention, running a full twenty minutes behind his closest competitor.

The Lozier's departure from the competition, if not the race, left the American challenge to the newcomers, Mercer and Stutz. But in the early stages of the race the underpowered pair found staying with the Europeans tough going. By lap six, Anderson and Hughes were running fourth and fifth, a minute or more ahead of George Clark's Mercedes, but three minutes down on DePalma and Wishart, who occupied second and third. DePalma, in turn, was two minutes behind Tetzlaff. Terrible Teddy was simply burning up the course in his big red machine, setting the lap record at 6:15 on lap three and equaling it again on lap six.

Despite the fact that the Grey Ghost had clearly demonstrated a speed advantage over Tetzlaff's Fiat at Indianapolis, DePalma seemed unable, or unwilling, to match Tetzlaff's speed as the laps unwound. Perhaps in the months since May, Terrible Teddy had found more speed from the Italian machine. Then again, perhaps DePalma had learned something from prior races where he had followed a tactic similar to Tetzlaff's only to have his machine falter for one reason or another. What the crowd didn't know was that the Mercedes' clutch was frozen. Unwilling to tax his machine unduly, DePalma let Tetzlaff go, contenting himself with a sharp dice with Wishart for second, while further back Anderson and Hughes, now well clear of Clark, waged their own scrap for fourth.

As the cars reached lap nineteen, Tetzlaff had a full ten minutes on Wishart's Mercedes, which had taken back second from DePalma. Hughes in the Mercer had pulled clear of Anderson's Stutz and was now matching the times of the Mercedes duo, holding position just three minutes back. At half distance, Tetzlaff was the first of the leaders to pit. As the red machine slowed and pulled in the crowd let out a groan, thinking it surely meant trouble. But the stop was routine, just gas, water, oil and rear tires. In less than two minutes the brute was away amid a thunder of exhaust and the cheers of its fans. A short while later Wishart came in, but his stop was a slow one, dropping him back of the Mercer in fourth. For the rest of the race the white Mercedes would lack the stamina to match the yellow racer from Trenton, falling back inexorably from the leaders over the final 150 miles.

As the race approached the 200-mile mark, twenty-five laps in, DePalma had shaved some time from Tetzlaff's lead, but it still stood at nearly seven minutes. Hughes' Mercer continued to mark the Grey Ghost, holding the gap at three minutes. Even so, the outcome seemed relatively certain, the gaps between the leaders too large for anyone to close in the hundred miles remaining. But as most race fans know, and as all drivers learn, it is just when things seem certain that they are certain to change. First, it was Tetzlaff's

"Terrible" Teddy Tetzlaff was unquestionably fast, but all too often he was simply too hard on the machinery (IMS Photo).

When commentators speak of tires of this era being "shredded" or "in tatters," it is not journalistic hyperbole. This Palmer tire has gone its last lap (IMS Photo).

Fiat — after two hundred miles at nearly 72 mph, the red monster blew up. Italian engineering had not created a car the equal of Tetzlaff's destructive talents after all.

Teddy's ouster handed the top spot to DePalma, but no sooner had he inherited what should have been a comfortable lead than it began to erode. Over the next seven laps, the lithe little Mercer found speed that the wounded Mercedes couldn't match. Like a wild dog running down its larger prey, the chrome-yellow Mercer tore time from the lead in huge chunks. DePalma's three-minute cushion became two, then one. By lap thirty-two it had shrunk to just forty-five seconds. If this kept up, DePalma's lead would last less than three laps — and there were still six remaining.

But Hughes' charge in the Mercer had taxed all of his skills. As DePalma found additional speed to hold off his rival, the Englishman caught his breath for a final assault. Over the next three laps, the gap between them stayed constant. Then, on lap thirty-six, Hughes renewed his attack, chopping nine seconds off DePalma's lead. Three more evaporated on lap thirty-seven. With one lap to go, though, it didn't seem enough, except for one thing — DePalma's tires were in shreds.

A pit stop was out of the question. So too was a cautiously slow lap with Hughes at his heels. With the memory of Bruce-Brown's fatal crash less than twenty-four hours old, Ralph DePalma had no choice but to flog his Mercedes for all it was worth over one final lap, knowing full well that a blow-out was likely, and its aftermath too ugly to contemplate. The crowd held its breath as the gray car disappeared in the distance, its tire treads flapping, then it looked to the loudspeakers for news as Hughes' Mercer sped past. A crash seemed inevitable. In retrospect, maybe it was the ghost of his friend who held the Mercedes together on that last fateful lap. Then again, it might simply have been Dago luck, evening things out for the heartbreak at Indianapolis. More likely it was the smoothness and speed of DePalma, displaying the skills of a master. He not only nursed his tires that last lap, he opened up his lead on Hughes' Mercer to forty-two seconds. Somehow the Grey Ghost stayed under him. Ralph DePalma had his first major victory.

Fifteen minutes behind Hughes, Wishart brought his Mercedes home third, with Gil Anderson's Stutz in fourth another three minutes back. Rounding out the field was George Clark's Mercedes. DePalma's victory for Mercedes marked the end of four years of American domination of the race and Germany's first time in the winner's circle. But there were few complaints among the hometown contingent. Even if Mercer had to settle for second, the little machine had shown it could run with the big dogs. In the end, it had outlasted Tetzlaff's Fiat and outrun two of the three German cars. In fact, only the skill and bravery of the great Ralph DePalma had kept it from coming home first.

16

Dago Luck (Part Three)

The Grand Prize was run three days after the Vanderbilt Cup. In the interim there had been the usual light car races, this year titled the Pabst and Wisconsin Trophy Races. Mortimer Roberts won the Pabst Trophy for 300-cubic inch cars in a Mason Special, followed by the F.A.L.s of Harry Hastings and Billy Chandler. In the Wisconsin Trophy for 230-cubic inchers, all three of the starters were Masons. Harry Endicott ran away with the race.

Also during the interim, there had been much talk about Ralph DePalma's chances in the Grand Prize. No one had ever pulled off the double, winning both Vanderbilt Cup and Grand Prize. In fact, only one man, Louis Wagner, could claim victories in both races in a career, let alone in one season. The accomplishment was made more difficult if, like DePalma, the driver was to use the same car in both races — the 600-cubic inch Vanderbilt Cup cars quite naturally gave up power to the larger-engined *grand prix* machines of the Grand Prize. But the memory of Ralph Mulford's near miss at the feat in 1911 fueled speculation, and there were those in the crowd and the press corps who thought Milwaukee, with its tight turns and narrow straights, might be a course where the additional power of the *grand prix* machines would not be such an advantage.

The installation of DePalma as a favorite for the 52-lap Grand Prize yielded an additional benefit for the organizers. In the wake of Bruce-Brown's fatal crash, the Fiat team had repaired his S-74. As his replacement at the wheel, the team selected that king of the fairgrounds, Barney Oldfield. The feud between Oldfield and DePalma was well known to most race fans. For the first time the two would be matched in a major race. It was a windfall for the promoters — DePalma, the favorite, just coming off his Vanderbilt Cup victory, facing Oldfield, the challenger, equipped with the Fiat that had set fastest time in practice. The script seemed sensational. Unfortunately, the duel would never develop.

As the prospect of a head-to-head match-up between DePalma and Oldfield was working the crowd into a frenzy, word from the Mulford camp was that his Knox would be withdrawn. Ignition problems continued to plague the car. Mulford's withdrawal reduced the starters to twelve and again dropped the weight of American hopes on Hughes'

Mercer and Anderson's Stutz. Few seemed to notice, however. With the large German population in the Milwaukee area, the prospect of seeing six German machines doing battle with three Italian Fiats was more than enough to hold the attention of the crowd of 150,000 that assembled for the start.

As the twelve cars boomed off, it was once again Tetzlaff who moved to the front, but this time there would be no runaway. Close behind was Caleb Bragg in his own S-74, followed by the best of the German machines: Bergdoll's Benz, Wishart's Mercedes, DePalma's Mercedes, Burman's Benz. Then came Hughes' Mercer and the rest of the field. And where was Oldfield? Dead last. He stayed there as Wishart began his predictable move to the front on lap two, getting by Bergdoll for third. It was as close to the lead as Wishart would get. On lap four, the white Mercedes snapped a rod. Still, he had lasted one lap longer than Burman, the other famed charger of the group. By lap three his Benz was already out, one of its enormous pistons disintegrated. Hughes, likewise, had trouble in the Mercer. A broken fuel line dropped him back to tenth, behind even Oldfield. By lap ten, the problem would be terminal.

At lap five, the leaders were still sorting themselves out. While Bragg continued to shadow the Terrible One at the front, maintaining the gap at just fifteen seconds, Gil Anderson pushed his Stutz past DePalma for fourth. DePalma then put on a burst of speed, retaking the position on the following lap. At the same time, Bergdoll, who had been lying third, stopped for tires, dropping back to sixth some five minutes behind. As DePalma continued to chase down the lead pair of Fiats, he opened up his lead over Anderson. By lap ten, the three at the front, Tetzlaff, Bragg and DePalma, were four minutes clear of the pack. At the back, Barney Oldfield had finally passed someone still running, taking over eighth from George Clark.

In the Vanderbilt Cup, Tetzlaff had made his tires last for nineteen laps. In his *grand prix* machine he could not. By lap eleven they needed replacement and in he came, handing a lead of a minute and change to Bragg. DePalma held position in third, ninety seconds further back. The rest, led by Anderson, were all four minutes or more in arrears and all losing ground to the leaders. Once out of his pit, Tetzlaff resumed his charge, setting the lap record at 6:07 on lap fourteen and retaking the lead on the following circuit. But just two laps later, he was back in the pits for more tires, again handing the lead back to Bragg. It seemed like the story of DePalma and Mulford at the 1911 Vanderbilt Cup. The difference was that Teddy had the speed to retake the lead between stops.

On lap twenty-two it was Bragg's turn to pit. Tetzlaff followed and got out ahead of his teammate. But ahead of them both was DePalma, holding the Grey Ghost at a comfortable pace. His lead lasted only three laps. On lap twenty-five he was into the pits — his scheduled stop. The Fiats retook control, then disappeared into the distance with Tetzlaff again leading Bragg, as DePalma had to pit again on lap twenty-six with ignition problems. At half-distance, the Fiats were twelve minutes ahead of the third-place Mercedes. DePalma's prospects for the win seemed dim.

At the front, Tetzlaff continued at his all-out pace, sliding the big S-74 through the turns in long lurid drifts, slamming it down the straights in bursts of acceleration. Try as he might, though, he simply couldn't shake his pursuer. Bragg was keeping it close without punishing his machine. Then, on lap thirty-one, the inevitable happened. Tetzlaff's Fiat, like its sister machine three days earlier, gave up under the relentless pounding, its suspension simply shattered. The retirement gave Bragg back the lead with a comfortable cushion of nine minutes on DePalma. For his part, DePalma had a lead of six minutes over Bergdoll in third. By this time Oldfield had finally found his rhythm in the big Fiat and was lying fourth, but he was fully twenty minutes behind Bragg. He would never pose a threat to the leaders.

With 165 miles left to run, the race had taken on much of the complexion of the Vanderbilt Cup only three days before. Only the faces and roles had changed, and they only slightly. As then, Tetzlaff had led until past half distance. His retirement had left the new leader, then DePalma and now Bragg, with a seemingly comfortable lead. And as in the Vanderbilt Cup, the man lying second in a smaller machine, then Hughes and now DePalma, would make it a race.

As Bragg cruised comfortably at the front, DePalma chased hard, the Grey Ghost clipping seconds from the Fiat lap by lap. In ten laps the lead shrank by nearly two minutes. Five laps more and another eighty seconds were gone. Still, Bragg's lead was over five minutes with just five laps remaining. DePalma's task looked impossible, but his charge was relentless, taking corners in terrifying

Teddy Tetzlaff led the Indianapolis 500, the Vanderbilt Cup, and the Grand Prize in 1912, the latter two for significant portions of the race. He was unquestionably fast, perhaps frighteningly so, but his hard-charging style routinely destroyed the equipment (IMS Photo).

slides, throwing rooster-tails of dirt on the crowd, airborne over the humps of Fond du Lac Road. By lap fifty, the gap was down to three minutes and change; DePalma's pursuit had shaved an unthinkable two minutes in just three laps. The Mercedes pit signaled "All Out!" as Bragg's blood-red behemoth disappeared in the distance. Bragg had three minutes in hand by virtue of his later start and still seemed unconcerned. He never put on speed despite his friend's frantic pursuit. The two took the green flag signaling one lap to go only seconds apart. True, Bragg's lead still seemed insurmountable, but who knew what DePalma could do if he could only get by?

Through the first half of the last lap, DePalma continued to close as Bragg kept to his pace. Down the backstretch they came, down the narrow and treacherous Fond du Lac Road, with DePalma now just mere feet behind Bragg. Then it happened — just a mile from the Graveyard Turn the cars touched. The Grey Ghost veered sharply, careening off the road, overturning in a cornfield. DePalma and mechanic Tom Alley were thrown clear, but all was not well. Alley's shoulder was broken, as was DePalma's leg. More seriously, a cornstalk had punctured DePalma's abdomen, and dirt had been driven deep into the wound.

None of this was known to Caleb Bragg as he felt the jolt of the Mercedes hitting

Caleb Bragg's victory in the 1912 Grand Prize was equal parts triumph and tragedy. First his friend David Bruce-Brown was fatally injured in a crash during practice; then close friend and mentor Ralph DePalma crashed and was seriously injured while trying to pass Bragg's Fiat on the last lap of the race. It was a crash for which Bragg felt partially responsible, despite DePalma's protestations to the contrary (IMS Photo).

the tail of his Fiat and turned to see the gray car roll and spit its occupants into the field. He feared that his good friend DePalma was dead — at nearly the same spot where Bruce-Brown had been killed. Losing two friends in five days was almost too much to bear. He motored on slowly for the final two miles, took the checker, stopped and ran to the officials, giving them a report of the crash. The crowd in the grandstands was mystified by Bragg's strange behavior until one of them noticed De-Palma was missing. As the ambulances for DePalma and Alley were set in motion, ferrying the duo to Trinity Hospital, the rest of the finishers limped home.

In second place, fully fifteen minutes behind Bragg, was Erwin Bergdoll in the Benz. Behind Bergdoll were Anderson's Stutz and Oldfield's Fiat. Still running, but flagged one lap short of the finish, was George Clark's Mercedes. But there was little celebration for the winner or other finishers. Bragg was given his trophy then hurried off to check on the condition of his friend.

At the hospital, as the still-bleeding DePalma was unloaded from the ambulance, he nevertheless had time for the reporters. "Boys," he told the gathered crowd of journalists, "don't forget that Caley Bragg wasn't to blame. He gave me all the road."[1] It was another display of DePalma's famed sportsmanship. It was also a lie calculated to absolve his friend of any blame. By Bragg's own admission, he hadn't given way for DePalma, never expecting him to attempt a pass on that narrow section of Fond du Lac Road on the last lap of the race just two miles from the finish.[2]

The news on the injured duo was optimistic, but guarded. Fortunately, both DePalma and Alley had escaped the crash with their lives. Alley's broken shoulder was painful, but not serious. Likewise, DePalma's leg was expected to heal without complication. The problem was DePalma's abdominal injury — while not life threatening of itself, it had required surgery and there remained a real risk of peritonitis. In 1912, before the advent of antibiotics, peritonitis was nearly always fatal. Nevertheless, DePalma, although obviously in pain, was in good enough spirits on the night of the race to meet with the press from his hospital bed. Ever the gentleman, he was quick to again absolve his good friend, Caleb Bragg, of all blame for the accident.

In the end, Ralph DePalma would heal completely, although he would spend several weeks in the hospital, and the bond between DePalma and Bragg would grow stronger than ever in 1913. But the Milwaukee Vanderbilt Cup and Grand Prize would go down in history as races filled with equal parts joy and pain, for their winners more than anyone else.

17

The Reason for Multiple Valves

The arts made big news in 1913. In February, the International Exhibition of Modern Art opened in New York City. It was the first display of the works of such artists as Picasso, Matisse, Braque and Brancusi on this side of the Atlantic. The American public was, by and large, unprepared for the experience, one visitor labeling paintings by Cézanne, Van Gogh, and Gauguin as the products of a "shabby French vagabond, a half-insane Flemish recluse and suicide, and a disreputable world wanderer."[1] This despite the fact that their work was among the tamest on display. Another likened Duchamp's *Nude Descending a Staircase* to "an explosion in a shingle factory."[2] But among the artistic community the show was a watershed, exposing American artists to a European avant-garde that could not be ignored. America's cultural isolation was at an end. Perhaps equally significantly, despite the criticism leveled at them by some, the European works at the show outsold American pieces four to one.

If New York was shocked by the International Exhibition, Paris was apoplectic over Igor Stravinsky's *The Rite of Spring*. First performed on May 29 at the *Théâtre des Champs-Élysées*, the ballet caused a riot. The well-heeled Parisian audience, which had received Stravinsky's earlier works, *The Firebird* and *Petrushka*, with acclaim, was as unprepared for its polyrhythmic score and the pagan images evoked by Vaslav Nijinsky's choreography as New Yorkers had been for Picasso and Braque. The audience drowned out the powerful music with thunderous volleys of boos and choruses of whistles, eventually becoming so unruly that Stravinsky was forced to flee backstage, fearing for life and limb. But like New Yorkers, Parisians demonstrated that they could adapt to the new artistic forms if given some time. Within the year, *The Rite of Spring* was again performed, this time as a symphony at the *Casino de Paris*. At its conclusion, Stravinsky was carried triumphantly from the theater on the shoulders of his fans. Music's Romantic Era was over; its Modern Era had arrived.

In England, D. H. Lawrence published *Sons and Lovers*, a tale of obsessive love between a son and his mother. The novel's sexuality, its indictment of modern industrial civilization, and its yearning for escape were subjects that would have been unthinkable just a few years before. Yet unlike Lawrence's later works, such as *The Rainbow* and *Lady Chatterley's Lover*, both of which were banned, *Sons and Lovers* was hailed as a masterpiece and Lawrence branded as one of the twentieth century's major writers.

Outside of the art world much was happening as well. Woodrow Wilson now occupied the White House. The twentieth century's first Democratic president had prevailed over a Republican party split by Teddy Roosevelt's third-party candidacy. Grand Central Terminal, the world's largest railway station and one of its most beautiful, opened in New York City. Olympic champion and toy maker A. C. Gilbert, inspired by the construction boom in New York, of which Grand Central was a part, introduced the Erector Set. It became the hit of the Christmas season. Henry Ford finally got his assembly line running, and the already popular Ford Model T dropped in price by nearly half. At a small Catholic college in Indiana, two undergraduates on the football team unveiled a new weapon in their game against powerhouse Army. The forward pass would lead to a 35–13 upset of the Black Knights of the Hudson, and while it wouldn't make Gus Dorais a household word, it would make Knute Rockne an icon of college football, and the little Catholic school, Notre Dame, the sport's unofficial capital.

On the political front, the brief but bloody Second Balkan War gutted the European holdings of the Ottoman Empire, redrew the map of southeastern Europe, and threatened to bring Austria and Russia into direct conflict, setting the stage for the world war that was now only one year away. In the United States, the Sixteenth Amendment to the Constitution was ratified, paving the way for a new federal tax. In 1913 only a small segment of the population was subject to the levy on incomes in excess of $3,000. The average American made just $800. Few, if any, saw the effect that the new income tax would have on that average American in years to come, or on the balance of power between the states and the federal government.

❖ ❖ ❖

Ralph DePalma had been driving for Mercer since 1911, but his drives in the yellow cars from Trenton had been confined to light car races. Whenever the big cars were running, DePalma could be found in a Fiat, or more recently the Schroeder Mercedes, unwilling to be saddled with the handicap of the Mercer's little 300-cubic inch engine despite its superb handling and renowned reliability. During much of 1912, DePalma had urged Mercer management to build a car to compete "with the big boys." After some initial reluctance, owing to their philosophy of racing what they sold to their customers, they agreed. By early 1913, their new racer, the Type 45, was ready. It featured a 445-cubic inch engine, just under the new Indianapolis limit of 450 cubic inches. The new engine was rated at a stout 150 horsepower. However, its design employed the older T-head valve arrangement of the Type 35, and its racing variant the Type F, with its valves in the block on either side of each cylinder, instead of utilizing the new overhead-cam design pioneered by Peugeot. This may have been, in part, due to the fact that the design of the Type 45 was already taking shape before anyone on this side of the Atlantic became aware of the radical new Peugeot. Mercer's designers, however, most notably Erik Delling, also had reservations about overhead cams. As Delling wrote in a 1913 article, "Simplicity and fewness of parts are ... absolutely necessary in high-speed motors.... I could never see the reason for multiple valves, and complicated overhead valve mechanism."[3]

Despite Mercer's adherence to older technology, the Type 45s looked sure to be fast,

Although the Mercer Type 45 was a new design in 1913, it still employed older technology. The valves were in a T-head arrangement with the cams set in the crankcase on either side of the engine, instead of in the more modern overhead-cam style pioneered by Peugeot. In addition, as can be clearly seen in this photo, the cylinders were cast in pairs, rather than as a four-cylinder unit (IMS Photo).

and DePalma, still healing from his abdominal injury and anxious to drive for a single team throughout the season, agreed to come on as team captain. Mercer management then asked DePalma to nominate two teammates to join him. He chose his friend Caleb Bragg, and fellow Mercedes campaigner Spencer Wishart, who had been doing some driving for Mercer since the summer of 1912. Thus Mercer not only had a powerful new car, they had the reigning Vanderbilt Cup and Grand Prize winners as their drivers. The team looked formidable indeed.

But if Trenton was putting together a serious contender, Indianapolis was not far behind. For 1913, Stutz wedged a 434-cubic inch Wisconsin engine under the hoods of its racers in place of the 390-cubic incher that had resided there in 1912. Mason, another successful marque from the light car ranks, retained the Duesenberg brothers, Fred and August, to design and build their new car. Within a few years, the pair would become famous building cars under their own name, both Indianapolis winners and, later, the incomparable road-going Model J. For Mason, the brothers designed a four-cylinder engine of innovative design that owed nothing to either the traditional American T-head or L-head designs or to the overhead cams of the Peugeots. The Duesenbergs' engine employed horizontal valves opening into the sides of the combustion chambers and actuated by long rocker arms, or walking beams, from a camshaft mounted low in the block.

Top: For 1913, Ralph DePalma joined the Mercer team. Here he is at Indianapolis in the new Type 45 (IMS Photo). *Bottom*: Unlike today, most of the drivers were intimately involved in the set-up, maintenance and repair of their machines: DePalma inspects the engine of his Type 45 Mercer (IMS Photo).

Top: DePalma weighs in the Type 45 Mercer prior to the 1913 Indianapolis 500 (IMS Photo).
Bottom: Spencer Wishart poses for the photographers prior to the 1913 Indianapolis 500. His Mercer would finish second, with the help of a relief drive from Ralph DePalma (IMS Photo).

Bob Burman's drive for the 1913 Indianapolis 500 was the radical Keeton, featuring wire wheels, shaft drive, and a radiator mounted behind the engine to permit a sloping, aerodynamic hood. In Burman's hands, it proved to be a formidable competitor, passing Jules Goux's Peugeot for the lead on lap forty and holding it past quarter-distance, until a carburetor fire dropped it from the ranks of the leaders (IMS Photo).

With their new machinery, both Stutz and Mason were counted on to be formidable, as was Bob Burman in the radical Wisconsin-powered Keeton, which featured a radiator mounted behind the engine to permit a sharply sloping aerodynamic hood. However, none of the American competition could boast the team of drivers that Mercer had assembled. Stutz retained Gil Anderson and Charlie Merz and added Don Herr, who had driven in relief for Joe Dawson in 1912, while Mason paired veteran Willie Haupt with Robert Evans and Jack Tower.

A changing of the guard was evident as the teams prepared for Indianapolis, the first major race of the season. Case would be returning with a three-car team for drivers Louis Disbrow, Joe Nikrent, and Bill Endicott, and Ralph Mulford had taken over DePalma's seat in the Schroeder Mercedes, repaired in the wake of DePalma's crash and now fitted with a 440-cubic inch engine featuring three overhead valves per cylinder. But Marmon and National, the winners of the previous two races at the speedway, were missing from the ranks of competitors. Gone too was Fiat, content to retire from American racing with two Grand Prize victories to its credit, and unwilling to build a new car to comply with the rules now in force at Indianapolis. In its place was Isotta-Fraschini, with new overhead-cam cars for Teddy Tetzlaff, Harry Grant, and 1908 *Targa Florio* winner Vincenzo Trucco. The real attention-getters were the European entries from the new *grand prix* power-houses, Peugeot and Sunbeam, the former fielding a pair of their overhead-cam machines for Jules Goux and Paolo Zuccarelli, the latter a single six-cylinder car for Albert Guyot. For the first time, Indianapolis would truly play host to an international field.

That fact was not lost upon the motoring press, which billed the race as one for "international supremacy."[4] One scribe, more carried away than most, likened the race to a medieval joust, with "plumed knights" from "foreign invader and American defender"

Top: The pride of the American side at Indianapolis, 1913 — the Stutz White Squadron posing in their Sunday best: Charles Merz (2), Gil Anderson (3), and Don Herr (8). Herr would retire on lap 7 with a broken clutch shaft, Anderson would retire on lap 187 with a sheared camshaft drive, and Merz would finish third with his car in flames (IMS Photo). *Bottom*: Bob Burman, Albert Guyot and Ralph DePalma eye Guyot's Sunbeam before the 1913 Indianapolis 500. The Sunbeam, which would go on to finish fourth, was one of the most radical racers present. It featured a six-cylinder engine, one of only three in the race. In addition, the coil atop the radiator cap is a condenser designed to cool escaping steam and allow it to funnel back into the radiator, and the two parallel pipes running the length of the body are an oil cooler. Note also the pinched, elongated nose for aerodynamics (IMS Photo).

The Sunbeam engine—although a modern design and one of only three six-cylinder engines entered in the 1913 Indianapolis 500, it still employed the older L-head valve arrangement, rather than Peugeot's overhead cams. The valve gear can be seen here below the finned intake manifold (IMS Photo).

proving their skill at "feats of arms." He called upon America's "champions of track and road to silence the challenge of the invaders and force the foreigners to bow in submission."[5] Another, less poetic and more demonstrative of the feelings of many Americans about Europeans in general, described the five drivers from across the Atlantic as "swarthy-skinned aliens."[6] But if the motoring press made much of the European challenge, most journalists picked the favorites to be Mercer and Stutz nonetheless, ignoring Peugeot's victory with the same machines in the 1912 *Grand Prix*. While acknowledging the fact that the Peugeots were fast, many experts opined that they were not strong enough to last the full 500 miles. Others pointed to the foreign teams' lack of speedway experience, despite the fact that Peugeot had retained veteran Johnny Aitken to handle race strategy. Their predictions were seemingly validated by Peugeot team manager M. Charles Faroux. In what may well have been one of the first instances of sandbagging, Faroux panned his team's chances, calling the cars "poorly balanced" for the Indianapolis track.

In practice the Peugeots were fast, with Goux posting a qualifying speed of 86.03 mph, a tick faster than teammate Zuccarelli. But the Mercers were faster, at least when they were healthy. Caleb Bragg spurred his Type 45 to a lap at 87.34 mph. DePalma, however, never got up to speed, his Type 45 displaying the teething problems common

Top: The beginnings of the European invasion at Indianapolis in 1913: Albert Guyot posing behind the wheel of his Sunbeam racer. He would go on to finish fourth (IMS Photo). *Bottom*: The invading "swarthy-skinned aliens"—the Peugeot team arrives at Indianapolis, 1913 (IMS Photo).

Top: Jules Goux's Peugeot at speed, Indianapolis 1913 (IMS Photo). Bottom: Jack Tower and mechanic Lee Dunning in the Mason-Duesenberg prior to the 1913 Indianapolis 500. A crash on lap fifty-one would leave Tower with a broken leg and Dunning with three broken ribs (IMS Photo).

to new designs. His qualifying speed was only 76.30 mph, fully five miles per hour slower than Spencer Wishart's Type F. The surprise of qualifying was Jack Tower's Mason-Duesenberg. While neither of his teammates could better 83 mph, Tower scorched the oval at a blazing 88.23 mph, nearly equaling David Bruce-Brown's 1912 qualifying record with an engine just two-thirds the size.

As with Bruce-Brown, however, Tower's display in qualifying would confer no advantage in the race. Indianapolis had yet to use qualifying speeds to determine starting positions. Instead, the spots were assigned in a drawing the evening before the race. Tower, the fastest qualifier, would start twenty-fifth, in the last row of the field. Bragg, second fastest, would start on the pole with Albert Guyot's Sunbeam next to him. The best placed of the Mason-Duesenbergs was Robert Evans' machine, starting fourth. Jules Goux in the Peugeot drew seventh.

As the record crowd of over 100,000 sweltered in the intense heat that would stress machines and cook tires throughout the day, the twenty-seven cars, paced by speedway president Carl Fisher, took their pace lap and readied for the red flag from starter Charles Root that would send them on their way. And then they were off in an explosion of color and a roar of exhaust, Caleb Bragg leading the way in his Mercer. But Bragg's lead would last just one lap. On lap two Robert Evans' Mason-Duesenberg caught and passed him. Evans' turn at the front lasted little longer. On lap four Jules Goux fought his way past Bragg and Evans to put his Peugeot in the lead.

Over the next four laps, Goux simply walked away from the field. On lap five, his

Caleb Bragg in the Type 45 Mercer prior to the 1913 Indianapolis 500. Bragg would start from the pole and lead the first lap, but thereafter would be mired mid-pack for most of the day and retire on lap 128 with a broken water pump (IMS Photo).

The field for the 1913 Indianapolis 500— Bragg's Mercer (19) on the pole, flanked by Guyot's Sunbeam (obscured by Stoddard-Dayton pace car), Liesaw's Anel (17) and Evans' Mason-Duesenberg (5). In row two are Herr's Stutz (8) (partially obscured by fence post), Clark's Tulsa (25), Goux's Peugeot (16) and Tetzlaff's Isotta-Fraschini (27) (IMS Photo).

lead was two hundred yards. On lap six, it was four hundred. By lap eight, he had a full thirty seconds on Willie Haupt's second-place Mason-Duesenberg, with DePalma's Mercer, Grant's Isotta, Tower's Mason, and Burman's Keeton in a bunch close behind.

On lap fourteen, the first of the Isotta-Fraschinis, Harry Grant's, retired with a ruptured gas tank. Unfortunately, the new Italian machines were not fully sorted. A strike at the factory had delayed their completion and they had only arrived at the track on the afternoon time trials began. A similar problem would sideline team leader Vincenzo Trucco on lap thirty-nine.

One lap later, that notorious charger, "Wild" Bob Burman, powered his Keeton past Goux's Peugeot to the front. Amid the excitement, few noticed Ralph DePalma's Mercer coasting into the pits. A cracked cylinder had ended the Type 45's day, but it would not end that of its driver. Three laps later, the second Peugeot, Zuccarelli's, blew its engine. The pundits nodded sagely, their predictions holding true. After all, the Peugeots were designed for road races, not for high-speed ovals where the throttle stays wide open virtually everywhere. But if Zuccarelli's retirement was a portent of trouble for Goux, it was not evident yet. The Frenchman's machine continued to look strong, running comfortably in second behind Burman.

As the race passed the one-quarter mark, another flurry of excitement brought the

Top: Paolo Zuccarelli poses for the photographers behind the wheel of his Peugeot in 1913. A burned main bearing would sideline his car from the third running of the Indianapolis 500, giving fans of the American side a glimmer of hope that a similar fate might befall teammate Jules Goux's Peugeot (IMS Photo). *Bottom*: Jules Goux in the Peugeot that would go on to win the 1913 Indianapolis 500. Note the round hole in the side of the hood: it is a hand hole to allow a mechanic to make adjustments to the engine without unbuckling the hood straps. The screened square hole above it is for ventilation and to allow the mechanic to see what he is doing while making adjustments (IMS Photo).

crowd to its feet. First Jack Tower's Mason-Duesenberg blew a tire and crashed in Turn One. Tower's leg was broken and mechanic Lee Dunning had fractured three ribs, but both of them would recover. No sooner had the crews cleaned up the wreck and ferried the pair off to Methodist Hospital than Bob Burman's Keeton caught fire on the backstretch. As Burman pulled off to extinguish the flames, then motored slowly back to his pit to replace his scorched carburetor, Goux once again sailed into the lead. If the Gallic machine had a weakness, it still had not shown it.

With Burman out, Ralph Mulford, Gil Anderson, and Albert Guyot took up the chase. The trio had been running comfortably some two and one-half minutes behind Goux, but as Burman pulled off Anderson spurred his Stutz toward the front. Between laps fifty-six and sixty-four, he passed the Grey Ghost Mercedes to move into second and narrowed the Peugeot's cushion to just forty-eight seconds. The experts from the motoring press smiled knowingly. While the Mercer Type 45s had not been the factor they anticipated (Bragg was running well back), Anderson's Stutz was headed for the front, just as they had predicted. Charlie Merz in the second Stutz was lying fifth, just thirty-one seconds behind Anderson. The team from Indianapolis looked poised to run down the French challenge.

The experts were in for a shock. Over the next ten laps Goux stretched his lead back out to more than a minute. By lap eighty, it was nearly two, and growing lap by lap. The

Charlie Merz in the Stutz that would go on to a flaming third place in the 1913 Indianapolis 500 (IMS Photo).

Peugeot was showing speed that the others couldn't match. As Anderson tried to hang on, the others in the lead group fell away one by one. By lap ninety, Merz' Stutz, now in fourth, was a full seven minutes back of the leader. Guyot's Sunbeam, now sixth, was another four minutes in arrears. The only car other than Anderson's Stutz that looked capable of giving the Peugeot a run for its money was Ralph Mulford's Grey Ghost Mercedes. Lying third, Mulford followed Anderson by just forty-five seconds.

On lap ninety-six, Goux pitted. Anderson took over the lead. The stop was routine, with Goux and his mechanic sharing a pint of champagne as his team filled the tank and hammered on new rubber, and the Peugeot returned to the fray in third place, 1:22 behind Anderson and just nineteen seconds behind Mulford. But within four laps, the French machine was back at the front, getting by the Mercedes with ease as Anderson stopped at his pit. On lap 105, Goux's lead stood at some thirty seconds over Mulford with Anderson ten seconds further back.

With just over half the race run, it looked like a three-way battle with none of the cars having any particular advantage. True, the Peugeot seemed fastest of the three, but its reliability was still an open question and Goux had had trouble keeping tires under the French machine in practice. An extra stop or two for new rubber would be more than enough to offset any speed advantage the Peugeot might enjoy on the track. Anderson's Stutz, second fastest through the first half of the race, was viewed as the more proven commodity.

As for Mulford in the Grey Ghost Mercedes, if he hadn't shown the outright speed of the others, he had an advantage all his own — a typically Mulford-like advantage. He was planning to run the race on one set of tires and to make just one stop for fuel. On lap 110, the Mercedes came in, taking on twenty gallons of gas. Mulford emerged still in

Between champagne breaks Jules Goux's Peugeot motors away from the field at the 1913 Indianapolis 500 (IMS Photo).

Gil Anderson in the Stutz prior to the 1913 Indianapolis 500. Anderson's Stutz would run second to Goux's Peugeot for most of the race, until a sheared camshaft drive would sideline it on lap 187 (IMS Photo).

third, some four minutes back of Anderson, but already the Peugeot was opening the gap once again. Just ten laps after taking the lead from the Stutz, Goux's advantage stood at nearly two minutes.

While the three at the front battled on, behind them the heat of the day and the strain of the race withered the field. On lap 118, it was Tetzlaff; his Isotta fell out with a broken drive chain. Ten laps later, it was Bragg. Mired back in the pack for most of the day, his Type 45's water pump finally gave up. Thirty laps further on it was Evans, the clutch of his Mason-Duesenberg destroyed. One notable exception to the carnage was Wishart's little Type F Mercer, now piloted by DePalma. Early in the race, it had been running outside the top ten, but since DePalma's takeover, its charge through the field had been truly remarkable. The yellow machine with the 300-cubic inch engine was lying eighth on lap fifty-five. Within ten laps it was fifth. By half distance it was closing on Charlie Merz' Stutz for fourth. Catching the leaders might be out of the question, but the little car from Trenton with the *maestro* at the wheel was putting on a show of its own.

On lap 125, Goux again pitted for tires and another quaff of champagne. Once again, the stop gave the lead to Anderson's Stutz. Back out on the track, the Peugeot slotted into second, nearly a minute behind Anderson, but comfortably ahead of Mulford's Mercedes. As before, he immediately began eating away at the lead of the Indianapolis product. By lap 136, Goux was back in the lead as Anderson took his turn in the pits. The stop was a slow one and the gap between Goux and Anderson, which had been hovering between

Billy Knipper pilots his Henderson past the grandstands in the 1913 500. A slipping clutch would sideline him on lap 125 (IMS Photo).

one and two minutes, now grew to four. And despite the pit stops by the frontrunners, Ralph Mulford had been unable to close the gap. Now forced to conserve his worn tires, he could do no more than nurse his machine around. He still held down third place, but he was a full three minutes behind Anderson, with Wishart's Mercer, which had finally gotten by Merz' Stutz, only three minutes back.

As the race passed three-quarter distance, the 150-lap mark, the gap between Goux and Anderson stood at four minutes. The gap between Anderson and Mulford had grown to five. Still the Stutz team remained confident. One of their number confidently predicted that the French machine would drop out just after four hundred miles, but as the Peugeot crossed the line to complete lap 160, its engine ran as smoothly as ever. The gap between it and the Stutz still stood at four minutes, while Mulford fell further behind the lead duo, now some eight minutes back of Anderson. With 100 miles left, it was a two-man race.

As the final laps unwound, Anderson tried to cut into the lead. By lap 168, he had it down to 3:22. But no sooner had the Stutz pilot shaved precious seconds from his deficit than the Peugeot found speed to keep him at bay. The gap again rose to four minutes and change, with the French machine in complete control. Meanwhile, behind the lead duo, the unthinkable had happened to Ralph Mulford. The man renowned for his meticulous preparation had somehow miscalculated and run out of gas on the backstretch. His mechanic was dispatched to the pits for a gas can, but half an hour would be lost before the Mercedes was back on the track.

With twenty laps remaining, the gap between Goux and Anderson held at four minutes. Try as he might, the Stutz pilot could not shrink it further. With the laps winding down and their captain unable to run down the "alien challenger," the Stutz pit clung desperately to their notion that reliability, not speed, would win the day. As it turned out, they were right — at least partly. The race between Goux and Anderson would be

Top: For the 1913 running of the Indianapolis 500, Ralph Mulford took over Ralph DePalma's seat in the Schroeder-owned "Grey Ghost" Mercedes. Now fitted with a new engine and an aerodynamic nose, the "Ghost" and Mulford looked poised to steal a victory in typical Mulford fashion, through brilliant race tactics, when the unthinkable happened — the man who planned to run the entire 500 miles on just one fuel stop ran out of gas (IMS Photo). *Bottom*: Gil Anderson's Stutz passes the famed pagoda in the 1913 Indianapolis 500. Anderson waged a race-long battle with the Peugeot of eventual race winner Jules Goux, until his Stutz sheared its camshaft drive and was forced to retire only thirteen laps from the finish (IMS Photo).

decided by mechanical failure, but it would not be the Peugeot that would succumb. With sixteen laps remaining, the Stutz pit looked on dejectedly as their machine began to slow. The Peugeot's four-minute lead became six. Finally, on lap 187, Anderson coasted silently into the pits, his camshaft drive sheared.

Anderson's retirement left Goux in a race of his own, now seven laps ahead of Wishart's second-place Mercer. For the entire second half of the race, the little Mercer had been locked in a battle with Charlie Merz' Stutz. With the winner decided, the crowd's attention now turned to this battle for second between the two American competitors — Merz' more powerful Stutz gaining ground on the straights; Wishart's superbly handling Mercer pulling away in the turns. Many in the crowd remembered a similar battle the previous year, when Hughie Hughes' Mercer and Charlie Merz' Stutz went hammer-and-tongs through a flurry of pit stops to a third-place finish for Mercer that Stutz still contested. Would Merz be denied again? Would Trenton again finish in front of the hometown marque? With just five miles to go, it was too close to call. Wishart clung to a slim lead,

Left: Charles Merz was a solid, if unspectacular, driver for most of his career, but his claim to fame came in the 1913 Indianapolis 500, when his Stutz caught fire with less than two laps to go while he dueled for second place with Spencer Wishart's Mercer. Ignoring the signals from his pit, Merz drove the final lap with flames streaming out of his racer's engine compartment to secure a third-place finish for Stutz (IMS Photo). *Right*: The son of a millionaire New York banker, Spencer Wishart began his big-time racing career at just nineteen, piloting his Mercedes to fourth place in the 1909 Vanderbilt Cup. He went on to lead the opening laps and finish fourth in the inaugural Indianapolis 500 and to place third in the 1911 Vanderbilt Cup, behind only Mulford and DePalma. Joining the Mercer team in the summer of 1912, he went on to finish second to Jules Goux's all-conquering Peugeot at Indianapolis in 1913. Sadly, he was killed while leading the National Trophy race at Elgin, Illinois, on August 22, 1914, when his Mercer crashed after touching wheels with a privately owned Mercer driven by Otto Henning. He was just twenty-four years old and had been married only two months (IMS Photo).

but Merz was only seconds behind. The Indianapolis crowd was on its feet, the home-town fans urging Merz to find speed, the eastern contingent willing Wishart to hold off the charge. Merz closed on Wishart down the backstretch, but as the cars entered Turn Three flames boiled from beneath the Stutz' hood. The car was on fire. One last time past the pits, Merz kept his foot to the floor, ignoring his pit crew as they signaled wildly for him to come in. With little thought for his safety, or that of his mechanic, Harry Martin, Merz set out on the final lap. Even if catching Wishart was now out of the question, he was determined to finish. Through Turns One and Two, down the back straight, then through Turn Three and Turn Four, the blazing machine motored on. Then, as Merz made his way toward the checker, Martin crawled out on the hood of the racer. Tongues of flame licked around him as he unbuckled the straps to enable the pit crew to put out the fire more quickly. The crowd cheered wildly as the smoke-blackened driver and mechanic took the flag — just twenty-six seconds behind Wishart's Mercer — then immediately headed for the fire extinguishers.

The battle between Wishart and Merz had been exciting, but in the end it had been all Peugeot. Behind Wishart and Merz, Guyot's Sunbeam came home fourth. In the wake of the race, Goux revealed just how dominant the French car had been, at least for those who were listening. He said that he could have gone faster and broken Dawson's record for the 500 miles, but that his pit had held him to a 77 mph pace at Aitken's instruction, then slowed him further once the race was in hand. Unfortunately, much of the American press was more interested in putting a good face on the situation than they were in reporting the realities of it. Citing the fact that the top four positions were equally divided between European and American entries, and that Dawson's record had not been broken, many of the experts opined that the Yank machines had shown that they were the equal of the Europeans. Some with particularly rose-colored glasses even went so far as to claim that Anderson would have caught Goux in the final laps if only his Stutz had held together — this despite the fact that the Peugeot had effortlessly held off the Stutz for the entire race.

Others took a completely different tack, giving the driver, rather than the car, all the credit. They hailed Goux as a "modern Napoleon" and anointed him "the hero of two continents."[7] As for the winner himself, after the kisses, hugs and handshakes of the victory celebration, he grabbed another pint of champagne from one of his teammates, his seventh of the day, and took a healthy swig. Then he gave the massed reporters his take on the race. "*Sans le bon vin,*" he said, "*je ne serais pas été en état de faire la victoire.*"[8] Loosely translated, it means, "Without the wine, I could not have won."[9]

Despite the fact that the American press wanted to put the win down to racing luck, or to a great driving performance, or perhaps even to the wine, the simple fact was that Peugeot's win signaled the return of French dominance in American racing. Wherever the Gallic cars appeared for the next three years, they would be a force to be reckoned with.

❖ ❖ ❖

At the French *Grand Prix* in July, the story was much the same. Held at the 19.65-mile Amiens circuit, the twenty-nine lap, 570-mile event was dominated by French machines. While no American cars or American drivers took part, a portent of the divergent paths the sport was taking on either side of the Atlantic, French cars swept four of the first five positions, with the Peugeot EX-3s of Georges Boillot and Jules Goux taking first and second, and the bull-nosed Delage Type Ys of Paul Bablot and Albert Guyot finishing fourth and fifth. The only blemish on a French sweep of the top five positions was Jean Chassagne's six-cylinder Sunbeam in third, ten minutes back of the leader.

❖ ❖ ❖

For 1913, the Vanderbilt Cup and Grand Prize were scheduled to return to Savannah. But once again disputes arose, this time well in advance of the race dates. After submitting their bid, Savannah authorities demanded terms unacceptable to the race's organizers. Drivers, citing European practice, demanded appearance money. In the end, the races were called off. For the second time since its inception in 1904, and for the first time since 1907, there would be no Vanderbilt Cup.

❖ ❖ ❖

Even though America was to go without two of its three crown jewels of motor racing, lesser events during the summer displayed the power and speed of the new generation of American iron — at least when they didn't have to compete with the likes of Peugeot or Delage. On July 4, Ralph Mulford took a Mason-Duesenberg to victory in the 200-mile race over Columbus, Ohio's, one-mile dirt oval. In early August, Earl Cooper's Stutz bested the Mercers of Barney Oldfield and Joe Nikrent at the 445-mile Santa Monica road race. It was Stutz again at the race for the National Trophy at Elgin, Illinois, in late August, as Gil Anderson brought his machine home ahead of Mulford's Mason-Duesenberg, with the Mercers of Wishart and DePalma placing third and fifth. At the AAA finale in Corona, California, Barney Oldfield's Type 45 ran away with the lead, averaging better than 80 mph for 180 miles, only to blow a tire, hit a curb and break a wheel, handing the win to Earl Cooper's Stutz. As the 1914 season approached, with a renewal of the Vanderbilt Cup and Grand Prize, the three American marques looked poised for battle. The question remaining was whether the Americans would have an answer for the power of Peugeot.

18

My All-Time Thrill

As the New Year rang in 1914, war was still seven months away. More to the point, the events that would light the fuse to this largest of conflagrations still lay five months off in the mist-shrouded future. Europe was perched precariously on the edge of the precipice, but no one yet knew when, if ever, the fall would come. Worse yet, no one had any idea just how terrible it would be.

But Europe was still a long way from America in 1914 — a five-day cruise on a fast ocean liner — and a still-insulated, if not isolated, American population was preoccupied with its own triumphs, trends and troubles. Chief among the troubles, at least to reform-minded politicians, was the monopoly power of big business. John D. Rockefeller's Standard Oil controlled 85 percent of the American oil industry. James Duke's American Tobacco Company ruled 80 percent of the tobacco market. George Pullman's corporation produced 85 percent of the nation's railroad cars. In response to this growing trend toward the concentration of wealth and power in the hands of a select few, Woodrow Wilson signed the Clayton Antitrust Act into law over strenuous opposition. The act wouldn't solve the problem entirely, but at least it would give the government a weapon to wield against the worst of the offenders.

Among the triumphs, the opening of the Panama Canal topped the list. After ten years of digging, disease, and death in the tropical jungle, Teddy Roosevelt's pet project was finally finished. But the completion of "the most important and ... formidable engineering feat in history,"[1] as Roosevelt called it, was not without its down side, at least in the eyes of the feisty ex-president. It galled him that a Democratic president was in office at the time of the canal's opening. It enraged him further that Woodrow Wilson proposed to compensate Colombia to the tune of $25 million for America's seizure of the Canal Zone. He attacked the plan stridently, calling it nothing less than "a crime against the United States." Roosevelt may not have spoken softly on this occasion, but he showed that he still carried a big stick. Congress rejected Wilson's proposal.

But big business, big money, and big ditches in malarial swamps were far removed from the day-to-day lives of most Americans in 1914. More important were the hot new trends in music, dance and literature. Black composer W. C. Handy had just published his classic *St. Louis Blues*, elevating the blues from a little-known regional musical type to one generating international attention. If folks weren't listening to the flattened notes of the blues, they were dancing the fox trot as the "dance craze" that had been gathering momentum around the nation reached its peak. And those with little interest in music or dancing could just curl up with a good book, like Edgar Rice Burroughs' new best-seller *Tarzan of the Apes*.

Then again, people who weren't interested in any of those things could always go out for a drive. And in 1914 they would finally know where they were going — Gulf Oil had just introduced the first road maps.

❖ ❖ ❖

The 1913 season had not been altogether satisfactory for the Mercer team. While the yellow cars from Trenton continued to have success in the light car races, victory with the Type 45 had eluded them. As the 1914 season began, Mercer management concluded that a change was needed. In a disastrous decision that is difficult to fathom in hindsight, they hired Barney Oldfield to drive for the team full time. Oldfield had handled some West Coast events for Mercer in 1913, and the hope was to join him with DePalma, giving the team the two marquee names of the day. It would seem that the Roeblings should have known such a thing was impossible. After all, the feud between DePalma and Oldfield was of long standing, well known, and very real. But Charles and Ferdinand Roebling, like other tycoons of that era, were men used to having their way. Then again, their primary preoccupation was with the Roebling Company; Mercer was a secondary venture. And the racing program was only a relatively minor part of Mercer's operations — it was the sale of its road-going cars that kept the black ink flowing. Perhaps most importantly, the Roeblings seemed to have lost touch with their racing program. Washington A. Roebling II, its primary proponent, was dead. Mercer's chief engineer, Finley Robertson Porter, who had designed the Type 35 Raceabout and was manager of the racing team, no longer enjoyed the complete support of his employers. The result was that Mercer management not only hired Oldfield without first consulting DePalma, they compounded the insult by instructing DePalma, as team captain, to decide which of his friends was to be fired to make room for his nemesis.

Rather than be part of a team with the hated Oldfield or oversee the firing of Wishart or Bragg, DePalma quit. Bragg followed. Thus a team that just a few days before had boasted both Vanderbilt Cup and Grand Prize winners among its drivers, now found itself composed of a fairgound and speed-record performer with not a single major road-race or oval-track victory to his credit; a rich young charger with speed and talent, but a poor record in getting to the finish line; and an empty seat. The problem was one that required immediate attention. For 1914, the Vanderbilt Cup and Grand Prize had been moved from the end of the season to its start. The races were scheduled to be held in Santa Monica, California, in late February. With so little time, Mercer management decided to look in-house to fill their vacancy. At the recommendation of Spencer Wishart, they gave the nod to Eddie Pullen. Pullen, a Trenton native, had started out as an apprentice at the Mercer factory. He had then been promoted to machinist, then to road-tester, then to a position as riding mechanic for Hughie Hughes. Finally, in July 1912, he had been given his own car at Tacoma. He repaid the favor by winning the light car race there. Still, this new promotion was a gamble. Until now, Pullen had never been trusted with anything approaching the power and speed of the Type 45. In retrospect, it would prove to be the only good decision that Mercer would make in those early days of 1914.

If DePalma's departure had left Mercer in the lurch, it left DePalma in an even bigger bind. With so little time before the races, any car worth driving already had a driver. (In fact, the situation was so acute that Caleb Bragg, the reigning Grand Prize champion, would be unable to defend his crown.) At a loss, DePalma called on his friend and former car owner, Ernest Schroeder, to inquire about the Grey Ghost. Schroeder said that the car was available and enthusiastically agreed to send it to Santa Monica, but warned DePalma that it had been collecting dust in a New Jersey barn for nearly a year. Moreover, it was still fitted with the 440-cubic inch engine it had carried at Indianapolis. DePalma arranged to have the original 597-cubic inch engine shipped along with the car, but even with its original powerplant the Grey Ghost's chances looked slim. After all, it was now six years old, a veteran from the days of the chain-drive behemoths. It was a dinosaur compared to the newer, faster, better-handling machines from Mercer, Stutz and Mason-Duesenberg, much as the front-engined Offy roadsters would be at Indianapolis in the late 1960s in the wake of the rear-engine revolution.

But DePalma was nothing if not game, and he had a plan—a long-shot perhaps, but a plan nonetheless. In the little time available, he reinstalled the original engine and added a new carburetor. Then he fitted the largest gas tank he could find. If he couldn't beat the newer cars from the factory teams with pure speed, maybe he could pull a page from Ralph Mulford's book and beat them with a carefully paced, non-stop run for the full thirty-five laps, 294 miles. It was a feat that had never been attempted in a race of that length.

When Oldfield learned that DePalma would be driving the Grey Ghost Mercedes in the Vanderbilt Cup, he was nearly beside himself with glee. He sought out reporters at every opportunity and boldly predicted victory for himself and the Mercer team. When questioned about DePalma's chances, Oldfield scoffed. "The Barber?" he sneered, "If he gets that old boat fixed, I'll run him clean off the course."[2] The press ate it up.

To hear Oldfield talk, you would have thought that Mercer had no competition in the Vanderbilt Cup outside of DePalma's Mercedes. The truth was quite different. Stutz had entered two of their successful 1913 cars for Gil Anderson and Earl Cooper. Mason-Duesenberg fielded two of their powerful, lightweight cars for Billy Carlson and Dave Lewis. Harry Grant would be at the wheel of an Isotta-Fraschini, the first racer to feature four-wheel brakes (prior to this time they had been fitted to just the rear wheels), and Englishman John Marquis had brought over one of the Sunbeams that had been finishing behind the Peugeots, but nothing else, in Europe for the past two seasons. The remaining five cars of the fifteen-car field may have been a rather mangy bunch—the ex-Harry Grant Alco, and aging representatives from Apperson, Fiat and Marmon—but any of the top ten competitors could easily walk away with the race.

If DePalma was under the gun in getting the Grey Ghost race-ready, the weather conspired to give him a hand. The Vanderbilt Cup and Grand Prize, originally scheduled for February 21 and 23, had to be postponed to Feb. 26 and 28 due to heavy rains and flooding. The concern was not for the drivers but for the organizers and fans. Flooding on the Pacific Electric Railroad streetcar lines had put 100 of its cars out of commission, crippled its lines and washed out several bridges. It was feared that many spectators would be unable to get to the track. But if the postponement was a boon to DePalma, it was a bane to the race's Italian contingent, both of which ran into trouble on the last day of practice. Harry Grant's Isotta-Fraschini broke a piston. With no replacement available, the piston was sent to Los Angeles to be welded, but it seemed unlikely that repairs could be completed in time for the race. The only other Italian machine entered, Frank Verbeck's Fiat, a veteran of the 1911 and 1912 races, suffered engine troubles as well, remaining in its garage all day.

Race day dawned clear and bright and conditions were perfect as a crowd of 120,000 filled the Ocean Avenue grandstand and lined the long straights of Nevada Avenue (now Wilshire Boulevard) and San Vincente Boulevard, the other two legs of the fast, triangular, 8.4-mile course. After an all-night thrash, the Isotta team had gotten their car back together, and Harry Grant was first away, followed at fifteen-second intervals by Wishart's Mercer, Anderson's Stutz, Pullen's Mercer, and the rest. Unfortunately, the repairs to the Isotta wouldn't last a lap — the welded but untested piston blew apart at full throttle, and Grant's day was over just as it began.

But Grant wasn't the only one in trouble. As the pack came around to complete lap one, led by Wishart's Type 45, with Anderson's Stutz and the Mercers of Pullen and Oldfield close behind, Dave Lewis' Mason-Duesenberg began to belch smoke. It would retire on lap two with a blown engine. On lap three, it was Wishart's turn to blow up, after falling to the tail of the field. With Wishart's departure, Eddie Pullen got his Mercer past Anderson's Stutz and took over the lead. Oldfield lurked just behind in third, with Frank Verbeck's Fiat fourth and Billy Carlson's Mason-Duesenberg rounding out the top five. DePalma was seventh, cruising at his own pace, but already falling back from the blistering, car-killing pace being set by the leaders.

Now in the lead, Pullen booted his Type 45 to a record on lap four, covering the 8.4 miles in just 6:03 — 83.3 mph. Behind him, Anderson, Oldfield, Verbeck and Carlson held station, but no one could stay with the rookie from Trenton in the flying yellow Mercer. On lap seven, DePalma, holding to his pre-determined 75 mph pace, got past Ball's Marmon for sixth, but the top five were opening the gap at ten seconds a lap. On lap nine, the aged Mercedes garnered fifth as Verbeck's Fiat dropped out with a burned bearing, but the front four were still pulling away. By lap thirteen, Pullen had opened up a lead of three minutes over Anderson's second-place Stutz. Oldfield and Carlson were nearly a lap back. By now, Marquis' Sunbeam, never a factor on this day, had broken its rear axle, and Goode's Apperson had retired with a ruptured oil line. Only nine of the starting fifteen still remained.

On lap fourteen, the nine became eight. As he passed the grandstand on Ocean Avenue and turned into notorious "Death Curve" at Nevada Avenue, the right front wheel of Eddie Pullen's Mercer collapsed. The crippled car nosed wide and crashed into an iron barricade. Pullen and his mechanic were unhurt, but their day was over. With Pullen out, Gil Anderson's Stutz inherited the lead. Behind him, Oldfield and Carlson were waved to their pits. Carlson's stop was routine. Oldfield's wasn't, his pit inspecting the Mercer's wheels carefully, wanting to avoid a repeat of Pullen's crash. But routine stop or no, neither one could get out of the pits before DePalma came past. The Grey Ghost Mercedes was now lying second.

Exiting the pits in sixth place, Oldfield began to charge through the field. On lap fifteen, he passed Ball's fading Marmon to take over fifth. On lap sixteen, he shouldered his way past Earl Cooper's Stutz for fourth. On lap seventeen, the victim was Billy Carlson's Mason-Duesenberg. Now only DePalma and Anderson lay between Oldfield and the lead.

On lap eighteen, it was only DePalma, as Anderson's Stutz coasted to a stop, its driveshaft in pieces. At just past half-distance DePalma had the lead — the pace and the plan looked like they were working. It was far too early to claim victory, however. Despite his slow pit stop, Oldfield was only twenty-nine seconds back on the track as the Mercedes and the Mercer flashed past the start-finish line on lap nineteen. And while DePalma had seventy-five seconds in hand by virtue of his later start, he didn't want to let Oldfield get past and give him a clear track any sooner than necessary. At some point the Mercer would catch him, there was no denying that. It was faster than the Grey Ghost and faster still since DePalma was maintaining his pace and saving his tires. It would take a deft touch and great skill to keep Oldfield at bay and still have something left for the finish.

Over the next four laps, Oldfield gnawed at DePalma's lead like a big dog on a small bone. By lap twenty-three, he was just eight seconds behind the gray Mercedes, but the charge through the field had shredded his tires. A quick stop for new rubber and Oldfield was back out, again storming down the straights, again sliding maniacally through the turns, again carving chunks from DePalma's shrinking lead. By lap thirty, the Mercer pilot again had the German machine in his sights. As the two cars approached Death Curve, Oldfield dove for the inside line and the pass. DePalma stayed wide, uncharacteristically giving the line to his foe. As the Mercer came alongside, DePalma glanced over and noticed "ragged rubber flailing the road."[3] Oldfield's charge to the front, like his last one, had damaged his tires. One look gave DePalma an idea — a "wonderful, awful" idea.

Standing on the gas, using more revs than he had throughout the race, DePalma surged into the lead as the two neared the pits. With the Mercer tucked in on the Mercedes' tail, DePalma signaled his pit that he was coming in next time. He was sure that Oldfield had seen the signal as well. The trap set, he let Oldfield barge past and resumed his carefully calculated pace as the Mercer disappeared in the distance.

Coming past the pits on lap thirty-one, DePalma grinned the sly grin of the wicked. There, up on jacks, was the No. 7 Mercer, like a queen bee surrounded by workers, its crew changing its tires. Without the slightest nod to his pit, DePalma kept going, fairly sure that his tires and fuel would last four more laps. Oldfield's stop was a quick one, and he stormed through the final four laps in pursuit, but the gap was too much to make up in just thirty-three miles. At the checker, Oldfield's Mercer was five seconds back of DePalma's "old boat."

Like Ralph Mulford's virtuoso performance in 1911, DePalma's non-stop run had set a new Vanderbilt Cup record at 75.49 mph. Once again, slow but steady had not only won the race, but somehow turned out to be fast in the end. But this year there was more to it than that. The crowd had seen DePalma's signal as plainly as Oldfield had. They were sure that old Barney had been snookered. When asked about the incident in the wake of the race, DePalma was uncharacteristically evasive, claiming that he had signaled his pit that he was "not" coming in.[4] Oldfield was no more forthcoming, claiming that he pitted because a tire had gone flat, not because of anything DePalma had done. But the press and the crowd weren't buying it, they knew what they had seen — DePalma, the master, at his absolute best.

Some time later DePalma owned up to the incident, admitting that the signal was a ruse, that he had let Oldfield by at Death Curve to get a look at his tires and then blasted back in front down the pit straight precisely so Barney would see his gesture. Then he went on to say something more. In twenty-seven years of racing, he said, spanning over 2,000 victories and 30,000 miles, beating Oldfield in the Vanderbilt Cup was "my all-time thrill."[5]

19

A Triumph of American Grit

Mercer's defeat in the Vanderbilt Cup was a bitter blow, especially since it came at the hand of the man who had abandoned the team. It was made little better by Oldfield's abrasive personality. Team manager Finley Robertson Porter held Oldfield accountable for the loss. His overly aggressive driving style had repeatedly torn up his tires, costing him over eight minutes in the pits. If Oldfield had just set a reasonable pace moving up through the field from the fourteenth lap on, the speed of his Mercer would easily have outdistanced DePalma and the rest. For his part, Oldfield, with only limited experience in races the length of the Vanderbilt Cup and much more accustomed to five-lap match races or speed-record runs, would have no part of it. Conserving his tires was not something he had learned, and he wasn't particularly interested in doing so now. As far as he was concerned, it was the job of the team to put a car under him that would stay together; it was his job to drive it as fast as possible. If the tires failed, it wasn't his fault — that was the team's responsibility. So the team manager blamed the driver, and the driver blamed the rest of the team. It was, and still is, a common malady in racing — and one that is usually a reliable omen of failure.

But if Porter and Oldfield were taking turns sniping at each other, Eddie Pullen and the crew of the No. 4 Mercer didn't have any time for such nonsense. They had a broken car to fix and only one full day to do it. Somehow they got the bent machine straightened and readied in time for the Grand Prize. Joining them on the starting grid would be most of the combatants of the Vanderbilt Cup, with some notable additions. The field would be every bit as fast as the earlier race and maybe faster, owing to the fact that it was still being run under the unlimited displacement rules.

The Stutzes of Anderson and Cooper would be back, as would DePalma's Mercedes, Marquis' Sunbeam and Verbeck's Fiat. Mason-Duesenberg would be represented by a fresh car driven by a young man named Eddie Rickenbacker (actually "Rickenbacher," he had yet to change the spelling). It would be "Rick's" first drive in a Grand Prize, but he had taken part in the 1912 Indy 500. In addition, two S-74 Fiats with their engines now enlarged to 904 cubic inches were entered for Teddy Tetzlaff and Dave Lewis. The S-74s were dinosaurs like the Grey Ghost, huge rolling barns with monstrous engines and chain drive, but there was no denying the fact that they were fast. After all, they had won every Grand Prize since 1911 and nearly whipped Boillot's Peugeot at the French *Grand Prix* in 1912. At any rate, in the wake of DePalma's performance in the Vanderbilt Cup, nobody was counting out the older machines.

In this, its fifth running, the Grand Prize had yet to be won by an American entry. Fiat had dominated, with wins in three of the four prior races, much in the same way the French Panhards and Darracqs had dominated the early years of the Vanderbilt Cup. But even the Cup had fallen to an American contender, Robertson's Old 16 Locomobile, in its fourth running, albeit against a field that lacked the cream of the European *grand prix* machines. To American fans of the sport, an American victory was long overdue. And for the first time, the American entries from Mercer, Stutz, and Mason-Duesenberg showed speed to match the Europeans. Then again, there was DePalma to consider. Going into the Vanderbilt Cup, no one had given him much of a chance. In the wake of his victory there, he had to be considered the favorite for the Grand Prize. There was also Tetzlaff's Fiat — always fast and now running on a track that the native Californian seemed to own. Few in the crowd gave much thought to John Marquis' Sunbeam after its dismal showing in the Vanderbilt Cup, but those in the know certainly did. They remembered Guyot's fourth-place finish at Indy and had read of Sunbeam's successes in Europe. Three makes of American cars, three makes of foreigners, all with a realistic chance for the win — it would be an interesting race.

The crowd that assembled for the forty-eight lap, 403-mile Grand Prize was, if anything, larger than the one that had swamped Santa Monica for the Vanderbilt Cup. This time it was Tetzlaff in the Fiat first away, followed by Wishart, Anderson, Pullen and the rest. To no one's surprise, at the end of lap one the scoreboard showed Terrible Teddy in the lead, but Wishart, just behind in the Type 45, had posted an equal time. The Mercers of Pullen and Oldfield filled out the top four places as the field tried to sort itself out. After two laps at the front, Tetzlaff's Fiat went sour. A quick stop at his pit cured the problem, but he found himself mired back in ninth.

With Tetzlaff's departure from the lead, the Mercers took control, with Wishart leading Oldfield and Pullen, the trio already opening a gap over DePalma and Anderson. No sooner had Tetzlaff re-entered the race, however, than he was again headed for the front. By lap five, he had carved his way back up to fourth, as DePalma dropped back behind Anderson, trying to maintain some sanity in the face of the blistering pace being set by the leaders. Further back, Eddie Rickenbacker in the lone Mason-Duesenberg, after a mediocre start, had run into problems that dropped his machine to the tail of the field. Showing consistent speed thereafter, he would climb as high as fifth before a broken crankshaft would end his day on lap thirty-four, but he would never be a threat to the leaders.

By lap seven, Tetzlaff had bullied his blood-red behemoth past Pullen and Oldfield to take over second. Dave Lewis in the second S-74 was not so fortunate. Its enormous engine already down on power, it dropped him to the back of the field. Before half distance, a burned bearing would end its day. But if Lewis was still soldiering on, his prospects remained better than those of Earl Cooper. His Stutz had already swallowed a valve, an early victim of the murderous pace. He would not be the last.

No sooner was Tetzlaff in second than his Fiat was back in the pits. Oldfield followed, but got out ahead of the Fiat, the pair now lying sixth and seventh. At the front, Spencer Wishart showed speed that no one could match, rocketing around the course at an average in excess of 85 mph. Behind him, Pullen, Anderson and DePalma hung on grimly, treading the fine line between cooking their machines and letting the leader get too far ahead. But by now they had been joined by another. After a mid-pack start, John Marquis now had his Sunbeam lying fifth, and closing.

Once out of the pits, Tetzlaff again made a rush through the field, passing Oldfield on lap ten, Marquis on lap eleven. On lap twelve, the victim was DePalma, as the Terrible One scorched the course in a blazing 5:49 — 86.6 mph. The big Fiat might be a dinosaur, but with Tetzlaff at the wheel the old monster could put even the most modern of machines in its dust. The California crowd cheered their native son wildly as he continued his chase toward the front.

As the leaders passed the 100-mile mark, quarter-distance, it became evident that the pace of this race was like nothing anyone had ever seen. Wishart's average was an incredible 84.48 mph, a speed unattainable for even one lap just a year or two earlier. And while the Mercers of Wishart and Pullen had opened gaps of roughly two minutes on each other and the rest of the leaders, the five just behind were only seconds apart. Anderson had nine seconds on a closing Tetzlaff. Tetzlaff, in turn, was thirty ahead of DePalma, who was fighting to stay ahead of Oldfield, now just nineteen seconds back and only five ahead of Marquis. And all of them were flying — even DePalma's average speed for the first hundred miles was within a whisker of 79 mph.

As Wishart and Pullen led the way, the gang of five behind them continued to battle. On lap thirteen, it was Tetzlaff past Anderson for third and off in pursuit of the Mercers. On lap fifteen, it was Oldfield by DePalma for fifth. On lap sixteen, a slow lap by Anderson cost him three places, as Oldfield, DePalma and Marquis got by. The racing was so close that the slightest mistake spelled disaster.

On lap eighteen, that disaster befell Teddy Tetzlaff. It was not a mistake per se, but the traditional Tetzlaff bugaboo — his Fiat's engine blew. The retirement left Oldfield in third at the head of the pack, but DePalma, Anderson and Marquis were still only seconds behind. Even so, the team from Trenton was ecstatic, its cars again occupied the top three positions, and both Wishart and Pullen had some cushion behind them.

Their joy was short-lived, however. As most of the teams made their scheduled pit stops, Oldfield's dropped him behind DePalma and Marquis. Worse yet, an "old soldier" walked out on the track right in front of Eddie Pullen.[1] The Mercer pilot veered hard to avoid a collision, but his Type 45 hit a curb, ripping up two of its tires. By the time he got his crippled machine around to the pits and back out on the course his cushion was gone and he was trailing the leaders in sixth.

While the others were pitting, DePalma stayed out, using the Grey Ghost's longer range to advantage. With the pit stops completed, he found himself lying second, behind only Wishart, and some ninety seconds ahead of Marquis' Sunbeam. One lap later, the Mercedes took over the lead as Wishart's Mercer coasted to a stop. The terrible pace had overcooked a bearing in the Type 45. If the Mercer pit had been jubilant just four laps before, it was now filled with dread. Could it be possible that DePalma and the Grey Ghost would beat them again? But mixed with the dread was new hope as Pullen now mounted a charge of his own. On lap twenty-two, he passed Anderson's Stutz. On lap twenty-three, it was Oldfield, his teammate. On lap twenty-four, Marquis' Sunbeam succumbed to his relentless pursuit.

As the race reached half-distance, DePalma held an eighty-five second lead over Pullen. Behind the flying yellow Mercer, the race was still closer than any that anyone could recall. Marquis' Sunbeam was barely nine seconds back, Anderson and Oldfield each just sixteen more in arrears. And the pace was still hideously fast, with DePalma covering the two hundred miles at 79.94 mph. By this time the lead group had simply left the others in the dirt. Among the five other cars that remained in the race, the leader was Rickenbacker's Mason-Duesenberg, and he was a full ten minutes behind Oldfield.

On lap twenty-five, it was Marquis' turn to show what his Sunbeam could do, as he forced his way past Pullen to take over second. Again Pullen looked for speed, but the charge through the pack had been taxing, he couldn't find any way by. On lap twenty-nine, as the gap between DePalma and the rest began to shrink, Pullen again nearly crashed. He kept it together, but lost valuable time. His Mercer was again behind Anderson and Oldfield in fifth. Then the engine note from the gray Mercedes at the front began blaring an ominous staccato. It was running on just three cylinders — an intake valve had burned. As Pullen again tore his way up from the back of the lead group, passing Oldfield on lap thirty, DePalma fell to second behind Marquis.

DePalma doggedly hung on to second as Pullen closed quickly, passing Anderson for third on lap thirty-one. But the crippled Mercedes had nothing left to fight with, and on lap thirty-two the Mercer was by and chasing down the Sunbeam at the front. Now it was Marquis' turn to feel the pressure of the surging Mercer. He did, and the pressure forced him into a mistake — a big one. Attempting Death Curve much too fast (estimates put his speed at 70 mph), he lost it. The Sunbeam barrel-rolled three times, spitting out mechanic Harry Hough. But Marquis was trapped in the car, and when it came to rest upside down against a fence, he was buried beneath it. At first, he was feared dead as his unconscious body was dug out from under the wreck. He looked so bad that the injured Hough buried his face in his hands and ran off, finally needing to be led to the ambulance. Marquis was indeed seriously injured, but miraculously no bones had been broken. He would make a full recovery.

With the Sunbeam now scrap, Pullen finally had inherited the lead he'd been chasing since Wishart's retirement, but all was not yet easy sailing. As DePalma pitted in a vain attempt to remedy his engine woes, Anderson took up the chase. Once again, it was Stutz against Mercer, but this time for the lead in the crown jewel of racing that no American machine had yet won. The importance of such a win was not lost for a second on either Harry Stutz or the Roeblings, nor on the teams from Indianapolis and Trenton. The Stutz pit signaled Anderson "flat out." Mercer did likewise to Oldfield, seeking to gain some protection for Pullen. The three leaders were now miles in front of the rest.

On lap thirty-five, Oldfield forced his faster Type 45 past the Stutz and into second. For the moment, the men in the Mercer pits could stop holding their breath — but just for a moment. Only two laps later, Oldfield was out with a burned engine bearing, the same malady that had befallen Wishart. It was now a two-man race, but the Mercer pit had cause for concern. Could Pullen's engine last for another ninety miles at this car-killing pace, or would the bearing problem rear its ugly head again?

As the laps unwound, Anderson kept the pressure on, spurring his Stutz for all it was worth. Still, he was unable to catch the yellow car from Trenton. For eight laps he chased, using every ounce of speed he could find, braking late, clipping turns as tightly as he dared, using every bit of road, searching for every rev his engine could produce. For his part, Pullen fought to hold him off, driving on the ragged edge and perhaps a bit beyond. Then on lap forty-five it was over, as only one engine still sang — but it was not

Perhaps no driver was more closely identified with a single team than was Gil Anderson with Stutz. Starting with the team at its inaugural race, the 1911 Indianapolis 500, and remaining team leader through the "White Squadron" years until Stutz abandoned racing at the close of the 1915 season, Anderson's fortunes mirrored those of Stutz, winning many lesser races and often finishing well at Indy and in the Vanderbilt Cup and Grand Prize, but unable to ever capture a win in the "Big Three" of American motor racing (IMS Photo).

the Mercer that had broken, it was Anderson's Stutz. A piston had shattered under the strain of his flat-out pursuit.

The final three laps were a walk-away. With no competition remaining, Pullen cruised to the finish. The murderous pace had so devastated the field that the second-place car, Ball's Marmon, was a half-hour behind at the finish. Third and fourth were Taylor's Alco and DePalma's crippled Mercedes. They were the only cars to complete the full forty-eight laps. Pullen's speed was a record, of course. Even though he cruised through the final three laps, it was still 77.2 mph. More representative of the true pace of the race, however, was his speed at 300 miles — 79 mph. It was a new world record for the distance.

It is not overstatement to say that the press and the public went a little bit cuckoo over the victory. Not only was it the inaugural triumph for American iron in a Grand Prize, it had been accomplished by a "virtually unknown ex-apprentice boy"[2] in a car he had wrecked only two days before at a speed even faster than the record set by the immortal Bruce-Brown at Savannah in 1911. It was a Horatio Alger tale come to life. As one journal trumpeted, "For [Pullen and Mercer] to come back and win the Grand Prize was a triumph of American grit and American engineering."[3] Another claimed, "When word was flashed across the country that the famous Grand Prize had been won by an American car and an American driver, every red-blooded motorist in this country was filled with pride."[4]

Whether those words were true nationwide, or merely reflective of some scribe's overactive imagination, it is not too much to say that Trenton was jubilant. The town on the Delaware had not had such cause for celebration since George Washington and his rag-tag Continental army had beaten the tar out of a bunch of hung-over, British-paid Hessians on the day after Christmas 1776. A holiday was proclaimed by the mayor. When the team got back to town, the city staged a huge celebration capped by a parade led by Pullen in his winning car. It was very nearly the finest hour for Eddie Pullen and Mercer. Nearly, but not quite. Their finest hour had come on the track at Santa Monica on February 28, 1914. Neither the man nor the marque would ever see its like again.

20

A Bad Day for America

Eddie Pullen's victory in the Grand Prize did nothing to put an end to the running soap opera that had existed at Mercer through the first two months of 1914. Within days of the race, Barney Oldfield was gone from the team. Team manager Finley Robertson Porter claimed to have fired him; Oldfield claimed he quit. By the time Indianapolis rolled around he would be driving for archrival Stutz. Before the end of March, Porter himself was gone, replaced as chief engineer and team manager by Erik Delling, the man who had seen no reason for overhead cam engines in 1912 (and still didn't). In just three months, the Mercer team — one that had started the year as a juggernaut — had completely disintegrated. With Oldfield's seat vacant, overtures were made to Caleb Bragg to return for Indianapolis. He agreed. The team would field Type 45s for Wishart and Bragg at the Brickyard.

For the 1914 edition of the Indianapolis 500, the French, spurred by the success of Peugeot in the 1913 race and by the huge payday that Indy represented, showed up in force. In addition to the two-car factory team of Peugeots for drivers Georges Boillot and Jules Goux, there was a two-car team from archrival Delage for drivers René Thomas and Albert Guyot, a single entry from Bugatti for Ernst Friedrich, and a privately entered "Baby" Peugeot for Arthur Duray. All featured overhead-cam engines, but Duray's displaced a mere 183 cubic inches, less than half the displacement of the big cars. Its small engine size earned it open contempt from Boillot and Goux, who felt the car had no chance to win and could only bring humiliation to the Peugeot name. Before the race was over they would be singing a very different tune.

But the French were not the only Europeans to take an interest in the 500. England was represented by Sunbeam, with cars for Harry Grant and Jean Chassagne. A privately entered Isotta-Fraschini for driver Ray Gilhooly represented Italy's interests. The Schroeder Mercedes, this time powered by a Peugeot engine, returned with Ralph Mulford again at the wheel. Even little Belgium had an entry, an Excelsior for Josef Christiaens. In all, eleven cars of the thirty-car field were of European manufacture. In its fourth year of existence, the Indianapolis 500 had supplanted the Grand Prize as America's international race.

Top: The final incarnation of the race car that wouldn't die — Ralph Mulford prepares for the 1914 Indianapolis 500 in the Schroeder-owned "Grey Ghost" Mercedes, now powered by a Peugeot engine. They would finish eleventh (IMS Photo). *Bottom*: Josef Christiaens' Excelsior takes on fuel at the 1914 Indianapolis 500 en route to a sixth-place finish, giving European teams five of the top six places (IMS Photo).

Opposing this horde from across the Atlantic were a number of American marques that, if not possessed of the speed of the Peugeots, looked competitive nonetheless. There were the Mercers, of course, and a three-car team from Stutz for Oldfield, Gil Anderson and Earl Cooper. Duesenberg, no longer running under the Mason banner, fielded cars for Eddie Rickenbacker and Willie Haupt, while a third Mason-owned car was entered for George Mason. In addition to these American stalwarts, newcomer Maxwell fielded two cars designed by Indianapolis winner Ray Harroun for Teddy Tetzlaff and Billy Carlson, and a privately owned Marmon was entered for 1912 winner Joe Dawson.

Perhaps most surprising was the notable name missing from the field. Ralph DePalma, now widely considered to be America's best driver, had originally been scheduled to compete in a 1913 Mercedes *grand prix* car. With its experimental six-cylinder engine, the car had been barred by the ACF from the 1913 French *Grand Prix*, but had later raced, without notable success, at the Sarthe *Grand Prix* held later that year. Powered by an aero-inspired 443-cubic inch engine, but still employing outdated chain drive, the car had been written off by Mercedes as a failure. DePalma's initial outing in practice for the 1914 Indianapolis 500 had been no more successful. Excessive vibration made the car nearly undriveable. Despite turning in a lap that would have put the Mercedes in the field, DePalma made the decision to withdraw it, and the car was shelved, at least until further development could be done. The withdrawal of the Mercedes left America's best driver, DePalma, a spectator in what was now clearly America's biggest race.

In qualifying, the factory Peugeots displayed their superior speed. Georges Boillot set the pace at a scorching 99.86 mph. His teammate Jules Goux was not far behind at 98.13. Surprisingly, the fastest American showing came, not from Mercer, but from the new Maxwell, with Teddy Tetzlaff posting third-fastest time at 96.36 mph. Behind him were René Thomas' Delage at 94.54 mph and Joe Dawson's Marmon at 93.55 mph. The speed of the Mercers, cast as pre-race American favorites, was somewhat disappointing. Bragg's best was a seventh-fastest 92.97 mph, followed by Wishart, eighth fastest at 92.69

Billy Carlson's Maxwell passes the grandstands during the 1914 Indianapolis 500. He would finish ninth (IMS Photo).

Top: Georges Boillot, winner of the 1912 French *Grand Prix*, pictured here in his Peugeot prior to the 1914 Indianapolis 500. Despite the French cars' dominance of the race, the day was not a good one for Boillot: his racer would be sidelined on lap 141 with a cracked frame (IMS Photo). *Bottom*: Veteran Stutz driver Gil Anderson readies his machine for the 1914 500. Sadly, hc would be forced to retire on the forty-second lap due to engine trouble (IMS Photo).

mph. Even Mercer's showing was better than Stutz, however. Only one of their three cars could crack the 90-mph barrier: Gil Anderson's eleventh-fastest 90.49 mph. Duesenberg found itself even further down the list, with Eddie Rickenbacker posting fastest time for the marque at 89.39 mph. If the qualifying speeds were indicative, it looked like a long day for the Yanks.

As in 1913, starting positions were determined by a drawing. And just as it had the previous year, the drawing resulted in the fastest qualifier starting at the back of the field. Georges Boillot's Peugeot would start twenty-ninth. The remainder of the French machines fared little better. Jules Goux's Peugeot drew the nineteenth slot; René Thomas' Delage the fifteenth. The best positioned of the French cars was Arthur Duray's "Baby" Peugeot in tenth. By comparison, the Maxwells of Tetzlaff and Carlson, third and sixth fastest in qualifying, drew the second and fifth starting spots. Veteran Bob Burman started twenty-second. As in prior years, with many of the quickest cars near the rear of the field, the opening laps would tell little until the field got itself sorted out.

With Teddy Tetzlaff sitting on the front row in the fastest American entry, many in the crowd of 110,000 were confident that the Maxwell pilot would own the early lead. Surprisingly, he didn't. At the start, Howdy Wilcox's Pope-Hartford jumped to the head of the pack from its position further out on the front row. His time in the lead would be short, however. By lap two, Christiaens' Excelsior had displaced him. All the while, Jules Goux's Peugeot was rocketing through the field from its nineteenth starting spot, taking the lead from the Belgian machine on lap five, only to see Christiaens re-take it on lap six and Caleb Bragg's Mercer pass them both on lap seven. It was the last lap an American would lead. Christiaens reclaimed it on lap eight, only to be

Bob Burman bends his Burman racer into Turn One in the 1914 500. Unfortunately, Burman's own car was no more able to withstand his hard-charging driving style than many of his other mounts had been. He was forced to retire on lap forty-seven with a snapped connecting rod (IMS Photo).

headed by René Thomas' Delage on lap thirteen. From here on, the blue cars from France took control.

On lap twenty, pole-sitter Jean Chassagne's Sunbeam rolled in Turn Four. Fortunately, neither Chassagne nor mechanic Albert Mitchell was seriously hurt. The crash slowed the furious pace of the leaders, at least temporarily, but did nothing to stop the French domination of the race. Only the Mercers seemed able to keep the Peugeots and Delages in their sights. On lap thirty, Duray's Peugeot displaced Thomas' Delage at the front. Three laps later, Tetzlaff's Maxwell was out with a broken rocker arm. On lap forty-five, Dawson's Marmon left the race in more spectacular fashion when Ray Gilhooly's Isotta blew a tire, hit the wall, and rolled on the back straight.

Dawson, close behind, dove for a narrow space between the wreck and the outside wall, but at the last minute the Isotta's mechanic began to crawl through the gap to safety. Dawson had no choice, he yanked the wheel hard left. The Marmon skidded wildly, then rolled twice, coming to rest on the soft ground at the inside of the track. Dawson escaped with nothing more serious than a broken collarbone, and the remainder of the participants had only minor injuries, but the Marmon's departure, coming so soon after the retirement of Tetzlaff's Maxwell, left the Americans without their two fastest cars before one quarter of the race had been run.

By lap sixty, French cars controlled three of the top four positions, with Duray's Peugeot leading the second- and fourth-place Delages of Albert Guyot and René Thomas. Only Caleb Bragg's third-place Mercer stood in the way of a complete Gallic stranglehold. On lap sixty-seven, Guyot took the lead as the "Baby" Peugeot made a pit stop for

The remains of pole-sitter Jean Chassagne's Sunbeam after it rolled in Turn Four on lap twenty of the 1914 Indianapolis 500. Neither Chassagne nor mechanic Albert Mitchell was seriously hurt (IMS Photo).

The wreckage of Ray Gilhooly's Isotta-Fraschini after the lap forty-five crash where it blew a tire, hit the wall, and rolled. Fortunately, Gilhooly and his mechanic escaped with only minor injuries (IMS Photo).

tires. Three laps later, Thomas joined his Delage teammate at the front after getting past Bragg and Duray. Then it was the "Baby" Peugeot's turn to find speed. As Guyot and Bragg pitted, dropping back from the lead group, Duray spurred his mount past Thomas. On lap eighty, the leaders were Duray's Peugeot followed by Thomas' Delage, with Wishart's Mercer and Boillot's Peugeot now occupying the third and fourth positions vacated by Bragg and Guyot. Once again, only a spot of Mercer yellow broke up the wall of French blue at the front.

But the Mercer's position among the top three would not last. By lap ninety, Wishart had fallen to fourth as Boillot's charge from the back of the field finally put him up among the leaders. At half-distance, while Duray continued to lead, Boillot closed on Thomas' Delage, threatening him for second as Bragg joined Wishart behind the lead trio. Thomas and Boillot continued to close on Duray until lap 116, when Duray pitted, handing Thomas the lead. Once again, the Mercers were lying third and fourth. With a little luck, they just might make it a race. Sadly, it wouldn't happen. One lap later, Bragg dropped out with a broken camshaft. Five laps further on Wishart fell victim to the same problem. The torrid pace set by the blue cars had torched the American challengers.

At 325 miles, 130 laps, Delage and Peugeot held the top four positions, with Thomas' Delage leading Boillot's Peugeot, Duray's "Baby" Peugeot third and Guyot's Delage fourth. The French cars' control of the race was complete. Even when Boillot retired from the race on lap 141 with his Peugeot's frame broken, another victim of the murderous pace, the Gallic stranglehold remained intact. Goux's Peugeot merely stepped up to take over fourth. They would hold those positions until the end, with Thomas crossing the stripe seven minutes ahead of Duray, and Guyot and Goux each another three minutes back. The best-placed American was Oldfield's Stutz in fifth, twenty minutes behind the leader and many laps in arrears.

Thomas' speed for the 500 miles, 82.47 mph, had simply shattered Joe Dawson's 1912 record. In fact, the top four finishers were all under Dawson's time. As in 1913, the

Top: The 1912 Indianapolis winner, Joe Dawson, poses for the photographers with his 1914 mount. Dawson was fifth fastest in practice for the 500 despite his Marmon's lack of up-to-the-minute technology (note the use of wooden-spoke wheels at a time when most teams had gone to lighter and stronger wire wheels), but his day ended on lap forty-five when he barrel-rolled his racer twice while trying to avoid the wreck of Ray Gilhooly's Isotta. Fortunately, Dawson would escape with only a broken collarbone (IMS Photo). *Bottom*: The Peugeot team, 1914 — Jules Goux (6) leads Georges Boillot (7) down the front straight at Indianapolis. Note the flags along the pit wall denoting each team's nationality. By 1914 Indianapolis had supplanted the Vanderbilt Cup and Grand Prize as America's international race (IMS Photo).

Top: Réne Thomas' Delage would go on to win the 1914 Indianapolis 500 (IMS Photo).
Bottom: French *Grand Prix* winner Georges Boillot's Peugeot in the pits during the 1914 Indianapolis 500. Running among the leaders for most of the race, Boillot would retire on lap 141, his racer's frame broken (IMS Photo).

By May 1914, Barney Oldfield had left Mercer and joined their archrival, the Stutz White Squadron. At Indianapolis, Oldfield would finish fifth, highest of any American entry, but still a full twenty minutes behind Réne Thomas' winning Delage (IMS Photo).

French machines had shown their superiority, but unlike the previous year there was no way to rationalize the result. No American car had even been close at the finish, and those that had tried to stay with the blue cars had blown up in the effort. Moreover, this year French dominance had not been confined to a single driver, or even a single marque. Among them, only Bugatti was missing from the front of the field at the end—and its single entry had run as high as second early on before retiring with a broken drive pinion. The Yanks had even been trounced by the "Baby" Peugeot with its little 183 cubic inch engine. *The Automobile* put it succinctly: "Today has been a bad day for America."[1]

❖ ❖ ❖

By the time of the running of the French *Grand Prix* on July 4, Europe was on the brink of war. At this point there was no denying it; someone had finally thrown the match into the bomb factory. Six days before the race, Archduke Franz Ferdinand, the heir to the Austro-Hungarian throne, had been assassinated along with his wife in Sarajevo, the capital of the newly annexed Austro-Hungarian province of Bosnia-Hercegovina. His assassin, Gavrilo Princip, was a Bosnian student with ties to the Black Hand, a terrorist group seeking to restore Bosnia-Hercegovina to Serbian control. The assassination further embittered already quarrelsome relations between the two neighboring nations. By late July, after a Serb

Top: Indianapolis 1914 — the scoreboard tells the tale: 16, 14, 10, 6 equals Delage, Peugeot, Delage, Peugeot, with the highest placed American entry, Oldfield's Stutz, a full twenty minutes behind and not yet appearing on the board (IMS Photo). *Bottom*: The blue cars roll on — Arthur Duray in the "Baby" Peugeot leads Réne Thomas' Delage and Georges Boillot's Peugeot in the 1914 Indianapolis 500 (IMS Photo).

rejection of Austria-Hungary's final ultimatum, Austria-Hungary would declare war, triggering the mutual protection provisions of treaties throughout Europe. By mid-August the continent would be awash in a tidal wave of troop trains and armies on the march.

War had not yet been declared when the racing fraternity convened at Lyons for the *Grand Prix*. Nevertheless, most people understood that it was imminent. For the French, that meant another fight with the hated Germans. Nationalism, long a part of the French attitude toward motor racing, whether it be *grand prix* or Gordon Bennett Cup, took on a new and sinister dimension. The *Grand Prix* now stood for something more than mere national pride. It was nothing less than a morality play with victory belonging to the righteous, an omen signaling the ordained outcome of the impending conflict. Such feelings were nonsense, of course, but feelings by their nature are irrational, and French feelings, perhaps, less rational still. It would not be the normal carefree crowd of spectators who attended this last race in Europe before the onset of hostilities. It would be a crowd possessed of the fever of war, demanding French victory in the race as though it were the opening battle of the conflict to come.

While the French, particularly Peugeot, had ruled the racing world for the past two seasons, the rest of Europe had used that time to catch up technologically. In fact, virtually all of the forty-one competitors at the French *Grand Prix* had developed their own Peugeot-style overhead-cam, four-valve-per-cylinder engines by 1914. Among the notables opposing the all-conquering Peugeots, which would be driven by Georges Boillot, Jules Goux and Victor Rigal, were Ralph DePalma in a British Vauxhall and Dario Resta in a Sunbeam. But the real threat to French domination came from Mercedes. The German marque brought a five-car team of their brand new four-cylinder cars for drivers Christian Lautenschlager, Max Sailer, Louis Wagner, Otto Salzer and Theodore Pilette. In practice, they looked marginally faster than the French machines, but it was difficult to gauge a clear favorite for the race. While the Mercedes had an edge in handling and in their acceleration out of the turns, the Peugeots were superior in straight-line speed and, equipped with front-wheel brakes, could out-brake the German cars going into the corners. Moreover, the Mercedes were an untested quantity. It remained to be seen whether they could last for the full 467 miles, twenty laps of the 23.38-mile Lyons circuit.

What the assembled crowd of 300,000 didn't know as the flag fell on the morning of the race was that Mercedes not only had a car to compete with the French, they had developed a carefully planned strategy to maximize the advantage of their five-car team. At the start, Max Sailer set a furious pace, establishing an early lead and forcing the Peugeots into flat out pursuit. After five laps, Sailer's Mercedes broke under the strain, but his run as the rabbit had taxed the Peugeots of Boillot and Goux. When Sailer retired, Lautenschlager lay just one minute behind Boillot in second. Goux, close behind in third, was followed by Wagner and Salzer. Now Lautenschlager put on the pressure. Lap after lap, he relentlessly chased down Boillot. All the while, Goux tried to hound him in every way possible. The Peugeot pilot tried to unsettle the German by braking late for corners, diving under the Mercedes, trying to force Lautenschlager into a mistake. The tactic proved useless. Lautenschlager would merely let Goux have the corner, then use his Mercedes' superior power to blast past the Peugeot down the straight.

Finally, on lap eighteen, Lautenschlager drove past Boillot for the lead. The Frenchman tried everything to catch him, but his blue car simply had nothing left. Just behind, the Mercedes of Wagner and Salzer caught and passed Goux's Peugeot. The early-lap chase of Sailer had taken the fine, fast edge from the French machines, leaving them vulnerable to the German onslaught at the finish. Finally, on the last lap, Boillot's engine gave out, letting Mercedes romp home first, second and third. Goux finished fourth, followed by Dario Resta's Sunbeam.

An eerie silence from the French crowd greeted Lautenschlager as he crossed the line victorious, followed by teammates Wagner and Salzer. The fans weren't simply dumbfounded, they felt somehow cheated — by God and the Germans. This race was to have been a demonstration of French invincibility, but, unbelievably, the unthinkable had happened — again. Could this be the omen the Gallic throng had sought — a prophecy of German victory in the war to come? Very nearly, as it would turn out — very nearly indeed.

❖ ❖ ❖

In America, the remainder of the summer saw a number of events that would have a major impact on the racing season to come in 1915. Perhaps first and foremost of these was Ralph DePalma's return to victory lane in E. C. Patterson's 1914 *grand prix* Mercedes, one of the cars (reputedly Wagner's) that had proven so successful at Lyons. For reasons which were not altogether clear, either then or now, the Mercedes had been "detained" in France after the running of the *Grand Prix*. Patterson purchased it shortly before the outbreak of hostilities. At the Elgin race meeting in August, the car and driver combination dominated the results, if not the races themselves. In the Cobe Trophy race, DePalma emerged victorious over Gil Anderson (Stutz) and Ralph Mulford, now at the wheel of a Peugeot, but not until Spencer Wishart's Mercer, which had built up an eight-minute lead, fell out with a split gas tank. On the following day in the National Trophy race, DePalma outdistanced Eddie Pullen, in a Mercer with a new, Delling-designed, L-head engine, and Barney Oldfield in a Stutz. The combination of DePalma and the E. C. Patterson Mercedes had established itself as a formidable force for the upcoming season.

Also at Elgin, tragedy once again struck the Mercer team. Spencer Wishart, now the team's nominal captain, was leading the National Trophy by four minutes at the eighteen-lap mark when he moved to overtake a privately owned Mercer driven by Otto Henning. While travelling down the backstretch at 110 mph, the hub of Wishart's left rear wheel touched Henning's right front. Wishart's Mercer shot twenty-five feet in the air, leaped a ditch, and smashed itself to pieces against a large elm tree. Wishart and mechanic John Jenter were killed. In five years of racing, it was the first accident the wealthy twenty-four-year-old had ever had. To make the loss even more tragic, Wishart had been married only two months. He had just returned from his honeymoon in Europe.

But if Mercer seemed alternately favored and cursed in this year of 1914, the wheel of fortune still had not made its final spin. At the last race of the season, in Corona, California, Eddie Pullen won again for the boys from Trenton, setting a new world's speed record of 87.89 mph in the process. Mercer newcomer Glover Ruckstell trailed Pullen for most of the race and seemed assured of second, until he ran out of gas six miles from the finish. Maybe the yellow cars would have something for the French and German machines in the upcoming season. Then again, maybe not — who knew where the spin of the wheel would land next.

21

As Dangerous a Drive as Has Ever Been Seen

As 1914 came to a close, the people of Europe finally began to realize the magnitude of the terrible tragedy in which they had become embroiled. By New Year's Day 1915, the tally of those killed, wounded and captured in the war had risen to well over a million men on each side — and the end was still nowhere in sight. Trench warfare had supplanted the land-swallowing offensives of the war's first few weeks. For the next four years, the slaughter would only worsen as Europe fed a generation of young men to the insatiable maw of the meat-grinder.

Fortunately, particularly for those of draft age, the United States remained neutral, at least for the time being. As most of the rest of the world occupied itself with the gruesome realities of the conflict that would come to be called World War I, American moviegoers found themselves enthralled by a film depicting their own Civil War. D. W. Griffith's *Birth of a Nation* was a sweeping epic unlike anything audiences had ever seen. Not only was it the first truly artistic film, it perfected many of the cinematic techniques that we today take for granted: the close-up; the long shot; the fade-in and fade-out; crosscutting to portray simultaneous action. As Lillian Gish, one of the film's stars, later put it, Griffith "gave us the grammar of filmmaking."[1]

But if the film was a technical and artistic masterpiece, its subject matter was cause for controversy. Griffith, the son of a Confederate colonel, told his tale from an unapologetically white-supremacist point of view. Most shocking of the scenes were those casting the formation of the Ku Klux Klan in a favorable light. The NAACP, in its most meaningful protest since its formation five years earlier, tried to block screenings of the film in major cities around the country. Their efforts would be only minimally successful, but the controversy itself would cause at least some white Americans to begin to rethink their preconceived notions of race.

Griffith's was not the only film causing controversy, however. In *A Fool There Was*, Theda Bara cemented her position in history as the cinema's first vamp. Her portrayal of

211

a *femme fatale* in the role where she uttered the now-famous (and often misquoted) line, "Kiss me, my fool," shocked and titillated audiences. The whole thing was cause for alarm among America's morally conservative. They feared that the film would despoil moral values. Meanwhile, moviegoers flocked to it by the thousands. They also packed theaters for another film that, if less controversial than *Birth of a Nation* or *A Fool There Was*, would prove more lasting than either of its notorious contemporaries — a little comedy called *The Tramp*, starring Charlie Chaplin, now Hollywood's highest paid star.

Outside of the fantasy world of the movies, Margaret Sanger faced trial for disseminating obscenity through the mail. The charge was based on her publication of an article espousing contraception in her magazine *Woman Rebel*. In September, Sanger, the originator of the term "birth control," returned to New York from London, where she had fled when first facing trial, to fight it out with the authorities. Much to her dismay, the district attorney dropped the charges against her. Within a year, she would open America's first birth-control clinic in Brooklyn, only to be arrested again ten days later.

In the world of sports, Jack Johnson lost the heavyweight boxing crown to Jess Willard, ending his seven-year reign at the top, and the Boston Red Sox, led by Babe Ruth, defeated the Philadelphia Phillies in the World Series. Over the next three years they would win two more championships, giving them a total of five crowns in the Series' first fifteen years, more than any other team in baseball. Then, in 1920, they would sell Babe Ruth's contract to the New York Yankees for $125,000. Over the century's remaining eighty years, they would never win another World Series.

❖ ❖ ❖

Nine years after its devastating earthquake and fire, the newly rebuilt city of San Francisco staged the Panama-Pacific International Exposition. Although ostensibly a celebration of the completion of the Panama Canal, it was, in truth, an excuse for San Franciscans to show off their new city to outsiders and to stage a grand party celebrating their achievement. Over eighteen million people flocked to the "World's Fair" to see such attractions as John Philip Sousa's band and the nation's first air show. Also among the events scheduled at the Exposition during the latter part of February were the Vanderbilt Cup and Grand Prize.

Unfortunately, the decision to hold the races on the grounds of the fair, while at first blush appearing to be a marketing coup which would benefit both the races and the Exposition, reflected a problem underlying road racing in America. The simple fact was that since its high-water mark in 1911, road racing, and more importantly the number of courses available to support those races, had been on the decline. In 1911, twenty-five events had been staged in locations all across the country, from Santa Monica, California, to Tacoma, Washington, and from Savannah, Georgia, to Lowell, Massachusetts. By 1915, that number had shrunk to five, nearly all of them in California. As ovals, board tracks and speedways proliferated around the nation, courses for road racing fell by the wayside. The reasons for this phenomenon were varied, but salient features stand out. Oval tracks could be privately built and races staged without the political involvement a road race entailed. For race organizers, ovals had the advantage of being enclosed — entrance fees could be charged of everyone, not just those with seats in the grandstands, and once inside the facility crowds were easier to control. For spectators, oval track racing had advantages as well — the cars could be seen for all or a large part of each lap and the racing was truly wheel-to-wheel, without the staggered start that road racing still employed. Most significantly, there was the phenomenon of the Indianapolis 500. By staging an oval track race with a purse vastly larger than any road race, Indianapolis had quickly secured to itself a position of preeminence in American racing. While it could not boast the history of the Vanderbilt Cup or the Grand Prize, a victory in either of those races paid less than fourth-place money at the Brickyard. Ralph DePalma's victory in the 1914 Vanderbilt Cup and Eddie Pullen's win in the Grand Prize netted each of them $3,000, exclusive of contingency prizes. By comparison, when René Thomas won the Indianapolis 500 that same year, he took home nearly $40,000. The result was that European manufacturers, which had first brought teams to America for the Vanderbilt Cup and, later, the Grand Prize, now came only for Indianapolis. A similar situation existed among American marques. With only limited resources to devote to racing, any car built by an American team had to be able to compete at Indianapolis. So it was that when Stutz and Mercer had built new cars with larger engines for the 1913 season, they had both stayed within the 450-cubic inch limit imposed at the Brickyard, despite the fact that the Vanderbilt Cup limit was 600 cubic inches and the Grand Prize unlimited.

All of this is a rather roundabout way of saying that the Panama-Pacific International Exposition was a less than ideal site for the Vanderbilt Cup and Grand Prize, despite the additional crowd that the tie-in with the Exposition might generate. It merely represented the best site still extant. First off, the course, a temporary circuit that wound through the grounds and started on a boarded-over section of horse track, was less than half the length of any of its predecessors — just 3.84 miles around. With the speed of the cars, the short lap length required the organizers to employ a three-by-three starting sequence, rather than the one-by-one start of previous races. In addition, the course was tight and narrow, with six sharp turns, a carousel around the loop of the horse track, and varying road surfaces and widths, more like Monaco or one of today's street circuits than a traditional road course of the time. It offered little chance for the cars to show their speed and made passing difficult and dangerous. The circuit was such that *The New York Times*, perhaps displaying a little envy that San Francisco was now hosting the race that New York had once called its own, sniffed that the Exposition course "can hardly be considered as filling the requirements of a road race."[2] In the end, the biggest problems would be caused by the boarded-over horse track, but those problems would be of a sort that no one had foreseen. But, then, nobody knew it would rain.

If the course was less than perfect, however, the entrants for the Vanderbilt Cup and Grand Prize featured as much up-to-date machinery as any within recent memory. Despite the war in Europe that made it impossible for European factory teams to compete and precluded their design of any new machinery even if they could have done so, the Vanderbilt Cup and Grand Prize included four privately owned representatives of some of the fastest of the European marques. Most notorious of these was still Peugeot, and Dario Resta was entered in one of their 345-cubic inch, 1913 *grand prix* machines.

The twenty-five-year-old Resta had been born in Trieste, Italy, but had spent most of his life in England. Since 1912, he had been driving for Sunbeam and had met with reasonable success, setting records at Brooklands and finishing fourth, sixth, and fifth in the French *Grands Prix* of 1912, 1913 and 1914, always just behind the fastest of the cars from France or Germany. After the outbreak of hostilities, the wealthy Resta, who was married to Spencer Wishart's sister, acquired a Peugeot and came to America to continue his racing career. But despite his European record, he was unknown in the United States and largely ignored. It was a situation that seems to have bothered the swarthy, taciturn foreigner. Unfortunately, in response to his lack of name recognition, Resta maintained a demeanor that appeared aloof and snobbish. Rarely smiling, and speaking English with a clipped British accent, he was certainly "not one of the boys," as one wag put it. Throughout his racing career in America, he would always be treated as the outsider, never particularly popular with the fans or the racing fraternity.

In addition to Resta's Peugeot, two other French machines were entered, a 298-cubic inch Bugatti for John Marquis, now recovered from the injuries he suffered at Santa Monica, and a 380-cubic inch Delage, identical to the most recent Indianapolis winner, for newcomer Claude Newhouse. The fourth of the foreigners was a Mercedes, with Ralph DePalma again at the wheel. But it was not the 1914 *grand prix* machine he had used with such success at Elgin the previous August. That car was being studied by its owners at Packard as part of the development of their aero engine program. For the Vanderbilt Cup and Grand Prize, DePalma would be back at the controls of the 1913 car he had been unable to qualify at Indy. Subsequent development had rendered the big six more manageable, but it was anyone's guess how fast it would be. All that could be said was that DePalma had undoubtedly gotten everything he could from the design. After winning the Vanderbilt Cup two times running, he desperately wanted to become the race's first three-time winner. If he did so, he would take permanent possession of the Vanderbilt Cup itself, as provided for in William K. Vanderbilt, Jr.'s, original charter.

Opposing this small but potent band of European machines were no less than twenty-six American entries. Most notable of these was Stutz with its three-car team dubbed the "White Squadron." For 1915, Stutz had developed an all-new car featuring more streamlined bodywork and the latest Wisconsin engine, a 294-cubic inch, single-overhead-cam, four-valve design similar in layout to the engine in the 1914 Mercedes *grand prix* cars. Unfortunately, only one of the new cars would be available in time for the Vanderbilt Cup and Grand Prize. That car would be driven by Gil Anderson, while teammates Earl Cooper and Howdy Wilcox would still be piloting the older 434-cubic inch machines.

Mercer and Maxwell fielded three-car teams as well. Maxwell had their Harroun-designed, 445-cubic inch cars for Barney Oldfield, Eddie Rickenbacker, and Billy Carlson. Mercer entered Type 45s for Eddie Pullen and Glover Ruckstell and a still-under-development, Delling-designed, L-head-engined car for team newcomer Louis Nikrent. In addition, Duesenberg fielded a two-car team for Eddie O'Donnell and DePalma's former mechanic Tom Alley, while Case entered cars for Harry Grant and Eddie Hearne, and Chevrolet, a newcomer to big-time racing, brought cars for Cliff Durant and Jack LeCain.

But if the best of the American factory teams were out in force, much of the rest of the field was a hodgepodge quite unlike anything seen in a Vanderbilt Cup or Grand Prize before. For the first time in either race there were cars listed as "Specials," mongrel combinations of engine and chassis, many of which were modified Mercers. In addition to the five machines specifically denoted as "Specials," several more of the genre were entered. Caleb Bragg would be at the wheel of a Californian, a modified Type 45 Mercer. Hughie Hughes was entered in an Ono, in reality Teddy Tetzlaff's old chain-drive Fiat powered by a 389-cubic inch Pope-Hartford engine. Louis Disbrow would pilot a Simplex, a name that hadn't been heard in top-flight racing circles in years. But once again, it was merely the Simplex "Zip" track racer that had been built for George Robertson in 1910, the "skeleton" car now clad in streamlined bodywork with a V-shaped radiator, angular hood, and rounded tail. Once again, America could be seen moving in its own direction in the sport, with automobile manufacturers being supplanted in racing circles by smaller (some would say backyard) operations bearing no connection to the production of road-going automobiles.

Originally, the Vanderbilt Cup was scheduled for Washington's Birthday, with the Grand Prize to be run five days later on February 27, but heavy rains and freezing temperatures forced a last-minute postponement. The weather had turned the tight course into something more akin to a skating rink than a race track. Two cars crashed in practice. More than a few drivers had complained that the course was unfit even before the rains came. Now they threatened a boycott, calling the circuit "utterly dangerous" in the foul weather.[3] Reluctantly, the organizers rescheduled the Vanderbilt Cup to March 6. Unfortunately, this meant that the Grand Prize would have to be run first. It could not be delayed further because many of the teams had commitments to run in the Venice, California, Grand Prix on March 11, and again threatened to boycott both races if their travel plans were further delayed. So it was that for the first and only time in history, the Grand Prize would be run as the preliminary for the Vanderbilt Cup.

In the days leading up to the running of the Grand Prize, the skies had cleared, giving the course a chance to dry out, but the soil beneath the top layer of dirt and below the wooden planks covering the horse track was still saturated from the recent storms. No matter, the weather for race day was predicted to be sunny, ideal conditions for the cars as they wound through the avenues of multicolored exhibition buildings with their columns, minarets, and towers, their baroque and Greek-revival facades, all laid out among acres of lush semi-tropical trees and flowers. It would be like racing through some fantasy kingdom, some early day Disneyland. With hay bales piled high at the outside of the turns and the circuit lined with reinforced iron railings "for the protection of the drivers and the public," the illusion might not be complete, but if the course itself left much to be desired, the site for the race was remarkable indeed.

Starter Fred Wagner flagged the first cars away on their 104-lap, 400.28-mile journey at 10:30 a.m. sharp. From his position on the front row, Glover Ruckstell in a Type 45 Mercer took the early lead. Earl Cooper, who had started beside Ruckstell, began to fall back almost immediately, suffering from engine trouble. His Stutz would be gone from the race by lap three. Behind Ruckstell, Tom Alley's Duesenberg, Gil Anderson's Stutz, Billy Carlson's Maxwell, and Dario Resta's Peugeot fought for the top five positions. By lap five, Resta had secured second, ahead of Alley, Carlson and Anderson, but the frontrunners all remained close. On lap seven, the Peugeot took over the lead from the Mercer, even as another of the French machines, Marquis' Bugatti, succumbed to ignition failure.

By lap ten, the field had sorted itself out. The order at the front was Resta's Peugeot, followed by Ruckstell's Mercer, Alley's Duesenberg, Carlson's Maxwell, DePalma's Mercedes and Rickenbacker's Maxwell. Anderson in the new Stutz had fallen to eighth. The problem was not with his car, however; in the tight confines of the circuit he had simply gotten tied up with slower traffic. Over the next four laps, he picked off his teammate Wilcox, then Rickenbacker and DePalma to settle into fifth as the lead four maintained their positions.

Next, it was Carlson's turn to put on a burst of speed, vaulting past Alley and Ruckstell into second. Behind him, Ruckstell and Anderson were both slowed by traffic, and at lap twenty the order was Resta, Carlson, Alley, Ruckstell, Wilcox, DePalma and Anderson holding the top seven positions. Uncharacteristically, DePalma was fighting just to hold onto sixth. Despite the development work, his six-cylinder Mercedes was still proving to be a handful in the tight confines of the Exhibition course. By lap twenty-five, he had fallen to eighth as both Oldfield's Maxwell and Anderson's Stutz blasted past. The duel between the old enemies, Oldfield and DePalma, was not without incident. As Anderson again fell back and DePalma attempted to get back around Oldfield, Barney spit tobacco juice at him. A few laps later, Ralph retaliated, ramming a front wheel of his Mercedes into the Maxwell's exhaust pipe, collapsing it.

Through the first quarter of the race, the leaders had been averaging over 65 mph, despite the tight confines of the circuit. But now the rains came, only moderate at first, yet still enough to make passing even more difficult, with wheels kicking up rooster-tails of spray, fogging goggles and blinding drivers. At lap thirty, as the rain began to intensify, the order was Resta's Peugeot with a two-and-one-half-minute lead over Carlson's Maxwell. Tom Alley's Duesenberg and Glover Ruckstell's Mercer were fighting it out for third, only six seconds apart but already four and one-half minutes behind the leader. Another minute back was Wilcox's Stutz with a cushion of two minutes over Hughie Hughes' Ono and DePalma's Mercedes. Somewhat improbably, Hughes and the Ono seemed comfortable in the deteriorating conditions. The Englishman at the wheel of the ancient Fiat chassis had picked up six positions in only five laps.

On lap thirty-one, with the rain still worsening, Resta pulled his Peugeot into the pits for non-skid tires. His stop put Carlson's Maxwell in the lead by twenty-four seconds. Meanwhile, Alley and Ruckstell fell back in the increasingly difficult conditions. Further back, Oldfield, who had been losing positions since his battle with DePalma, dropped out with a burned piston. On lap thirty-five, it was Carlson still holding a slight lead on Resta's Peugeot, with Wilcox's Stutz now lying third, followed by Alley's Duesenberg, Hughes' Ono (still climbing in fifth), Ruckstell's Mercer and Disbrow's Simplex. DePalma's Mercedes, difficult to handle even in the dry and now all but impossible in the wet, had fallen to ninth as Eddie Pullen, who had had a hideous start in the other Type 45 Mercer, was finally up to eighth. At the rear of the field, Caleb Bragg's Californian, never a factor in the race, retired with a broken crankshaft.

By lap forty, the course had become saturated. Worse yet, the wooden planking on the horse track was now afloat on a soup of mud and manure. The board surface came adrift from its moorings and would rise and fall as each car passed. Some cars became airborne projectiles over the heaving surface; drivers and mechanics were pelted with the ooze that lay beneath as spurts of it shot from between the loosened boards. Conditions were atrocious. The rain had become a monsoon, with gusts of wind whipping spray everywhere. The crowd retreated to points of shelter. As the drivers attempted to navigate in these blinding conditions, Resta somehow pushed his Peugeot back past Carlson's Maxwell to take over first and open up a sixteen-second lead. Behind the lead duo, Wilcox grimly clung to third as Hughes continued his climb through the field, displacing Alley's Duesenberg for fourth. Most of the rest were just trying to hang on, sure that the race would be stopped.

Despite lying seventeenth, Eddie Rickenbacker continued on, even in the wake of a frightening spin he had had on the rain-slick course. At least his battle in the awful conditions would be short, his Maxwell stalled permanently by soaked ignition wires on lap forty-one. Others, less fortunate, continued to soldier on, but by now the Grand Prize had become more endurance trial than race. Among them, only Resta seemed unfazed by the weather. As he passed half distance, he pulled in for his scheduled pit stop. The stop again gave Carlson a slight lead, this time just seven seconds. And again, over the next five laps the Peugeot pilot methodically ran down the Maxwell to retake his place at the front.

The race was already four hours old when Resta passed the stripe for lap sixty. Behind him lay Carlson, now nearly two minutes back, with Wilcox another two minutes in arrears. A further three minutes behind was Hughes, his Ono finally among cars of equal speed in the awful conditions. Another two minutes down lay the duo of Alley and Ruckstell, now merely hanging on. But the two early frontrunners were now joined by a third as Eddie Pullen continued to spur his Mercer up the field. The ex-apprentice from Trenton was on the move, his Type 45 lying sixth.

Since lap forty, a parade of team managers had been making their way to the judge's stand to demand that the race be stopped. The conditions were too bad, they argued, the drivers simply couldn't see in the blinding spray that now hung everywhere, and the cars were nearly uncontrollable, skidding on the slick surface at the slightest provocation. It was simply too dangerous to men and machinery. Besides, they argued, it was already 2:30 p.m. and the race still had over forty laps to run. At this rate, it would be dark before the finish. There was no point in continuing. Despite the teams' demands, the organizers refused to flag the race. Upon learning of this, a whole host of racers began to withdraw. First it was Eddie Hearne on lap sixty-four. He was followed by DePalma on lap sixty-six. Pulling his Mercedes up in front of the grandstand, DePalma was deluged with questions regarding the reason for his retirement. "Nothing is wrong with my car," he said, "but the condition of the track is such that a racer is foolish to continue."[4] DePalma's retirement was followed by those of Mercer pilots Ruckstell and Pullen on laps sixty-seven and seventy-one. Despite gaining over twenty positions since his terrible start, climbing as high as fifth in the miserable conditions, and remaining one of the few drivers on the course who was still really racing, even Pullen, the reigning Grand Prize champion, saw no point in continuing.

With Pullen's withdrawal, the order at the front was Resta's Peugeot, now followed by Hughes' Ono, Wilcox's Stutz, Carlson's Maxwell, Anderson's Stutz, and Disbrow's Simplex. Carlson had begun to experience the same ignition problems that had sidelined Rickenbacker. Over the remainder of the race, he would slide back to ninth before withdrawing on lap ninety-nine. Wilcox was beset by indecision regarding tire choice. Before the race was over, he would make five stops, changing back and forth between non-skids and smooth treads. It would cost him over eleven minutes.

With Carlson and Wilcox falling back, Resta's seven-minute lead over the second-place Hughes was completely secure. For the remainder of the race, he would be in control. In fact, over the race's final thirty laps, the only real racing would be between Wilcox and Hughes, and that would degenerate into a comedy of errors. After getting past the Ono to take over second, the Stutz pilot again pulled into the pits on lap ninety-four for a final tire change, handing the position back to Hughes. With just ten laps to go, the Englishman's place looked secure, but then he ran out of gas and coasted to a stop a quarter-mile from his pit. In a flash, his mechanic was sprinting to the pits and back with a can of gasoline, but the time lost gave second back to Wilcox. At the flag, it was Resta's Peugeot the winner, nearly seven minutes ahead of Wilcox's Stutz. Hughes' Ono was third another seven minutes back, with Anderson's Stutz eight minutes further behind, and Disbrow in the Simplex "Zip" rounding out the finishers.

Resta's victory was met with a smattering of applause, but no great ovation. Most of the spectators had fled the horrible conditions. Many of those who remained were little impressed by the methodical race run by the unknown foreigner in the French machine. In truth, Resta's drive had not been spectacular. In fact, it had been rather slow — at an average speed of only 56.13 mph it was the slowest winning speed ever for a Grand Prize and faster than only George Heath's 1904 victory in the Vanderbilt Cup. And while the lack of speed had been due to the conditions and the tight confines of the course, and Resta's Peugeot had been sliding all over the road at times, in the end he had just motored away from the field, seemingly oblivious to the weather. Several self-proclaimed experts called the win a fluke. In fact, only *The New York Times* seemed willing to give the Anglo-Italian the credit he was due. Recognizing Resta's obvious skill and bravery in the hostile conditions, their correspondent minced no words. He called it "as dangerous a drive as has ever been seen in a big automobile race."[5]

22

The Most Remarkable Performance

Perhaps the best measure of how bad conditions had been for the running of the Grand Prize is demonstrated by the story of Earl Cooper. Despite lasting for only three laps in the race, the Stutz pilot had hung around the pits throughout the storm, available in case either of his teammates should need a relief driver. Weakened by the cold, wet conditions, he had contracted pneumonia. His condition was so serious that Harry Grant would take his place on the Stutz team for the March 6 running of the Vanderbilt Cup.

Other than Grant's replacement of Cooper and the addition of another "Special," one that had not made the Grand Prize and would last just fifteen laps in the Vanderbilt Cup, the fields for both races were identical. Yet remarkably few among the experts, or in the crowd of 100,000 that attended the Vanderbilt Cup, considered the combination of Dario Resta and Peugeot the favorite. Perhaps it was nationalism, perhaps it was the fact that, with the exception of the "fluke" one week previously, America's two road racing classics had been won by American drivers every year since 1908, but most in the crowd looked to DePalma's Mercedes, or Pullen's Mercer, or one of the White Squadron of Stutzes to take the victory. They were in for a shock.

The day was fair and warm as the racers gathered before a capacity crowd that filled every inch of space around the circuit. Among the assemblage was William K. Vanderbilt, Jr. Since the race that bore his name had left Long Island, Willie K. had had little involvement. But today he was seated in a box in the grandstand, rubbing elbows with San Francisco's politically important and ready to personally present the Vanderbilt Cup to Ralph DePalma should the Brooklyn Italian attain a third successive victory. As in 1904, the starting ceremonies were marred by an interruption as a top-hatted spectator wandered onto the course. At Fred Wagner's signal, armed guards manhandled the intruder and began to hustle him off the track until they realized who he was — San Francisco's Mayor Rolf, belatedly looking to join Governor Johnson in the official box.

The interruption in the ceremonies quickly quelled, the racers got away on their seventy-seven lap, 296.3-mile quest just one minute late, at 12:31 p.m., as Wagner sent off the first three — DePalma's Mercedes, Durant's Chevrolet, and Resta's Peugeot. Row by row, the remainder roared away at fifteen-second intervals. No sooner had the last of them departed than the leaders could be heard approaching: the little circuit was literally awash in a swarm of speeding, brightly colored machines. Cars cut and thrust, jockeying for position everywhere. The scoreboard had Rickenbacker's Maxwell in the lead, but behind him the order changed moment to moment. It was not until lap five that the field began to sort itself out. Rickenbacker was still leading, but behind him Pullen's Mercer, Oldfield's Maxwell, Resta's Peugeot, DePalma's Mercedes, Disbrow's Simplex, Ruckstell's Mercer, Burman's Case, Carlson's Maxwell, and Bragg's Californian were all within seconds of each other. Missing from the mix were the Duesenberg and Stutz contingents, however. Eddie O'Donnell in the best placed of the Duesenbergs was no better than eleventh, with teammate Alley back in twenty-fourth. The Stutz trio had fared even worse at the start, with Howdy Wilcox leading the team in fourteenth and Grant and Anderson mired back in twenty-third and twenty-ninth.

Rickenbacker's early speed had been spectacular, but it would not last. As Resta pushed his Peugeot toward the front, a ruptured fuel line put the Maxwell on the sidelines. At the same time, Louis Disbrow and Bob Burman began putting on speed as Wilcox's Stutz and O'Donnell's Duesenberg climbed through the pack from their dismal starts. At the ten-lap mark, it was Resta leading, followed by Pullen's Mercer, Disbrow's Simplex, Oldfield's Maxwell, Burman's Case, Ruckstell's Mercer, DePalma's Mercedes, and Carlson's Maxwell, with Wilcox and O'Donnell rounding out the top ten.

Over the next five laps, Wilcox continued his climb through the field as DePalma fell back to ninth. As it had in the Grand Prize, the Mercedes was proving to be a handful, especially through the tight corners of the Exposition circuit. The board portion of the track had dried and been repaired, but by now oil thrown from the cars had the planking as treacherous as it had been in the wet. But as DePalma clung grimly to his spot in the pack, it was Carlson and then Burman who put on the show, the Maxwell pilot picking up two spots to take over fifth, while Wild Bob blasted his Case past Oldfield to land in third as Disbrow pulled his Simplex into the pits, giving up three positions. On lap twenty, the order was Resta, still in the lead, followed by Pullen's Mercer, Burman's Case, the Maxwells of Oldfield and Carlson, Disbrow's Simplex, Wilcox's Stutz, Ruckstell's Mercer, DePalma's Mercedes and O'Donnell's Duesenberg.

Like Disbrow, Ruckstell had pitted before lap twenty, giving up two positions in the process. Now it was Pullen's turn to pit. His stop dropped him from second back to sixth, where he tucked in just behind Ruckstell. But even Pullen's pit stop was better than Barney Oldfield's. Problems with the Maxwell dropped him from fourth to thirteenth. For the rest of the day he would be mired well back in the pack. By lap twenty-five, Resta's lead over Burman's second-place Case stood at 1:36. Another minute back, Disbrow, again on the charge, and Carlson, fighting vainly to hold off the Simplex, waged a battle for third with only eight seconds separating them. Thirty seconds further down came the Mercers of Ruckstell and Pullen, with Wilcox's Stutz only four seconds behind. Then it was another minute to DePalma's Mercedes, followed by the Duesenbergs of Alley and O'Donnell, each some twenty seconds further in arrears. The racing among most of the leaders was close, with knots of cars fighting for position, but alone at the front the blue Peugeot with the Anglo-Italian at the wheel motored on, simply too much for his American competitors to handle.

His pit stop completed, it was now Pullen's turn to make a rush through the field. By lap thirty, he had powered his Mercer past his teammate, Carlson's Maxwell and Disbrow's Simplex to take over third. As he did so, Disbrow again made a call at the pits, dropping five places in the process. Next it was Alley, finding more speed in the Duesenberg than it had shown all day. From ninth, DePalma's ex-mechanic strong-armed his way past his old boss' Mercedes and Disbrow's Simplex. The pace proved too much for the Duesie, however. No sooner had he taken over seventh than he began to fall back. He would retire on lap forty-one with broken steering.

Despite the tight confines of the course and the dangerous conditions in which the Grand Prize had been run, neither race had been marred by any serious incident. All that was about to change. On lap forty, "Cap" Kennedy's Edwards Special, running back in twenty-first, threw a wheel into the crowd. It hit a spectator, knocking him unconscious. Three laps later, Bob Burman, vainly trying to close the gap between his Case and Resta's Peugeot, got a little too wild at the turn near the Palace of Machinery. The Case rolled. Burman and mechanic Joe Cleary were both knocked unconscious. While Wild Bob's injuries would prove not to be serious, Cleary wasn't so lucky. He would survive, but he had taken quite a beating: two broken legs, a broken shoulder and two broken ribs.

With Burman's crash, Eddie Pullen again lay second, but by now the leader had a lap on the field. Pullen spurred his Mercer for all it was worth to get past the blue car and un-lap himself, but it was all he could do. After letting Pullen past, Resta merely tucked his Peugeot to the Mercer's tail and rode that way, safe and secure with all of the field save one a lap down and his only competition within sight. Behind the frontrunners, now running in inverse order on the track (and confusing some fans in the process), Ruckstell pushed his Type 45 past Wilcox's Stutz and Carlson's Maxwell into third. On this day, the Mercers looked to be the class of the American contingent, but not even they could match the speed and handling of the French machine. Resta and the Peugeot were simply in a league all their own.

By lap fifty, Resta had again passed Pullen to put the entire field a lap down and had opened up a gap of five minutes over the second-place Mercer. Ruckstell, another ninety seconds back, nursed an eleven-second lead over Carlson's Maxwell. The rest, Wilcox, DePalma, Disbrow, and O'Donnell, now joined by Grant's Stutz and Newhouse's Delage, were all minutes further behind. Little would change without mechanical casualties, but they would come quickly. On lap fifty-four, O'Donnell's Duesenberg succumbed to broken steering, like his teammate's. Harry Grant, making a routine pit stop, had his day ended when a pit worker poured water in his Stutz' fuel tank. Billy Carlson's stop went more smoothly, but it cost the Maxwell pilot three positions and put an end to the battle with Ruckstell's Mercer, the only close racing anywhere near the front.

For the next eighteen laps, the race was little more than a procession, broken only by another push by Louis Disbrow past DePalma's Mercedes to take over fifth, and another inevitable pit stop, dropping the Simplex back to ninth. Then, with just five laps remaining, the Mercer team ran into bad luck as only the Mercer team could. First Ruckstell hit a curb in front of the Massachusetts Building and broke an axle on his Type 45. Three laps later, Pullen was forced to pit. His gas tank had broken loose from its mounts, a result of the incessant pounding over the boards. Quick work by his crew would salvage third for the Trenton boys, but it was a bitter third indeed. Not only had the Mercers had nothing for Resta's Peugeot, they had been snaked out of second in the end by Howdy

Dario Resta, seen here at the wheel of his Peugeot in 1915, never garnered much support from the American fans despite his Vanderbilt Cup and Grand Prize victories (IMS Photo).

Wilcox's Stutz. Rounding out the field behind Resta, Wilcox and Pullen were DePalma, Carlson, and Newhouse, with Barney Oldfield finally climbing into seventh after spending most of the day in mid-pack. The last of the finishers, in eighth place, was Louis Disbrow's Simplex, a full twenty-six minutes back of the winner.

Resta's victory should have been met with an ovation like no other. After all, he had done what no man in history had ever done before, won the Vanderbilt Cup and Grand Prize back to back. But the crowd, while more jubilant than those that had greeted his Grand Prize victory, was still strangely subdued. They just couldn't seem to work up much enthusiasm for the foreigner in the French blue machine. Perhaps only *The New York Times*, in Resta's corner all along, could accurately put the race in perspective. "Resta's feat," their correspondent wrote, "in winning the two big races in eight days is one of the most remarkable performances in the history of automobile racing."[1]

It certainly was — and Dario Resta wasn't done yet.

23

The World's Best Race

On May 7, 1915, twenty-two days before the scheduled running of the fifth Indianapolis 500, the British ocean liner *Lusitania*, making its way from New York to Southampton, was torpedoed and sunk by a German U-boat off the coast of Ireland. Among the 1,198 passengers and crew killed in the attack were 128 Americans. And although the German government claimed that the sinking was justified, inasmuch as the *Lusitania* had been secretly carrying munitions, the American people weren't buying it. Public opinion was shifting toward war. Everywhere you looked the word was "preparedness."

❖ ❖ ❖

For 1915, Indianapolis issued regulations limiting engine size to 300 cubic inches. The new rules made virtually all existing American machinery immediately obsolete. European *grand prix* machines, which had been running under a 4.5-liter (274.5 cubic inch) formula since 1914, suffered no such handicap. After two straight wins at the Brickyard, the French cars were again considered the favorites, but that is not to say they were without competition. Three Peugeots were entered, two by their American importer, a 1914 *grand prix* car for Dario Resta and a "Baby" Peugeot for George Babcock. A third privately owned, and much modified, machine would be driven by Bob Burman. The flight of Peugeots was joined by single, privately owned entries from Bugatti, with George Hill at the wheel, and Delage, with John DePalma, Ralph's brother, manning the controls.

But France wasn't the only European nation with cars in the race. Britain was represented by a trio of Sunbeams. Like Peugeot, two of their numbers were entered by their American importer for drivers Noel Van Raalte and Jean Porporato, while a third privately owned car would be driven by Harry Grant. But the car that looked most likely to give the Peugeots trouble was the one from Germany. Ralph DePalma was back at the wheel of a Mercedes — and not the experimental nightmare from San Francisco. Instead, it was the E. C. Patterson-owned, 1914 *grand prix* car he had driven to back-to-back wins at Elgin the previous August.

Opposing these nine foreigners were fifteen Americans, headed by full three-car teams from Duesenberg, Maxwell and Stutz. Ralph Mulford joined stalwarts Eddie O'Donnell and Tom Alley at the wheel of the Duesies, while Tom Orr was added to the Maxwell team of Billy Carlson and Eddie Rickenbacker. The White Squadron Stutz team was the same that had started the year, with Gil Anderson, Howdy Wilcox, and the now-healthy Earl Cooper at the controls. This time, however, they would all have the new cars with the streamlined bodywork and overhead-cam engines. New cars were all well and good, but given Anderson's rather disappointing showing in San Francisco, there were those in the crowd who speculated that they might not be much of an asset.

Missing from the list of starters was Mercer. Such a state of affairs was particularly surprising in light of the new regulations mandating the reduction in engine size. After all, the 300-cubic inch engine had been a Mercer specialty in its early days of competition. But technology had moved on and left Mercer behind. Initially, the team had entered three of its L-head-powered cars for Eddie Pullen, Glover Ruckstell and Louis Nikrent. In practice, all three had set lap times that would have made the field easily, but just five days before the race Erik Delling announced their withdrawal. He cited weather problems that had limited the team's ability to tune and prepare the machines for a five-hundred-mile run, but the rumor among insiders was that the Delling-designed engine had reliability problems in sustained high-speed runs. Whether true or not, the team from

Now recovered from the bout of pneumonia that kept him out of the Vanderbilt Cup, Earl Cooper provides a photo opportunity in his White Squadron Stutz prior to the 1915 Indianapolis 500. Fastest of the American entries in the race, the White Squadron still could not match the speed of DePalma's Mercedes or Resta's Peugeot. At the finish, Anderson and Cooper would be credited with third and fourth, respectively (IMS Photo).

Trenton bid adieu to the Brickyard. After taking part in every race since the 1911 inaugural and finishing eleventh, third and second in the first three 500s, Mercer would never race at Indianapolis again.

For the first time at Indy, qualifying speeds were used to determine starting positions, giving these solo laps a new level of importance. To no one's surprise, Resta's Peugeot was fast, setting third-quickest time at 98.47 mph. Oddly, neither teammate George Babcock nor even Bob Burman was anywhere close. Burman's best was only 92.40 mph, good for seventh spot, and Babcock, in the "Baby" Peugeot, couldn't even crack ninety. He would start back in twelfth. The other French machines, Hill's Bugatti and John DePalma's Delage, fared even worse, placing twenty-second and thirteenth on the grid. If a blue car was destined to reach victory lane for a third straight year, it seemed sure to be Resta's Peugeot and none other.

But if most of the French cars were having their problems in getting up to speed, so too were the British Sunbeams. Both Harry Grant and Noel Van Raalte turned in sub-ninety speeds. They would start no better than tenth and fourteenth. Only Jean Porporato could come up with a quick lap. His 94.74 mph was good for sixth starting position. But faster than either the French or British machines was the lone German entry. To no one's surprise, DePalma's Mercedes cracked the whip an eye-blink quicker than Resta's best time. His 98.58 mph netted him second place.

So if the pole hadn't been won by Resta's Peugeot, or DePalma's Mercedes, then just who had taken it? It wasn't a Duesenberg; only Tom Alley had broken ninety, and he just barely. In fact, Art Klein in a privately owned Duesie had bested the factory trio with a lap at 90.45 mph, good for eighth. Nor was it a Maxwell; Billy Carlson's sixteenth-best 84.11 mph was the most they could do. To the surprise of many, it was the White Squadron's Howdy Wilcox. He had blasted the oval within a whisker of the century mark at 98.90 mph. His Stutz teammates were not far behind. Earl Cooper had posted a fourth-fastest 96.77 mph, while Gil Anderson was fifth-best at 95.14 mph. Obviously, Harry Stutz and his boys had used the time between March and Memorial Day to advantage. The new car that had had such an inauspicious debut at San Francisco was now strong and well-sorted.

The White Squadron's performance left the odds-makers in somewhat of a quandary. It had been difficult enough to pick a favorite between DePalma's Mercedes and Resta's Peugeot. True, the German machine had bested its French rival in their *Grand Prix* debut, but that could be put down to team tactics more than any significant advantage in speed. Moreover, the Peugeot's strengths, particularly its higher top speed, looked to be more of an asset at the Brickyard than it had been at Lyons. Nor was there much to choose between the drivers. While DePalma was widely considered the world's finest driver, Resta's unprecedented victories in the Vanderbilt Cup and Grand Prize could not be ignored. Even in the department of "speedway experience," the match-up looked fairly close. While DePalma had three "500s" on his résumé, Resta had considerable experience at the even faster oval at Brooklands. The argument could be made either way.

And now the Stutz team's performance in qualifying had added a new dimension to the mix. If anything, the American machines looked slightly faster than their European counterparts. And while Anderson, Wilcox and Cooper could not boast the record of a DePalma or a Resta, they had numbers on their side, much as Mercedes had had at Lyons. It could prove to be a significant asset in a race of 500 miles.

The race was originally scheduled for Saturday, May 29, but inclement weather forced its postponement to Monday. Race day dawned little better, with cold temperatures and a sky threatening rain. A "Scotch mist," one scribe called it. The chill conditions coupled with the postponement of the race kept the crowd down to 75,000, and those who did come were bundled in overcoats and winter wraps, but the rain that had threatened would never materialize. In the end, the conditions would prove ideal for power and speed.

As in years past, Speedway owner Carl Fisher led the pace lap, and at 10:00 a.m. sharp starter Tom Hay flagged away the twenty-four machines. Quickly to the front from his spot near the outside of row one was Resta's Peugeot, closely followed by DePalma's Mercedes and the Stutzes of Anderson and Wilcox. But the American team would waste little time in overtaking their European rivals. On lap two Wilcox, the fastest of the White Squadron, wrested the lead from Resta. He, in turn, was supplanted at the front by Anderson five laps later.

The Squadron leader's Stutz was simply flying. Lapping at over 90 mph, by the thirty-mile mark he had a full straightaway lead on the field. The White Squadron had adopted the tactics used to such advantage by Mercedes at Lyons. Anderson had been designated the rabbit. His job was to force Resta and DePalma to overtax their machines giving chase, while Wilcox and Cooper waited just behind, ready to use their numerical advantage to pounce when the time was ripe. There was only one problem. DePalma and Resta were both veterans of European racing. They had seen such tactics before and refused to play into the White Squadron's hand. Instead, they let Anderson's Stutz pull away at its murderous pace, sure in the knowledge that worn tires or mechanical problems would soon bring it back to the field.

Fifty miles into the race, Anderson was nearly a full lap in front, but already his speed was slackening somewhat, his average now 89.91 mph. Behind him, the tight knot formed by Resta's Peugeot, DePalma's Mercedes and the Stutzes of Wilcox and Cooper was joined by Porporato's Sunbeam. The top six qualifiers now occupied the top six positions; the cream was indeed coming to the top. Then on lap thirty-three the inevitable happened: Anderson's Stutz pulled into the pits. The killing pace had shredded its tires. With the stop, Resta's Peugeot took over the lead, but the blue car had company. DePalma's Mercedes was pushing it hard, while Wilcox's Stutz lay just behind in third.

Seven laps later, the first of the leaders fell victim to mechanical woes, but it wasn't the Peugeot or Mercedes, the intended victims of the White Squadron's strategy. It was one of the Squadron's own. Howdy Wilcox's Stutz dropped a cylinder. Despite running on only three for the remaining four hundred miles, the Stutz would finish seventh, but its day as a threat to the leaders was over. Still, no sooner had Wilcox dropped back than his teammates, Anderson and Cooper, took up the chase. Stutz might have lost its fastest entry, but its remaining two were right in the thick of it.

A blue car at the front of a race was an all too familiar phenomenon to the Indianapolis fans. It was one they had seen far too often in recent years. And worse yet, it seemed that once a blue car took over, it inevitably motored away from the field. This time it would be different. Resta found himself unable to open a gap on DePalma. Instead, the Mercedes was closing, making up more ground in the turns than the Peugeot, with its superior top speed, could offset on the straights. For eighteen laps, the white German car hounded the French blue machine, closing the gap down to nothing in the corners,

Dario Resta in his Peugeot prior to the 1915 Indianapolis 500. After winning the Vanderbilt Cup and Grand Prize, he had to be considered the favorite. In the race, Resta's Peugeot and DePalma's Mercedes were the class of the field, putting on a remarkable show, with first one and then the other in the lead (IMS Photo).

tucking in behind down the straights. On the nineteenth lap, DePalma shouldered his way past Resta's Peugeot and began opening a lead of his own. For the first time since the Gallic return to American racing in 1913, a non–French machine had actually run down one of the blue cars to take over a race. The crowd went wild. DePalma, always a crowd favorite, was clearly their man, even if he was driving a car created by the now-hated Germans.

At half-distance, DePalma still led, but the gap over Resta had stopped growing. The two leaders, who had refused to chase Anderson's Stutz early on, were now both flat out in their duel with each other. By lap 120, DePalma had again raised the race average to over 90 mph, and Resta was just a few yards behind. The Stutzes of Anderson and Cooper were still third and fourth, but by now they were a lap in arrears. Barring accident or mechanical failure, it was a two-man race — with two hundred miles to go.

Behind the leaders, the attrition had started in earnest, the high-speed chase too much for many. On lap 111, Klein's Duesenberg had blown up spectacularly, leaving a fog worthy of London hanging over the track. Six laps later it was Babcock's "Baby" Peugeot, a cylinder cracked from the strain. Seven laps further on it was Mulford's Duesenberg snapping a connecting rod. One by one they fell out, their engines exploding like grenades. Yet still at the front, the leaders kept charging, DePalma still trying to open the gap, Resta still trying to close it. The White Squadron Stutzes of Anderson and Cooper now circled the track like two vultures, waiting for the leaders to blow up.

On lap 128, the Mercedes pulled into the pits. The stop was routine: four tires, gas, oil and water. But before DePalma could get back on the track, Resta's Peugeot had opened a sizeable lead. Their positions now reversed, it was DePalma trying to run down the blue car and Resta trying to hold off the white one. And it was here, finally, that the crowd would witness the incredible speed of the Mercedes in the hands of a driver like DePalma. Lap by lap, the master closed the gap on his rival, speeding down the straights, drifting through the turns without lifting, swallowing precious distance in huge chunks. In front of him, Resta was pushing the Peugeot for all it was worth, pouring on the power, sliding within inches of the wall in the turns. Still, it was to no avail. The Mercedes closed the gap inexorably. Within five laps, the white car sat square on the tail of the blue one, like a cat all too ready to pounce. Searching for more speed, Resta pushed even harder — too hard. The Peugeot slid wide to the wall in Turn Four, scuffing its tires on the concrete. The right rear blew and it spun. In a flash, DePalma was past, as Resta guided his mount to the pits for replacements.

The stop was a quick one, but it still gave DePalma a lead of nearly a lap. Once again, it was Resta in the role of pursuer, but this time there was just too much ground to make up and the contact with the wall had damaged the Peugeot's steering. Still, he fought gamely, narrowing the gap to three-quarters of a lap by the four-hundred-mile mark. It was as close as he would get. Unable to catch the flying Mercedes in the few miles remaining, and with the Stutzes of Anderson and Cooper now a full three laps back, he put the Peugeot on cruise control, holding his position and hoping for disaster to again befall DePalma.

Ralph DePalma in the Patterson Mercedes, the 1914 *Grand Prix* car that would take him to victory in the 1915 Indianapolis 500 (IMS Photo).

Resta's prayers went unanswered until lap 197. Then the specter of DePalma's 1912 heartbreak again surfaced to plague him. Almost unimaginably, the Mercedes began to falter, its engine running on only three cylinders. Post-race inspection would reveal two holes in the crankcase where a broken connecting rod had punched through. The fans in the stands let out a huge groan. It seemed impossible, but maybe DePalma was truly jinxed. Maybe he just couldn't win at the Brickyard.

But this year there would be no ominous silence from the backstretch. The German machine, although crippled, would keep running somehow. And as the laps finally unwound to 200 and DePalma took the flag, the crowd was on its feet cheering wildly. After crossing the stripe, he drove straight to his garage, locking it behind his broken white racer. But the throng that pursued him would not be denied a glimpse of their champion. They burst open the doors and engulfed the garage, demanding a speech from their hero. Exhausted after over five hours at the wheel and three laps of nursing his crippled machine, the first words DePalma could think of were in praise of his mechanic. He was as much a gentleman in victory as he had been in defeat three years before. The crowd loved it.

In the end, DePalma's margin of victory had been over two laps. His time, 5:33:55.5, was good for an average speed of 89.84 mph, shattering René Thomas' year-old race record by over 7 mph, a huge margin, particularly since it had been accomplished with an engine just two-thirds the size. Resta's second-place time was 5:37:24.9, just under three and one-half minutes back, with the Stutzes of Anderson and Cooper another five minutes in arrears. In fact, the pace had been so fast that the top four had all finished under Thomas' old record. Rounding out the paying positions were O'Donnell's Duesenberg in fifth; Burman's Peugeot sixth; Wilcox's wounded Stutz seventh; Alley's Duesenberg eighth; Carlson's Maxwell ninth; and Van Raalte's Sunbeam tenth.

The experts opined that the incredible speed of the race had been due to the chilly conditions, which had helped to save tires and to keep engines cool. Citing the cooperative weather, they speculated that the record was one that would not be broken anytime soon. But no one was discounting the magnificent performance put on by DePalma. While the weather and the white machine may have conspired to give him a fast track to run on and a fast horse to ride, there was no mistaking the bravery and skill that went into the feat. *The New York Times* put it all quite succinctly in their headline: "DePalma Drives World's Best Race."[1]

24

Dago Luck Revisited

By 1916, the war in Europe had taken a horrible turn, the possibility of which no one had foreseen just eighteen months before. In February, the German high command, in a stroke of hideous lunacy, embarked on an offensive aimed at the fortress city of Verdun. The attack was not designed to break the formidable French lines in the area, nor to bring victory to Germany or an end to the war, but rather to bog the French forces down in an unwinnable battle from which they could not retreat. As one German general put it, "We'll bleed France white." Unable to devise a strategy to break the stalemate on the Western Front, the high command on both sides now resorted to a "war of attrition," the idea being not to gain territory or to bring about victory, but to kill or maim so many of your enemy that they could not be replaced — and to hope that the last man left standing was one of your own. One French lieutenant, with a clearer understanding of the situation than most, wrote in his diary, "Humanity ... must be mad to do what it is doing."[1]

An ocean away from the horrors of Verdun and the Somme — an equally futile and bloody offensive undertaken by the British — the United States military, after a year of "preparedness," found itself all dressed up with no place to go. By no means were America's armed forces ready to join in the conflict in Europe; they would remain far from ready until months after war was finally declared in April 1917. But the focus on military readiness seems to have provoked an urge to put American forces to the test — a trial run, so to speak, to see what they could do. A perfect candidate for such a test was the Dominican Republic. It had been crippled by an unstable government and successive revolutions for a decade or more. In fact, it was little more than an American protectorate. The United States was its only foreign creditor and had run its customs operations since 1905. Determined to restore order and to protect American political and economic interests from the most recent revolt, President Wilson ordered in the Marines. Unfortunately, no sooner had they landed than President Juan Isidro Jimenez, the very person whom the Marines had come to protect, resigned in protest, thus putting the United States in the somewhat awkward position of having invaded a friendly nation and deposed its elected leader.

Undaunted, the American invasion would lead to an occupation of the country that would last until 1924.

While the Marines were invading and occupying the Dominican Republic, the United States Army was embarking on an invasion of its own. In the early morning hours of March 9, 1916, the Mexican revolutionary Francisco "Pancho" Villa had led his band of guerrillas on a raid on Columbus, New Mexico. To this day, no one is quite sure why. Some speculate that the raid was motivated by revenge against an American arms dealer in the town who had taken Villa's money for weapons and then refused to deliver. Others claim that the raid was calculated to involve the United States in the Mexican civil war (although why Villa would want the United States allied with the Mexican government against him is something that is rather difficult to fathom). In any event, the raid, although a military defeat for Villa, who lost over 100 of his men, resulted in a call for American retaliation. General John "Black Jack" Pershing, in command of a force of 12,000 men, was ordered to conduct a punitive expedition into Mexico to kill or capture Villa. Among his troops was Vanderbilt Cup winner George Robertson, now an Army captain. Unfortunately, after wandering over most of Mexico for nearly a year, Pershing would be unable even to find the elusive "bandit," let alone capture or kill him. In the face of rising Mexican resentment, President Wilson would order the expedition home.

But if war and other lesser armed conflicts were filling the front pages of the newspapers in 1916, other significant events were happening as well. At his garden in Giverny, France, little more than one hundred miles from the no-man's land of the Western Front, artist Claude Monet, the man whose 1873 painting, *Impression, Sunrise*, had given the Impressionist movement its name, began work on the project that would consume much of the last ten years of his life. His *Waterlilies*, a series of monumental paintings depicting the subject at different times of day and under different light conditions, would later be called "the Sistine Chapel of Impressionism."[2]

Eleven years after the publication of his special theory of relativity, in which he described what we now call the space-time continuum, Albert Einstein published his general theory of relativity, in which he established and quantified the relationship between matter and energy. In doing so, he would give us the twentieth century's most famous scientific formula: $E=MC^2$.

Perhaps less significant than great art or monumental science, but equally important in transforming the world into one we would recognize today, was the second Rose Bowl, held in Pasadena, California, after a fourteen-year suspension in the wake of its 1902 debut. So began an annual tradition for this oldest of football classics that continues to this day. Washington State defeated Brown 14–0. Elsewhere, America was introduced to windshield wipers, Keds sneakers, Lincoln Logs, and lipstick in metal tubes.

❖ ❖ ❖

In 1916, the Vanderbilt Cup and Grand Prize were returned to the autumn dates they had enjoyed until 1914. That made the Indianapolis 500 the first of the crown jewels of American racing on the calendar. But even as Indy's star was rising and those of the older duo were on the wane, 1916 would be a far from stellar year at the Brickyard. It would prove even more fateful for the two older races, but those events still lay some months in the future.

The problem was one of participation. The 1916 Indianapolis "500," still so named although it had been shortened to 300 miles for 1916, in part a reflection of management concerns over the quality of the machinery, would be as much remembered for the cars and drivers that did *not* take part as it would for its winner. Most glaring of the absences was that of the White Squadron from Stutz. In the wake of their second-place finishes in the 1915 Grand Prize and Vanderbilt Cup, and their third- and fourth-place finishes at Indianapolis, the team had been hugely successful over the remainder of the previous season. At Elgin in August, Earl Cooper and Gil Anderson had finished first and second, ahead of Barney Oldfield's Delage, in the 301-mile Chicago Automobile Club Trophy Race. They had followed that up with another one-two finish, this time with the order reversed, in the National Trophy, where they beat out Eddie O'Donnell's Duesenberg and DePalma's Mercedes. In early September, Earl Cooper headed another Stutz one-two finish in the 500-mile race at the new concrete track at Minneapolis owned by former Indianapolis co-owner Frank Wheeler. Then in October, at the two-mile, board speed-bowl at Sheepshead Bay, Long Island, White Squadron members Gil Anderson and Tom Rooney had come home first and second again in the inaugural running of the 350-mile Astor Cup. Anderson's victory there at an average speed of 102.56 mph had set a world record for the distance.

But there would be no Stutz cars at Indianapolis in 1916. In the wake of their 1915 successes, the decision had been made to curtail the racing program. In the mind of Harry Stutz it had simply become too expensive, and the public's perception of Stutz as a winner was now secure. Like Locomobile, Alco and Lozier before it, Stutz saw no point in continuing to devote huge sums of money to racing when the team had been visited with considerable success. Moreover, Harry Stutz had other concerns. Since mid-1915 demand for Stutz' road cars had far outstripped supply. Stutz was now in the middle of a refinancing plan to permit further expansion. By June, the Stutz Motor Car Company of America would be formed to acquire the Stutz Motor Car Company of Indiana. Harry Stutz would remain president, financial wizard Alan A. Ryan would become vice-president, but most significantly, the new company's stock would be publicly traded. The sale of stock would give Stutz the capital it needed, but it would also weaken Harry Stutz' control of the company.

If Stutz, like Mercer, was now gone from Indianapolis, the fortunes of the other American mainstays of racing's second decade, Duesenberg and Maxwell, appeared to be on the wane as well. Duesenberg entered a three-car team, but could qualify only two. Then Eddie O'Donnell's car broke, leaving the factory with but a single car for Wilbur D'Alene, augmented by a privately owned Duesie entered for Tom Alley. Two Maxwells were entered for Eddie Rickenbacker and Pete Henderson, but both of them were running under Carl Fisher's and James Allison's Prest-O-Lite Racing banner.

Chief among the missing drivers was Ralph DePalma, the victim of a power play by speedway president Carl Fisher. As the reigning champion, DePalma had demanded $5,000 in appearance money and threatened to hold out when his demand was refused. Fisher became furious. DePalma backed off from his demand a couple of days after the deadline for entries and submitted his forms, but Fisher refused to accept them. It would be 1919 before DePalma would compete at Indianapolis again.

But DePalma's was not the only famous face absent from the ranks of competitors. Grand Prize winners Caleb Bragg and Eddie Pullen were missing as well. So too were crowd favorite "Wild" Bob Burman, killed (along with mechanic Eric Schroeder) in a

Top: Wilbur D'Alene's Duesenberg, the factory's sole entry in the 1916 Indianapolis 500, was fast enough to finish second to Dario Resta's Peugeot, but at the checker he was over a lap in arrears (IMS Photo). *Bottom*: The Prest-O-Lite team at Indianapolis in 1916, featuring Eddie Rickenbacker and Pete Henderson (IMS Photo).

crash at Corona in April when the wheel of his Peugeot collapsed as he chased down Eddie O'Donnell's Duesenberg for the lead, and that old master of pace, Harry Grant, dead of injuries suffered at Sheepshead Bay the previous September. In fact, of the twenty-one cars to start the 500 in this smallest-ever field, eight would be piloted by "rookies." No former winners would be represented, and only the Peugeots of Dario Resta and Ralph Mulford would be piloted by drivers with a Vanderbilt Cup or Grand Prize win on their résumé. The main problem was the scarcity of first-class machinery and car owners willing to put up the money for an effort at Indianapolis. The situation was so acute that the Indianapolis Motor Speedway had fielded two teams of its own — a two-car team of Peugeots for Charlie Merz and Johnny Aitken, and a three-car team of Premiers for the old White Squadron, Gil Anderson, Howdy Wilcox and Tom Rooney.

On a brighter note, the Chevrolet brothers, Louis, Arthur and Gaston, had entered three of their new Frontenacs. Louis, now divorced from his alliance with General Motors founder William C. Durant, and the production of the car bearing his name, had decided to go back into racing in a car of his own. Over the next decade, Frontenacs in the hands of the Chevrolets and others would populate the tracks of America. At Indianapolis, only Louis and Arthur would qualify, but at least their entry signaled some new blood on American racing's horizon.

The field pitted eight foreign entries against thirteen Americans. Most feared among the foreigners, of course, were the Peugeots, but two Delages had also been entered, one by Barney Oldfield for himself, and a second by Harry Harkness for Jules DeVigne. Of lesser concern to the experts were the Sunbeam entered for Belgian Josef Christiaens and the Sunbeam-powered Peugeot entered and driven by Aldo Franchi. On the American side, the fastest of the cars looked to be the Maxwells and Duesenbergs, with the Premiers and Frontenacs remaining unknown quantities. Also unknown, but given serious consideration because of their Duesenberg power, were the three Crawford-Duesenbergs entered by Billy Chandler for himself, Art Johnson and Dave Lewis. Still, in the eyes of the experts, the class of the field were the Peugeots, and the class of the Peugeots was Resta's.

In qualifying, now on a best-lap-of-three format, the Peugeots didn't disappoint, but the particular Peugeot that took home the pole was a bit of a surprise. It was Johnny Aitken, not Dario Resta, who

Indianapolis Motor Speedway President Carl Fisher was not a man to be trifled with. Ralph DePalma discovered that fact in 1916, after demanding $5,000 in appearance money from Fisher in the wake of his victory in the 1915 500. Not only was his demand rejected, he found himself a spectator for the race when Fisher refused to accept his belated entry forms (IMS Photo).

New for 1916 was the Frontenac, designed and built by the Chevrolet brothers, Louis, Arthur and Gaston. Only Louis and Arthur would qualify for the Indianapolis 500, and neither would be a factor in the race, but over the next decade Frontenacs would be a mainstay of American racing (IMS Photo).

set fastest time at 96.69 mph. Alongside him on the four-wide front row would be Eddie Rickenbacker's Maxwell with a speed of 96.44 mph, Gil Anderson's Premier at 95.94 mph, and, surprisingly, Resta, his qualifying speed a fourth-best 94.40 mph. Row two would find Oldfield's Delage (94.33 mph) flanked by Wilcox's Premier (93.81 mph), Rooney's Premier (93.39 mph), and Merz' Peugeot (93.33 mph), with Henderson's Maxwell (91.33 mph) and the fastest of the Duesenbergs, Wilbur D'Alene's (90.87 mph), rounding out the top ten on row three. The other Duesies, both Alley's and the three Crawford-Duesenbergs, were mired well back in fifteenth or below. Also missing from the mix at the front was Ralph Mulford. It wasn't that his Peugeot wasn't fast; it was just that he had set his time late, on the day before the race. Under Indy's rules, his tardiness would put him at the back of the pack. Despite his 91.09 mph speed, he would start twentieth, right next to Louis Chevrolet's Frontenac.

Intermittent rain in the days before the race had washed down the track and turned the infield to mud, but on race day a bright sun beamed down, drying puddles and firming the ground. A crowd of 90,000 filled the stands to witness this late-starting shortened version of the 500. With Frank E. Smith at the wheel of the pace car, the racers were off

Barney Oldfield campaigned a Delage at the 1916 Indianapolis 500. He was fifth fastest in qualifying, and started inside on row two, but he would never be a factor in the race (IMS Photo).

at 1:30 p.m. on the first of their 120 laps. From the middle of the front row, Eddie Rickenbacker's Maxwell jumped to the early lead, with Johnny Aitken's Peugeot holding down second and Dario Resta snaking his way under Gil Anderson's Premier for third.

The opening laps were all Rickenbacker. By lap eight he had a full straightaway on Aitken. Unfortunately, it wouldn't last. One lap later, the Maxwell was sidelined with damaged steering. Still, the early leader would not finish last; Aldo Franchi's Peugeot-Sunbeam was already parked, a blown engine ending its day. Rickenbacker's retirement handed the lead to Aitken's Peugeot, and the pole-sitter continued to hold it for a time, but on lap seventeen a shredded right rear tire forced him into the pits, passing the baton to Resta's Peugeot. He would never be headed again.

As Aitken fought his way back up through the pack in an effort to catch Resta and make a battle of the race, the inevitable attrition began to take its toll. On lap twenty-five it was Charlie Merz' Peugeot out with oiling problems. Ten laps later Arthur Chevrolet's Frontenac was sidelined with a faulty magneto. Still, both of them were luckier than Tom Rooney. On lap forty-eight, the former White Squadron pilot's Premier blew a tire and hit the wall in Turn One. The force of the impact catapulted his mechanic, Thane Houser, over the wall, but he escaped with nothing more serious than cuts and bruises. Rooney was caught in the wreckage. He would survive, but with a broken leg and a dislocated shoulder to serve as mementos.

By lap sixty, Aitken had climbed back to second and appeared poised to give Resta a run for his money. Then just one lap later, Jack LeCain, driving in relief of Jules DeVigne,

Dario Resta in his Indianapolis-winning Peugeot, 1916. The victory at Indy would make Resta the only driver to win all three of America's premier races, the Vanderbilt Cup, the Grand Prize and the Indianapolis 500 (IMS Photo).

crashed in a big way in the short chute between Turns Three and Four. LeCain was pinned underneath as the Delage rolled, fracturing his skull and causing internal injuries. His condition was serious, but he would survive.

No sooner had the wreckage been cleared and the race resumed than Aitken's Peugeot burned a valve. His retirement nine laps past half distance gave Resta a lead of a lap on the field. Assuming the Anglo-Italian's Peugeot stayed together, the only real race was the one for second, with Mulford's Peugeot leading Henderson's Maxwell and Wilbur D'Alene's Duesenberg. The Maxwell was now being driven by Eddie Rickenbacker, who had taken over at the first pit stop. The trio held position to the two-thirds mark, eighty laps, then D'Alene began to pressure the others. Rickenbacker was the first to fall, slowed with mechanical problems. Then Mulford succumbed to the Duesenberg's power.

At the finish, it was Resta's Peugeot with a lap on D'Alene's Duesenberg. Mulford's Peugeot, in third, was nearly another full lap in arrears. Behind the top three were Christiaens' Sunbeam, Oldfield's Delage, Henderson's Maxwell, Wilcox's Premier, and the Crawford-Duesenbergs of Art Johnson and Billy Chandler. Resta's time for the three hundred miles, 3:36:10.82, was far off the record set by DePalma a year earlier. As with his victory in the Grand Prize in 1915, the slow speed, coupled with the race's lack of drama, seemed to quiet the crowd. Despite the fact that Resta had become the only man to win all three of American racing's crown jewels, there was no wild cheering, no throngs of admirers clamoring to get near him, as there had been for DePalma just one year before. No matter what he did, Dario Resta just couldn't seem to get the crowd behind him. It was a curse that would haunt him throughout his career — perhaps his own particular form of "Dago luck."

25

Return to Santa Monica

If conflict was rampant throughout Europe and Latin America in 1916, it touched the world of motor racing as well, centered around the Vanderbilt Cup and Grand Prize. The tenuous relationship between the AAA and the ACA had been tranquil, if not harmonious, since the formation of the Motor Cups Holding Company in 1909. Now, hostilities brewed anew between the two organizations, as the AAA usurped control of the Grand Prize to make it, along with the Vanderbilt Cup, the penultimate rounds of their new season-long championship. With the AAA's vast control of motor racing and racing venues in America, there was little the older organization could do about the takeover except to quarrel about its unfairness, but quarrel they did, with much of the gusto that had marked the early days of the Vanderbilt Cup.

Nineteen sixteen also shaped up as the final running of the Vanderbilt Cup. Willie K. Vanderbilt had announced his intention to retire the trophy, citing waning fan interest in road racing and the proliferation of speedway races on the AAA calendar. His announcement was not taken entirely seriously, however. He had threatened to retire the cup in 1915 as well, at one point even expressing a desire to throw it in the ocean. In the end, cooler heads among the leadership of the Motor Cups Holding Company had prevailed, but it remained to be seen whether the race could survive another season.

Since Indianapolis, the 1916 season had been dominated by the Peugeots, with the French machines taking eleven victories in the twenty events leading up to the Vanderbilt Cup and Grand Prize, now scheduled for Santa Monica in mid-November. It had not been all Dario Resta, however. Johnny Aitken's Peugeot from the Indianapolis stable had equaled the Anglo-Italian in wins, and his second-place finishes at Minneapolis and the Grand American gave him a slim 240-point advantage in the championship standings, at 3,440 to Resta's 3,200. With the Vanderbilt Cup and Grand Prize each worth 900 points to the winner, and the only race remaining on the calendar a 150-miler at Ascot on November 30, it was anticipated that the championship would be decided once and for all at Santa Monica.

Both Resta and Aitken would be at the wheel of 4.5-liter (274 cubic inch) Peugeots,

1914 *grand prix* machines featuring four-wheel brakes as well as their trademark double-overhead-cam engines. They would be the only foreign cars entered. Arrayed against them were entries from Mercer, Stutz, Duesenberg and newcomer Hudson, as well as four of the "Specials" that continued to populate the bottom of the standings. But even the factory-built American iron was not of the caliber it had been just a year or two previously.

The only full factory teams were from Mercer and Hudson. Mercer was now campaigning its new cars with the four-valve-per-cylinder, overhead-cam engine that had spent over a year in development and kept the team out of most of the 1916 season. The Trenton marque brought cars for Eddie Pullen, Glover Ruckstell, and Mercer newcomer Joe Thomas, but the meticulous preparation and attention to detail that had been the hallmark of the team in previous years was absent. Two devastating fires at the Roebling works in 1915 had forced Charles and Ferdinand Roebling to devote virtually all of their time to rebuilding that enterprise, leaving Mercer without supervision at the uppermost levels. To make matters worse, chief engineer and racing team manager Erik Delling had left the firm in July. His replacement was Locomobile veteran A. C. Schultz, but Schultz had had little time to get matters organized and had little recent experience with motor racing.

Hudson, in its first venture into big-time racing, fielded three of its Super Six cars and a team supervised by Ralph Mulford, but the effort appeared weak behind the wheel. Professional Ira Vail would be teamed with amateurs Clyde Roads and A. H. Patterson at the controls of the three machines. Duesenberg would have four cars in the race, but the team was not factory-backed. Instead, it was sponsored by Virginia millionaire William Weightman, who fielded cars for himself, Eddie Rickenbacker, and unknowns George Buzane and Mike Moosie. Of more lasting significance than either of Weightman's unknown drivers was his riding mechanic, Jimmy Murphy, who would go on to star in the twenties, winning at both Indianapolis and the French *Grand Prix* at Le Mans. Earl Cooper had wangled a lone Stutz, but factory support was still minimal, the firm remaining committed to its decision to curtail its racing program. In addition, there would be a privately entered National driven by Bill Cody, and an aging Marmon for Lewis Jackson in his first venture into big-time racing, but these, like the "Specials," were expected to be also-rans at best.

Once again missing from the race would be Ralph DePalma. His affiliation with Packard in their work on aero engines was now taking up all of his time. And while it would deprive him of a chance to win a third Vanderbilt Cup, his expertise would at least tangentially assist Packard's chief engineer, J. G. Vincent, in his collaboration with E. J. Hall of the Hall-Scott Motor Company. That collaboration would produce one of the most famous aero and marine motors of all time, the Liberty engine.

A crowd of 100,000 packed the temporary grandstands along Ocean Avenue and formed "two deep hedges" along the sides of the course as the nineteen cars were fired up for their thirty-five-lap, 294-mile journey over the 8.4-mile circuit. Although a mass standing start was still considered too dangerous, the cars would be sent off at ten-second intervals, minimizing the crowd's need to factor in time differentials in determining who was ahead. In the final analysis, it wouldn't matter anyway. As in every race since the 1911 Grand Prize, the winner would be first to the stripe.

Johnny Aitken's Peugeot took the lead from the start with Earl Cooper's Stutz slotted in second, closely pursued by the Mercers of Glover Ruckstell and Joe Thomas. But the favorite, Dario Resta, was nowhere to be found. After a simply horrendous start, he was eleventh past the grandstands on the opening lap. But his time in mid-pack would not last long. As the slower cars among the early starters, notably Jackson's Marmon and Moosie's Duesenberg, fell back toward the tail of the procession, Resta rocketed through the field. By lap three, he was seventh. By lap five, he had blasted past Rickenbacker's

With Eddie Rickenbacker between them, 1916 AAA points leaders Johnny Aitken and Dario Resta smile for the cameras (IMS Photo).

Coming to Santa Monica for the Vanderbilt Cup and Grand Prize in 1916, Johnny Aitken's Peugeot, pictured here, led Dario Resta's sister machine by 240 points in the standings for the inaugural AAA championship (IMS Photo).

Duesenberg and the Mercers to take over third. By lap seven, he had shouldered his Peugeot past Earl Cooper's Stutz into second. Now came the duel that everyone expected, the fight between Resta and Aitken for the win and the lead in the all-important AAA championship.

Behind the front-running Peugeots, Cooper continued to hold down third, with the Mercers still hot on his heels. They were followed by Rickenbacker, at least until lap seven when a stripped high gear ended his Duesenberg's day. By this time, three of the four "Specials" were out as well, suffering from a variety of ailments. The fourth would leave the race on lap nine with a burned bearing. But the attrition wasn't confined to the unlucky Rickenbacker and the "Specials" alone; the pace being set by Aitken in his bid to outdistance Resta was decimating the competition. On lap nine, Ruckstell's Mercer succumbed to ignition failure and Jackson's Marmon coasted to a stop with a burned-out clutch. On lap twelve, Thomas' Mercer was sidelined, its radiator holed. By half-distance, over half of the starters would be parked.

Despite Aitken's record-shattering pace at the front (88.8 mph through 90 miles), Resta's chase of the leading Peugeot was relentless. Lap by lap, the gap between the two cars shrank. Aitken, the speedway expert, was pushing his car's limits as hard as he dared, booming down the San Vicente straight, sliding within inches of the curbing at notorious Death Curve. Behind him, Resta, the veteran road-racer, seemed entirely in his element, carving smooth lines through the curves, accelerating, braking and turning with the precision of a surgeon. And at the end of each lap, he was closer, ever closer, to the fleeing No. 16 Peugeot.

Finally, on lap fourteen, came the inevitable ending to the relentless pursuit, as Resta sliced past Aitken's Peugeot to take over the lead. Behind the lead duo, Cooper's Stutz, Weightman's Duesenberg, Pullen's Mercer and Roads' Hudson were all nearly a lap in arrears. What had been a two-car race for the past seventy miles now seemed all but decided. Yet Resta was unable to open the gap on his rival. For the next five laps, the two Peugeots screamed around the circuit nose to tail, with Aitken tucked in just yards behind the Anglo-Italian. The crowd watched entranced — maybe Aitken could make a race of it yet. Maybe, like DePalma at Indy in 1915, he could run down Resta and retake the lead. Spectators waited breathlessly for the pair to come around, then carefully measured the distance between them. Was Aitken catching up? Was Resta pulling away? The gap stood at only twelve seconds.

And then it was over. On lap twenty, Aitken's Peugeot began sputtering a three-cylinder staccato, the sure sign of a swallowed valve. With a five-minute lead over the second-place Stutz of Earl Cooper, Resta could easily cruise to the finish. But with fifteen laps remaining, the American contingent was not about to go quietly. The retirement of one of the Peugeots had given them hope: perhaps Resta's was vulnerable as well. In turn, the Stutz, Duesenberg, Mercer and Hudson pits signaled their drivers "All Out." And in turn Cooper, Weightman, Pullen and Roads tried to put pressure on Resta. It was pointless. The Anglo-Italian's Peugeot was the class of the field, and try as they might, the American machines simply had no response.

Resta pitted on lap twenty-five, taking on fuel and a right rear tire. The well-orchestrated stop cost him just fifty seconds. Then Pullen came in for a similar stop, and the pit men from Trenton fairly flew around the car. Thirty-two seconds later the Mercer was back on the road. The grandstand crowd cheered with delight, but it would be the last hurrah for an American entry. Through the final fifteen laps, Resta motored away as he had done so often over the past two years. The only deviation from the procession would come on lap thirty-one, when Pullen's Mercer retired with a broken gearbox. At the wire, it was Resta's Peugeot with a lap in hand on Earl Cooper's Stutz. The only other finishers were Weightman's Duesenberg and Clyde Roads' Hudson.

Resta's time, 3:22:48.4, an average speed of 86.98 mph, had shattered Ralph DePalma's two-year-old Vanderbilt Cup record by some eleven miles per hour and Eddie Pullen's Grand Prize record by nine — an even wider margin than DePalma's record-smashing Indianapolis run in 1915. And yet, while the cheering for the victor was enthusiastic, there was none of the uproar that would have attended a win by either Pullen or DePalma. Maybe it was blatant nationalism, with war looming on the horizon. Maybe it was the fact that Resta always seemed to have vastly superior equipment. Maybe he just made it look too easy. Whatever the reason, Dario Resta, despite a record of wins in the Indianapolis 500, Vanderbilt Cup and Grand Prize that no one could match, would never gain the public acclaim that was certainly his due. Even today, while the names DePalma, Oldfield, Chevrolet and Rickenbacker are familiar to most fans of American motorsports, the name of the only man to win all three of American racing's crown jewels remains largely unknown.

26

Winners and Losers

The Grand Prize was scheduled for November 18, just two days after the Vanderbilt Cup. There would be little time to repair broken machinery or to refurbish tired racers after a season of competition. Most significantly, there would be no time to find speed to match the Peugeots — and there would be three of them in this round, with Howdy Wilcox joining Johnny Aitken on the Indianapolis team. The short interval between the races also meant that the Mercer team was down to two machines. Eddie Pullen's blown gearbox could not be repaired, so his No. 4 car was fitted with the one from Joe Thomas' No. 2. Thomas would sit out the Grand Prize. Otherwise, except for some minor shuffling of cars that would have no bearing on the outcome and the addition of a Stutz for Cliff Durant, the field was identical to the Vanderbilt Cup.

Despite Dario Resta's victory in the Vanderbilt Cup, which had given him a 660-point lead in the championship chase, Johnny Aitken was still in the hunt for the $14,000 prize. A victory in the forty-eight lap, 403-mile Grand Prize would give him enough points to regain the lead. Anything less would leave him all but eliminated. Thus, as the crowd of over 100,000 assembled for the final major race of the year, its focus was on the Peugeots which had dominated the racing all season, but overriding the race itself was the showdown between Resta and Aitken for the lucrative season-long championship.

Unfortunately, the expected duel never materialized. Aitken's Peugeot broke a piston on lap one. But instead of deciding the championship issue, Aitken's retirement would only serve to complicate it. As Glover Ruckstell's Mercer took the early lead, the Indianapolis pit began scrambling for a solution to Aitken's problem. Within four laps they had found one — Aitken would take over Wilcox's Peugeot. Meanwhile, out on the circuit Ruckstell had faded to eighth on lap two as Resta inevitably took over at the front, followed by Pullen's Mercer, Cooper's Stutz and Vail's Hudson. Howdy Wilcox was lying fifth.

On lap five, the Indianapolis team gave Wilcox the signal to pit. He ignored it. Positioned just behind the leading trio of Resta, Pullen and Cooper, he was locked in a battle for fourth, with Ruckstell's Mercer just ahead of him and Rickenbacker's Duesenberg just behind. A pit stop now would cost him not only time but track position. Even so, he was unable to hold off the charging Rickenbacker, and on lap seven he fell back to sixth as the Duesenberg sped past.

Since the opening lap, Eddie Pullen had been chasing Resta's Peugeot for all he was worth. On lap eight, it all came undone. Entering a corner too fast, his Mercer skidded wide, then crashed through a barrier and caught fire. Neither Pullen nor his mechanic was hurt, but their race was over. Pullen's crash slowed Earl Cooper, who had been following closely, but it never slowed Glover Ruckstell for an instant. In a flash, the Mercer pilot was past the Stutz into second and on his way after the fleeing Peugeot at the front.

Resto was unable to pull away from the pack in the early laps of the Grand Prize, as he had in many of his previous races. First, Pullen had put on the pressure. Now it was Ruckstell, with Cooper, Rickenbacker and Wilcox in a bunch close behind. Then came a large gap to the rest of the runners, Buzane, Patterson, Jackson, Durant and Weightman. Moosie's Duesenberg and three of the "Specials" were already parked. Wilcox, at the tail of the lead group, chose this moment to honor his pit's signal to come in. What happened next is the source of conflicting reports.

Some sources say that Howdy Wilcox refused his pit's request that he hand over his car to his friend and mentor, Johnny Aitken. Others say Wilcox was ill and wanted Aitken to take over, but that Referee Brady refused to allow the change. Whatever the truth of the matter, Wilcox stayed in the car and Aitken on the sidelines, but the machinations were only beginning. Back on the course, Wilcox found himself still in fifth, but now some distance behind Rickenbacker. Ahead of them, the leading trio, Resta's Peugeot, Ruckstell's Mercer and Cooper's Stutz, continued to lap within seconds of each other. Almost immediately, Wilcox began to make up ground at a phenomenal rate, shrinking the gap between his Peugeot and Rickenbacker's Duesenberg. By lap twelve, he was back on its tail.

Behind the gang of five at the front, Lewis Jackson was having the race of his life. His lifelong ambition had been to race in the Grand Prize. He had been a riding mechanic for several racers in the East and had even been spilled out of an overturned car at Indianapolis, but the Vanderbilt Cup two days earlier had been his first big chance behind the wheel. His aging Marmon had run surprisingly well, but it had lasted only nine laps. Today, while not positioned as well as he had been in the Vanderbilt Cup, he was fighting for eighth with Cliff Durant's Stutz and just ahead of William Weightman's Duesenberg when he overcooked it at the Ocean Avenue turn on lap eleven. His Marmon jumped the curbing and climbed onto the street car tracks, breaking a wheel. Hastily, he fitted a spare and set off to make up the time lost. For his part, Durant had had troubles of his own, and on lap twelve Jackson nosed past the Stutz and was off in pursuit of Patterson's Hudson. He would never complete another lap.

As his Marmon rocketed down the San Vincente straight at 110 mph toward the flat-out bend at Seventh Street, it inexplicably ran wide. Some authorities have speculated that the earlier incident at the Ocean Avenue turn had damaged the Marmon's steering. Others claim that Jackson just lost it. Whatever the cause, the car hit the curb at terrific speed, breaking its left front wheel. The crippled Marmon then careened along the curbing, shearing off two trees, smashing its way through a lemonade stand and hurling the now-lifeless body of its proprietor, Leana Juratch, over a hundred feet down the road.

Without seeming to slow in the slightest, the murderous machine then ran down cameraman L. D. Jenkins and smashed itself to pieces against the trunk of a big pepper tree. Mechanic John Chianda was thrown clear and escaped with only slight injuries, but Jackson was not so lucky. His body was crushed between the car and the tree and nearly cut in two. Still, the instrument of mayhem had not finished its spree of injury and death. Upon impact with the tree, the car's engine and radiator tore free and were thrown further down the street. They hit two spectators, J. S. Hannigan and Harold Edgerton. Hannigan was struck a glancing blow and only slightly injured, but Edgerton was hit full force by the flying projectile. He died an hour later.

Despite the swath of death and destruction along San Vincente Boulevard, the race never slowed. Howdy Wilcox continued his march to the front as Ruckstell and Cooper fell back. By lap fourteen, he was second behind only Resta, with Rickenbacker just behind in third and Cooper and Ruckstell rounding out the top five. And although the order behind Resta had shuffled, the Anglo-Italian still had not managed to open a gap on his pursuers. He was being crowded from behind. It was now Wilcox's Peugeot doing the crowding in place of the Mercers.

After finishing second to Dario Resta's Peugeot in both the 1915 Grand Prize and Vanderbilt Cup, Howard "Howdy" Wilcox traded his "White Squadron" Stutz for an Indianapolis-sponsored Peugeot for the 1916 Grand Prize and came away with the win, despite the fact that teammate Johnny Aitken drove the car from lap twenty onward (IMS Photo).

The order at the front stayed the same through lap sixteen, but on lap seventeen Resta dived into the pits for a change of two spark plugs. The stop took a mere thirty seconds, but by the time the Peugeot was back on the track both Rickenbacker, the new leader, and Wilcox had come by, dropping Resta to third. From there it was all downhill for the Anglo-Italian. On lap eighteen, he was into the pits again, but his Peugeot emerged running only on three cylinders. On lap nineteen, he retired for good — the cause, ignition failure. Still, things weren't all bad. With Aitken already out, the championship was all but his — or so he thought.

By lap twenty, Wilcox had retaken the lead from Rickenbacker's Duesenberg, while Ruckstell's Mercer had fallen from the lead group. It would last until lap thirty-nine before a burned valve would finally end its day, but it would never again be a threat. It was time for scheduled pit stops, and the leaders, Wilcox, Rickenbacker and Cooper, all came in. But Wilcox did more than just get fuel and change tires. In the interim between lap nine and lap twenty, the Indianapolis pit had been hard on the ear of Referee Brady, arguing that driver changes were legal under the rules, and citing their use in the Indianapolis 500 as precedent. Brady relented and allowed Wilcox, now claiming illness, to hand the car over to Aitken. Upon learning of the driver change, it was Resta's turn to protest. As Aitken, Rickenbacker and Cooper circled the track, Brady explained to Resta that there was nothing in the rules to prevent driver changes. Resta thereupon seized on a strategy of his own in an effort to combat the team tactics being used against him. He stomped down to the Stutz pits and tried to buy Cooper's machine on the spot. His offer was flatly refused. Still fuming at Brady's ruling, he joined his wife in the grandstand to brood.

The pit stops had done nothing to separate the leaders, and Rickenbacker continued to hound Aitken as he had Wilcox. By lap twenty-six, the future flying ace had muscled his Duesie past the Peugeot. From the stands, Dario Resta breathed a sigh of relief—Aitken needed a win to rob Resta of the points lead. But just one lap later,

that good feeling was gone as the Duesenberg pulled to the side of the road — stripped gears had ended Rickenbacker's day and handed the lead back to Aitken.

Now only Earl Cooper had a chance to catch the lone remaining Peugeot. For a time it appeared that he would, but slower pit stops over the final twenty laps offset the small speed advantage his Stutz displayed on the road. In the end, it was Aitken's Peugeot first across the line, with a winning margin of 6:12 over Earl Cooper's Stutz. The only other finishers, the Hudsons of Patterson and Roads, were both well off the pace, with Patterson over twenty minutes behind Cooper and Roads a full hour in arrears. It appeared that Johnny Aitken had won the race and retaken the lead in the championship points chase. But had he?

Locked in a duel with Dario Resta for the inaugural AAA championship in 1916, Johnny Aitken saw his point lead evaporate when his Peugeot burned a valve in the Vanderbilt Cup. In the Grand Prize, held just two days later, Aitken took over teammate Howdy Wilcox's Peugeot after his own mount broke a piston and spurred it on to victory. Unfortunately, the points for the win would be credited to Wilcox, not Aitken, and Resta would garner the championship (IMS Photo).

Race officials quickly huddled to try to sort out the question of whom to credit with the victory — Wilcox who started the race, or Aitken who finished it. Once again, the precedent they looked to was Indianapolis. At the race there in May, Rickenbacker had taken over Henderson's Maxwell and had finished in the points, but the points had been awarded to Henderson, not Rickenbacker. Using that reasoning, the race officials awarded the victory in the Grand Prize to Howdy Wilcox. With it, the 1916 AAA Championship would go to Dario Resta. As for the odd man out, Johnny Aitken, he would never have another chance to capture the crown. The veteran racer would die in the influenza epidemic of 1918.

❖ ❖ ❖

In the end, the race and all question of winners and losers would be overshadowed by Jackson's horrendous crash. Like Herbert Lytle's crash in practice for the 1904 Vanderbilt Cup that had killed Harold Rigby and almost derailed big-time racing in America at its very inception, or the blood-bath of the 1910 Vanderbilt Cup that had banished the race from Long Island, Jackson's crash and the three bystander fatalities had the public up in arms. Within days, there were calls in the California legislature for a ban on all racing on public roads. It was the end of the road racing era in America. With oval tracks now commanding the public's attention and no venue to call home, the Grand Prize was doomed. So too was any chance for the Vanderbilt Cup's resurrection. Motor racing in America would be suspended with the nation's entry into World War I in April 1917, but when it resumed for the 1919 season only one of the three crown jewels would remain: the Indianapolis 500. The Vanderbilt Cup and Grand Prize, the two great races that had started it all, would be consigned to the dustbin of history.

27

Epilogue

So ended the first great era of American racing. Although largely forgotten today, in many ways the era of the Vanderbilt Cup and Grand Prize before World War I was the golden age of motor racing in America. Never again would factory teams compete, as they would continue to do in Europe. Never again would American manufacturers like Locomobile, Alco, Lozier, Mercer and Stutz go head to head with Europe's finest marques, among them Panhard, Darracq, Fiat, Benz, Mercedes and Peugeot, vying for attention in America's greatest races as well as in showrooms across the country. And never again would road races in America attract crowds numbering a quarter-million or more.

In the final analysis, Willie K. Vanderbilt's race had accomplished its goals and done much more besides. It did, indeed, do much to make American automobiles the equals of their European counterparts, both on the track and in the showroom. One need only trace the improvement of American finishes in the race, from being completely outclassed by Panhard and Darracq in the races of 1904 and 1905; to the setting of fastest lap by Tracy's Locomobile in 1906; to George Robertson's win, albeit against lesser competition, in the same car in 1908; to Harry Grant's back-to-back victories in 1909 and 1910; and finally culminating with Ralph Mulford's win in the stock-chassis Lozier in the face of competition from the factory might of Fiat and from all-out Mercedes racers piloted by Ralph DePalma and Spencer Wishart in 1911. The fact that Mulford and Lozier very nearly pulled off another victory in that year's Grand Prize against a factory-backed Benz team as well as the Fiat and Mercedes contingents only serves to underscore the fact that the Americans had, indeed, arrived. And while it is true that the resurgence of *grand prix* racing in Europe between 1912 and 1914 would foster a new breed of smaller, more powerful machines from Peugeot, Delage and Mercedes that were superior to America's best, the entries from Mercer, Stutz and Duesenberg were never far behind. More importantly, America's sporting marques had established themselves in the eyes of the public as every bit the equal of their European cousins. Young men of means with a penchant for speed, who in the early days of the century would have driven creations from Panhard, Darracq, or Richard-Brasier, or a few years later machines from Fiat, Mercedes, or Benz, were now behind the wheel of a Mercer or a Stutz.

But perhaps more significant than the Vanderbilt Cup's contribution to the improvement of the American automobile were its role in establishing motor racing as a major sport in America and its role, along with that of the Grand Prize, in helping to perpetuate the infant sport worldwide. The Vanderbilt Cup elevated motor racing from a fairgrounds spectacle of only local interest to one of national or international significance. It continued an American presence at the highest level of the sport at a time when the Gordon Bennett Cup was meeting its demise at the hands of the French. And it, along with the Grand Prize, provided a venue for top-flight international competition in the face of the French boycott between 1908 and 1912. One is left to wonder what fate motor racing might have suffered without these two races.

❖ ❖ ❖

One cannot read the names of the American marques referred to in this book without being struck by the fact that virtually all of them are names which are no longer part of the automotive scene. Unlike their European counterparts, such as Renault, Peugeot, Fiat, Mercedes and Benz, all of which are still active manufacturers, nearly all of the Americans are gone, and long gone at that. Of the cars with any significant presence in the Vanderbilt Cup or Grand Prize, only Buick and Chevrolet remain, protected by their positions within the Goliath of General Motors. Of the others, only Hudson survived World War II before foundering, along with Packard, in the face of increased competition from the Big Three. As for the others, some, like Alco and Lozier, were defunct even before the end of the pre–World War I era. Alco, a product of the American Locomotive Company, was never the financial success that its parent envisioned. The last one rolled out of the shop at Bridgeport, Connecticut, in 1913.

In 1911, Lozier expanded its production capacity to meet with increased demand, due, in part, to its racing successes. Unfortunately, the expansion required outside capital, and that meant a loss of control by its founder, Harry Lozier, and his chief engineer, John Perrin. When profits weren't forthcoming at the rate sought by the money men, they pressed for a mass-market car, but Lozier was in no position to compete in that arena with Ford and General Motors. By August 1914, the "real" Lozier Company had shut down. Perrin, who had been with Lozier since its inception, quit. Speculators closed in, took over what was left and tried to keep the company afloat, but it was useless. By 1918, the company from Plattsburgh, N.Y., was but a memory.

Stutz would suffer a similar fate, but would survive and even prosper until the 1930s. The public issuance of stock authorized by Harry Stutz in 1916 to increase the company's production facilities inevitably eroded his control of the company. Financial interests headed by Alan A. Ryan took control and by 1919 Harry Stutz was gone from the company that bore his name. In 1920, Ryan cornered the market on Stutz shares, in the process driving the price up from $70 to an outrageous $724 per share. In 1922, he sold out at top dollar to Charles Schwab, the president of Bethlehem Steel, and a small group of bankers, but no sooner had this new group taken over than Stutz' fortunes nose-dived. Customers for the Speedway Six which Schwab's engineers had designed were few and far between.

Fortunately, in 1924 a Hungarian-born engineer by the name of Frederic Erwan

Moscovics approached Schwab with an idea for a new car. Moscovics had worked for Daimler in Germany and Marmon and Franklin in the United States, and he had been associated with Charles Kettering in the development of ethyl gasoline and with Ralph DePalma in racing. His résumé was superb, and Schwab was a smart enough business-man to know a good idea when he heard it. So began Stutz' second era of greatness, with models such as the Vertical Eight, the Safety Stutz of 1926, and the Blackhawk Speedster of 1927. The company also returned to racing, with a second-place finish at the 1928 Le Mans Twenty-four Hours, behind only Woolf Barnato's 4½-liter Bentley. In fact, the Stutz, driven by Frenchmen Édouard Brisson and Robert Bloch, was leading until forty-two miles from the finish, when Brisson stripped a gear. Three supercharged Blackhawks were entered at Le Mans in 1929, with one of them, driven by Guy Bouriat and George Philippe, finishing fifth, behind a parade of four Bentleys.

While the twenties were a successful decade for Stutz, in the early years of the Great Depression the company found itself in a quandary. Cars in its price class from Packard, Cadillac and Lincoln were being offered with twelve- and, in Cadillac's case, sixteen-cylinder engines. Stutz could not afford the development of such an engine, especially at a time when customers for luxury cars were dwindling. It attempted to combat the prob-lem by offering a twin-cam straight eight with four valves per cylinder known as the DV-32, but sales were dismal. By 1935, the Indianapolis firm's doors were closed.

Like Stutz, Duesenberg would enjoy considerable success in the era from the end of World War I until the latter days of the Great Depression. The firm would begin build-ing road-going cars in 1920 with the pricey straight-eight Model A. A Duesenberg piloted by Jimmy Murphy would win the French *Grand Prix* at Le Mans in 1921, and Duesen-bergs would go on to win at Indianapolis in 1924, 1925, and 1927. Unfortunately, the passenger car business, located across the street from the race car shop, fared less well. It was constantly on the edge of bankruptcy and went into receivership in 1924. In 1926, Errett Lobban Cord, the "Boy Wonder" of American business, purchased the passenger car business, then known as Duesenberg Motors Corporation, and made Fred Duesen-berg its vice-president in charge of engineering. Cord's idea was for the new company, Duesenberg, Inc., to divorce itself completely from racing and to concentrate on mak-ing the world's finest car. While brother August continued with the Duesenberg Broth-ers racing operation, Fred began work on the car that was to become the icon of American automotive design — the incomparable Model J.

Unfortunately, Fred would die on July 26, 1932, as a result of a road accident while driving a Model J back to Indianapolis. On a rain-slick mountain road just west of Jen-nerstown, Pa., two approaching cars crested a hill in front of him almost abreast. He swerved to avoid them, but hit the mountainside, bouncing off it several times. He was thrown from the car, fracturing two ribs and a lumbar vertebra and dislocating his shoul-der. While his injuries were serious, they didn't appear life-threatening, but during his convalescence at a hospital in Johnstown, he developed a case of pneumonia that proved fatal.

Fred's death robbed Duesenberg of a great leader and brilliant engineer. As a con-sequence, there was no replacement for the Model J when the initial production run of nearly 500 cars had been sold. By this time, 1936, E. L. Cord was under investigation for stock manipulation, the sales force had run out of cars to sell, and the executives at the parent Cord Corporation had lost interest in Duesenberg as a product. In 1937, the Cord

Corporation sold the Duesenberg factory to the Marmon-Herrington Company and moved the remaining parts, one remaining chassis, and seventeen used cars to its Auburn headquarters, from which they were subsequently sold to a DeSoto dealership in Chicago. The day of the Duesie was over.

Perhaps the saddest story of all about the demise of the great American marques of the pre–World War I era is the one concerning Mercer, Simplex and Locomobile. Certainly, no three marques can claim more of a racing heritage than these, particularly Locomobile, with its victory in the 1908 Vanderbilt Cup, and Mercer, with the first and only victory for America in the 1914 Grand Prize. Mercer, although beset by the loss of key personnel from the time of Washington Roebling II's death on the *Titanic* in 1912, and having suffered through the departure of successive chief engineers, was still a healthy and profitable company in 1916. But the following year Ferdinand Roebling died, followed in 1918 by brother Charles. The Roebling family interests came under the control of their ill and aging older brother, Washington A. Roebling, the man who had given his health and a large part of his life to the creation of the Brooklyn Bridge. The elder Roebling, a Civil War hero as well as a brilliant engineer, was a man much more of the nineteenth century than the twentieth. He had no interest in these new-fangled machines called automobiles. In 1919, he sold the Roeblings' interest in Mercer to a Wall Street syndicate headed by Emlen Hare.

Hare, a former Packard salesman, had a plan to acquire a number of smaller independent marques with famous names and merge them into a single company to compete with the giants of Ford and General Motors. He depleted Mercer's cash reserves and leveraged the company to purchase Locomobile and Crane-Simplex (Simplex had been purchased by Goodrich, Lockhart & Smith in 1912, and the new owners had acquired Crane as well). Unfortunately, the shaky little conglomerate that was Hare's Motors was undercapitalized from the start and had acquired at least two marques, Locomobile and Simplex, whose glory days were behind them. They were cars of the bygone chain-drive era. Despite Emlen Hare's machinations and grandiose schemes, Hare's Motors was never in any position to compete with the big boys. When the post-war recession years of 1921 and 1922 softened the market for sporting and luxury automobiles, Hare's Motors was unable to satisfy its creditors. Locomobile and Crane-Simplex died with it. Mercer limped along in receivership until 1925, but its financial woes were too severe to remedy, and finally the doors of the Trenton marque that had given America its first true sports car were closed for good.

❖ ❖ ❖

If many of the cars and the companies that made them are now gone, what of the drivers of that long-ago era? As witnessed in these pages, many, far too many, died behind the wheel before the era was over. The names of David Bruce-Brown, Spencer Wishart, Harry Grant and Bob Burman come quickly to mind. Others, like Eddie Pullen, vanished into obscurity. More than a few, most notably Ralph DePalma, Howdy Wilcox, Eddie Hearne, and Ralph Mulford, would continue to race well into the twenties. DePalma would go on to assist in the design of the Packard V-12, which he drove to a land speed record of 149.87 mph at Daytona in 1919. He would compete in the Indianapolis 500 until 1925 and would continue to attempt to qualify for the race until 1931. His last race in a dirt-track car came in 1934, at age 51, and he would continue to make record runs in stock cars until 1936. He ended his career with over 2,000 victories to his credit, 24 of which would now be considered "AAA Championship" wins. He died of natural causes in 1956 at age 73.

In the wake of his victory in the 1916 Grand Prize, Howdy Wilcox would go on to win the Indianapolis 500 in 1919. Unfortunately, he would die behind the wheel on September 4, 1923, when his Duesenberg blew a tire at the inaugural race at the 1¼-mile board track at Altoona, Pennsylvania. Eddie Hearne would go on to win that day at Altoona in a Cliff Durant-owned Miller on his way to the 1923 AAA Championship. In a fine sporting gesture, Hearne donated $1,000 from his winnings to each of his friend Howdy Wilcox's children. Like Ralph Mulford, Hearne, the man they called "Grandpa," would continue to race until 1927.

Perhaps best known is the story of Eddie Rickenbacker, who would go on to become America's "Ace of Aces" over the skies of Europe in World War I. Credited with shooting down 26 enemy planes in his SPAD, he would eventually rise to command of the 94th Aero Squadron, the famous "Hat in the Ring" Squadron. He would ultimately receive the Congressional Medal of Honor for his exploits on September 25, 1918, when, flying alone, he engaged seven German fighters in a dogfight, shooting down two. After the war, Rickenbacker began the manufacture of an automobile bearing his name. Despite good initial sales, the firm failed in the mid-1920s, leaving Rickenbacker a quarter-million dollars in debt. Rebounding quickly, he purchased the Indianapolis Motor Speedway in 1927 and

By 1914 Eddie Rickenbacker was the young lion of the Duesenberg team, finishing tenth that year in the Indianapolis 500. But racing driver was only the first of several remarkable lives led by this remarkable man. Some of the others: World War I flying ace, Congressional Medal of Honor winner, owner of the Indianapolis Motor Speedway, and founder of Eastern Airlines (IMS Photo).

was instrumental in shepherding that facility and America's last great race through the often difficult inter-war years. During World War II, he became a special envoy for the Army Air Corps, making inspection tours of air bases around the world. In November 1942, the B-17 carrying Rickenbacker and seven others on a tour of Pacific bases ran out of fuel and ditched, forcing the group to spend twenty-four days on life rafts. The ordeal only served to enhance Rickenbacker's reputation for bravery and determination. At war's end, he sold the Indianapolis Motor Speedway to Anton Hulman, Jr., and returned to his interest in civil aviation. He had purchased a small air carrier by the name of Eastern Air Transport in 1938. By the time of his retirement in 1963, it had changed its name to Eastern Air Lines, and Rickenbacker was its chairman. He died in Zurich, Switzerland, in 1973, having never possessed a driver's license.

Among the Europeans who came to America in those early years to take part in its greatest races, many of the later arrivals, including Jules Goux, René Thomas, Albert Guyot, Jean Chassagne, Victor Rigal and Arthur Duray, fought for France in World War I. Georges Boillot became a fighter pilot. He was shot down and killed over Verdun in 1916. Of the remainder, Goux, Thomas, Guyot and Chassagne would continue to race into the twenties, making yearly pilgrimages to Indianapolis. Likewise, Dario Resta, after a short period of retirement from racing, would return to Indianapolis in 1923. Unfortunately, his Packard would leave the race after eighty-eight laps with differential problems. It would be his last visit to the Brickyard. In 1924, he would be killed at Brooklands when his Sunbeam overturned and caught fire during a record run.

Alsatian Louis Wagner, like his French compatriots, fought on the side of France in the war and continued to race in Europe well into the twenties, but for forty years after his second-place finish as part of the Mercedes team in the 1914 French *Grand Prix*, he was shunned by many in his own country. Finally, in 1955, the stigma that had caused Wagner so much pain and embarrassment through the years was lifted when the French government belatedly awarded him the Legion of Honor.

Wagner contemporary Camille Jenatzy, the "Red Devil," gave up racing in 1908, although he continued to compete in sprints and hillclimbs until 1910, when he quit racing entirely to devote himself full-time to his thriving tire company. A renowned practical joker, Jenatzy was entertaining guests at his hunting preserve in the Ardennes in 1913 when he decided that it would be amusing to scare them by sneaking off into the bushes and imitating a wild boar. Apparently, his imitation was too realistic. He was fatally shot by one of his party.

Perhaps the most interesting and least well known story of the great racing drivers of that era is that of Caleb Bragg. As World War I approached, Bragg became infatuated with airplanes, eventually becoming the seventieth licensed pilot in America and garnering an executive position in the Wright Aeronautical Company. In the post-war years, Bragg turned his attention to powerboat racing, and specifically that most prestigious of events, the Gold Cup. Beginning in 1922, the rules for the Gold Cup were revised to eliminate the unlimited hydroplanes in which Gar Wood had dominated the race, winning it five times consecutively. In their place, the American Power Boat Association adopted a new formula for "gentleman's runabouts," boats without the stepped hulls of the hydroplanes or their multiple Liberty engines. The 1922 race was won by Packard's J. G. Vincent, now Colonel Vincent, in *Packard Chris-Craft*, powered by a Packard V-12. The following year, *Packard Chris-Craft* won again, this time powered by a purpose-built

Louis Wagner, pictured here in a Ballot prior to the 1919 Indianapolis 500, had a long and sto-ried career as a race driver, being one of only two drivers to win both the Vanderbilt Cup and Grand Prize. Sadly, his second-place finish for Mercedes in the 1914 French *Grand Prix* caused many of his fellow Frenchmen to shun him (IMS Photo).

Packard six-cylinder. For the 1924 race, Caleb Bragg commissioned designer George Crouch to build a boat for him, powered by a Wright-built, Hispano-Suiza V-8 aircraft engine. The result was one of the most beautiful boats of that, or any, era—*Baby Boot-legger*. With Bragg at the helm, *Baby Bootlegger* finished second on the water to another Crouch design, *Rainbow IV*, but *Rainbow IV* was disqualified for employing lapstrake con-struction in such a way that several of the outlawed steps were created in her hull. Bragg and *Baby Bootlegger* were declared the winners, making Bragg the only man to have won Gold Cups both on land and on water. Bragg and *Baby Bootlegger* would go on to win the Gold Cup again in 1925, this time without need for the judges' intervention. Today, *Baby Bootlegger* resides in the boathouse of Mark Mason at Center Harbor on Lake Win-nipesauke, New Hampshire. Saved from a Quebec City junkyard, this most desirable of antique speed boats lives on, much like its Vanderbilt Cup counterpart, Old 16.

❖ ❖ ❖

And what of the man who started it all, William Kissam Vanderbilt, Jr.? He and his wife, Virginia, separated in 1910, although her Catholic faith precluded them from get-ting a divorce. Their three children lived with Virginia in a Fifth Avenue mansion, while Willie K. leased out the Deepdale estate and began the construction of a new residence in Centerport, Long Island, he called "Eagle's Nest." When the Vanderbilt Cup left Long Island in 1911, Willie K.'s involvement with the race diminished to practically nothing, although he would make appearances at the 1915 and 1916 races. By that time, his Motor

Parkway stretched for forty-five miles, from Queens to Lake Ronkonkoma, where Vanderbilt had built an inn that was a copy of the *Petit Trianon* of Versailles.

In 1917, Willie K. was named president of the New York Central Railroad, but he was never much more than a figurehead, leaving the actual running of the company to others. By this time, he had become enamored of the sea, as both a sailor and an amateur naturalist. He took navigation classes at the Merchant Marine Academy, made five Atlantic crossings on his yacht, and began collecting marine specimens. In 1926, he hired a curator from New York's American Museum of Natural History and set sail for the Galapagos Islands to witness the unique animal life there.

In 1927, he and Virginia finally divorced and he married Rosamund Warburton, described in at least one newspaper as "a youthful blonde edition" of Virginia. Rosamund set about expanding the Eagle's Nest into a mansion of Vanderbilt stature while Willie K. continued to oversee the further expansion of the Motor Parkway. Although it had seen little use in its early days, compelling Vanderbilt to reduce tolls from $2.00 to $1.50, and later to $1.00, by the mid-twenties the Parkway played host to over 150,000 cars a year. Unfortunately, at about this same time, New York's transportation guru, Robert Moses, began planning his Northern State Parkway, a toll-free road that would render the older Motor Parkway redundant. Vanderbilt could read the handwriting on the wall and offered to sell, but Moses expressed interest in only one small section of the road. When Willie K. balked, Moses told him he would end up giving the whole thing to the state for nothing. By 1933, the Northern State Parkway ran from Queens to Mineola, and traffic on Vanderbilt's parkway was so sparse that he lowered the toll to forty cents in an effort to attract more cars. It was no use. Fewer and fewer automobiles traveled over the narrow older road, and in 1937 Vanderbilt turned it over to Nassau, Suffolk and Queens counties in lieu of $80,000 in back taxes. Moses' prediction had been fulfilled. On Easter 1938, the road closed. The tiny toll lodges where the toll-takers and their families had resided were offered to them for $500. Despite an investment of $10 million in building and improving the road, neither Vanderbilt nor any of the investors who had heeded the gilt-edged predictions of Arthur R. Pardington ever made a penny on the enterprise.

Today, little evidence of the Motor Parkway remains. Disconnected stretches of pavement run through backyards, alongside apartment complexes and behind shopping malls. Only a twelve-mile-long portion of the road in Suffolk County is in use. Nassau County sold much of its portion to the Long Island Lighting Co. for a power line right-of-way. Elsewhere, portions have been converted to bike trails. Evidence of the existence of America's first automobile highway has all but vanished. A small but dedicated group of Long Islanders takes pleasure in retracing the route of the road, and attempts have been made to preserve what is left, but without some designation as a historical landmark, the few remnants of the Parkway that still exist disappear bit by bit, year by year.

If the remainder of the twentieth century was kinder to Willie K. than it was to his highway, it was nevertheless unkind to the family fortune. Despite inheriting an additional $21 million on the death of his father in 1920, over the remaining twenty-four years of his life, Willie K. presided over the incessant and inevitable erosion of his family's great wealth. The root cause was that little-noticed 1913 amendment to the U.S. Constitution, the one that had provided for a federal income tax, but other factors conspired with it to deplete the family fortune — railroads came under increasing federal regulation, unions obtained wage increases for railroad workers. The day of the industrial tycoon was over.

Vanderbilt acknowledged that fact in 1934. "There is no point in dodging facts," he said. "In another ten years there won't be a single great fortune left in America. The country will come back — it always does. But we won't."[1]

By the time of his death from a heart attack in 1944, the Fifth Avenue mansions built by his parents and grandparents had fallen to the wrecker's ball. Marble House, his mother's opulent summer retreat at Newport, Rhode Island, had been sold in 1932. None of the family could afford to maintain it, or any of the other great estates that earlier Vanderbilt generations had built. Rosamund continued to live at Eagle's Nest until her death in 1947. Thereafter, the estate was given to Suffolk County. Today, it is used as a museum, and the expansive garage that once held Willie K.'s collection of luxury cars is an educational center. And Willie K.'s splendid sterling silver trophy? It is housed today at the Smithsonian Institution, along with other icons of American automotive history.

❖ ❖ ❖

The Vanderbilt Cup was resurrected on Long Island in 1936, after a twenty-six-year absence, but not by Willie K. The donor this time was his cousin George Vanderbilt, who commissioned the creation of an even larger trophy and guaranteed prize money totaling $85,000. The event was held at Roosevelt Raceway, billed as the finest racing facility yet constructed, and attracted seventy-three entrants from five nations. This renewal of the Vanderbilt Cup was the dream of George Robertson, who had spent his days since his service with Pershing in Mexico in various capacities in racing, most notably as team manager for Duesenberg in 1921, when Jimmy Murphy won the French *Grand Prix*. Now he was Roosevelt Raceway's general manager. And so it was that as the masses assembled to see these new machines from Mercedes, Auto-Union and Alfa Romeo do battle with America's best, they were treated to a visit by a ghost from the past — a fast lap of honor by America's first champions, the Locomobile "Old 16" with George Robertson at the wheel.

Chapter Notes

Chapter 1

1. Sylvia Adcock, "Driving in the Fast Lane," http://www.newsday.com/community/guide/lihistory/ny-history_motion_road1,0,7025640.story?coll=ny-lihistory-navigation.

2. Sylvia Adcock, "The Age of the Auto," http://www.newsday.com/community/guide/lihistory/ny-history-hs701a,0,6567870.story?coll=ny-lihistory-navigation.

3. "Auto Race Supporters Win at the Hearing," *New York Times*, October 5, 1904.

Chapter 2

1. Adcock, "Driving in the Fast Lane."

2. "Auto Cars Ready for 300-Mile Race," *New York Times*, October 8, 1904.

3. "Heath Auto Wins; One Man Killed," *New York Times*, October 9, 1904.

Chapter 3

1. "Speed Average High over 283-Mile Course; Three Cars Were Excluded," *New York Times*, October 15, 1905.

2. "Vanderbilt Race Won by Hemery; Race May Be the Last," *New York Times*, October 15, 1905.

3. "Vanderbilt Race Won by Hemery; Straightaway at the Start," *New York Times*, October 15, 1905.

4. "Speed Average High over 283-Mile Course; Lancia Will Protest," *New York Times*, October 15, 1905.

5. "Vanderbilt Race Won by Hemery; Tire of Wagner's Car Burst," *New York Times*, October 15, 1905.

6. "Vanderbilt Race Won by Hemery; Lancia's Tremendous Speed," *New York Times*, October 15, 1905.

7. "Speed Average High over 283-Mile Course; Keene's Startling Gains," *New York Times*, October 15, 1905.

8. "Vanderbilt Race Won by Hemery; Heath Was Close Behind," *New York Times*, October 15, 1905.

9. "Vanderbilt Race Won by Hemery; Sleepers Line the Course," *New York Times*, October 15, 1905.

Chapter 4

1. "Autos Make Fast Time over Racing Circuit," *New York Times*, October 3, 1906.

2. "Shepard's Auto Kills a Spectator; Dr. Weilschott Stopped," *New York Times*, October 7, 1906.

3. "Auto Cup Race Won by Wagner," *New York Times*, October 7, 1906.

4. Ibid.

5. "Shepard's Auto Kills a Spectator."

6. Louis Wagner, "Early Adventures with the Automobile; Winning the Vanderbilt Cup, 1906," http://www.eyewitnesstohistory.com/auto.htm.

7. Peter Helck, *The Checkered Flag* (New York: Charles Scribner's Sons, 1961), 74.

Chapter 5

1. "Auto Cup Race Won by Wagner."

2. Ibid.

3. Adcock, "The Age of the Auto."

4. A. R. Pardington, "The Modern Appian Way for the Motorist," *Harper's Weekly*, March 16, 1907, 390.

5. Adcock, "The Age of the Auto."

6. Ibid.

7. Ibid.

Chapter 6

1. "Bad Management at the Auto Race; Society Well Represented," *New York Times*, October 25, 1908.

2. "America Wins Big Auto Race," *New York Times*, October 25, 1908.

3. Ibid.

Chapter 7

1. Tim Considine, *American Grand Prix Racing; A Century of Drivers & Cars* (Osceola, WI: Motorbooks International Publishers, 1997), 15.

Chapter 8

1. John Bentley, *Great American Automobiles* (New York: Prentice-Hall, 1957), 264.

2. "Robertson Wins Big Lowell Race," *New York Times*, September 2, 1909.

3. "Grant Wins Vanderbilt Cup; Jack Johnson on Hand," *New York Times*, October 31, 1909.

Chapter 9

1. Dennis David, "David Bruce-Brown," http://www.ddavid.com/formula1/ brown.htm.

2. John Chuhran, "History: The Grey Ghost's Greatest Race/Part 1," *iRace*, http://www.irace.com/gatheringplace/rearview/gryghst1.htm.

3. Helck, *The Checkered Flag*, 87.

4. "Crowds Flock to Vanderbilt Race," *New York Times*, October 1, 1910.

5. Fred J. Wagner, "Savannah Begins Carnival To-Day," *New York Times*, November 27, 1911.

6. "Grant's Steadiness Wins the Cup Race," *New York Times*, October 2, 1910.

7. "4 Dead, 20 Hurt in Vanderbilt Race," *New York Times*, October 2, 1910.

Chapter 10

1. "Dawson and Knipper Win Auto Races," *New York Times*, November 12, 1910.

2. Helck, *The Checkered Flag*, 127.

3. Considine, *American Grand Prix Racing*, 21.

Chapter 11

1. Bentley, *Great American Automobiles*, 218.

2. Russell Jaslow, "Who Really Won the First Indy 500?" *North American Motorsports Journal*, http://www.na-motorsports.com/Journal/1997/RussellJ.html.

3. Ibid.

Chapter 12

1. Bentley, *Great American Automobiles*, 263.

2. Wagner, "Savannah Begins Carnival To-Day."

3. Louis Wagner, Forward to "Grand Prize—1908," *The Checkered Flag*, 116.

4. Fred J. Wagner, "Ralph Mulford Wins Vanderbilt Race," *New York Times*, November 28, 1911.

5. Wagner, "Savannah Begins Carnival To-Day."

Chapter 13

1. Ralph Mulford, Forward to "Vanderbilt Cup Race—1911," *The Checkered Flag*, 90.

2. Ibid.

Chapter 14

1. Lorraine Glennon, ed., *Our Times; The Illustrated History of the 20th Century* (Atlanta: Turner Publishing, 1995), 95.

2. Ibid., 96.

3. Fred J. Wagner, "Drivers and Cars Ready for Race," *New York Times*, May 30, 1912.

4. Ibid.

5. "Ranch for Dawson, DePalma is Game," *Trenton Evening Times*, May 31, 1912.

6. Ibid.

7. Ibid.

Chapter 15

1. "Bruce-Brown Killed in Auto Race Trial," *New York Times*, October 2, 1912.

2. David, "David Bruce-Brown."

Chapter 16

1. "DePalma Proves His Sportsmanship," *Motor Age*, June 15, 1913, 53.

2. Caleb Bragg, "Bragg's Version of the Accident," *Horseless Age*, October 9, 1912, 540.

Chapter 17

1. Glennon, ed., *Our Times*, 100.
2. Ibid.
3. E. H. Delling, "Light Motors Show Efficiency and Power," *Automobile*, October 16, 1913.
4. "Starters Ready for 500 Mile Race at Indianapolis," *Motor Age*, May 29, 1913, 36.
5. Ibid.
6. Ibid.
7. J. C. Burton, "Champagne, Castor Oil and Gasoline," *Motor Age*, June 5, 1913, 50.
8. Ibid.
9. While reporters at the race never raised the question of Goux's sobriety, some later commentators have done so. As pointed out elsewhere in these pages, it was common practice among European drivers of that era to employ champagne as a refreshment, much as a modern athlete might use a sports drink. Nevertheless, with the temperance movement gaining great strides in America, Goux's comment was not particularly good for public relations. For the 1914 season, the AAA passed a regulation banning all alcoholic beverages from the pits.

Chapter 18

1. Glennon, ed., *Our Times*, 110.
2. John Chuhran, "History: The Grey Ghost's Greatest Race/Part 4," *iRace*, http://www.irace.com/gatheringplace/rearview/gryghst4.htm.
3. Ralph DePalma, Forward to "Vanderbilt Cup Race—1914," *The Checkered Flag*, 99.
4. Considine, *American Grand Prix Racing*, 30.
5. DePalma, Forward to "Vanderbilt Cup Race–1914," 99.

Chapter 19

1. "Pullen Wins Fifth Grand Prize Race," *New York Times*, March 1, 1914.

2. "Pullen Started as Apprentice," *Trenton Times-Advertiser*, March 1, 1914.
3. Helck, *The Checkered Flag*, 138.
4. Ibid.

Chapter 20

1. J. Edward Schipper, "Thomas, in Delage, Wins," *Automobile*, June 4, 1914, 66.

Chapter 21

1. Glennon, ed., *Our Times*, 112.
2. "Resta's Peugeot Wins Grand Prix," *New York Times*, February 28, 1915.
3. Helck, *The Checkered Flag*, 105.
4. "Resta's Peugeot Wins Grand Prix."
5. Ibid.

Chapter 22

1. "Resta's Peugeot Car Wins in Cup Race," *New York Times*, March 7, 1915.

Chapter 23

1. "DePalma Drives World's Best Race," *New York Times*, June 1, 1915.

Chapter 24

1. Glennon, ed., *Our Times*, 112.
2. Ibid., 119.

Chapter 27

1. Adcock, "Driving in the Fast Lane."

Bibliography

Adcock, Sylvia. "The Age of the Auto." http://www. newsday.com/community/ guide/lihistory/ny-history-hs701a,0,6567870.story?coll=ny-lihistory-navigation.

_____. "Driving in the Fast Lane." http://www.newsday.com/ community/guide/lihistory/ny-history_motion_road1,0,7025640.story?coll=ny-lihistory-navigation.

_____. "Fast Forward; Discoveries of a Road's Scholars." http://www .newsday.com/community/guide/lihistory/ny-history-hs701c,0,6698944. story?coll=ny-lihistory-navigation.

_____. "The Vanderbilt Tollhouses." http://www.newsday.com/ community/guide/lihistory/ny-history-hs701e,0,6830018.story?coll=ny-lihistory-navigation.

"Alco Again Wins Vanderbilt Cup but Race Death Toll Is High." *New York Times*, October 2, 1910.

"America Wins Big Auto Race." *New York Times*, October 25, 1908.

"Anderson, O'Donnell and DePalma Break Records in Elgin Race." *Trenton Sunday Times-Advertiser*, August 22, 1915.

"Auto Cars Ready for 300-Mile Race." *New York Times*, October 8, 1904.

"Auto Cup Race Won by Wagner." *New York Times*, October 7, 1906.

"Auto Derby Won by Delage Car, Thomas Driving." *Trenton Sunday Times-Advertiser*, May 31, 1914.

"Auto Dispute Settled; Pope-Toledo Withdraws." *New York Times*, October 4, 1906.

"Auto Race Course Under Strict Patrol." *New York Times*, October 10, 1905.

"Auto Race Supporters Win at the Hearing." *New York Times*, October 5, 1904.

"Auto Racers Angry at American Drivers." *New York Times*, October 12, 1905

"Auto Racing Course Has Few Bad Places." *New York Times*, October 9, 1905.

"Auto Speed Kings Arrayed for Race." *New York Times*, May 30, 1916.

"Auto Speed Trials Fast." *New York Times*, Oct. 1, 1912.

"Autoists Guests of W. K. Vanderbilt, Jr." *New York Times*, October 28, 1909.

"Automobile Wrecked on Way to Cup Race." *New York Times*, October 14, 1905.

"Automobiles Guarded for Vanderbilt Race." *New York Times*, October 13, 1905.

"Autos Dashed Daringly Around Neil Drive Turn." *Philadelphia Inquirer*, October 11, 1908.

"Autos Make Fast Time Over Racing Circuit." *New York Times*, October 3, 1906.

"Autos to Race in Great Park Speed Contest." *Philadelphia Inquirer*, October 10, 1908.

"Bad Management at the Auto Race." *New York Times*, October 25, 1908.

"Barney Oldfield." *International Motorsports Hall of Fame*, http://www .motorsportshalloffame.com/main/03_halloffame.htm.

Beecroft, David. "How the Sweepstakes Was Run and Won," *Motor Age*, June 5, 1913.

Bentley, John. *Great American Automobiles*. New York: Prentice-Hall, 1957.

"Big Auto Race Won by Resta." *Trenton Sunday Times-Advertiser*, February 28, 1915.

"Big Autos Battling at Point Breeze." *Philadelphia Inquirer*, June 29, 1907.

"Big Crowds Gather at Danger Points," *New York Times*, October 25, 1908.

"Bragg and DePalma Win at Milwaukee." *Horseless Age*, October 9, 1912.

Bragg, Caleb, "Bragg's Version of the Accident." *Horseless Age*, October 9, 1912.

"Bragg Sends His Fiat Home First in Grand Prize." *Horseless Age*, October 9, 1912.

"Brilliant Work by Mercer Cars." *Trenton Evening Times*, August 31, 1912.

"Bruce-Brown Killed in Auto Race Trial." *New York Times*, October 2, 1912.

"Bruce-Brown Wins Grand Prize Race." *New York Times*, November 13, 1910.

"Bruce-Brown Wins His Second Grand Prize Auto Race." *Trenton Evening Times*, December 1, 1911.

Burgess-Wise, David. *The Ultimate Race Car*. New York: DK Publishing, 1999.

Burton, J. C. "Champagne, Castor Oil and Gasoline." *Motor Age*, June 5, 1913.

"Carl G. Fisher Out of Speedway." *Trenton Evening Times*, August 26, 1915.

Chuhran, John. "History: The Grey Ghost's Greatest Race/Part 1." *iRace*, http://www.irace.com/gatheringplace/rearview/gryghst1.htm.

———. "History: The Grey Ghost's Greatest Race/Part 2." *iRace*, http://www.irace.com/gatheringplace/rearview/gryghst2.htm.

———. "History: The Grey Ghost's Greatest Race/Part 3." *iRace*, http://www.irace.com/gatheringplace/rearview/gryghst3.htm.

———. "History: The Grey Ghost's Greatest Race/Part 4." *iRace*, http://www.irace.com/gatheringplace/rearview/gryghst4.htm.

Clayden, A. Ludlow. "Overhead Valves Triumph." *Automobile*, June 3, 1915.

Considine, Tim. *American Grand Prix Racing: A Century of Drivers & Cars*. Osceola, WI: Motorbooks International Publishers, 1997.

"Course Was Clear Says Harry Grant." *Philadelphia Inquirer*, October 9, 1910.

"Crowds Early for Auto Race." *New York Times*, October 30, 1909.

"Crowds Flock to Vanderbilt Race." *New York Times*, October 1, 1910.

"Dario Resta Wins Indianapolis Race." *Trenton Evening Times*, May 31, 1916.

David, Dennis. "David Bruce-Brown." http://www.ddavid.com/formula1/brown.htm.

Davidson, Donald. "Money Demand in 1916 Backfired." *Indianapolis Star/News*, May 16, 1998.

"Dawson and Knipper Win Auto Races." *New York Times*, November 12, 1910.

"Dawson in a National Wins Thrilling 500-Mile Indianapolis Race." *Horseless Age*, June 5, 1912.

"Dawson Makes New Speedway Records." *New York Times*, May 31, 1912.

"Dawson's National New King of Auto Speedway; Record." *Trenton Evening Times*, May 31, 1912.

"Delage Car Wins; New Race Record." *New York Times*, May 31, 1914.

Delling, E. H. "Light Motors Show Efficiency and Power." *Automobile*, October 16, 1913.

"DePalma Drives World's Best Race." *New York Times*, June 1, 1915.

"DePalma First in Vanderbilt Race." *New York Times*, February 27, 1914.

"DePalma in a Mercedes Wins Vanderbilt from Hughes in Mercer." *Horseless Age*, October 9, 1912.

"DePalma, in Mercedes, Wins at 89.84 m.p.h." *Automobile*, June 3, 1915.

"DePalma, in Mercer Broke Auto Record at Santa Monica." *Trenton Evening Times*, May 6, 1912.

"DePalma Proves His Sportsmanship." *Motor Age*, June 15, 1913.

DePalma, Ralph. Foreword to "Vanderbilt Cup Race—1914." in Helck, *The Checkered Flag*. New York: Charles Scribner's Sons, 1961.

"DePalma Wins Vanderbilt Race." *New York Times*, October 5, 1912.

"Drivers and Cars Ready for Race." *New York Times*, May 30, 1912.

"Drivers in 1913 Sweepstakes." *Motor Age*, May 29, 1913.

"Drivers in Vanderbilt Cup Race and Sweepstakes on Long Island Course." *New York Times*, October 24, 1909.

Duncan, Robert Bruce. *Cutwater: Speedboats and Launches from the Golden Age of Boating*. Novato, CA: Top Ten Publishing, 1993.

"E. Bergdoll Wins Park Auto Race; Sets New Record." *Philadelphia Inquirer*, October 10, 1911.

"E. Shepard's Auto Kills a Spectator." *New York Times*, October 7, 1906.

"Earl Cooper Won Elgin Auto Race." *Trenton Evening Times*, August 26, 1915.

"Eddie Pullen, Trenton Boy, Wins Grand Prize Race, with Mercer Car, Establishing New Record." *Trenton Sunday Times-Advertiser*, March 1, 1914.

"Eighty-Eight Tires Changed During the 500-Mile Race." *Motor Age*, June 5, 1913.

"Enter Three Mercers in Speedway Classic." *Trenton Sunday Times-Advertiser*, May 9, 1915.

"Expect New Record in Big Auto Race." *New York Times*, May 31, 1915.

"Explosion of Auto Tire Causes Bruce-Brown to Be Killed at Milwaukee Track." *Trenton Evening Times*, October 2, 1912.

Faroux, Charles. "Sidelights on Big Race by French Motoring Authority." *Motor Age*, June 5, 1913.

"Fast Speed Trials in Cup Practice." *New York Times*, October 27, 1909.

"4 Dead, 20 Hurt in Vanderbilt Race." *New York Times*, October 2, 1910.

"Four Pilots Drive Complete Race." *Motor Age*, June 5, 1913.

Glennon, Lorraine, ed. *Our Times; The Illustrated History of the 20th Century*. Atlanta: Turner Publishing, 1995.

"Grand Prix Today." *New York Times*, February 27, 1915.

"Grant Wins Vanderbilt Cup." *New York Times*, October 31, 1909.

"Grant's Steadiness Wins the Cup Race." *New York Times*, October 2, 1910.

"Great Crowd Starts for the Auto Battle." *New York Times*, October 6, 1906.

"Half Million Spectators Line Racers' Course." *Philadelphia Inquirer*, October 10, 1909.

"Half Million View Thrilling Park Auto Race." *Philadelphia Inquirer*, October 9, 1910.

Hatch, Darwin S. "Scenes and Incidents Noted at the Pits During the Race." *Motor Age*, June 5, 1913.

_____. "Tuning Up the Cars for the Memorial Day Motor Marathon." *Motor Age*, May 29, 1913.

"Heath Auto Wins; One Man Killed." *New York Times*, October 9, 1904.

Helck, Peter. *The Checkered Flag*. New York: Charles Scribner's Sons, 1961.

"History of Indianapolis Motor Speedway." *Motor Age*, May 29, 1913.

"How Lancia Lost Lead When 30 Miles Ahead." *New York Times*, October 15, 1905.

"Hughes in Mercer 30 Third in Big Elgin Race." *Trenton Evening Times*, August 29, 1911.

"Hughie Hughes in Mercer Car Second to Ralph DePalma." *Trenton Evening Times*, October 3, 1912.

"Indianapolis Motor Speedway." *Automobile*, June 1, 1911.

"Inquirer First in News of Race." *Philadelphia Inquirer*, October 10, 1911.

"Inquirer to Give Auto Race News." *Philadelphia Inquirer*, October 10, 1908.

"Italian Repeats Victory." *Trenton Sunday Times-Advertiser*, March 7, 1915.

Jarrott, Charles. "The Race to Death; Paris-Madrid Race of 1903." http:// www.ddavid.com/formula1/paris1903.htm.

Jaslow, Russell. "Who Really Won the First Indy 500?" *North American Motorsports Journal*, http://www.na-motorsports.com/Journal/1997/RussellJ.html.

"Keene's Auto Damaged, May Not Enter Race." *New York Times*, October 2, 1906.

"Local Boy Favors Italian Drivers." *Trenton Evening Times*, May 15, 1915.

"Louis Chevrolet." *International Motorsports Hall of Fame*, http://www.motorsportshalloffame.com/halloffame/1992/Louis_Chevrolet_main.htm.

"Lozier Wins 24-Hour Race; Frayer-Miller Close Second." *Philadelphia Inquirer*, June 30, 1907.

Ludvigsen, Karl. *Classic Grand Prix Cars*. Stroud, England: Sutton Publishing, 2000.

"Machines Trying Course." *New York Times*, October 7, 1904.

"Mason Cars Lead in Two Cup Races." *New York Times*, October 1, 1912.

"Mercer a Betting Favorite as Speed Demons Get Away." *Trenton Evening Times*, May 30, 1912.

"Mercer Car Driver Is Killed in Race." *Trenton Sunday Times-Advertiser*, August 23, 1914.

"Mercer Car Withdrawn from Indianapolis Race." *Trenton Evening Times*, May 25, 1915.

"More Auto Troubles for the German Team." *New York Times*, October 11, 1905.

"Motorists Praise Course Policing." *Philadelphia Inquirer*, October 10, 1909.

Mulford, Ralph. Foreword to "Vanderbilt Cup Race—1911." In Helck, *The Checkered Flag*. New York: Charles Scribner's Sons, 1961.

"Nassau Residents Get Anti-Auto Race Order." *New York Times*, October 7, 1904.

"New Speed Records Predicted for the Park Auto Course." *Philadelphia Inquirer*, October 7, 1911.

"Nineteen Cars in Race." *New York Times*, October 14, 1905.

"No Credit for Aitken Winning Tragedy Race." *Trenton Sunday Times-Advertiser*, November 19, 1916.

Oldfield, Barney. "1911 an "Off" Year for Race Drivers." *Philadelphia Inquirer*, October 8, 1911.

"Oldfield to Pilot Foreign Car in Race." *Trenton Sunday Times-Advertiser*, May 9, 1915.

Pardington, A. R. "The Modern Appian Way for the Motorist." *Harper's Weekly*, March 16, 1907.

"Park Auto Race Postponed Until Tomorrow Noon." *Philadelphia Inquirer*, October 8, 1911.

"Park Auto Race Starts at Noon." *Philadelphia Inquirer*, October 8, 1910.

"Park Was like Soldiers' Camp Before Race." *Philadelphia Inquirer*, October 11, 1908.

"Peugeot Car Wins $50,000 Auto Race." *New York Times*, May 31, 1913.

"Postponed Park Auto Race to Be Run Off Today." *Philadelphia Inquirer*, October 9, 1911.

"Powerful Autos All Ready for Races at Point Breeze." *Philadelphia Inquirer*, June 28, 1907.

"Pullen Is Victor of Grand Prize Race." *Motor Age*, March 5, 1914.

"Pullen Started as Apprentice." *Trenton Times-Advertiser*, March 1, 1914.

"Pullen Wins Fifth Grand Prize Race." *New York Times*, March 1, 1914.

"Racing Auto Hits Man at Brighton." *New York Times*, October 3, 1908.

"Racing Auto Leaps Track; Four Killed." *New York Times*, November 19, 1916.

"Ralph DePalma." *International Motorsports Hall of Fame*, http://www.motorsportshalloffame.com/main/03_halloffame.htm.

"Ralph DePalma Captures Auto Classic and Sets a New Record for Course." *Trenton Evening Times*, June 1, 1915.

"Ralph de Palma—Sportsman." *Motor Age*, March 5, 1914.

"Ralph Mulford at Last Wins a Big Automobile Race." *Trenton Evening Times*, November 28, 1911.

"Ranch for Dawson, DePalma Is Game." *Trenton Evening Times*, May 31, 1912.

Rendall, Ivan. *The Power and the Glory: A Century of Motor Racing*. London: BBC Books, 1991.

"Resta Sets Mark in Auto Cup Race." *New York Times*, November 17, 1916.

"Resta Takes Lead with His Peugeot." *Trenton Evening Times*, May 31, 1915.

"Resta Winner of Vanderbilt Cup." *Trenton Evening Times*, November 17, 1916.

"Resta's Peugeot Car Wins in Cup Race." *New York Times*, March 7, 1915.

"Resta's Peugeot Wins Grand Prix." *New York Times*, February 28, 1915.

"Resta's Peugeot Wins Sweepstakes." *New York Times*, May 31, 1916.

"Rickenbacher to Drive a Maxwell." *Trenton Sunday Times-Advertiser*, May 9, 1915.

"Robertson Wins Big Lowell Race." *New York Times*, September 2, 1909.

Schipper, J. Edward. "Thomas, in Delage, Wins." *Automobile*, June 4, 1914.

"Several Accidents to Machines Occur along Neil Drive." *Philadelphia Inquirer*, October 9, 1910.

"Shepard's Auto Kills a Spectator." *New York Times*, October 7, 1906.

"Simplex Car Wins 24-Hour Auto Race." *New York Times*, August 1, 1909.

Sinsabaugh, C. G., "Speedway Honors Go to French Car." *Motor Age*, June 5, 1913.

"Six Persons Killed in Automobile Race." *New York Times*, May 25, 1903.

"Six Races Broke Record of Course." *Philadelphia Inquirer*, October 10, 1911.

"Society All There and in Gay Colors." *New York Times*, October 7, 1906.

"Speed Average High Over 283-Mile Course." *New York Times*, October 15, 1905.

"Speedy Loco Sets New Mark in Park." *Philadelphia Inquirer*, October 9, 1908.

"Starters Ready for 500 Mile Race at Indianapolis." *Motor Age*, May 29, 1913.

"The Story of the Race — A Fierce Battle from the Start." *Automobile*, June 4, 1914.

"Supreme Attack on Verdun Is Launched, Using 1,000,000 Men." *Trenton Evening Times*, May 31, 1916.

"Thirty-Two Cars Tuned Up for 200-Mile Race in Fairmount Park Tomorrow." *Philadelphia Inquirer*, October 7, 1910.

"Thomas Car Eligible in Spite of Protest." *New York Times*, October 5, 1906.

"3000 Cars Filled with Spectators Line Course." *Philadelphia Inquirer*, October 11, 1908.

"Thrills in Plenty Stir Onlookers." *Philadelphia Inquirer*, October 10, 1909.

"Track Record by DePalma." *New York Times*, October 3, 1908.

"Trenton Men Aboard Giant Titanic Which Meets Disaster in Ice." *Trenton Evening Times*, April 15, 1912.

"Twenty-Four Cars in Speedway Race." *New York Times*, May 30, 1915.

"Twenty-Seven Cars in 500-Mile Race." *New York Times*, May 30, 1913.

"22 Motor Cars Race Today in Fairmount Park." *Philadelphia Inquirer*, October 9, 1909.

"Twenty-Two Starters in Indianapolis Automobile Race; Resta Is Favorite." *Trenton Evening* Times, May 30, 1916.

"200,000 Persons Viewed Terrific Speed Flights." *Philadelphia Inquirer*, October 11, 1908.

"Two Mercers Start at Santa Monica." *Trenton Evening Times*, May 4, 1912.

"Vanderbilt Cup Auto Race To-Day." *New York Times*, February 26, 1914.

"Vanderbilt Cup Race Now a Reality." *Philadelphia Inquirer*, October 10, 1909.

"Vanderbilt Cup Racer Overturned." *New York Times*, October 29, 1909.

"Vanderbilt Race Won by Hemery." *New York Times*, October 15, 1905.

Wagner, Fred J. "Bruce-Brown Wins Grand Prize Race." *New York Times*, December 1, 1911.

_____. "Drivers and Cars Ready for Race." *New York Times*, May 30, 1912.

_____. "Hemery Picked to Win Grand Prize." *New York Times*, November 30, 1911.

_____. "Ralph Mulford Wins Vanderbilt Race." *New York Times*, November 28, 1911.

_____. "Savannah Begins Carnival To-Day." *New York Times*, November 27, 1911.

Wagner, Louis. "Early Adventures with the Automobile; Winning the Vanderbilt Cup, 1906." http://www.eyewitnesstohistory.com/auto.htm.

_____. Foreword to "Grand Prize — 1908." In Helck, *The Checkered Flag*. New York: Charles Scribner's Sons, 1961.

"Wagner's Fiat Wins Gold Cup." *New York Times*, November 27, 1908.

"Weary Wait for Autos at Long Island Ferry." *New York Times*, October 7, 1906.

"Winner of Auto Race Makes Fast Time for Course." *Philadelphia Inquirer*, October 11, 1908.

"Zengle Victor; Lowers Record of Park Course." *Philadelphia Inquirer*, October 9, 1910.

Index